# EGON RONAY'S GUINNESS PUB GUIDE 1985

D1362481

Food and accommodation

First published by Egon Ronay Organisation Ltd 1985
Greencoat House, Francis Street, London SW1P 1DH, in association with
Mitchell Beazley London, Mill House, 87–89 Shaftesbury Avenue, London W1V 7AD
Copyright © Egon Ronay 1985
All rights reserved

The contents of this book are believed correct at the time of printing and every effort has been made to ensure the information is correct. Nevertheless, the Publisher can accept no responsibility for errors or omissions or for changes in the details given.

Printed and bound in Great Britain by Cox & Wyman Ltd, Reading
Filmset by JH Graphics Ltd, Reading
Produced by Egon Ronay Organisation Ltd
Cartography revised by Intermap P.S. Ltd
All road maps are based on the Ordnance Survey Maps, with the permission of the Controller of H.M. Stationery Office, Crown Copyright Reserved.

Layout and typography by Barbara Ronay

Except in the United States of America, this book is sold subject to the condition that it shall not, by way of trade or otherwise, be lent, re-sold, hired out, or otherwise circulated without the publisher's prior consent in any form of binding or cover other than that in which it is published and without a similar condition including this condition being imposed on the subsequent purchaser.

# THE EGON RONAY ORGANISATION

Our researches have included the whole field of catering, from de luxe hotels and restaurants to inns, pubs, transport and motorway cafés, hospital meals, international airlines, European airports, car ferries, theatres, the British Armed Forces, etc. Our four annual Guides are the present one, as well as

***Egon Ronay's Lucas Guide 1985* to Hotels and Restaurants.**
***Just a Bite, Egon Ronay's Lucas Guide 1985***
**for Gourmets on a Family Budget**
***Egon Ronay's TWA Guide 1984* to Good Restaurants**
**in Major Cities, Europe & United States.**

Our researches are carried out by full-time professional inspectors with catering backgrounds and proven knowledge of international cooking, which we test before training them for many weeks in the Organisation to achieve common standards of judgement with as much objectivity as this field allows. Their professional identities are not disclosed until they seek information from the management after paying their bills.

To find establishments for our Guides, we normally rely partly on re-inspection of current listings and a research programme drawn up from many sources, such as readers' recommendations and requests for visits from proprietors of establishments (these latter two categories being subject to careful vetting).

The Organisation maintains complete independence in its editorial selection and judgements. It is sustained, in addition to sales, by sponsorship and advertising, without which the price of our Guides would be prohibitive, but we do not accept advertising, payment or free hospitality from any of the establishments we cover.

# CONTENTS


| | |
|---|---|
| The Egon Ronay Organisation | 3 |
| Continuing success | 7 |
| How to use this Guide | 8 |
| Explanation of symbols | 10 |
| Summing up | 11 |
| Pub survey | 15 |
| Pub of the Year | 16 |
| Food much above average | 17 |
| The English Cheese Pub Award 1985 | 19 |
| Good English cheeseboards | 20 |
| Schweppes family pub guide | 23 |
| Restaurants at pubs | 33 |
| Waterside pubs | 35 |
| **LONDON** | **37** |
| London pubs by area | 38 |
| **ENGLAND** | **67** |
| UK maps | following 160 |
| **SCOTLAND** | **281** |
| **WALES** | **295** |

| | |
|---|---|
| **CHANNEL ISLANDS** | **308** |
| **ISLE OF MAN** | **309** |
| Special offer for a Guide next year | 311 |
| For readers' comments (tear-out pages) | 313 |
| Advertisers' index | 319 |

**WE CORDIALLY INVITE**

# establishments not in this Guide

to write to us if they would like to be considered for inclusion next year – provided their standard of food *served in the bar* is exceptionally high, or their bedrooms clean and very pleasant, or both.

Write to **Egon Ronay's Guinness Pub Guide, Greencoat House, Francis Street, London SW1P 1DH**

We do not accept advertising, payment or free hospitality from any of the establishments we recommend.

# Continuing success

After the success of our first joint venture in 1984, we look forward to further developing the role of Egon Ronay's Guinness Pub Guide, which reflects all that is best about British pubs.

The Guide's relentless search for pub food of the highest quality has, we hope, contributed to the improving standards achieved in recent years. Guinness has been synonymous with beer of the finest quality for more than two centuries.

And it is no coincidence that pubs featured within these pages for the food they prepare have an equally high reputation for the beer they serve.

Good food and good beer make natural partners. Similarly, the Egon Ronay Organisation and Guinness Brewing make an ideal team in their pursuit of excellence.

*Ernest Saunders*
*Group Chief Executive*
*Arthur Guinness & Sons plc*

*Egon Ronay*

# HOW TO USE THIS GUIDE

**GOOD BAR FOOD**
We include establishments where our team of professional inspectors found excellent-quality bar food. Such pubs are indicated by '*Food*' following the locality. We did not cover pub restaurants, as they fall within the scope of *Egon Ronay's Lucas Guide 1985 to Hotels and Restaurants.*

Two typical dishes are listed, with prices valid at the time of our visit. However, prices may well have risen since our researches. We also indicate any restrictions on availability of food, for instance, only sandwiches at Sunday lunch time. Additionally, it is advisable to check the hours at which food is served. Last order times refer to bar food where it is served in the evening.

Those establishments serving outstanding – 'Much Above Average' – food are shown with a star.

**GOOD ACCOMMODATION AT PUBS**
We also tried the accommodation and we list the number of bedrooms for those pubs we can recommend for an overnight stay, such pubs being indicated by '*B & B*' following the locality. When looking for accommodation, bear in mind that the publican's free time is traditionally in the afternoon, when he or she is usually not available.

The accommodation is rated Grade 1 or Grade 2 (if the rooms vary, we use Grades 1 & 2), and we indicate where dogs are not allowed in bedrooms. The symbol £A+, £A, £B or £C shows the price of bed and a cooked English breakfast in a double room for two occupants:

£A+ over £37
£A from £31 to £37
£B from £24 to £30
£C under £24
(including VAT)

Some hotels included for their bar snacks do not offer pub style accommodation but are recommended in *Egon Ronay's Lucas Guide 1985 to Hotels and Restaurants*. This is indicated in their write-up.

**ATMOSPHERIC PUBS**
These pubs are recommended as pleasant or interesting places for a drink rather than for their bar food or accommodation. Entries are denoted by the figure to the right:

**SUITABLE FOR FAMILIES**
Those pubs we suggest as suitable for families are ones that have a room or indoor area where children are allowed whether eating or not. Many pubs welcome children if they are eating bar food and some pubs make a feature of outdoor play areas, but readers should note that these are not the qualifications on which we base our **Family pub** category. Restrictions on children staying overnight are mentioned in the entries.

**BEERS AND CIDER**
We print whether an establishment is a free house or brewery-owned. After the ▮ symbol are listed the names of a number of beers, lagers and cider on draught. *Real ale* appears if one or more of the beers offered can be defined as such.

*continued*

**OPENING TIMES**
Opening hours vary throughout the country. Some pubs have a six-day licence. As many pubs close at some time during Christmas and the New Year, it is advisable to check. Also, some pubs choose to close one or more days a week.

**ORDER OF LISTING**
In London, listings are in alphabetical order by the establishment's name. Out of London listings are in alphabetical order under the names of localities within the regional divisions of England, Scotland, Wales, the Channel Islands and the Isle of Man.

**MAP REFERENCES**
Entries contain references to the map section located in the middle of the Guide.

# SYMBOLS

*Food* Recommended for bar food

*B & B* Recommended for accommodation

★ Bar food much above average

On draught

**Family pub** Suitable for families (see also preceding page)

# SUMMING UP

We wrote to the 950 pubs in our 1984 Guide asking about the importance of their food sales. *85% of the replies stated that they could not survive without them!* A quarter have increased their food turnover by more than 50%, half by more than 25% – all in the last two years. The speed with which this change has occurred is surprising.

Even though these statistics refer to only a small proportion of pubs in Britain, the significance of the findings cannot be overestimated. The pubs they mirror represent the best in the country – those which set the trend.

**Dramatic changes**

Snack-type bar food is rapidly giving way to full meals. Three-course meals, tables laid and waitress service bring to mind the atmosphere of German-type brasseries or, in many cases, French bistros.

The number of what we call 'family pubs' has increased, and they have improved their facilities for children. There is a dramatic change in publicans' attitudes to welcoming – as opposed to tolerating, let alone barring – children. 88% of landlords said that they favour serving food to families with children; about a third would welcome children even under four years old! (Results of our survey on licensing are on page 15.)

All this points to a more radical and faster change in the traditional face of the British pub and its social function than is realised. Within ten to fifteen years traditional British pubs, as we know them, may well be reduced to a fraction of their former number.

So much for the changing face of pubs. How about the food they offer?

*continued*

**The chips are down**
Though food keeps improving, the progression is slower and still has a long way to go. Certainly numerous pubs are a very satisfactory answer to bistros in France. There is more home-made food and fewer commercial pies. There are often more interesting dishes than the predictable prepacked fare. But there are still far too many houses with dull, carelessly prepared food, seas of peas, mountains of smothering cress, artificial-looking salads to match mock beams and plastic ferns, and *practically no good chips to be found.* The phenomenon of British inability to produce a modest dish of decent chips instead of the undercooked, frozen, greasy, flabby, stuck-together, reheated stuff purveyed by 'cooks' who ought to be ashamed of themselves is absurd.

**Fetish of microwave**
Naive brewers exemplify the British delusion that money poured into improved kitchens, into stainless steel, and the fetish of microwave ovens, will result in improved quality. If a quarter of the investment had gone into the training of kitchen staff, if brewery-owned pubs employed cooks half as skilled as those turned out by the Armed Forces schools of catering, pub food could be a joy almost everywhere.

But breweries do deserve praise for the way they maintain and keep improving accommodation. Free houses, too, have been conspicuously investing in creating very good bedrooms and bathrooms. Annexes are being built, and rooms at the inn have now become much more than a romantic notion.

**Creature (dis)comforts**
Yet there are still at least as many rooms crying out to be refurbished. While automatic breakfast kettles (somewhat incongruous with the country inn image) are universal, they are often a source of frustration when it comes to locating the electrical socket. And – please – could more and warmer blankets, as well as something better than depressingly battered coat hangers, be provided?

Television is by no means general in rooms – and long may it remain blissfully absent as a matter of policy: people who seek out a lovely country inn for spending a night or two and yet want to stay in their room to watch snooker may well have a split personality.

Clearly, rooms at the inn are entering the phase of serious business. What puzzles me is that no one has yet thought of popularising them through cooperative marketing groups.

# JUST A BITE

## Egon Ronay's Lucas Guide

**for Gourmets on a Family Budget**

**— 1985 —**

for the best British light meals and snacks in some 1,000 cafés, tearooms, wine bars, wholefood and vegetarian restaurants, fish and chip shops, pizzerias and hamburger places, coffee shops and many other modest eating places serving high-quality food:

including **EATING ON & OFF MOTORWAYS**

With many new recommendations replacing the old ones after reappraisal.

£3.95 from bookshops everywhere or £4.50 to include postage and packing (limited to addresses in the United Kingdom) from:

Egon Ronay Organisation Ltd,
Greencoat House, Francis Street
LONDON SW1P 1DH

*See colour pages following page 96 for news of another 1985 Egon Ronay publication.*

# Changes in the licensing laws: what the publicans think

*Results of our researches conducted in October 1984, compiled from nearly 700 answers received from landlords in our 1984 Guide*

86% are in favour of changes

14% are against changes

74% do *not* want *all* restrictions abolished

93% favour the landlords deciding their own opening hours

73% think that greater flexibility in hours would *not* result in greater consumption of alcohol

27% think that greater flexibility *would* result in greater consumption of alcohol

67% think flexibility in hours would increase the consumption of food

58% think the increase in food consumption would be about 20%

# PUB OF THE YEAR

Our annual award is a Pewter Plate, a floating trophy engraved with the winner's name and retained until next year. Since it would be impossible to name 'the best pub in the land', we are choosing one from the short list below, and the final choice is announced on the day of publication. As previously, the main criteria are a very high standard of bar food and a congenial atmosphere fostered by the appealing personality of the landlord. The short list is as follows: *Henley-on-Thames, Little Angel; Shipton-under-Wychwood, Lamb Inn; Staddle Bridge, McCoys; Tetbury, Gentle Gardener; Yattendon, Royal Oak; Llanfihangel Crucorney, Skirrid Inn.*

*Previous winners*

1984 Rhydspence Inn, Whitney-on-Wye, Hereford & Worcester
1983 No winner
1982 Rock Inn, Haytor Vale, Devon
1981 Greyhound Inn, Staple Fitzpaine, Somerset
1980 Fox Inn, Ansty, Dorset

# FOOD MUCH ABOVE AVERAGE

# ★ PUB FOOD MUCH ABOVE AVERAGE

**ENGLAND**

Ansty, Dorset: Fox Inn
Biddenden, Kent: Three Chimneys
Box, Wilts: Chequers
Brightwell Baldwin, Oxon: Lord Nelson Inn
Broad Oak, H & W: Broad Oak Inn
Burham, Kent: Golden Eagle
Burton, Wilts: Plume of Feathers
Chenies, Herts: Bedford Arms Thistle Hotel
Fawley, Bucks: Walnut Tree
Fowlmere, Cambs: Chequers Inn
Fulking, W Sussex: Shepherd & Dog
Great Waltham, Essex: Windmill

Henley-on-Thames, Oxon: Little Angel
Huntingdon, Cambs: Old Bridge Hotel
Kirkby Stephen, Cumb: King's Arms Hotel
Langley Marsh, Som: Three Horseshoes
Little Walden, Essex: Crown Inn
Maidensgrove, Oxon: Five Horseshoes
Moulton, N Yorks: Black Bull Inn
Rockbourne, Hants: Rose & Thistle
Saffron Walden, Essex: Saffron Hotel
Shipston-on-Stour, Warwicks: White Bear
Staddle Bridge, N Yorks: McCoy's at the Tontine
Stamford, Lincs: George of Stamford
Stanford Dingley, Berks: Old Boot Inn
Stanton Harcourt, Oxon: Harcourt Arms
Staple Fitzpaine, Som: Greyhound Inn
Stapleton, Co. Durham: Bridge Inn
Stow Bardolph, Norfolk: Hare Arms
Stuckton, Hants: Three Lions Inn
Tetbury, Glos: Gentle Gardener
Whitney-on-Wye, H & W: Rhydspence Inn
Yattendon, Berks: Royal Oak

**SCOTLAND**

Dulnain Bridge, H'land: Muckrach Lodge Hotel
Tarbert, S'clyde: West Loch Hotel
Wester Howgate, Lothian: Old Howgate Inn

**WALES**

Llanfihangel Crucorney, Gwent: Skirrid Inn
Llowes, Powys: Radnor Arms

# THE ENGLISH CHEESE PUB AWARD 1985

With new names like Lymeswold, Melbury and Ash Barrow appearing regularly on the market, it's clear that the art of English cheesemaking is a constantly developing one. The public continue to show great interest in both the established and the new varieties, and pubs have long played a major role in popularising this fine, nourishing product.

English cheese and English beer are natural companions, and the traditional lunchtime fare of cheese, bread and pickles with a glass of ale remains a favourite throughout the land.

Our inspectors have again taken a close look at pub cheeseboards, taking note of quality, variety and presentation. Our recommendations for good English cheeseboards follow.

We award an annual trophy to the pub with the best English cheeses and are pleased to announce this year's winner:

## RHYDSPENCE INN
## WHITNEY-ON-WYE

An impressive range of perfectly kept cheeses – at least ten in the prime months – is offered at this fine old Welsh Border inn.

**Previous winners**
1981 The Park, Bedford
1982 The Plough, Rusper
1983 Lamb & Flag, London WC2
1984 Black Bull, Moulton

# GOOD ENGLISH CHEESEBOARDS

**LONDON**
Admiral Codrington, SW3
Lamb & Flag, WC2

**ENGLAND**
Bedford, Beds: Park
Biddenden, Kent: Three Chimneys
Bowdon, Ches: Griffin
Braintree, Essex: Retreat
Bridge Trafford, Ches: Nag's Head
Brockton, Shrops: Feathers Inn
Brome, Suffolk: Oaksmere
Burtonwood, Ches: Fiddle i'th Bag Inn
Byworth, W Sussex: Black Horse
Chenies, Herts: Bedford Arms Thistle Hotel
Chiddingfold, Surrey: Swan
Constable Burton, N Yorks: Wyvill Arms
Cottesmore, Leics: Sun Inn
Cumnor, Oxon: Bear & Ragged Staff
Dorchester-on-Thames, Oxon: George Hotel
East Haddon, Northants: Red Lion
Etton, Cambs: Golden Pheasant
Faugh, Cum: String of Horses Inn
Fenay Bridge, W Yorks: Star
Fulking, W Sussex: Shepherd & Dog

Grantchester, Cambs: Green Man
Harpenden, Herts: Silver Cup
Hildenborough, Kent: Gate Inn
Horley, Surrey: Ye Olde Six Bells
Hungerford, Berks: Bear at Hungerford
Kenley, Surrey: Wattenden Arms
Kingsclere, Berks: Crown
Kinver, Staffs: Whittington Inn
Lacock, Wilts: Red Lion
Ledsham, Ches: Tudor Rose
Lickfold, W Sussex: Lickfold Inn
Longparish, Hants: Plough Inn
Mark Cross, E Sussex: Mark Cross Inn
Marsh Gibbon, Oxon: Greyhound Inn
Millthorpe, Derbys: Royal Oak
Moulton, N Yorks: Black Bull Inn
Murcott, Oxon: Nut Tree Inn
Nassington, Northants: Black Horse Inn
Naunton, Glos: Black Horse
Nottingham, Notts: Lord Nelson
Nunney, Som: George Inn
Peppard Common, Oxon: Red Lion
Perranarworthal, Corn: Norway Inn
Philleigh, Corn: Roseland Inn
Rushlake Green, E Sussex: Horse & Groom
Sambourne, Warwicks: Green Dragon
Semley, Wilts: Benett Arms
Shalfleet, I of W: New Inn
Shelley, W Yorks: Three Acres Inn
Shepperton, Surrey: Thames Court
Slaithwaite, W Yorks: White House
Sonning-on-Thames, Berks: Bull Inn

*continued*

Staple Fitzpaine, Som: Greyhound Inn
Stapleton, Co. Durham: Bridge Inn
Testcombe, Hants: Mayfly
Timperley, Ches: Hare & Hounds
Waltham St Lawrence, Berks: Plough Inn
Washbrook, Suffolk: Brook Inn
Westbury, Bucks: Reindeer Inn
Weston, Ches: White Lion
Whitney-on-Wye, H & W: Rhydspence Inn
Wilson, Derbys: Bull's Head Inn
Wincham, Ches: Black Greyhound Hotel
Yattendon, Berks: Royal Oak Hotel

**SCOTLAND**
Canonbie, D & G: Riverside Inn
Killiecrankie, Tayside: Killiecrankie Hotel

**WALES**
Abergavenny, Gwent: Crowfield Inn
Llowes, Powys: Radnor Arms

**Traditional Country Cheeses**

For further information about English cheeses, contact the English Country Cheese Council, 5–7 John Princes Street, London W1M 0AP

# The Schweppes® Family Pub Guide

SELECTED BY THE
EGON RONAY ORGANISATION

Below is a list of pubs which the Egon Ronay Organisation has selected as being particularly suitable for families. All have an *indoor* area or special room where children are allowed whether eating or not, and all of them serve Schweppes soft drinks.

These and other pubs in the Guide which have facilities for children are denoted by the words **Family pub**. Many pubs welcome children if they are eating bar food and some pubs make a feature of outdoor play areas, but readers should note that these are not the qualifications on which our **Family pub** category is based.

In recent years, the Egon Ronay Organisation has drawn attention to the trend towards more family pubs. The demand for making pubs more and more suitable for the whole family is growing and special facilities for children are improving all the time.

**LONDON**
Albion, N1
Cock Tavern, EC1
City Barge, W4
Hand in Hand, SW19
King's Head & Eight Bells, SW3
Paxton's Head, SW1
Prospect of Whitby, E1
Shepherd's Tavern, W1
Ship, SW14 (until 7pm)
Ye Olde Cheshire Cheese, EC4

**ENGLAND**
**Avon**
Tormarton, Compass Inn (lunchtime)
**Berkshire**
Ascot, Stag (lunchtime)
Chaddleworth, Ibex
Great Shefford, Swan
Highclere, Yew Tree Inn
Hungerford, Bear at Hungerford
Upper Basildon, Beehive Inn
Wickham, Five Bells
Yattendon, Royal Oak Hotel

**Buckinghamshire**
Cheddington, Rosebery Arms
Fawley, Walnut Tree
Fingest, Chequers Inn
Forty Green, Royal Standard of England
Hambleden, Stag & Huntsman Inn
Hartwell, Bugle Horn
Skirmett, King's Arms
Stewkley, Swan
Stony Stratford, Cock Hotel
Westbury, Reindeer Inn
Winslow, Bell Hotel
**Cambridgeshire**
Elsworth, George & Dragon
Fowlmere, Chequers Inn
Grantchester, Green Man
Holywell, Ye Olde Ferry Boat Inn
Huntingdon, George
Huntingdon, Old Bridge Hotel
Keyston, Pheasant Inn
Madingley, Three Horseshoes
Molesworth, Cross Keys
Needingworth, Pike & Eel
Newton, Queen's Head

These and other pubs in the Guide which have facilities for children are denoted by the words **Family pub.**

*It can only be...*
*Schhh...you-know-who*

St Neots, Chequers Inn
St Neots, Stephenson's Rocket
Wansford, Haycock Inn
Whittlesey, Falcon Hotel
Wisbech, Rose & Crown Hotel

**Cheshire**

Burtonwood, Fiddle i'th Bag Inn
Congleton, Lion & Swan Hotel
Disley, Dandy Cock Inn
Goostrey, Olde Red Lion Inn
Parkgate, Ship Hotel
Weston, White Lion
Wincham, Black Greyhound Hotel (lunchtime)

**Cleveland**

Guisborough, Fox Inn

**Cornwall**

Boscastle, Wellington Hotel
Helston, Angel Hotel
Lanreath, Punch Bowl Inn
Manaccan, New Inn
Marhamchurch, Bullers Arms
Perranarworthal, Norway Inn
Philleigh, Roseland Inn
St Mawes, Rising Sun Inn
St Mawgan, Falcon Inn
Sennen Cove, Old Success Inn
Trebarwith, Mill House Inn

**Cumbria**

Askham, Queen's Head Inn
Barbon, Barbon Inn
Bassenthwaite Lake, Pheasant Inn
Boot, Woolpack Inn
Calderbridge, Stanley Arms
Cartmel Fell, Mason's Arms
Casterton, Peasant Inn
Elterwater, Britannia Inn
Faugh, String of Horses Inn
Hawkshead, Queen's Head
Levens, Hare & Hounds Inn (lunchtime)
Loweswater, Kirkstile Inn
Lowick, Farmers Arms (lunchtime)
Metal Bridge, Metal Bridge Inn
Sandside, Ship Inn
Talkin, Hare & Hounds Inn
Wasdale Head, Wasdale Head Inn
Winster, Brown Horse Inn

**Derbyshire**

Bamford, Rising Sun Hotel
Fenny Bentley, Bentley Brook Inn
Hope, Poachers Arms

**Devon**

Alswear, Butchers Arms
Beer, Anchor Inn
Branscombe, Masons Arms
Brendon, Stag Hunter's Inn
Christow, Artichoke Inn
Croyde, Thatched Barn Inn
Eggesford, Fox & Hounds Hotel
Georgeham, Rock Inn
Hatherleigh, George Hotel
Haytor Vale, Rock Inn
Hexworthy, Forest Inn
Lifton, Arundell Arms
Lydford, Castle Inn
Lynton, Crown Hotel
Moretonhampstead, White Hart Hotel

These and other pubs in the Guide which have facilities for children are denoted by the words **Family pub**.

North Bovey, Ring of Bells
Sandygate, Blue Ball Inn
South Zeal, Oxenham Arms
Staverton, Sea Trout Inn
Stokenham, Tradesman's Arms
Woodbury Salterton, Digger's Rest (till 8pm)
Yarde Down, Poltimore Arms

**Dorset**

Ansty, Fox Inn
Bridport, Bull Hotel
Cerne Abbas, New Inn
Cranborne, Fleur de Lys Hotel
Dorchester, King's Arms
Fiddleford, Fiddleford Inn
Kingston, Scott Arms
Milton Abbas, Hambro Arms
Poole, Inn in the Park
Shave Cross, Shave Cross Inn
West Bexington, Manor Hotel
Winfrith Newburgh, Red Lion

**Co. Durham**

Barnard Castle, Red Well Inn
Durham, Traveller's Rest
Greta Bridge, Morritt Arms Hotel
Piercebridge, George
Romaldkirk, Rose & Crown
Sedgefield, Nag's Head Inn
Stapleton, Bridge Inn

**Essex**

Braintree, Retreat
Coggeshall, White Hart Hotel
Dedham, Marlborough Head
Easthorpe, House Without a Name
Gestingthorpe, Pheasant
Great Waltham, Windmill
Saffron Walden, Eight Bells
Saffron Walden, Saffron Hotel

**Gloucestershire**

Bibury, Catherine Wheel
Bledington, King's Head
Broadwell, Fox Inn
Chedworth, Seven Tuns
Chipping Campden, Kings Arms Hotel
Coln St Aldwyns, New Inn
Elkstone, Highwayman
Frampton Mansell, Crown Inn
Kineton, Halfway House (lunchtime)
Kingscote, Hunter's Hall Inn
Little Washbourne, Hobnails Inn
Nailsworth, Tipputs Inn
North Cerney, Bathurst Arms (lunchtime)
Stow-on-the-Wold, Royalist Hotel
Stowe Green, Traveller's Rest Inn
Tetbury, Gentle Gardener
Toddington, Pheasant
Upper Oddington, Horse & Groom Inn
Withington, Mill Inn

These and other pubs in the Guide which have facilities for children are denoted by the words **Family pub**.

*It can only be...*
*Schhh... you-know-who*

**Greater Manchester**
Hawk Green, Crown (lunchtime)
**Hampshire**
Beauworth, Milbury's
Damerham, Compasses Inn
Ibsley, Old Beams Inn
Ovington, Bush Inn
Ringwood, Original White Hart
Rotherwick, Coach & Horses
Stockbridge, Vine Inn
**Hereford & Worcester**
Abberley, Bell at Pensax
Bewdley, Black Boy Hotel
Bromyard, Hop Pole Hotel
Carey, Cottage of Content
Chaddesley Corbett, Talbot Inn
Fownhope, Green Man Inn
Hereford, Cock of Tupsley
Kingsland, Angel Inn
Knightwick, Talbot Hotel
Ledbury, Ye Olde Talbot Hotel
Leominster, Royal Oak Hotel
Malvern, Foley Arms Hotel
Mamble, Sun & Slipper
Pembridge, New Inn
Ross on Wye, Rosswyn Hotel
Sellack, Loughpool Inn
Weobley, Red Lion Hotel
Woolhope, Butchers Arms (lunchtime)
**Hertfordshire**
Ashwell, Three Tuns Hotel
Chenies, Bedford Arms Thistle Hotel
Flamstead, Three Blackbirds
Great Chishill, Pheasant Inn (lunchtime)
Puckeridge, White Hart
**Humberside**
Bishop Wilton, Fleece Inn
Driffield, Bell Hotel
Howden, Bowmans Hotel
Market Weighton, Londesborough Arms
Pocklington, Feathers Hotel
Skidby, Half Moon Inn
Sutton upon Derwent, St Vincent Arms
**Isle of Wight**
Chale, Clarendon Hotel
**Kent**
Biddenden, Three Chimneys
Chilham, Woolpack
Fairbourne Heath, Pepper Box
Harriestsham, Ringlestone Inn
Hawkhurst, Royal Oak Hotel
Hawkhurst, Tudor Arms Hotel
Ickham, Duke William
Marshside, Gate Inn
Newenden, White Hart
Smarden, Bell
Tenterden, White Lion Hotel
Wingham, Red Lion Inn
Wye, Kings Head Hotel
Wye, New Flying Horse Inn
**Lancashire**
Forton, New Holly Hotel
Mellor, Millstone Hotel
Newton-in-Bowland, Parkers Arms Hotel
Slaidburn, Hark to Bounty Inn
Whitewell, Inn at Whitewell
**Leicestershire**
Cottesmore, Sun Inn
Empingham, White Horse
Kegworth, White House (lunchtime)
Langham, Noel Arms
Old Dalby, Crown Inn
Waltham-on-the-Wolds, Royal Horseshoes
**Lincolnshire**
Boston, New England Hotel
Grimsthorpe, Black Horse Inn
Lincoln, Wig & Mitre
Newton, Red Lion Inn
Silk Willoughby, Horseshoes
Stamford, Bull & Swan Inn
Stamford, Crown Hotel
Stamford, George of Stamford
**Middlesex**
Isleworth, London Apprentice
Shepperton, Anchor Hotel
Shepperton, Thames Court
Teddington, Clarence Hotel (lunchtime)

These and other pubs in the Guide which have facilities for children are denoted by the words **Family pub**.

*It can only be...*
*Schhh...you-know-who*

Twickenham, White Swan

**Norfolk**

Blickling, Buckinghamshire Arms
Briston, John H. Stracey
Great Ryburgh, Boar Inn
Hunworth, Bell Inn
Scole, Scole Inn
Stow Bardolph, Hare Arms
Winterton-on-Sea, Fisherman's Return

**Northamptonshire**

Blakesley, Bartholomew Arms
Collyweston, Cavalier
Fotheringhay, Falcon Inn
Nassington, Black Horse Inn
Weedon, Crossroads Hotel
Weldon, George Hotel

**Northumberland**

Cornhill-on-Tweed Collingwood Arms Hotel
Seahouses, Olde Ship Hotel
Wall, Hadrian Inn
Wooler, Tankerville Arms

**Nottinghamshire**

Bottesford, Red Lion
Newark, Robin Hood Hotel

**Oxfordshire**

Ashbury, Rose & Crown Hotel
Asthall, Maytime
Charlbury, Bell at Charlbury
Chipping Norton, Crown & Cushion
Clanfield, Clanfield Tavern
Cumnor, Bear & Ragged Staff
Dorchester-on-Thames, George Hotel
Duns Tew, White Horse Inn
Faringdon, Bell Hotel
Fifield, Merrymouth Inn
Frilford Heath, Dog House Hotel (lunchtime)
Fyfield, White Hart
Henley-on-Thames, Victoria
Oxford, Turf Tavern
Peppard Common, Red Lion
Pyrton, Plough Inn
Shenington, Bell
Shiplake, Baskerville Arms
South Leigh, Mason Arms
Stanton Harcourt, Harcourt Arms
Towersey, Three Horseshoes
Weston on the Green, Chequers Inn
Witney, Butchers Arms
Woodstock, Black Prince
Woodstock, Marlborough Arms
Woodstock, Punch Bowl Inn

**Shropshire**

Bridgnorth, Falcon Hotel
Brockton, Feathers Inn
Hopton Wafers, Crown Inn
Market Drayton, Corbet Arms Hotel
Pulverbatch, White Horse

**Somerset**

Brendon Hills, Ralegh's Cross Inn
Burtle, Ye Olde Burtle Inn
Croscombe, Bull Terrier
Glastonbury, George & Pilgrims Hotel

These and other pubs in the Guide which have facilities for children are denoted by the words **Family pub**.

*It can only be...*
*Schhh...you-know-who*

Knapp, Rising Sun
Leigh on Mendip, Bell Inn
Long Sutton, Devonshire Arms
Montacute, Kings Arms Inn
North Petherton, Walnut Tree Inn
North Wootton, Crossways Inn
Nunney, George Inn
Stoke St Gregory, Rose & Crown
Williton, Egremont Hotel
Wincanton, Hunters' Lodge Inn
Woolverton, Red Lion

**Staffordshire**

Alrewas, George & Dragon
Leek, Three Horseshoes Inn
Onecote, Jervis Arms
Sandon Bank, Seven Stars Inn
Stafford, Swan Hotel
Tutbury, Ye Olde Dog & Partridge

**Suffolk**

Brome, Oaksmere
Bromeswell, Cherry Tree
Cavendish, George
Long Melford, Crown Inn Hotel
Mildenhall, Bell Hotel
Needham Market, Limes Hotel
Newton, Saracen's Head
Pin Mill, Butt & Oyster
Southwold, Crown Hotel
Stoke-by-Nayland, Crown
Woodbridge, Bull Hotel

**Surrey**

Alford Crossways, Napoleon Arms
Chiddingfold, Crown Inn
Cobham, Plough
Downside, Cricketers
Farnham, Spotted Cow
Gomshall, Black Horse Inn
Holmbury St Mary, Royal Oak
Oakwoodhill, Punchbowl Inn
Ockley, King's Arms

**East Sussex**

Bexhill, Wilton Court
Brightling, Fullers Arms (lunchtime)
Burwash, Bell Inn
Framfield, Barley Mow
Hartfield, Anchor
Mark Cross, Mark Cross Inn
Offham, Blacksmith's Arms

These and other pubs in the Guide which have facilities for children are denoted by the words **Family pub**.

*It can only be...*
*Schhh...you-know-who*

Old Heathfield, Star Inn
Winchelsea, Winchelsea Lodge Motel

**West Sussex**

Ashington, Red Lion
Clayton, Jack & Jill Inn
Lancing, Sussex Pad
Lickfold, Lickfold Inn
Lurgashall, Noah's Ark
Midhurst, Angel Hotel
Petworth, Angel
Stopham Bridge, White Hart

**Warwickshire**

Coleshill, Coleshill Hotel
Dunchurch, Dun Cow Hotel
Priors Hardwick, Butchers Arms
Sambourne, Green Dragon
Shipston on Stour, White Bear
Stratford-upon-Avon, Slug & Lettuce
Wellesbourne, King's Head
Wilmcote, Swan House Hotel

**West Midlands**

Stourbridge, Talbot Hotel

**Wiltshire**

Box, Chequers
Bratton, Duke
Broad Hinton, Crown Inn
Burton, Plume of Feathers
Castle Combe, Castle Hotel
Chiseldon, Patriots Arms
Corsham, Methuen Arms Hotel
Devizes, Bear Hotel
Fonthill Bishop, Kings Arms
Ford, White Hart
Fovant, Cross Keys Inn
Holt, Old Ham Tree
Lower Woodford, Wheatsheaf
Malmesbury, Suffolk Arms
Mere, Old Ship Hotel
Pewsham, Lysley Arms
Ramsbury, Bell at Ramsbury
Salisbury, Haunch of Venison
Salisbury, High Post Hotel
Semley, Benett Arms

**North Yorkshire**

Appletreewick, Craven Arms
Arkengarthdale, C. B. Hotel
Askrigg, Kings Arms Hotel
Bainbridge, Rose & Crown Hotel (lunchtime)
Constable Burton, Wyvill Arms
Coxwold, Fauconberg Arms
East Layton, Fox Hall Inn
Elslack, Tempest Arms
Gargrave, Anchor Inn
Great Ayton, Royal Oak Hotel
Harome, Star Inn
Horton in Ribblesdale, Crown Hotel
Hovingham, Worsley Arms Hotel
Hubberholme, George Inn
Kettlewell, Bluebell Hotel
Kettlewell, Racehorses Hotel
Malham, Buck Inn
Malton, Green Man Hotel
Middleham, Black Swan Hotel
Osgodby, Barn (summer)
Oswaldkirk, Malt Shovel Inn
Pickhill, Nags Head
Richmond, Castle Tavern
Rosedale Abbey, Blacksmith's Arms
Rosedale Abbey, White Horse Farm Hotel
Sleights, Salmon Leap
Snainton, Coachman Inn
Staddle Bridge, McCoy's at the Tontine
Starbotton, Fox & Hounds
Staveley, Royal Oak
Terrington, Bay Horse Inn
Wath in Nidderdale, Sportsman's Arms Hotel
West Witton, Wensleydale Heifer

**South Yorkshire**

Sutton, Anne Arms

**West Yorkshire**

Darrington, Darrington Hotel
Holywell Green, Rock Hotel
Linton, Windmill Inn
Shelley, Three Acres Inn

**SCOTLAND**

**Borders**

Eddleston, Horse Shoe Inn
Melrose, Burts Hotel
Melrose, George & Abbotsford

These and other pubs in the Guide which have facilities for children are denoted by the words **Family pub**.

*It can only be...*
*Schhh...you-know-who*

**Central**
Killin, Clachaig Hotel
Killin, Queen's Court Hotel (till 9pm)
Kippen, Cross Keys
Strathblane, Kirkhouse Inn
**Dumfries & Galloway**
Castle Douglas, King's Arms Hotel
Moffat, Balmoral Hotel
New Abbey, Criffel Inn
**Fife**
Anstruther, Craw's Nest Hotel
**Grampian**
Elrick, Broadstraik Inn (till 7.30pm)
Fochabers, Gordon Arms Hotel (lunchtime)
**Highland**
Dulnain Bridge, Muckrach Lodge Hotel
Glenfinnan, Stage House Inn
Invergarry, Inn on the Garry
Invermoriston, Glenmoriston Arms
Lewiston, Lewiston Arms Hotel
Lybster, Bayview Hotel
Muir of Ord, Ord Arms Hotel
Onich, Onich Hotel
Portree, Rosedale Hotel (lunchtime)
Spean Bridge, Letterfinlay Lodge Hotel
Spinningdale, Old Mill Inn
Uig, Ferry Inn
Ullapool, Argyll Hotel
**Lothian**
Balerno, Marchbank Hotel
Edinburgh, Rutland Hotel
Linlithgow, Champany Inn
Wester Howgate, Old Howgate Inn
**Strathclyde**
Airdrie, Staging Post
Busby, Busby Hotel
Loch Eck, Coylet Inn
Tarbert, West Loch Hotel
Tayvallich, New Tayvallich Hotel
**Tayside**
Killiecrankie, Killiecrankie Hotel

**WALES**
**Clwyd**
Bodfari, Dinorben Arms Inn
Holywell, Stamford Gate Hotel
Llanarmon DC, West Arms Hotel
Mold, Arches Inn
**Dyfed**
Cardigan, Black Lion Hotel
Cenarth, White Hart
Henllan, Henllan Falls Inn
Llanarthney, Golden Grove Arms
Llandovery, King's Head Inn
Wolf's Castle, Wolfe Inn
**Gwent**
Llanfihangel Crucorney, Skirrid Inn
Monmouth, Queens Head Hotel
Raglan, Beaufort Arms Hotel
Whitebrook, Crown at Whitebrook
**Gwynedd**
Beaumaris, Ye Olde Bull's Head
Penmaenpool, George III Hotel
**Mid Glamorgan**
Nottage, Rose & Crown
**Powys**
Crickhowell, Nantyffin Cider Mill Inn
Hay-on-Wye, Old Black Lion
Llanfrynach, White Swan
Penybont, Severn Arms (lunchtime)

**CHANNEL ISLANDS**
Pleinmont, Guernsey, Imperial Hotel
St Aubin's Harbour, Jersey, Old Court House Inn

**ISLE OF MAN**
Peel, Creek Inn

These and other pubs in the Guide which have facilities for children are denoted by the words **Family pub**.

*Schweppes*®
The First Name in
Fruit Juice

# RESTAURANTS

## RECOMMENDED IN OUR HOTEL & RESTAURANT GUIDE

# AT PUBS

**ENGLAND**

Chenies, Herts: Bedford Arms Thistle Hotel
Chipping Campden, Glos: Kings Arms Hotel
Coggeshall, Essex: White Hart Hotel
Corton, Wilts: Dove
Cumnor, Oxon: Bear & Ragged Staff
Grimsthorpe, Lincs: White Hart
Harome, N Yorks: Star Inn
Hildenborough, Kent: Gate Inn
Hungerford, Berks: Bear at Hungerford
Huntingdon, Cambs: Old Bridge Hotel
Kintbury, Berks: Dundas Arms
Lifton, Devon: Arundell Arms
Llanfair Waterdine, Shrops: Red Lion Inn
Moulton, N Yorks: Black Bull Inn
Ockley, Surrey: King's Arms
Orford, Suffolk: King's Head Inn
Pett Bottom, Kent: Duck Inn
Ramsbury, Wilts: Bell at Ramsbury
Ripponden, W Yorks: Old Bridge Inn
Saffron Walden, Essex: Saffron Hotel
St Mawes, Corn: Rising Sun Hotel
Scole, Norfolk: Scole Inn
Shipton-under-Wychwood, Oxon: Lamb Inn
Staddle Bridge, N Yorks: McCoy's at the Tontine
Stamford, Lincs: George of Stamford
Stanton Harcourt, Oxon: Harcourt Arms
Stapleton, Co. Durham: Bridge Inn
Tarrant Monkton, Dorset: Langton Arms
Tetbury, Glos: Gentle Gardener Restaurant
Timperley, Gtr Manch: Le Bon Viveur
Troutbeck, Cumb: Mortal Man Hotel

*continued*

Tunbridge Wells, Kent: Royal Wells Inn
Winkleigh, Devon: King's Arms
Yattendon, Berks: Royal Oak Hotel

**SCOTLAND**
Canonbie, D & G: River Inn
Dulnain Bridge, H'land: Muckrach Lodge Hotel
Dysart, Fife: Old Rectory Inn
Linlithgow, Lothian: Champany Inn
Tayvallich, Strathclyde: New Tayvallich Inn
Wester Howgate, Lothian: Old Howgate Inn

**WALES**
Crickhowell, Powys: Nantyffin Cider Mill Inn
Three Cocks, Powys: Three Cocks Hotel

**CHANNEL ISLANDS**
St Aubin's Harbour, Jersey: Old Court House Inn

# WATERSIDE PUBS

**LONDON**
Anchor, SE1
Angel, SE16
Bull's Head, W4
City Barge, W4
Dickens Inn, E1
Dove, W6
Grapes, E14
King's Head & Eight Bells, SW3
Mayflower, SE16
Prospect of Whitby, E1
Samuel Pepys, EC4
Ship, SW14
Trafalgar Tavern, SE10
Yacht, SE10

**ENGLAND**
Armathwaite, Cumb: Duke's Head Hotel
Beaulieu, Hants: Montagu Arms Hotel, Spats Bar
Bedford, Beds: Embankment Hotel
Beer, Devon: Anchor Inn
Bewdley, H & W: Black Boy Hotel
Bexhill, E Sussex: Wilton Court
Bidford-on-Avon, Warwicks: White Lion Hotel
Bledington, Glos: King's Head
Brendon, Devon: Stag Hunter's Inn
Buckler's Hard, Hants: Master Builders House Hotel
Burnham-on-Crouch, Essex: Ye Olde White Harte
Calderbridge, Cumb: Stanley Arms
Chappel, Essex: Swan Inn
Eskdale, Cumb: Bower House Inn
Felixstowe, Suffolk: Fludyer Arms Hotel
Fiskerton, Notts: Bromley Arms
Ford, Wilts: White Hart
Fossebridge, Glos: Fossebridge Inn
Gargrave, N Yorks: Anchor Inn
Great Shefford, Berks: Swan
Helford, Corn: Shipwright's Arms
Holywell, Cambs: Ye Olde Ferry Boat Inn
Horley, Surrey: Ye Olde Six Bells
Hubberholme, N Yorks: George Inn
Hungerford, Berks: Bear at Hungerford
Huntingdon, Cambs: Old Bridge Hotel
Ightham, Kent: George & Dragon
Isleworth, Middx: London Apprentice
Kegworth, Leics: White House
Kettlewell, N Yorks: Bluebell Hotel
Kettlewell, N Yorks: Racehorses Hotel
Kintbury, Berks: Dundas Arms
Knightwick, H & W: Talbot Hotel
Lamberhurst, Kent: Chequers Inn
Lamberhurst, Kent: George & Dragon
Langdale, Cumb: Pillar Hotel, Hobson's Pub
Llanfair Waterdine, Shrops: Red Lion
Loweswater, Cumb: Kirkstile Inn
Marshside, Kent: Gate Inn
Metal Bridge, Cumb: Metal Bridge Inn
Needingworth, Cambs: Pike & Eel Inn
Newbridge, Oxon: Maybush
Newenden, Kent: White Hart
North Cerney, Glos: Bathurst Arms
Onecote, Staffs: Jervis Arms
Ovington, Hants: Bush Inn
Parkgate, Ches: Ship Hotel
Piercebridge, Co. Durham: George
Pin Mill, Suffolk: Butt & Oyster
Pooley Bridge, Cumb: Crown Hotel
Porlock Weir, Som: Anchor Hotel & Ship Inn
Port Gaverne, Corn: Port Gaverne Hotel

*continued*

Pulborough, W Sussex: Waters Edge
Ripponden, W Yorks: Old Bridge Inn
St Mawes, Corn: Rising Sun Inn
Sandside, Cumb: Ship Inn
Sennen Cove, Corn: Old Success Inn
Shepperton, Middx: Thames Court
Sleights, N Yorks: Salmon Leap
Smarden, Kent: Chequers Inn
Stockbridge, Hants: Vine Inn
Stopham Bridge, W Sussex: White Hart
Testcombe, Hants: Mayfly
Trebarwith, Corn: Mill House Inn
Twickenham, Middx: White Swan
Umberleigh, Devon: Rising Sun Inn
Wansford, Cambs: Haycock Inn
Wasdale Head, Cumb: Wasdale Head Inn
Whitewell, Lancs: Inn at Whitewell
Whitney-on-Wye, H & W: Rhydspence Inn
Winkton, Dorset: Fisherman's Haunt
Withington, Glos: Mill Inn
Woodstock, Oxon: Black Prince

**SCOTLAND**

Canonbie, D & G: Riverside Inn
Catterline, Grampian: Creel Inn
Edinburgh, Lothian: Cramond Inn
Inverbeg, S'clyde: Inverbeg Inn
Killin, Central: Clachaig Hotel
Killin, Central: Queen's Court Hotel
Loch Eck, S'clyde: Coylet Inn
Onich, H'land: Onich Hotel
Portree, H'land: Rosedale Hotel
Spean Bridge, H'land: Letterfinlay Lodge Hotel
Tarbert, S'clyde: West Loch Hotel
Tayvallich, S'clyde: New Tayvallich Inn

**WALES**

Aberaeron, Dyfed: Harbourmaster Hotel
Brockweir, Gwent: Brockweir Inn
Dolgellau, Gwynedd: Gwernan Lake Hotel
Felindre Farchog, Dyfed: Old Salutation Inn
Llanarmon Dyffryn Ceiriog, Clwyd: West Arms Hotel
Llangorse, Powys: Red Lion
Menai Bridge, Gwynedd: Gazelle Hotel
Penmaenpool, Gwynedd: George III Hotel

**CHANNEL ISLANDS**

Pleinmont, Guernsey: Imperial Hotel
St Aubin's Harbour, Jersey: Old Court House Inn

**ISLE OF MAN**

Peel: Creek Inn

# LONDON

# LONDON PUBS BY AREAS

**BAYSWATER & NOTTING HILL**
Victoria, 10a Strathearn Place, W2
Windsor Castle, 114 Campden Hill Road, W8

**BLOOMSBURY & HOLBORN**
Lamb, 94 Lamb's Conduit Street, WC1
Museum Tavern, 49 Great Russell Street, WC1
Ye Olde Mitre Tavern, Ely Court, Ely Place, EC1

**CHELSEA**
Admiral Codrington, 17 Mossop Street, SW3
King's Head & Eight Bells, 50 Cheyne Walk, SW3

**CITY**
Black Friar, 174 Queen Victoria Street, EC4
Cock Tavern, Poultry Market, Central Markets, EC1
Crowders Well, Fore Street, EC2
Dirty Dick's, 202 Bishopsgate, EC2
Fox & Anchor, 115 Charterhouse Street, EC1
Hand & Shears, 1 Middle Street, EC1
Railway Tavern, 15 Liverpool Street, EC2
Samuel Pepys, Brooks Wharf, Upper Thames Street, EC4
Three Compasses, 66 Cowcross Street, EC1
Ye Olde Dr Butler's Head, Masons Avenue, Coleman Street, WC2
Ye Olde Watling, 29 Watling Street, EC4

**COVENT GARDEN**
Lamb & Flag, 33 Rose Street, off Garrick Street, WC2
Maple Leaf, 41 Maiden Lane, WC2
Nag's Head, 10 James Street, WC2
Nell of Old Drury, 29 Catherine Street, WC2
Salisbury, St Martin's Lane, WC2

**EAST LONDON**
Black Lion, 59 High Street, Plaistow, E13
Dickens Inn, St Katharine's Way, E1
Grapes, 76 Narrow Street, E14
Prospect of Whitby, 57 Wapping Wall, E1

**FLEET STREET**
Old Bell Tavern, 95 Fleet Street, EC4
Printer's Devil, 98 Fetter Lane, EC4
Seven Stars, 53 Carey Street, WC2
Ye Olde Cheshire Cheese, 145 Fleet Street, EC4
Ye Olde Cock Tavern, 22 Fleet Street, EC4

**KNIGHTSBRIDGE**
Grenadier, 18 Wilton Row, SW1
Paxton's Head, 153 Knightsbridge, SW1

**MAYFAIR & MARYLEBONE**
Prince Regent, 71 Marylebone High Street, W1
Red Lion, 1 Waverton Street, W1
Shepherd's Tavern, 50 Hertford Street, W1
Thistle, 11 Vigo Street, W1
Ye Grapes, 16 Shepherd Market, W1

**NORTH & NORTH-WEST LONDON**
Albion, 10 Thornhill Road, N1
Bull & Bush, North End Way, NW3
Eagle, 2 Shepherdess Walk, N1
Flask, 77 Highgate West Hill, Highgate, N6
Jack Straw's Castle, North End Way, NW3
Spaniards Inn, Spaniards Road, NW3

**ST JAMES'S**
Red Lion, 23 Crown Passage, Pall Mall, SW1
Two Chairmen, Warwick House Street, off Cockspur Street, SW1

**SOHO & TRAFALGAR SQUARE**
Sherlock Holmes, 10 Northumberland Street, WC2
Tom Cribb, Panton Street, SW1

*continued*

**SOUTH-EAST LONDON**
Anchor, 1 Bankside, Southwark, SE1
Angel, 101 Bermondsey Wall East, SE16
Fox & Firkin, 316 Lewisham High Street, SE13
George, 77 Borough High Street, Southwark, SE1
Mayflower, 117 Rotherhithe Street, SE16
Trafalgar Tavern, Park Row, SE10
Yacht, Crane Street, SE10

**SOUTH-WEST LONDON**
Hand in Hand, Crooked Billet, Wimbledon Common, SW19
Ship, 10 Thames Bank, Riverside, SW14
Sun Inn, 7 Church Road, Barnes, SW13
White Horse on Parsons Green, 1 Parsons Green, SW6
Ye Olde Windmill Inn, Clapham Common Southside, SW4

**VICTORIA & WESTMINSTER**
Albert, 52 Victoria Street, SW1
Orange Brewery, 37 Pimlico Road, SW1
St Stephen's Tavern, 10 Bridge Street, SW1
Two Chairmen, 39 Dartmouth Street, SW1

**WEST LONDON**
Bull's Head, Strand-on-the-Green, W4
City Barge, Strand-on-the-Green, W4
Dove, 19 Upper Mall, W6

## *Admiral Codrington* *(Food)*

17 Mossop Street, SW3 · Map 12 B1
01-589 4603

*Brewery* Bass
*Landlords* Melvyn & Sue Barnett
T-bone steak £5.25 Steak & mushroom pie & vegetables £2.75 (Last order 10.45pm. No bar food Sun)
Bass; Charrington's IPA; Stones Bitter; Guinness; Carling Black Label; Tennent's Extra; Taunton cider. *Real ale*

The gas-lit bar and flower-filled covered patio are equally delightful settings for enjoying the excellent food served at this sociable Victorian-style pub. Steaks are always very popular, grilled to a T over charcoal, and other hot dishes might include curries, pies and lemon sole. Cold cuts and well-kept cheeses widen the choice further, and to round things off there's a refreshing fruit salad.

## *Albert*

A handsome and much photographed Victorian survival in a street largely taken over by modern office blocks. The Albert opened as a pub in 1867, having been bought five years earlier from the Dean and Chapter of Westminster, and there are many period features to admire, including carved woodwork and fine engraved glass windows.

52 Victoria Street, SW1 · Map 12 C1
01-222 5577
*Owner* London Host *Landlords* Mr & Mrs E. Jones
Watney's Stag Bitter, Special; Combe's Bitter; Websters Yorkshire Bitter; Ben Truman; Guinness; Holsten; Foster's. *Real ale*

## *Albion* *(Food)*

10 Thornhill Road, N1 · Map 10 C1
01-607 7450

*Owners* London Hosts
*Landlords* Michael & Shirley Parish

Steak & kidney pudding £2.85 Steamed syrup pudding 80p (Last order 10.30pm)
Ruddle's County; Webster's Yorkshire Bitter; Watney's Special; Ben Truman; Guinness; Holsten; cider. *Real ale*

Lunchtime crowds flock to this charming Victorian pub to enjoy some splendid traditional home cooking. Hot salt beef is the treat on Monday and Friday, steak and kidney pudding on Thursday; other delights include hearty soups, bangers and mash, succulent roast lamb and fried fish, with sandwiches and ploughman's for lighter snacks and always a good old-fashioned English pud. Less evening choice. Garden. **Family pub**

## *Anchor*

Customers watched the Great Fire of London from the original Anchor, which was later replaced by a Georgian building. The famous Clink Prison and Globe Theatre stood nearby, and Russian Imperial Stout, Dr Johnson's favourite drink, originated at the neighbouring brewery. Superb river views from the terrace. **Family pub**

1 Bankside, Southwark, SE1 · Map 11 C2
01-407 1577
*Brewery* Courage *Landlord* Gary Lloyd
Courage Director's Bitter, Best Bitter; John Smith's Bitter; Guinness; Kronenbourg; Hofmeister; Taunton cider. *Real ale*

## Angel

Views of the Thames come no better than those enjoyed by this popular pub, whose prominent patrons down the years have included Samuel Pepys and Captain Cook, Judge Jeffreys and Laurel and Hardy. There was a tavern here in the 15th century, and the Angel of today is a brick-built pub with an open-plan interior.

101 Bermondsey Wall East, Rotherhithe, SE16 · Map 10 D2
01-237 3608
*Owner* Imperial Inns & Taverns *Landlord* Mr Derek Davies
Courage Best Bitter, Directors Bitter; John Smith's Bitter; Guinness; Taunton cider. *Real ale*

## Black Friar

A 13th-century Dominican priory formerly occupied the site of this 300-year old pub, re-decorated at the turn of the century. Five types of Italian marble, mosaics, and bas reliefs of jolly friars are an antiquarian's delight. Closed Sat lunch (in winter), Sat eve, all Sun & Bank Holidays.

174 Queen Victoria Street, EC4 · Map 11 C1
01-236 5650
*Free House* *Landlord* Mr Doug Walls
Tetley's Bitter; Morrell's Bitter; Guinness; Oranjeboom; Holsten; cider. *Real ale*

## Black Lion *(Food)*

59 High Street, Plaistow, E13. Map 10 D1
01-472 2351

*Brewery* Courage
*Landlord* Mr R. Hales
Prawn omelette & chips £1.50 Steak & kidney pie or pudding £1.50 (Last order 7.30pm. No bar food Sat eve & all Sun)
Courage Directors Bitter, Best Bitter; Guinness; Kronenbourg; Hofmeister; Taunton cider. *Real ale*

The steak and kidney pudding is a must at this friendly, down-to-earth pub. Light, well-cooked suet crust, plenty of tender meat and lovely rich gravy make a dish to remember. Other super snacks include home-made bubble and squeak, hearty chicken and vegetable soup, freshly cut sandwiches and fluffy omelettes served with lovely chips. Blackberry and apple pie for a splendid finish. Less evening choice. Beer garden.

## Bull & Bush

Immortalised in the old music hall song 'Down at the Old Bull & Bush', this plush pub lined with prints and photographs of show-biz personalities attracts lively crowds in the evening. Set on the edge of Hampstead Heath, the former 17th-century farmhouse was once the home of painter William Hogarth. Beer garden.

North End Way, NW3 · Map 9 B1
01-455 3685
*Brewery* Taylor Walker *Landlord* Graham Dove
Taylor Walker Bitter; Burton's Bitter; Guinness; Löwenbräu; Oranjeboom; Skol; cider. *Real ale*

## *Bull's Head*

Right on the towpath on a delightful stretch of the Thames at Chiswick, this 350-year-old pub gained fame as the headquarters of Oliver Cromwell during the Civil War. The comfortable panelled bar affords pleasant views of the river.

Strand-on-the-Green, W4 · Map 9 A3
01-994 1204
*Owner* London Host *Landlords* Mr & Mrs Ward
Watney's Stag, Combes Bitter; Webster's Yorkshire Bitter; Guinness; Carlsberg; Foster's; Holsten. *Real ale*

We have raised our standards considerably since last year. The omission of some houses that appeared in last year's Guide is no reflection on their standing.

## *City Barge*

This popular tavern on the Thames towpath was named after the Lord Mayor's official barge which used to be moored nearby. Largely rebuilt after World War II, the pub still features some fine antiques, beams and brassware. There are two comfortable bars, one in period style and the other smartly up to date. **Family pub**

Strand-on-the-Green, W4 · Map 9 A3
01-994 2148
*Brewery* Courage *Landlord* Mr J. MacDonald
Courage Directors Bitter, Best Bitter, JC; Guinness; Kronenbourg; cider. *Real ale*

## *Cock Tavern* *(Food)*

The Poultry Market, Central Markets, EC1
Map 11 C1
01-248 2918
*Free House*
*Landlord* Mr A. Burrows
Salt beef, pease pudding & potatoes £4.50
Sirloin steak & vegetables £6.50 (No bar food eves)
Courage Best Bitter; Young's Special; John Bull Bitter; John Smith's Bitter; Guinness; Hofmeister. *Real ale*

Succulent salt beef brisket is the speciality at this cheerful pub under Smithfield poultry market: served generously with potatoes, carrots and pease pudding, it's an outstanding pub dish. Steaks, game and roast turkey provide further lunchtime choice, and soup, sandwiches and salads are available for lighter snacks till 3pm. From 6am there's a good breakfast selection. Closed Saturday, Sunday & Bank Holidays.
**Family pub**

## *Crowders Well* *(Food)*

Fore Street, EC2 · Map 11 C1
01-628 8574

*Brewery* Vintage Inns
*Landlord* Mr A. D. Cregg

Lasagne £2.20 Chilli con carne £2.20 (No bar food eves)
Bass; Charrington IPA; Worthington 'E'; Guinness; Carling Black Label; Tennent's Extra; Taunton cider. *Real ale*

Lunchtime in the comfortable pantry bar of this popular city pub sees a good choice of tasty, well-prepared snacks. Lasagne and calf's liver veneziana are two of the Italian chef's homeland specialities, and there are also salads and sandwiches, smooth pâté, quiches and chilli. The bar opens on to a terrace and the Barbican's lake complex. Closed Saturday and Sunday.

## *Dickens Inn* *(Food)*

St Katharine's Way, E1 · Map 10 C2
01-488 9936

*Free House*
*Landlord* Michael Harwood
Ploughman's lunch £1.45 Steak & kidney pie with vegetables £2.95 (Last order 10pm)
Dickens Own, Special; Ruddle's County, Ordinary; Fuller's London Pride; Sam Smith's Old Brewery Bitter; Guinness; Tennent's Extra; Carling Black Label; cider. *Real ale*

Tiered wooden balconies create a distinctive frontage at this modern conversion of a dockland warehouse, and a terrace overlooking the river makes it very popular with tourists. The busy bars offer a wide variety of simple, tasty pub food, from pâté and quiche to steak and kidney pie, casseroles and meatballs.

## *Dirty Dick's*

Nathaniel Bentley, who became landlord in 1761, earned the nickname Dirty Dick when he renounced cleanliness – both personal and territorial – after the death of his prospective bride. Genuine period atmosphere remains in the stone-floored cellar, while the main bar is in Victorian style. Closed Sat and Sun eves.

202 Bishopsgate, EC2 · Map 10 C2
01-283 5888
*Free House* *Landlord* Mr J. Clapham
Charrington's IPA; Greene King IPA; Courage Director's, Best Bitter; Guinness; Skol, Tennent's; Taunton cider. *Real ale*

## *Dove*

Turner is said to have painted the Thames from here and James Thomson, who wrote the words of 'Rule Britannia', occupied a room at the inn in 1725. The pub stands in a group of fine Georgian houses beside the river, with a vine-clad terrace from which to admire the view.

19 Upper Mall, W6 · Map 9 A2
01-748 5405
*Brewery* Fuller, Smith & Turner *Landlord* Mr Lovrey
Fuller's ESB, London Pride. *Real ale*

## Eagle

The comedienne Marie Lloyd made her debut at the Eagle in the days when it was one of London's best-known variety theatres. Perhaps an even greater claim to fame of this popular pub off the City Road is its mention in the lyrics of 'Pop Goes the Weasel'.

2 Shepherdess Walk, N1 · Map 10 C1
01-253 4715
*Brewery* Charrington *Landlord* Mr Lajune
Charrington's IPA, Bass, Toby Bitter; Guinness; Carling Black Label; Tennent's Extra; Taunton cider. *Real ale*

## Flask

Named after the flasks of spa water which could be bought here or at the nearby spring, this 18th-century Highgate pub is especially popular in summer for its hedge-rimmed forecourt. The interior is beamed and cosy. Among famous former patrons was the painter William Hogarth.

77 Highgate West Hill, N6 · Map 9 B1
01-340 3969
*Brewery* Taylor Walker *Landlord* Mrs G. Light
Taylor Walker Bitter; John Bull's Bitter; Ind Coope Burton Ale; Guinness; Löwenbräu; Oranjeboom; Skol; cider. *Real ale*

## Fox & Anchor *(Food)*

115 Charterhouse Street, EC1 · Map 11 C1
01-253 4838

*Brewery* Taylor Walker
*Landlord* Mr P. Zeid

Lamb chump chop £4.25 Mixed grill £5.50
(No bar food eves)
Taylor Walker Bitter; Ind Coope; Burton Ale; Friary Meux; Guinness; Löwenbräu; Skol; cider. *Real ale*

Grills feature strongly on the menu at this friendly, well-run pub that's open from 6am for huge breakfasts. Lamb chump chop – charcoal-crisp outside, pink and tender within – is typical of the high-quality fare available till 2.30pm, and lighter snacks include sandwiches and salads. Apple pie or good Stilton to finish. Closed evenings, weekends, 1st 2 weeks August & 1 week Christmas.

## Fox & Firkin *(Food)*

316 Lewisham High Street, SE13 · Map 10 D3
01-690 8925

*Free House*
*Landlord* Mr John Barlow

Roast beef & vegetables £3 Home-made quiche & salad £1.25 (Last order 10.30pm)
Fox Best Bitter; Dogbolter; Vixen; Murphy's Stout; Kronenbourg; Hofmeister; John Young's Lager; Taunton cider. *Real ale*

They brew their own beer at this large, sociable pub furnished with old church pews and a pulpit. The real ale's not the only attraction, though, because the food is tasty, nourishing and largely home-prepared: filled baps, well-baked quiches, good fresh salads, crusty pies and a lunch-time hot special like pork chop, curry or roast beef. Live music at night. Patio.

## *George Inn*

The only surviving galleried inn in London, the George is built round a courtyard where Shakespeare's plays were once performed. It was probably known to the Bard, being no more than 500 yards from the site of the Globe Theatre. It's certainly one of the capital's most interesting pubs, manifesting a sense of history throughout.

**Family pub**

77 Borough High Street, Southwark, SE1 · Map 11 C2
01-407 2056
*Brewery* Whitbread *Landlord* Mr & Mrs Davis
Flower's Original; Wethered's Bitter; Fremlins Tusker; Guinness; Stella Artois; Heineken; cider. *Real ale*

## *Grapes*

There's plenty of character in this peaceful little 16th-century pub tucked away by the river in the heart of dockland. Once a popular literary haunt, it is said to have been the model for the 'Six Jolly Fellowship Porters' in Charles Dickens' *Our Mutual Friend.*

76 Narrow Street, E14 · Map 10 D2
01-987 4396
*Brewery* Taylor Walker *Landlord* Mr Frank Johnson
Taylor Walker Bitter; Ind Coope Burton Ale; Friary Meux Bitter; Guinness; Löwenbräu. *Real ale*

## *Grenadier* *(Food)*

18 Wilton Row, SW1 · Map 12 C1
01-235 3074

*Owners* London Hosts
*Landlord* Mr Ken Woodhams

Steak & kidney pie £1 Cauliflower cheese 95p
(Last order 10pm)
Ruddle's County; Watney's Special, Stag; Combes Bitter; Webster Yorkshire Bitter; Guinness; Carlsberg; Holsten; cider. *Real ale*

A military theme runs through the bars of this famous pub that was once the mess for the Duke of Wellington's officers. Regulars troop in nowadays to enjoy the convivial company, the good beer and the simple, sustaining bar fare. Sandwiches are freshly cut to order, there's quiche with a salad garnish, and hot dishes include tasty cauliflower cheese and home-made steak and kidney pie. Patio.

## *Hand & Shears*

Dating back to Tudor times, this pub just off Cloth Fair gets its name from the emblem of the Guild of Merchant Tailors. A less happy association is that in the 19th-century, condemned prisoners from the notorious Newgate prison nearby were allowed to take their last drink here. Closed Sat & Sun.

1 Middle Street, EC1 · Map 11 C1
01-600 0257
*Owner* Imperial Inns *Landlord* Mr Latimer
Courage Directors Bitter, Best Bitter; Guinness; Hofmeister; Kronenbourg; Taunton cider. *Real ale*

## *Hand in Hand* *(Food)*

7 Crooked Billet, Wimbledon, SW19 · Map 9 A3
01-946 5720

*Brewery* Young's
*Landlords* Mr & Mrs D. A. Miles

Chilli con carne £1.50 Pizza £1.95 (Last order 8.30pm)
Young's Bitter, Special, Winter Warmer; Ruddle's Rutland Bitter; Guinness; Young's Lager; Taunton cider. *Real ale*

Standing in a row of little houses on the southern edge of Wimbledon Common, this sociable pub is a very popular place for lunchtime snacks. Ploughman's platters come in four varieties, and other favourites include shepherd's pie, salads, pizzas and various things with chips. The last two are the only items available in the evening. There's a cosy panelled bar, as well as a patio for pleasant weather. **Family pub**

## *Jack Straw's Castle*

Perched on the heights of Hampstead Heath, this weatherboarded pub is a famous tourist attraction. Said to be named after Wat Tyler's second-in-command during the Peasants' Revolt of 1381, it later succoured highwaymen and was also the haunt of Dickens and Thackeray. Rebuilt in 1964, the pub retains many original fittings.

North End Way, NW3 · Map 9 B1
01-435 8374
*Brewery* Charrington *Landlord* Brian Hillyard
Charrington's IPA, Bass; Stones Bitter; Guinness; Carling Black Label; Tennent's Extra; Taunton cider. *Real ale*

## *King's Head & Eight Bells* *(Food)*

50 Cheyne Walk, SW3 · Map 12 B2
01-352 1820

*Brewery* Whitbread
*Landlord* Mary Timmons

Turkey, ham & cranberry pie £1.85 Fridge cake 85p (Last order 9.30pm)
Flower's Original; Whitbread Bitter; Wethered's Bitter; Fremlins Tusker; Guinness; Stella Artois; Heineken; cider. *Real ale*

Savoury pies take top billing at this delightful Victorian pub by the Thames. Ham, turkey and cranberry, Huntingdon fidget, all-vegetable harvest – these and others are appetisingly displayed at one end of the comfortable bar, together with cold cuts, pâtés and big bowls of good fresh salads. There are simple hot snacks, too, such as baked potatoes and beef roll, plus cheese and usually a pudding or two. **Family pub**

## *Lamb*

Charles Dickens lived just around the corner from this inviting little pub. Victorian cut-glass snob screens are a noteworthy feature and hundreds of sepia photographs of stage and music hall personalities gaze down upon the busy throng at the bar.

94 Lamb's Conduit Street, WC1 · Map 11 B1
01-405 0713
*Brewery* Young *Landlord* John Jeffery
Young's Bitter, Special Bitter, Winter Warmer (winter only); Guinness; John Young's London Lager; Taunton cider. *Real ale*

**Welcome to the Guinness section of this Guide. The following ten pages are intended to tell you a little about our famous dark brew and suggest, through recipes, drinks ideas and some travel tales how you can enjoy some of the good things in life with Guinness. Cheers!**

# GUINNESS WITH FOOD

**Cooking with Guinness**
"The flavour and body of Guinness make it an excellent ingredient in a wide variety of dishes" says cookery expert, Sonia Allison *(right)*.

True aficionados of the dark brew already know that the addition of Guinness to a hearty stew does wonders for the end result.

But there are scores of other dishes, both savoury and sweet, which can be enhanced by the subtle use of Guinness.

Here are some hints to guide you along the way to better cooking with Guinness. Try them and surprise your palate!

**All the better with Guinness**
To bind a better *Pastry,* especially shortcrust or wholemeal, Guinness is great – for both savoury and sweet dishes. *Casseroles of Meat or Poultry* – one part Guinness to three parts stock really enhances the flavour.

*Rich Soups* such as oxtail, mixed vegetable or fish really deserve their Guinness. They're never quite the same without it. And if you take your game seriously, Guinness as a base ingredient makes superb gravy too. Tastier *Pasta*? Try a tablespoon of Guinness in the cooking water.

What else? *Marinades* for meat and poultry and *Desserts* such as Coffee Cheesecake – versatile Guinness adds flavour and all-round improvement to both with equal aplomb. *Batters* made with Guinness turn out beautifully crisp and tasty.

**How to avoid wasting Guinness**
*Never* put Guinness into casseroles destined for the freezer – add it when you reheat for serving. That way you get the full benefit. *Neat* Guinness on its own is not recommended as stock for casseroles or sauces. Even the best ideas can be carried too far. Full-strength Guinness is best served separately – in a glass.

GUINNESS

# COUNTRY QUICHE

**Wheatmeal Pastry**
6oz wholemeal flour
6oz self raising flour
3oz margarine
3oz lard
10 tblsp GUINNESS
pinch of salt

**Filling**
8oz cheddar cheese (grated)
8oz streaky bacon (diced)
4 spring onions (diced)
6 eggs
¾pt milk or cream
salt & pepper
4oz cheddar cheese (grated)

Make the pastry by rubbing the fats into the flours. Bind to a pliable dough with the GUINNESS. Knead lightly – roll out on a floured board and use to line a 12″ flan ring or dish. Prick the base lightly. Place the 8oz of cheddar cheese over the base of the pastry. Fry the bacon with the onions for 3 minutes and place on top of the cheese. Beat the eggs and add the milk or cream – season – pour over the flan. Top with the remaining cheese and bake 400°F, 200°C, gas mark 6 for 35/40 minutes.

Serve either hot or cold.

Serves 10

GUINNESS

# CARBONADE FLAMANDE

6 large onions (finely sliced)
2 cloves garlic crushed – optional
4 tblsp beef dripping or vegetable oil
3lb stewing beef (cut into 1″ wide strips)
4 tblsp flour
1pt GUINNESS
3 tsp vinegar
salt & pepper
2 tblsp brown sugar
bouquet garni

Serves 10

Cook the onions with the garlic and half the sugar in the dripping or oil until soft. Dust the beef with the seasoned flour and brown with the onions. Blend in the remaining flour, add the GUINNESS and vinegar. (If meat is not covered add extra beef stock). Season, add the bouquet garni. Cover closely and cook gently for 1½ hours. For extra flavour toast slices of french bread spread with french mustard on top of the casserole.

GUINNESS

# BARBECUE MARINADE

½ pt GUINNESS
4 tblsp oil
2 tblsp honey
2 tblsp tomato purée
juice and rind of 2 large oranges

Blend all the ingredients together and marinate 2lb of cubed meat or 10 steaks in this for a minimum of 2 hours, but preferably overnight. Drain from the marinade. Thread the cubes on kebab skewers with a selection of vegetables or fruit before cooking on the grill.

Sufficient for 10 kebabs or 10 steaks

GUINNESS

# STEAK & KIDNEY PIE

2lb stewing steak
(cut into ½" cubes)
10 lamb's kidneys
(skinned, cored and diced)
3 medium size onions
(finely chopped)
1pt beef stock
2 tsp Worcestershire Sauce
¼pt GUINNESS
8oz mushrooms (finely sliced)
salt & pepper
cornflour to thicken
chopped parsley
2lb puff pastry
beaten egg to glaze

Serves 10

Put the meat, kidney and onion into a saucepan and brown well. Add beef stock, Worcestershire Sauce and GUINNESS. Cover, and simmer gently for about 1 hour until meat is tender. Add mushrooms and seasoning, cook for a further 15 minutes. Remove a little of the stock and blend with about 2 tblsp cornflour. Add the blended cornflour to the steak and kidney. Bring to the boil, stir and cook for 1 minute. Place into one large pie dish or 10 individual dishes. Roll out the pastry and use to cover the cooled steak and kidney, brush with the beaten egg and bake in a hot oven 425°F, 220°C, gas mark 7 for 20 minutes until the pastry is golden brown.

# GUINNESS MIXERS

**The art of Guinness-mixing is as old as the famous brew itself and it seems that there's scarcely a drink that hasn't shared the same glass at one time or other. Many of the mixtures have provoked cries of delight. We suggest you experiment with these three first, then move on to more adventurous combinations.**

## Black Velvet

Guinness mixed fifty-fifty with champagne. This famous drink was invented in 1861 at Brooks's Club on the day Prince Albert died. The steward of the Club, with due decorum, ordered the champagne to be put in mourning and proceeded to mix it with Guinness with unexpectedly delicious results.

## Guinness Shandy

Guinness mixed with lemonade. Rumoured to have been invented by the New Zealand rugby team during a British tour. Ordering Guinness and lemonade (instead of bitter), they found the drink extremely refreshing. An appropriate drink for the All Blacks!

Try Guinness mixed with ginger beer too. That's called a Top Hat.

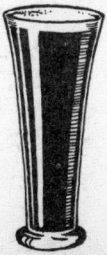

## Longship

Guinness halved with lager. A long, refreshing thirst-quencher, favoured by the Danes who find it makes their own pale brew more interesting.

It could make a Viking of you too!

# GUINNESS

# PUB PSYCHOLOGY

The British pub may *seem* like a quiet haven for relaxation, and cracking a joke or two, but is in fact a maze of subtle gestures, guarded postures and secret conflicts. These are some of the findings of a psychologist and sociologist who were commissioned by Guinness to unravel what really goes on in pubs.

The researchers visited pubs up and down the country inviting groups of drinkers to talk about themselves and their drinks. They spent a year collecting thoughts and impressions on the subject of pubs and drinks – here are some of the results.

What you drink is an expression of who you are: 'you are', they found, 'what you drink'. Each drink carries with it subtle messages about the sort of person you are, your mood and the way you drink.

For example the Guinness drinker sees himself as mature and self-confident – a man who knows what he wants and with the inner security to take time out to enjoy it. He sees other drinks as less distinctive in every way, and lager drinkers in particular as immature whizz kids.

The pub is seen as a man's 'playground'. It offers an escape from the hassles of everyday life, and a chance to recharge batteries, spiritually and physically, and partake of male camaraderie.

# GUINNESS TRAVELLERS

**Thankfully, there are few places in the world, except perhaps the most far flung, where the desire for a pint of the dark brew cannot be met.**

Here are a few interesting possibilities:

Visit *The Guinness Tavern* near the Pompidou Centre in France. The sensible *patron* is reputed to sell little else, with the possible exception of the odd dram of Irish Whiskey.

When further afield, a sojourn in the *La Toc Racquet Club of St Lucia* will improve more than your forehand drive. The tennis professional, a man of sound principles and boundless common sense, appreciates the pleasure a cool Guinness brings after a hard game of mixed doubles.

In America, head for the *Epcot Centre,* the result of a visionary dream by Walt Disney to create a world brotherhood. Guinness is available here in the British pub, just the thing after a hectic tour around this astounding complex.

If night-clubbing is more your style then the *Café des Sports* in Douala, Cameroon serves a mean glass of Guinness to refresh you after the exertions of the dance floor.

Finally, the betting man will be fascinated to know that a visit to the *Cock and Bull Tavern* in Sydney, Australia will answer two needs. You can quench your thirst for a Guinness *and* place a bet on the horses without losing your place at the bar. If you win a modest amount, you'll be paid there and then from the till. A major windfall, on the other hand, will necessitate a visit from a security van to award you your winnings!

# GUINNESS

# 200 YEARS ON...

## Still the Perfect Pint of Guinness

The original brewery was opened by Arthur Guinness in 1759 in Dublin on a 9,000 year lease.

Nearly two centuries later, in 1936, the brewery at Park Royal, London opened its doors. Today Guinness is the biggest-selling brand of beer in the British Isles, and indeed 7 million glasses a day are consumed by discerning drinkers, in over 110 countries.

The brewing of Guinness has changed little over the years; barley, water, hops and yeast are the four ingredients used. But it takes more than wholesome, natural ingredients to create the perfect pint. The craftsmanship of the Guinness brewer and his team is of paramount importance.

At each stage of the lengthy brewing process, the brewers and tasters measure, assess and improve. Only when the brewer is satisfied that the distinctive taste, aroma and appearance are perfect is his job complete. The quality control chain is then completed in the pub when the Guinness salesman visits to test samples, check serving temperatures, and help the landlord to get the best from his Guinness.

This route to a perfect Guinness is followed meticulously. The reward comes at the end in that superb pint of cool creamy Guinness.

# WHAT THE FAMOUS THINK OF GUINNESS

**The list of people – famous or otherwise – who enjoy a glass of Guinness is endless and each has his or her own special reason.**

Actor Terence Brady recently divulged in a Daily Mail article his recipe for Sorbet à la Guinness. He is also quoted there as saying: "Just as every oyster eater will tell you the only drink to take with the mollusc is Guinness, the serious curry consumer never takes wine with spice."

Cyril Ray, prolific author and authority on food and wine, says: "What do I love more than anything else in the world? Guinness! What else can you drink in the middle of the morning? With your lunch? As an aperitif before dinner? With your dinner? Before you go to bed? Guinness."

Sporty lady Jane Furniss, who ran in the women's 3000 metres at the Los Angeles Olympics, often drinks Guinness in the evening on the advice of her Irish coach Jim Madigan "because of the goodness in it and I enjoy it".

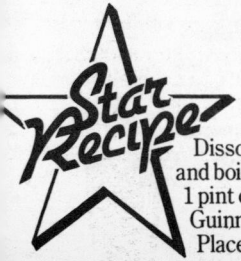


Terence Brady's
**Sorbet à la Guinness**

Dissolve 1lb sugar in 2 pints water to make syrup, and boil to reduce by one third. Allow to cool. Add 1 pint of Guinness and taste. Bitterness of Guinness must come through taste of syrup. Place in ice cream machine or simply freeze.

## *Lamb & Flag* *(Food)*

33 Rose Street, Covent Garden, WC2
Map 11 B2
01-836 4108

*Brewery* Courage
*Landlord* Loraine Baldwin
Stilton ploughman's £1.25 Hot pasty 70p (Last order 10.30pm)
Courage Directors Bitter, Best Bitter; John Smith's Bitter; Guinness; Kronenbourg; Hofmeister; Taunton cider. *Real ale*

Dickens, Dryden and Samuel Butler are among the literary luminaries linked with this famous little pub, whose selection of English cheeses really is something to write home about. Cheddar and Red Leicester, Sage Derby, Blue Shropshire and other prime varieties are served with pickles and either crisp baguettes or wedges of hot bread. There are other lunchtime dishes, but it's definitely the cheese that takes the biscuit.

## *Maple Leaf* *(Food)*

41 Maiden Lane, WC2 · Map 11 B1
01-240 2843

*Brewery* Grand Met
*Landlord* Mr Noel Healy

Roast beef £2.95 Beef & ale cassoulet £2.95 (Last order 10pm. No bar food Sun eve)
Webster's Yorkshire Bitter; Ruddle's County; Eldridge Pope Royal Oak; Guinness. *Real ale*

Portions are hearty at this friendly pub with a Canadian theme. Granary-bread sandwiches packed with roast beef or lean, succulent ham are just the thing for aspiring lumberjacks, and hot dishes include lasagne, Suffolk hot pot and tourtière – thin pastry enveloping tasty minced beef and served with fresh vegetables or a salad. The servery is at one end of the cheerful, well-furnished bar.

## *Mayflower*

In 1611 the *Mayflower's* captain was enjoying a pint at this riverside pub when he received his assignment to transport the Pilgrim Fathers to America. The 17th century is faithfully recalled in the black-beamed bars, and there's an interesting collection of nautical memorabilia. A jetty affords super views of the Thames. **Family pub**

117 Rotherhithe Street, SE16 · Map 10 D2
01-237 4088
*Brewery* Vintage Inns *Landlord* Mr Benson
Charrington's IPA; Bass; Guinness; Carling Black Label; Tennent's Lager. *Real ale*

## *Museum Tavern*

Karl Marx is said to have taken breaks from his studies to visit this popular pub, which stands opposite the British Museum. Today's students and tourists can enjoy an excellent range of well-kept real ales in smartly revamped Victorian surroundings, with carved wood, frosted and stained glass, gilded columns and ceiling fans.

49 Great Russell Street, WC1 · Map 11 B1
01-242 8987
*Owner* Clifton Inns *Landlord* Mr Price
Greene King IPA; Brakspear's Special; Ruddle's County; Guinness; Carlsberg; Foster's; Taunton cider. *Real ale*

## *Nag's Head*

This 18th-century pub has seen many different faces over the years. Once an early-morning haunt of workers from Covent Garden Market, it now attracts a lively pre-theatre crowd. The decor is plush Edwardian in style, with etched mirrors catching the eye along with opera and ballet playbills.

10 James Street, WC2 · Map 11 B1
01-836 4678
*Brewery* McMullen *Landlord* Mr M. P. Conway
McMullens Coventry Bitter; Guiness; Steingold; Hartsman; cider. *Real ale*

## *Nell of Old Drury*

Nell Gwyn, later to become mistress of Charles II, used to sell her oranges on the steps of the Theatre Royal, across the road from this old tavern. Playbills line the walls of the simply furnished bar, and Richard Sheridan is said to have been a patron. Closed Sunday.

29 Catherine Street, WC2 · Map 11 B1
01-836 5328
*Brewery* Courage *Landlord* Mr M. P. Dunphy
Courage Directors Bitter, Best Bitter; John Smith's Bitter; Guinness; Kronenbourg; Hofmeister. *Real ale*

**Prices given are as at the time of our research and are comparative indications rather than firm quotes.**

## *Old Bell Tavern*

Sir Christopher Wren's workmen were the first customers of this busy Fleet Street inn during the building of the church of St Bride's next door. An earlier house on the same site was used as a workshop by one of Caxton's assistants. Closed Sat eve and all Sun.

95 Fleet Street, EC4 · Map 11 C1
01-353 3796
*Free House* *Landlord* Mrs N. Healy
Morrell's Bitter; Adnams Bitter; Courage Directors Bitter; Guinness; Oranjeboom; Löwenbräu; Carlsberg. *Real ale*

## *Orange Brewery* *(Food)*

37 Pimlico Road, SW1 · Map 12 C2
01-730 5378

*Owners* Clifton Innkeepers
*Landlords* John & Avril Fletcher

Hot roast pork sandwich £1.50 Beef bourguignon £2.50 (Last order 10.30pm)
Orange Brewery SW1, SW2, Pimlico Porter; Guinness; Holsten; Foster's; cider. *Real ale*

A popular Pimlico pub with two bars, its own range of real ales and a daily changing selection of tasty snacks. Sandwiches with fillings of freshly cooked roasts are the favourite lunchtime choice, and other offerings include soup and ploughman's platters, salads and hearty hot specials like chilli con carne or beef bourguignon.

## *Paxton's Head*

This busy Knightsbridge pub is named after Sir Joseph Paxton, a man of many talents who is best remembered as the designer of the Crystal Palace, which originally stood not far away in Hyde Park. The Victorian-style bar with its central serving area features some delightful etched mirrors in mahogany frames. There's also a cellar bar.

**Family pub**

153 Knightsbridge, SW1 · Map 12 B1
01-589 6627
*Owners* H. H. Finch & Co *Landlord* George Redgewell
Ind Coope Burton Ale, Special Bitter; John Bull; Double Diamond; Guinness; Löwenbräu; Skol. *Real ale*

## *Prince Regent*

Portraits and caricatures of the Prince Regent abound in this smartly refurbished and ever-popular corner pub. There are also royal warrants, medals and many other memorabilia, and another interesting feature is a collection of little brass plaques engraved by a former landlord with the names of his staunchest regulars. Patio.

71 Marylebone High Street, W1 · Map 11 A1
01-935 2018
*Brewery* Charrington *Landlords* Mr & Mrs P. Lewis
Charrington's IPA; Mitchells & Butlers Springfield Bitter; Guinness; Carling Black Label; Taunton cider. *Real ale*

## *Printer's Devil*

Printing workers from nearby Fleet Street crowd into this busy pub, named after the traditional nickname for a printer's errand boy. The main bar features a splendid display of woodcuts, old books and models of printing presses. Rare for the City, there is also a public bar. Closed Sunday.

98 Fetter Lane, EC4 · Map 11 C1
01-242 2239
*Brewery* Whitbread *Landlord* Mr A. Fletcher
Wethered's Bitter; Flower's Original; Whitbread Best Bitter, Trophy Bitter, Mild. *Real ale*

## *Prospect of Whitby*

Foreign visitors flock to this old waterside inn, once a den of thieves and smugglers. Turner painted the river from here, and Judge Jeffreys reportedly watched the execution of pirates from a balcony while dining. The one large bar has a beamed ceiling and flagstone floor. **Family pub**

57 Wapping Wall, E1 · Map 10 D2
01-481 1095
*Owner* Sovereign Host *Landlord* Mr Trevor Chapman
Watneys Stag, Combes Bitter; Ben Truman's Bitter; Ruddle's County; Guinness; Carlsberg; Holsten; Foster's; cider. *Real ale*

## *Railway Tavern*

Train enthusiasts should schedule a stop at this mid-Victorian pub near Liverpool Street Station. Photographs, models of steam locomotives and crests of 19th-century railway companies revive memories of pre-diesel days. Closed Sat, Sun & eves from 9pm.

15 Liverpool Street, EC2 · Map 10 C2
01-283 3598
*Brewery* Whitbread *Landlord* Mr Hanley
Flowers Original; Wethered's Marlow Bitter; Whitbread Trophy; Brakspear's Bitter; Greene King Abbot Ale; Guinness; Stella Artois. *Real ale*

## *Red Lion* *(Food)*

23 Crown Passage, Pall Mall, SW1 · Map 11 A2
01-930 8067

*Brewery* Watney Combe Reid
*Landlords* Gerard & Michael McAree

Steak & kidney pie, salad or jacket potato £3.50
Roast turkey £3.15 (Last order 10.30pm)
Ruddles County; Webster's Yorkshire Bitter; Combes Bitter; Guinness; Foster's; Carlsberg. *Real ale*

Tucked away in a passage off Pall Mall, this snug little pub does a roaring trade in tasty, home-cooked bar snacks. Pride of place undoubtedly goes to the splendid hot meat pies – steak and kidney, beef and ale, chicken with gammon and mushroom – served with a jacket potato or crisp salad. Sandwiches (choose from ten fillings) are made to order, and there are excellent cold meat salads.

## *Red Lion*

Built in 1723 to accommodate builders working on Chesterfield House, this cosy pub has a delightfully British atmosphere, with dark panelling, wooden settles and tables, leaded windows and prints of old London. In fine weather chairs and tables made out of barrels are set out on the little patio. Closed 1 week Christmas.

1 Waverton Street, Mayfair, W1 · Map 11 A2
01-499 1307
*Owners* London Hosts *Landlord* Mr David Butterfield
Webster's Yorkshire Bitter; Watney Stag Bitter; Ruddle's County; Combe's Bitter; Guinness; Foster's; Cider. *Real ale*

## *St Stephen's Tavern*

Beside Westminster pier, this old tavern is a favourite with civil servants and political journalists. The cellar bar was once connected to the Houses of Parliament by a tunnel said to have been used by Guy Fawkes; the upstairs bar sports an ornately carved bar counter and fine engraved glass. Closed Sunday evening.

10 Bridge Street, SW1 · Map 11 B2
01-930 3230
*Brewery* Whitbread *Landlord* Mr Christopher Gent
Webster's Yorkshire Bitter; Watneys Stag Bitter; Combes Bitter; Guinness; Carlsberg; Foster's; Holsten; cider. *Real ale*

## *Salisbury*

This handsome Victorian pub has a style and atmosphere very much in keeping with its location in London's theatreland. It's long been a favourite pre-performance rendezvous and is also popular with the acting profession and its acolytes. The lavish decor is authentic 1890s, with plush velvet, engraved glass screens and moulded ceilings.

90 St Martin's Lane, WC2 · Map 11 B2
01-836 5863
*Owner* Clifton Inns *Landlord* Mr Gerry Wynne
Ind Coope Burton Ale, Double Diamond; Taylor Walker Bitter; John Bull Bitter; Guinness; Oranjeboom; Löwenbräu; cider. *Real ale*

## *Samuel Pepys*

At the end of a narrow alley, this Thames-side pub is a skilful reconstruction of a 17th-century inn. A nautical theme in the cellar bar recalls Samuel Pepys' service as a naval secretary, and extracts from his diary line the walls. The verandah provides splendid river views.

**Family pub**

Brooks Wharf, Upper Thames Street, EC4 · Map 11 C2
01-248 3048
*Owners* Vintage Inns *Landlord* Mr Spencer
Charrington's IPA; Bass; Stones Bitter; Guinness; Carling Black Label; Tennent's Pilsner, Export; Taunton cider. *Real ale*

## *Seven Stars*

Between the Law Courts and Lincoln's Inn Fields, this tiny pub first licensed in 1602 is a favourite haunt of lawyers and accountants. The ever-busy little bar is enlivened by Spy cartoons of eminent members of the legal profession. Closed Sat, Sun and Bank Holidays.

53 Carey Street, WC2 · Map 11 B1
01-242 8521
*Brewery* Courage *Landlord* Mr J. A. Crawley
Courage Best Bitter, Directors Bitter, JC; Guinness; Hofmeister; Kronenbourg; Taunton cider. *Real ale*

O.G. 1031·5°
Brewed in Salford

O.G. 1032·6°
Brewed in Faversham

O.G. 1033·7°
Brewed in Marlow

O.G. 1035·9°
Brewed in Cheltenham

O.G. 1035·9°
Brewed in Sheffield

O.G. 1043·7°
Brewed in Cheltenham

O.G. 1042·6°
Brewed in Cheltenham

O.G. 1038·42°
Brewed in Castle Eden

O.G. 1041·5°
Brewed in Faversham

O.G. 1030·4°
Brewed in Salford

# When travelling, be sure to observe local customs.

While you're drinking in some of the local atmosphere, try drinking in some of the local brew.

Chesters, for example, if you're visiting Greater Manchester.

Pompey Royal or Flowers Original, when you're heading towards the West Country.

All over England we brew cask conditioned ales to regional recipes. (A selection is shown above.)

We believe the extra effort involved is worthwhile.

Recently, three of our beers were singled out for praise by no less an authority than CAMRA themselves.

But not only do we satisfy their demanding tastes. We satisfy local tastes, too.

**WHITBREAD**

**Our reputation has been brewing since 1742.**

## *Shepherd's Tavern*

A fine old corner pub between Park Lane and Piccadilly. Bull's eye window panes add a period touch to the mellow, pine-panelled bar, and a notable feature upstairs is a sedan chair that once belonged to the Duke of Cumberland. It's now used as a telephone booth.

**Family pub**

Hertford Street, W1 · Map 11 A2
01-499 3017
*Owners* London Hosts *Landlord* Mr Ken Woodhams
Ruddle's County; Watneys Stag; Mann's IPA; Webster's Yorkshire Bitter; Guinness; Holsten; cider. *Real ale*

## *Sherlock Holmes*

A must for devotees of the dauntless detective, this well-known pub is filled with Holmesiana; there's also a fascinating collection of early forensic equipment. Sir Arthur Conan Doyle was a regular visitor here when it was the Northumberland Arms and mentions it in *The Hound of the Baskervilles.* Outside drinking in summer.

10 Northumberland Street, WC2 · Map 11 B2
01-930 2644
*Brewery* Whitbread *Landlord* Mrs J. R. Hardcastle
Fremlins Tusker; Flower's Original; Whitbread Winter Royal; Guinness; Stella Artois; Heineken; cider. *Real ale*

## *Ship*

A position right opposite the finishing post makes this pleasant riverside pub one of the most popular places in London on Boat Race day. A long history goes back to Elizabethan times. **Family pub** (until 7pm)

10 Thames Bank, Riverside, SW14 · Map 9 A3
01-876 1439
*Owner* London Host *Landlord* Roger Smart
Combes Bitter; Ruddle's County; Webster's Yorkshire Bitter; Guinness; Foster's; cider. *Real ale*

## *Spaniards Inn*

Close to Hampstead Heath, this famous old pub stood beside a toll-gate over which Dick Turpin leapt on horseback while fleeing from London. Keats, Byron and Shelley all frequented the inn, which still has its weatherboarded frontage and beamed bars. **Family pub**

Spaniards Road, NW3 · Map 9 B1
01-455 3276
*Brewery* Charrington *Landlords* Mr & Mrs Culver
Charrington's IPA; Bass; Guinness; Carling Black Label; Tennent's Extra; Taunton cider. *Real ale*

## *Sun Inn*

Legend has it that Drake and Walsingham taught Elizabeth I to play bowls on the green in front of this popular pub opposite Barnes Pond. The cellar bar is modern, but ground-floor rooms retain their traditional style.

7 Church Road, Barnes, SW13 · Map 9 A3
01-876 5893
*Brewery* Taylor Walker *Landlords* Mr & Mrs J. Fisher
Taylor Walker Bitter; Ind Coope Burton Ale; John Bull; Guinness; Löwenbräu; Oranjeboom; cider. *Real ale*

## *Thistle* *(Food)*

11 Vigo Street, W1 · Map 11 A2
01-734 1947

*Brewery* Younger
*Landlords* Mr & Mrs B. K. E. Banyai

Honey roast gammon & salad £3.50 Fruit pie 75p (No bar food eves)
Younger's IPA, Tartan; McEwan's Export; Guinness; Cavalier; Becks. *Real ale*

A popular place for escaping the bustle of Regent Street, this comfortable pub has an outstanding cold table. Succulent honey-roast gammon, beautifully tender beef, turkey pie and quiche are served with a selection of simple fresh salads, and sandwiches are available for a quicker snack. The fruit pie is delicious, too, and there's a hot special on Saturdays. Closed Saturday evening, all Sunday and Bank Holidays.

## *Three Compasses* *(Food)*

66 Cowcross Street, EC1 · Map 11 C1
01-253 3368

*Brewery* Trumans
*Landlord* Mr W. I. Hutchinson
Shepherd's pie 99p Quiche & salad £1.25 (Last order 11pm)
Trumans Bitter, Best Bitter; Sampson Hanbury Strong Ale; Ben Truman Export Lager; Guinness; Foster's, Holsten; cider. *Real ale*

Seven-day opening is a rarity among City pubs, and the constant availability of excellent home-cooked snacks is a further bonus at the Three Compasses. In the attractively restored panelled bar you can enjoy freshly prepared sandwiches and salads, the quiche of the day – crisp, light and full of flavour – or a splendid shepherd's pie packed with lots of lean, tasty mince.

## *Tom Cribb*

Once barefist boxing champion of England, Tom Cribb became landlord of this busy corner pub upon retiring from the ring in 1811. Posters and prints still recall his and others' pugilistic exploits. Tables with parasols are set out on the pavement in fine weather.

36 Panton Street, SW1 · Map 11 B2
01-839 6536
*Brewery* Charrington *Landlords* Mr & Mrs A. M. S. Talbot
Charrington's IPA, Bass; Stones Bitter; Guinness; Carling Black Label; Tennent's Extra; Taunton cider. *Real ale*

## *Trafalgar Tavern*

Built in 1837 and restored in 1965, this smart riverside pub in Greenwich has a distinctly nautical flavour. Bars are named after Nelson's admirals, and the Hawke and Howe is strikingly designed to resemble the forecastle of an 18th-century man-o'-war. Bay windows provide panoramic views of the river. **Family pub**

Park Row, SE10 · Map 10 D2
01-858 2437
*Owner* Gateway Hosts *Landlord* Mr Frederick Davies
Young's Special Bitter; Ruddle's County; Webster's Yorkshire Bitter; Guinness; Carlsberg; cider. *Real ale*

## *Two Chairmen*

A colourful sign depicting two sedan chairmen hangs outside this handsome pub in a dignified Westminster Street, and the theme is continued inside with delightful murals of bucks and grandees being carried in sedan chairs. Darkwood panelling and an open fire contribute to the period charm. Closed Sunday.

39 Dartmouth Street, SW1 · Map 11 B2
01-222 8694
*Owner* Clifton Inns *Landlord* Miss P. Allcorn
Ruddles County; Webster's Yorkshire Bitter; Watney's Stag Bitter; Combe's Bitter; Guinness; Carlsberg; Foster's. *Real ale*

## *Two Chairmen*

Tucked away in a narrow street near Trafalgar Square, this congenial little pub was built in 1683 and reconstructed 200 years later. Its name refers to the sedan chairmen who plied their trade about the city in the 17th and 18th centuries. The intimate, simply furnished bar is a congenial place for a good pint of real ale. Closed Sunday.

Warwick House Street, off Cockspur St, SW1 · Map 11 B2
01-930 1166
*Brewery* Courage
Courage Best Bitter, Directors Bitter; Guinness; Hofmeister; Kronenbourg. *Real ale*

## *Victoria*

Built in 1835, this splendid pub still features etched glass, mahogany panelling and a moulded plaster ceiling, while fittings from the old Gaiety Theatre adorn the upstairs bar. Queen Victoria, after whom the pub was named, visited here when she opened nearby Paddington Station.

10a Strathearn Place, W2 · Map 9 B2
01-262 5696
*Brewery* Charrington *Landlords* Mr & Mrs Byrne
Charrington's IPA; Bass; Stones Bitter; Guinness; Carling Black Label; Harp; cider. *Real ale*

# Let TWA be your guide to the USA.

## TWA helps you see America on wheels.

It may seem strange for a great airline to offer you travel by car.

But TWA offers you terrific car hire deals in America.

TWA knows that flying is a fine way to get from place to place. But as every good guide-reader knows, you have to get around by car to see it all properly. Find the little-known places. Take in the spectacular scenery.

TWA's Getaway Fly/Drive programmes are among the best in the business. All part of our guide to America.

Enjoy it.

See your TWA Main Agent

You're going to like us TWA

## *White Horse on Parsons Green* *(Food)*

1 Parsons Green, SW6 · Map 9 A3
01-736 2115

*Free House*
*Landlord* Mrs Sally Cruickshank
Fish pie & vegetables £2.60 Eggplant Parmesan £2.20 (Last order 9pm. No bar food Sat & Sun eves)
Bass; Charrington's IPA; Springfield Bitter; Tennent's Extra; Stones Bitter; Guinness; Taunton cider. *Real ale*

The menu is long and varied at this attractive, spacious pub, where the crowds testify to Sally Cruickshank's skills in the kitchen. Standard favourites – quiche, jacket potatoes, cold meats and salads – are supplemented by imaginative choices like fish and banana pie, liver casserole and stuffed vegetarian pancakes. Rare roast beef in a bun is a popular Saturday lunchtime snack. **Family pub** (lunchtime)

## *Windsor Castle*

Built on the site of what was once Kensington spa, this friendly little pub brings a breath of country air to city streets. Oak and elm panelling and wooden settles add to the old-fashioned charm.

114 Campden Hill Road, W8 · Map 12 A1
01-727 8491
*Brewery* Charrington *Landlord* Mr Gavriel
Charrington's IPA; Bass; Guinness; Carling Black Label; Tennent's Extra. *Real ale*

## *Yacht*

Dating back to the 17th century and rebuilt after World War II bomb damage, this pleasant Thames-side pub stands near Greenwich's major tourist attractions. The mahogany-panelled bar has a strong maritime theme, with portholes, ship's instruments and yachting photographs. The terraces command splendid views along the river. **Family pub**

Crane Street, SE10 · Map 10 D2
01-858 0175
*Owner* Gateway Hosts *Landlord* Mr T Ryan
Ruddle's County; Webster's Yorkshire Bitter; Guinness; Holsten; Foster's; cider. *Real ale*

## *Ye Grapes* *(Food)*

16 Shepherd Market, W1 · Map 11 A2
01-629 4989

*Free House*
*Landlords* A. F. Wigram & P. L. Jacobs

Cottage pie £1.85 Tandoori chicken £2.15 (No bar food Sun & eves)
Fremlin's Tusker; Wethered's Bitter; Ind Coope Burton Ale; Arkell's BBB; Guinness; Stella Artois; Heineken; cider. *Real ale*

On the corner of Shepherd Market, this well-preserved Victorian pub is a delightful spot for a lunchtime bite. The carvery is the centre of attraction, with excellent cold meats and fresh salmon to accompany crunchy coleslaw and other super salads. There's a good selection of sandwiches, too, plus seasonal oysters and winter warmers ranging from vegetable soup to chilli con carne. Patio.

## *Ye Old Dr Butler's Head*

Dr William Butler, physician to James I and a great believer in the medicinal properties of ale, founded this hostelry in 1610. Today, City workers throng the sawdust-strewn bar with its black beams and old brewery mirrors. Closed Sat, Sun and evenings from about 8pm.

Mason's Avenue, Coleman Street, EC2 · Map 11 C1
01-606 3504
*Free House* *Landlords* Nigel & Carolina Field
Bass; Courage Best Bitter; Guinness; Tennent's Extra; Carling Black Label. *Real ale*

## *Ye Olde Cheshire Cheese*

Rebuilt in 1667 after the Great Fire of London, this famous Fleet Street pub looks much as it did when Dr Johnson used to pop in from his house round the corner, with panelling, scrubbed tables, and sawdust on the floors. Congreve, Pope and Voltaire are among other famous patrons. Closed Sat and Sun. **Family pub**

145 Fleet Street, EC4 · Map 11 C1
01-353 6170
*Free House* *Landlord* Mr L. Kerly
Marston's Pedigree, Burton Bitter, Pils Lager. *Real ale*

## *Ye Olde Cock Tavern*

Built in 1549 and a narrow survivor of the Great Fire of London, this famous tavern is rich in history. Two features of special note are a superb Tudor chimney piece and a handsomely carved and gilded cock. Its literary links are impressive, too, with Samuel Pepys, Dickens and Tennyson familiar faces in their day. Closed Sat and Sun.

22 Fleet Street, EC4 · Map 11 C1
01-353 3454
*Owners* London Host *Landlord* Mr P. M. Kelly
Truman's Best Bitter, Bitter, Mild; Guinness; Holsten; Carlsberg; Foster's. *Real ale*

## *Ye Olde Mitre Tavern*

This little gem of a pub is tucked away down an alley between Hatton Garden and Ely Place. Originally built in 1546 for the Bishop of Ely, it later saw service as a prison and Civil War hospital. The present 18th-century building has a great deal of old-world charm, with dark-wood panelling and fine old seating. Closed Sat, Sun & Bank Hols.

1 Ely Court, Ely Place, Holborn, EC1 · Map 11 C1
01-405 4751
*Brewery* Ind Coope *Landlord* Mr F. Rix
Ind Coope Burton Ale, Double Diamond; Friary Meux Bitter; Guinness; Skol. *Real ale*

## *Ye Olde Watling*

This richly historic pub in the oldest street in London provided food and lodgings for the builders of St Paul's. Little has changed in 300 years – massive beams, arched doorways and leaded windows remain in the bars. Closed Sat eve, all Sun, evenings from about 8pm and Bank Holidays.

29 Watling Street, EC4 · Map 11 C1
01-248 7524
*Owners* Vintage Inns *Landlord* Mr R. G. Wale
Charrington's IPA; Bass; Guinness; Carling Black Label; Tennent's Extra; Taunton cider. *Real ale*

## *Ye Olde Windmill Inn* *(B & B)*

Clapham Common Southside, SW4
Map 9 B3
01-673 4578

*Brewery* Young
*Landlords* Mr & Mrs Tobin

**BEDROOMS 13 Grade 1 £B** (No dogs)
Young's Special Bitter, Ordinary, Young John's Ale, Winter Warmer (winter only); Guinness; London Lager. *Real ale*

Standing by the edge of Clapham Common, this large, sturdily built pub is well placed for travellers to the south of London. The spacious bars have a solid Victorian feel, with their rich decor, mahogany tables and stained glass, and there's a pleasantly secluded beer garden. Bedrooms are smartly modern, with neat fitted furniture, attractive matching fabrics, colour TVs and tea-makers. One has a full bathroom, the others shower units.

# ENGLAND

CRUGGLEWICK
CRICKET CLUB
DINNER AND
SMOKING CONCERT
AT
THE JOLLY FEATHER
HOTEL
ON SAT. SEPT 1ST
AT 7.0 P.M.
TICKETS FROM

## Abberley *(Food)* — *Bell at Pensax*

Near Worcester · *Hereford & Worcester*
Map 7 D1
Great Witley (029 921) 677

*Free House*
*Landlords* Robert & Pamela Eaton
Pâté £1.25 Sausage & parsley pie £2 (Last order 10pm)
Hook Norton Best Bitter; Taylor's Landlord; Wood's Special; Guinness; Tuborg; cider. *Real ale*

Pamela Eaton does all the cooking at this smart red-brick pub, which lies between the villages of Abberley and Pensax. Her pâté is a popular starter or light snack, along with soup and garlic mushrooms, and for heartier appetites there are things like chilli con carne and beef goulash. Anyone with space to spare should try the toothsome treacle tart. Patio. **Family pub**

## Abbots Bromley *(B & B)* — *Crown Inn*

Market Place · *Staffordshire* · Map 4 C4
Burton-on-Trent (0283) 840227

*Brewery* Bass
*Landlords* Mr & Mrs Finch

**BEDROOMS 6 Grade 2 £C** (No dogs)
Bass; Mitchells & Butlers Mild; Worthington 'E'; Guinness; Carling Black Label; Taunton cider. *Real ale*

This friendly half-timbered pub stands facing the village market place where a performance of the ancient Horn Dance is a traditional attraction every September. Paintings and antlers adorn the comfortable bar which offers a fine selection of malt whiskies. Simply furnished bedrooms have TVs and share a single public bathroom. Local sausages are a feature of Mr and Mrs Finch's home-cooked breakfasts. Garden.

## Abingdon *(Food)* — *Ox Inn*

15 Oxford Road · *Oxfordshire* · Map 6 A3
Abingdon (0235) 20962

*Brewery* Morland
*Landlord* Mr J. P. Conway

Steak & mushroom pie £2.80 Chicken in white wine sauce £3.45 (Last order 10pm)
Morland's Ordinary Bitter, Best Bitter, Dark Mild, Artist; Guinness; Stella Artois; Heineken; cider. *Real ale*

Steaks delivered straight from the next-door butcher top the popularity charts at this welcoming roadside inn. Mrs Conway also provides a good choice of home-cooked dishes such as steak and mushroom pie or pork chop in cider sauce. Steaming apple crumble makes a satisfying finish. The choice is smaller on Sundays. Patio and garden.

## Ainsworth *(Food)* — *Duke William*

Wells Road, Near Bolton · *Greater Manchester*
Map 3 B3
Bolton (0204) 24726

*Brewery* Whitbread
*Landlords* Ann & Basil Collier-Brown
Roast lamb £2.50 Steak & kidney pie £2 (No bar food eves or lunch Sat–Mon)
Whitbread Trophy; Dutton's Light; Chester's Best Mild; Heldenbrau; Stella Artois; Heineken; cider.

Customers come from far and wide to enjoy the splendid lunchtime bar snacks that have made this cosy Georgian pub so popular. Home-made savoury pies are great favourites, along with pâté, grills and daily specials like roast lamb or poached halibut with shrimp sauce. Good fresh vegetables accompany main courses. Book, and remember that the early bird has the widest choice. Terrace.

## Aldenham *(Food)* — *Game Bird*

Hartspring Lane · *Hertfordshire* · Map 6 B3
Watford (0923) 25826

*Brewery* Benskins
*Landlord* Mr L. Mortiss

Game Bird pie £2.50 Filled potatoes £1.95 (Last order 7.30pm. No bar food Sun eve)
Ind Coope Burton Ale; Benskins Bitter; John Bull Bitter; Guinness; Löwenbräu; Skol; Oranjeboom; cider. *Real ale*

The heart of this zippy pub with intimate alcove seating is a large island bar dispensing world-wide lagers. A cold buffet offers a self-service selection of cooked meats and salads, while hot choices include filled jacket potatoes (Sultry Sophia comes with a tangy bolognese topping), special duckling pie and daily dishes like cauliflower cheese. Freshly cut sandwiches, too – perhaps sausage and sauerkraut.

## Alfold Crossways *(Food)* — *Napoleon Arms*

Near Cranleigh · *Surrey* · Map 6 B3
Loxwood (0403) 752357

*Free House*
*Landlords* Wilf & Mary Forgham

French onion soup £1.30 Curry with rice & vegetables £2.75 (Last order 10pm)
Fuller's London Pride; Webster's Yorkshire Bitter; Wilson's Great Northern Bitter; Carlsberg; cider. *Real ale*

Tables outside and an ornamental pool make this low-built roadside pub particularly attractive in summer. The wide choice of snacks available in the bar ranges from French onion soup to baked potatoes with various fillings and an expertly prepared herb omelette. More substantial dishes like beef curry cater for the truly hungry, and there's ice cream to finish. **Family pub**

## Alfriston *(B & B)* — *George Inn*

*East Sussex* · Map 6 C4
Alfriston (0323) 870319

*Owners* Hotels of the Cinque Ports
*Landlord* Mr Robin Harriott

**BEDROOMS 8 Grade 2 £C** (No dogs)
Watneys Stag Bitter, Special, Special Mild; Usher's Bitter; Ben Truman; Guinness; Carlsberg; cider. *Real ale*

Steeped in history and once notorious as a haunt of smugglers, this 15th-century timber-framed inn stands in the main street of a pretty Sussex village. Oak beams abound, and a blazing fire keeps winter at bay in the comfortable main bar. The mood is similar in the bedrooms, most of which have fine old furnishings. There's a pleasant garden. **Family pub**

## Allensmore *(Food, B & B)* — *Three Horseshoes*

Near Hereford · *Hereford & Worcester*
Map 7 D2
Wormbridge (098 121) 329
*Free House*
*Landlords* Mr & Mrs Sloggett
**BEDROOMS 4 Grade 2 £C** (No dogs)
Home-made soup 95p Chilli con carne £3 (Last order 10pm. No bar food Sun lunch)
Mitchells & Butlers Brew XI; Bass, Allbright; Younger's Tartan; Guinness; Tennent's; Carling Black label; cider. *Real ale*

A cordial welcome awaits visitors to the Sloggetts' whitewashed country pub near the junction of the A465 and B4348. Bar snacks are a popular feature, ranging from made-to-order sandwiches and ploughman's platters to delicious French onion soup, chicken and chips, curries and a gorgeous treacle tart. The four spotless bedrooms (no children accommodated) have attractive floral decor and sturdy furnishings. Excellent breakfasts.

## Alresford *(Food)* — *Horse & Groom*

Broad Street · *Hampshire* · Map 6 B3
Alresford (096 273) 4809

*Brewery* Whitbread
*Landlords* Mr & Mrs P. Clements

Steak & kidney pie £2.45 Chicken & tomato casserole £2.50 (Last order 9.30pm)
Flower's Original; Whitbread Strong Country Bitter; Guinness; Heineken; Stella Artois; cider. *Real ale*

The mood is friendly and relaxed at the Clementses' popular pub, whose exterior is adorned with colourful flower tubs and hanging baskets. Inside, in the brick-walled bar, a good choice of snacks is always available, the pick perhaps being hearty daily specials like spiced lamb, pasta italienne or flavoursome chicken and tomato casserole served with nicely cooked fresh vegetables. Garden.

## Alrewas *(Food, B & B)* — *George & Dragon*

Main Street, Near Burton-upon-Trent
*Staffordshire* · Map 4 C4
Burton-on-Trent (0283) 790202
*Brewery* Marston, Thompson & Evershed
*Landlords* Mr & Mrs R. G. Stanbrook
**BEDROOMS 13 Grade 1 £A**
Steak & kidney pie £1.50 Pork & liver pâté £1.20 (Last order 10pm. No bar food Sun)
Marston's Pedigree, Albion Mild, Lager; Guinness; Heineken; cider. *Real ale*

The Stanbrooks are charming hosts at this pleasant country pub, which offers plenty of atmosphere along with good food and comfortable accommodation. In a setting replete with Royal Family souvenirs you can enjoy bar snacks ranging from a super roast beef sandwich to burgers, salads and pies, both savoury and sweet. Neatly fitted bedrooms have tea-makers and colour TVs. Garden. Accommodation closed 1 week Christmas. **Family pub**

## Alsager *(Food, B & B)* — *Manor House*

Audley Road, Near Stoke-on-Trent · *Cheshire*
Map 3 B4
Alsager (093 63) 78013
*Free House*
*Landlords* Mr & Mrs A. Cottingham
**BEDROOMS 8 Grade 1 £A+** (No dogs)
Hot seafood platter £2.25 Beef & onion batch 90p (Last order 10pm)
Ansells Bitter; Double Diamond; Tetley's Bitter; Burton Bitter; Guinness; Skol; Löwenbräu; cider. *Real ale*

Only five minutes from the M6, this striking red-brick inn offers a good selection of tasty snacks in its characterful main bar. Seafood, both hot and cold, is a popular choice, along with sandwiches, pâtés, cold meats and a daily roast. The oak-beamed bedrooms with handsome fitted units are splendidly comfortable, having central heating, TVs, well-appointed shower rooms as well as lots of extras. **Family pub**

## Alswear *(B & B)* — *Butchers Arms*

Near South Moulton · *Devon* · Map 8 C3
Bishop's Nympton (076 97) 477

*Free House*
*Landlords* Peter & Jean Gannon

**BEDROOMS 3 Grade 2 £C**
Usher's Best Bitter, Triple Crown; Whitbread Trophy; Guinness; Carlsberg; cider. *Real ale*

Once a flour mill, this pleasant village inn on the A373 is a friendly, welcoming place. The rustic public bar and quiet lounge bar provide a choice for the thirsty, and there's a popular games room with pool and skittles. Three prettily decorated bedrooms have washbasins and tea-makers, and guests can watch TV in the Gannons' lounge. Garden. **Family pub**

## Alton *(Food)* — *Eight Bells*

Church Street · *Hampshire* · Map 6 B3
Alton (0420) 82417
*Free House*
*Landlords* Mr & Mrs Moxley
Home-made soup & French bread 85p Filled jacket potato with side salad £1.60 (Last order 10pm)
Hall & Woodhouse Badger Best Bitter; Bass; Courage Best Bitter; John Smith's Bitter; Kronenbourg; Guinness; Taunton cider. *Real ale*

Rosemary Moxley's wholesome, freshly prepared bar snacks make this rustic roadside inn an ideal stopping place. Specialities include jacket potatoes with tasty fillings like chilli con carne, and there is a wide choice of plain and toasted sandwiches. You can also have pizza, a burger or a seafood platter. Garden.

## Anslow *(Food)* — *Brickmakers Arms*

Beamhill Road, Near Burton upon Trent
*Staffordshire* · Map 4 C4
Burton-on-Trent (0283) 813799

*Brewery* Marston, Thompson & Evershed
*Landlord* Mr K. W. Woolley

Pâté with toast 75p Farmhouse grill £1.90 (Last order 8.45pm. No bar food Sun)
Marston's Pedigree, Low C, Lager. *Real ale*

Real ale makes a welcome accompaniment to Mrs Woolley's excellent home-made snacks, and the two combine to keep this yellow-brick pub constantly busy. Pastry is particularly recommended, whether in a meat pie or a delicious blackberry and apple pie. The menu also offers steak, heaped mixed grills, salads and ploughman's. Sandwiches only on Monday–Thursday evenings. Swings in the Garden.

## Ansty *(Food, B & B)* ★ — *Fox Inn*

Near Dorchester · *Dorset* · Map 8 D3
Milton Abbas (0258) 880328
*Free House*
*Landlords* Peter & Wendy Amey
**BEDROOMS 10 Grades 1 & 2 £B**
Cold table £4 Barbecued steak £4 (Last order 10pm)
Ansty Ale; Fox Ale; Hall & Woodhouse Badger Best Bitter, Tanglefoot; Hector's Bitter; Guinness; Carlsberg; Brock; Taunton cider. *Real ale*

An outstanding village pub, whose spectacular cold buffet is known far and wide. A dozen or more delicious cooked meats, including seasonal game, are served with amazing variety of super salads, and there are appetising filled jacket potatoes, too. The convivial bars are also notable for a fine collection of plates and Toby jugs. Comfortable bedrooms, most with private facilities, have TVs and tea-makers. Garden. **Family pub**

## Appleby *(Food, B & B)* — *Royal Oak*

Bongate · *Cumbria* · Map 3 B2
Appleby (0930) 51463

*Free House*
*Landlord* Colin & Hilary Cheyne

**BEDROOMS 8 Grade 2 £C**
Crofter's pie £1.75 Prawns St Jacques £1.50 (Last order 9pm)
Younger's XXPS; McEwan's Mild, Export, Lager; Guinness; Taunton cider. *Real ale*

This attractive old black and white inn stands on the southern edge of Appleby. Meat dishes are a good bet among the bar snacks, thanks to an excellent local butcher, and other choices include salads and sandwiches, shellfish and home-made lasagne. Bedrooms (three with TV) offer simple comforts, and there are two welcoming bars and a pleasant terrace.

## Appletreewick *(Food)* — *Craven Arms*

Near Skipton · *North Yorkshire* · Map 4 C2
Burnsall (075 672) 270

*Free House*
*Landlords* Paul & Jane Emsley
Gammon & eggs £3.25 Steak & kidney pie £2.75 (Last order 9.30pm. No bar food Sun & Mon eves in winter)
Tetley's Porter; Theakston's Old Peculier, Best Bitter; Younger's Scotch Bitter; Guinness; Carlsberg; cider. *Real ale*

Paul Emsley takes care of the cosy bar while his wife Jane does the cooking at this charming creeper-clad inn which lies between Burnsall and Bolton Abbey. Tasty, wholesome snacks range from soups and pâté to ploughman's, salads, sandwiches, fried haddock and an excellent steak and kidney pie. There are some delicious desserts, too. Garden. **Family pub**

## Arkengarthdale *(B & B)* — *C. B. Hotel*

Reeth, Near Richmond · *North Yorkshire*
Map 4 C2
Richmond (0748) 84265

*Free House*
*Landlords* Mr G. Gilbraith & Mr W. Dixon

**BEDROOMS 8 Grades 1 & 2 £C** (No dogs)
Webster's Pennine Bitter, Yorkshire Bitter; Guinness; Carlsberg; cider.

Scenically situated in the heart of the Yorkshire Dales, this friendly, welcoming inn is a popular base for walking holidays. Good-sized bedrooms are bright and cheerful, with plenty of cupboard space. One has its own bathroom, two others shower cubicles. The beamed bar has a warm, traditional appeal, and there's an ample lounge with a section for tele-viewing. No under-threes overnight. Patio.
**Family pub**

## Armathwaite *(B & B)* — *Duke's Head Hotel*

Near Carlisle · *Cumbria* · Map 3 B1
Armathwaite (069 92) 226

*Brewery* Whitbread
*Landlords* Mr & Mrs D. B. Taylor

**BEDROOMS 8 Grade 2 £C**
Whitbread Mild, Trophy; Heineken; cider.

Trout and salmon fishing are popular pastimes at this peaceful pub by the banks of the river Eden. There's a lot of angling talk in the pleasant lounge bar, which features a grandfather clock and some splendid antique chairs and tables. Eight neatly kept little bedrooms, all with tea-makers and washbasins, provide simple comforts for an overnight stay. Garden.

## Ascot *(Food)* — *Stag*

63 High Street · *Berkshire* · Map 6 B3
Ascot (0990) 21622

*Brewery* Friary Meux
*Landlords* Mr & Mrs T. McCarthy

Chicken & ham hot pot £1.70 Vegetarian jacket potato £1.10 (Last order 10.45pm)
Friary Meux Bitter; Ind Coope John Bull, Double Diamond; Guinness; Skol. *Real ale*

Enjoy Ann McCarthy's daily blackboard specials in the main bar or, in summer, at one of the pavement tables at this welcoming main street pub. The choice might range from pizza or a pasta dish to beef Stroganoff, fish pie or Chinese chicken. Home-made granary bread makes a good accompaniment, and there are also sandwiches and burgers, as well as homely desserts to round things off.
**Family pub** (lunchtime)

## Ashburton *(B & B)* — *Exeter Inn*

26 West Street · *Devon* · Map 8 C4
Ashburton (0364) 52559

*Free House*
*Landlords* Mr & Mrs A. Shepherd

**BEDROOMS 3 Grade 2 £C** (No dogs)
Palmer's IPA, Bitter; Badger Best Bitter; Usher's Best Bitter; Tetley's Bitter; Guinness; Skol; cider. *Real ale*

Built more than 800 years ago to accommodate the builders of the village church, this friendly inn retains a great deal of its original charm. The beamed bar is delightfully old-fashioned and the comfortable bedrooms are equally appealing, with sloping floors and ceilings and odd little corners. The bathroom they share is modern and spotless. Patio. **Family pub**

## Ashbury *(Food, B & B)* — *Rose & Crown Hotel*

Near Swindon, Wiltshire · *Oxfordshire*
Map 6 A3
Ashbury (079 371) 222

*Free House*
*Landlord* Mr Marcel Klein
**BEDROOMS 10 Grade 2 £B**
Steak & kidney pie £1.70 Ploughman's £1.35
Charrington's IPA; Stones Bitter; Worthington 'E'; Guinness; Carling Black Label; Tennent's Extra; Taunton cider. *Real ale*

Bar food is a popular feature at this sturdy whitewashed village inn, which lies about four miles from junction 15 of the M4. Baked potatoes with various fillings provide tasty quick snacks, and more substantial items include bangers with bubble and squeak, Cotswold hot pot and turkey curry. Centrally heated bedrooms (all with TVs and tea-makers) are in simple modern style. Patio. **Family pub**

## Ashcott *(Food)* — *Ashcott Inn*

Near Bridgwater · *Somerset* · Map 8 D3
Ashcott (0458) 210282
*Free House*
*Landlords* Peter, Allison & David Milne
Stuffed fillet of sole with salad £3.50 Oriental ginger ice cream 75p (Last order 10pm. No bar food Sun lunch)
Flowers Original; Eldridge Pope Dark Brown; Dorchester Bitter; Guinness; Heineken; Stella Artois; Taunton cider. *Real ale*

There's no shortage of choice on the bar menu of this trim 17th-century pub. Starters include soup, ratatouille and garlicky baked mushrooms, and besides main courses like rainbow trout and lamb cutlets there is a tempting range of daily specials such as lasagne with herb bread or pork chop with barbecue sauce. Garden.

## Ashington *(Food)* — *Red Lion*

*West Sussex* · Map 6 B4
Ashington (0903) 892226

*Free House*
*Landlords* Nigel & Cathy Evans

Country casserole £2.45 Fish & meat salads from £2.50 (Last order 10pm. No bar food Mon)
Hall & Woodhouse Badger Bitter, Tanglefoot; King & Barnes Festive; Guinness; Carlsberg; Foster's; cider. *Real ale*

Children are especially well catered for at this large friendly pub on the A24, with a TV room and light snacks like mini-burgers on the bar menu. There are also sandwiches, ploughman's, jumbo sausages, and more substantial choices like grilled gammon, savoury pancakes or steak and cider stew. Closed Monday 1 Oct–1 May. Garden.
**Family pub**

## Ashwell *(Food)* — *Bushel & Strike Inn*

Mill Street, Near Baldock · *Hertfordshire*
Map 5 B2
Ashwell (046 274) 2394

*Brewery* Wells
*Landlords* Sandra & Tony Lynch
Cold roast rib of beef £2.75 Lamb & pork brochette £2.50 (Last order 10pm)
Wells Eagle Bitter, Bombardier, Silver Eagle; Guinness; Red Stripe; Kellerbräu. *Real ale*

The garden is delightful in summer at this charming village inn and the two cosy bars provide a warm welcome on colder days. Food from the buffet bar includes starters like home-made soup, avocado with prawns, salads, fried chicken and lamb brochettes, as well as daily specials such as a hot pot or pork in cider. Sandwiches too.

## Ashwell *(B & B)* — *Three Tuns Hotel*

6 High Street · *Hertfordshire* · Map 5 B2
Ashwell (046 274) 2387

*Brewery* Greene King
*Landlord* Mrs E. M. Harris

**BEDROOMS 11 Grade 1 £B**
Greene King Abbot Ale, IPA, Light Mild; Guinness; Harp; Kronenbourg; Taunton cider. *Real ale*

This two-storey brick-built hotel is the social hub of a village that is both attractive and historic. The quarry-tiled public bar is a favourite local meeting place, and there's a lounge bar with old lamps and prints. There's some fine period furniture in the comfortable bedrooms, four of which are in a nearby Victorian house; all have TV.
**Family pub**

## Askham *(Food, B & B)* — *Punch Bowl*

Near Penrith · *Cumbria* · Map 3 B2
Hackthorpe (093 12) 443

*Brewery* Whitbread
*Landlords* Aubrey & Diana Zalk

**BEDROOMS 5 Grade 2 £C** (No dogs)
Chicken curry £2.75 Rump steak £4.65 (Last order 9.30pm)
Whitbread Best Mild, Trophy Bitter; Guinness; Heineken; cider.

Not far from the M6, this village pub is winning friends with some very good cooking. In the cottagy bar or out on the patio you can enjoy anything from sandwiches and steaks to a pancake tastily filled with ham, chicken and mushrooms. The home-made ice cream is delicious, too. Five tidy bedrooms offer simple overnight comforts. **Family pub**

## Askham *(Food, B & B)* — *Queen's Head Inn*

Near Penrith · *Cumbria* · Map 3 B2
Hackthorpe (093 12) 225

*Brewery* Vaux
*Landlords* John & Anne Askew
**BEDROOMS 6 Grade 1 £B** (No dogs)
Cottage pie with red cabbage £2 Oriental pork & rice £3.50 (Last order 9pm)
Vaux Sunderland Bitter, Samson, Mild; Lorimer's Scotch; Guinness; Tuborg; Taunton cider. *Real ale*

Set in a peaceful village, this smartly kept pub retains plenty of character in its old beamed bars. Sandwiches, generous salads and hot dishes like cottage pie are always available and there are steak suppers in the evening. The bedrooms are pleasantly furnished and six of them have their own well-fitted bathrooms. Children under seven not accommodated overnight.
**Family pub**

## Askrigg *(B & B)* — *King's Arms Hotel*

Market Place · *North Yorkshire* · Map 4 C2
Wensleydale (0969) 50258

*Free House*
*Landlords* Ray & Liz Hopwood

**BEDROOMS 11 Grade 1 £B**
Scottish & Newcastle Exhibition; Younger's Scotch Bitter; McEwan's 80/-, Export Lager; Taunton cider.

Scenes for a popular TV series were filmed at this 17th-century coaching inn, where the public bar with its huge fireplace and cosy settles, and the panelled lounge with ancestral portraits and a grandfather clock, are full of character. Bedrooms, off steep stairs and quaint passages, are handsomely furnished with antiques and quality fabrics; all have TVs, tea-makers and good private bathrooms. **Family pub**

## Asthall *(Food)* — *Maytime Inn*

Near Burford · *Oxfordshire* · Map 5 A2
Burford (099 382) 2068

*Free House*
*Landlords* Tim & May Morgan

French onion soup £1.50 Breast of chicken in lobster sauce £5.25 (Last order 10.30pm)
Wadworth's Special Bitter, 6X; Morrell's Varsity Bitter; Webster's Yorkshire Bitter; Younger's Tartan; Foster's. *Real ale*

All ages and appetites are catered for at this plush old stone pub, where the Morgans present a bar menu of exceptional variety. Smooth, creamy chicken liver pâté makes an excellent starter or snack, and there are pizzas and pasta, ploughman's and omelettes, plus vegetarian specials and substantial main-course dishes served with good fresh vegetables. Simple sweets, and a special children's menu. Garden.
**Family pub**

## Aston Cantlow *(Food)* — *King's Head*

Near Stratford-upon-Avon · *Warwickshire*
Map 5 A2
Great Alne (078 981) 242

*Brewery* Whitbread
*Landlords* Di & Joe Saunders
Fisherman's pie £2.30 Red cherry cheesecake roll £1 (Last order 9.45pm)
Flower's IPA, Best Bitter; Whitbread Best Bitter; Guinness; Heineken; Stella Artois. *Real ale*

The welcome could not be warmer at the Saunders' black and white half-timbered inn, where Shakespeare's parents held their wedding breakfast in 1557. The food is still a very popular feature, with snacks in the beamed bars including soup and ploughman's, cod bake and a well-seasoned chilli con carne with rice. Red cherry cheesecake roll makes an unusual and delicious dessert. Garden.

## Aswarby *(B & B)* — *Tally Ho*

Near Sleaford · *Lincolnshire* · Map 4 D4
Culverthorpe (052 95) 205

*Free House*
*Landlords* Mr & Mrs C. Davis

**BEDROOMS 6 Grades 1 & 2 £B**
Adnams Bitter; Bateman's Bitter; Guinness; Ayingerbräu; Samuel Smith's Diät Pils; cider. *Real ale*

Generations of eager feet, including those of the Belvoir Hunt, have worn down the stone steps leading into the cosy beamed bar of this characterful 17th-century stone inn. Bedrooms, in a converted stable block, are contrastingly modern, with pretty fabrics, tea-makers, colour TVs and neat tiled bathrooms or showers. Standards of housekeeping are impressively high. Garden.

## Bainbridge *(B & B)* — *Rose & Crown Hotel*

Leyburn · *North Yorkshire* · Map 4 C2
Wensleydale (0969) 50225

*Free House*
*Landlord* Mr B. C. C. Thorpe

**BEDROOMS 13 Grade 2 £A**
Younger's No. 3 Ale, Scotch Bitter; Newcastle Exhibition; McEwan's Export; Kestrel; Taunton cider. *Real ale*

Yorkshire is renowned for its hospitality, and you'll find it in abundance at this fine old village inn. The famous Bainbridge horn – traditionally blown to guide lost travellers – is one of many curios that adorn the entrance hall and bars. Spotlessly clean bedrooms, furnished in a variety of styles, modern to traditional, have colour TVs and six have their own neat little shower rooms. Patio. **Family pub** (lunchtime)

## Bamford *(B & B)* — *Rising Sun Hotel*

Hope Road, Hope Valley · *Derbyshire*
Map 4 C3
Hope Valley (0433) 51323

*Free House*
*Landlords* John & Teresa Ellis

**BEDROOMS 11 Grade 1 £B**
Webster's Yorkshire Bitter, Dark Mild; Guinness; Foster's; Carlsberg.

Outside Bamford on the A625, this low half-timbered pub enjoys breathtaking views of the surrounding Peak District. You can sit out on the terrace in fine weather and there are two cosy, relaxing bars. Attractively furnished bedrooms have central heating, fitted carpets, colour TVs and tea-makers. Five have neatly fitted private bathrooms, the rest shower cabinets. Good breakfasts. **Family pub**

## Bantham *(B & B)* — *Sloop Inn*

Near Kingsbridge · *Devon* · Map 8 C4
Kingsbridge (0548) 560489

*Free House*
*Landlord* Mr Neil Girling

**BEDROOMS 5 Grade 2 £C**
Bass; Usher's Best Bitter; Worthington Best Bitter; Guinness; Carlsberg Hof; Carling Black Label; cider. *Real ale*

Once associated with the smuggling trade, this welcoming old inn is just a short stroll over the dunes from the beach. Black beams and wooden benches add old-world charm to the bar, where locals like to chat or have a game of crib. Pretty bedrooms (four with well-equipped bathrooms) have simple contemporary furnishings and tea-makers. Accommodation closed Christmas. Patio. **Family pub**

## Barbon *(Food, B & B)* — *Barbon Inn*

Near Kirkby Lonsdale · *Cumbria* · Map 3 B2
Barbon (046 836) 233

*Free House*
*Landlord* Mr K. Whitlock
**BEDROOMS 11 Grade 1 £B**
Morecambe Bay potted shrimps £1.85 Grilled sirloin steak £4.95 (Last order 9pm.
No bar food Sat eve)
Theakston's Real Ale, Best Bitter, Old Peculier; Foster's; cider. *Real ale*

This old whitewashed coaching inn enjoys a quiet rural setting between the Lakes and the Dales. The little residents' lounges are cosy and intimate, and the bar offers some enjoyable fare, from good thick mushroom soup to salads, steaks and a delicious fruit pie, plus a roast for Sunday lunch. Comfortable, prettily papered bedrooms are attractively furnished and equipped with tea-makers. Garden. **Family pub**

## Barnard Castle *(Food)* — *Red Well Inn*

Harmire Road · *Co. Durham* · Map 4 C2
Teesdale (0833) 37002
*Free House*
*Landlords* Mr & Mrs M. J. Rudd & Mr & Mrs K. M. Thompson
Mussels in white wine & garlic butter £1.90 Fried beef in hot pepper sauce with rice £3.20 (Last order 9.30pm. No bar food Sun & Mon eves)
John Smith's Bitter, Magnet; Theakston's Best Bitter; Guinness; Hofmeister; Harp; Taunton cider. *Real ale*

Standards remain high in the pleasant lounge bar of this creeper-clad pub. Staff cheerfully dispense substantial main courses, grills and salads – perhaps braised ham florentine, richly flavoured steak and kidney pie or stuffed Whitby lemon sole. Smooth chicken liver pâté, filled seafood pancake or a quiche salad for a lighter bite. **Family pub**

## Bassenthwaite Lake *(Food, B & B)* — *Pheasant Inn*

Near Cockermouth · *Cumbria* · Map 3 B1
Bassenthwaite Lake (059 681) 234

*Free House*
*Landlords* Mr & Mrs W. E. Barrington-Wilson

**BEDROOMS 20 Grade 1 £A+** (No dogs)
Pâté £1.45 Cumberland pork, ham & egg pie £1.60 (No bar food eves)
Theakston's Best Bitter; Bass; Guinness; Carlsberg. *Real ale*

Open fires and well-polished furniture make the three lounges of this peaceful lakeside inn very inviting and the cheerful bedrooms provide homely comfort. Simple lunchtime snacks available in the cosy bar range from potted shrimps, pâté, and savoury quiche to smoked trout, a Cumberland sausage platter or a hot daily special. Garden. **Family pub**

## Bath *(Food)* — *Park Tavern*

3 Park Lane · *Avon* · Map 8 D3
Bath (0225) 25174

*Brewery* Courage
*Landlords* Mr & Mrs D. Collins

Chicken livers £1.85 Devilled kidneys £1.85 (Last order 9.30pm)
Courage Best Bitter, Directors Bitter, JC; John Smith's; Guinness; Hofmeister; Taunton cider. *Real ale*

Mrs Collins' tasty and imaginative bar meals draw the crowds to her simple pub with its own garden. Choices on a hugely varied menu might include mussels in white wine, pasta dishes, curries, an assortment of pizzas and the ever-popular devilled kidneys. For a lighter snack, there are jacket potatoes, ploughman's and salads. No sweets, however.

## Bawburgh *(Food)* — *Kings Head*

Harts Lane, Near Norwich · *Norfolk*
Map 5 D1
Norwich (0603) 744977

*Free House*
*Landlords* Mr & Mrs A. A. Wimmer
Beef chasseur £3.60 Crab quiche & salad £2.20 (Last order 10.30pm)
Wethered's Bitter; Adnams Bitter; Stewart & Paterson Bitter; Whitbread Mild; Guinness; Foster's; Carlsberg; cider. *Real ale*

Some very enjoyable snacks are to be found in the quaint old bars of this charming pub opposite the village green. For a quick bite there's pâté and various ploughman's, and you can also tuck into beef chasseur, spicy lamb casserole and crab in a wine sauce. There's a squash court and bowling green for the energetic, and a garden for fine weather. **Family pub**

## Beaulieu *(Food)* — *Montagu Arms Hotel*

*Hampshire* · Map 6 A4
Beaulieu (0590) 612324

*Free House* Greenclose Hotels
*Landlord* Mr J. Talbot
Venison sausages & vegetables £2.25
Curry £1.75 (No bar food eves)
Wadsworth 6X; Flower's Original Bitter; Whitbread Best Bitter; McEwans's Export; Guinness; Heineken; Löwenbräu; cider. *Real ale*

Spats Bar is a lively, popular spot for lunchtime snacks at this comfortable former monk's hostelry and coaching inn. Start with the day's soup – our broccoli was really delicious – and go on to roast chicken, venison sausages, perhaps a curry in winter. Other choices include open sandwiches, interesting salads and yummy sherry trifle. *For accommodation see Egon Ronay's Lucas Hotel & Restaurant Guide 1985.*

## Beauworth *(Food, B & B)* — *Milbury's*

Near Cheriton · *Hampshire* · Map 6 B4
Bramdean (096 279) 248

*Free House*
*Landlords* Greg & Jaqueline Gregory
**BEDROOMS 6 Grade 2 £C**
Crab salad £2.95 Chilli con carne £2.65 (Last order 10.30pm)
Wethereds Bitter; Flowers Original; Marston's Pedigree; Gale's Horndean Special Bitter; Wadworth's 6X. *Real ale*

Standing on the Cheriton-Bishops Waltham road on the site of an old mill, this listed building boasts many fascinating features, including a huge treadwheel and a 300-foot-deep well. Tasty bar fare ranges from French onion soup to salads, grilled trout and sirloin steak, and sweets include a scrumptious lemon and sultana cheesecake. Recently restored bedrooms have pretty decor and solid traditional furnishings. **Family pub**

## Beckley *(Food)* — *Abingdon Arms*

Near Oxford · *Oxfordshire* · Map 6 A3
Stanton St John (086 735) 311

*Brewery* Halls
*Landlords* Mr & Mrs Greatbatch

Spiced game pie with port sauce £2.65
Roast beef £4.65 (Last order 10.15pm. No bar food Sun eve)
Halls Harvest Bitter; Ind Coope Burton Ale, Double Diamond; Guinness; Skol. *Real ale*

Mrs Greatbatch's excellent home cooking attracts a loyal following to this delightful converted house with a large and pretty garden. Rare roast rib of beef is a perennial favourite, along with ploughman's, prawns in creole sauce, quiche lorraine and chicken, ham and mushroom pie. Fish soup is a popular winter warmer, seafood salad a summer treat for two. Puds include a nice raspberry torte.

## Bedford *(B & B)* — *Embankment Hotel*

The Embankment · *Bedfordshire* · Map 5 B2
Bedford (0234) 217791

*Brewery* Charrington
*Landlord* Mr J. Bradnam

**BEDROOMS 20 Grade 1 £A**
Charrington's IPA, Stones Bitter, Worthington 'E'; Carling Black Label; Tennent's Extra. *Real ale*

Built in Victorian times, but with a mock-Tudor facade, this recently refurbished hotel stands near the centre of town overlooking the river Ouse. Bedrooms of various sizes provide accommodation of a high standard: modern fitted units, direct-dial telephones, remote-control TVs, trouser presses. Nearly all have their own neat bath or shower rooms. Public rooms include a smart reception area and comfortable bar.

## Bedford *(Food)* — *Park*

98 Kimbolton Road · *Bedfordshire* · Map 5 B2
Bedford (0234) 54093

*Brewery* Wells
*Landlord* Mr E. Cheeseman
Choice of 3 cheeses, pickles, bread £1.65
Pâté, pickles, bread £1.35 (No bar food eves or Sun)
Wells Eagle Bitter, Bombardier, Noggin; Guinness; Kellerbräu; Red Stripe; cider. *Real ale*

A selection of more than 20 fine English cheeses is the strong point of this smart beamed pub. Served with pickles and fresh granary bread, they make a splendid lunch-time snack. If you're not in the mood for cheese, there are also home-made pies, quiche, soup and warming winter specials like Lancashire hot pot. Simple sweets to finish. Patio.

## Beer *(B & B)* — *Anchor Inn*

Fore Street · *Devon* · Map 8 C3
Seaton (0297) 20386

*Free House*
*Landlords* Mr & Mrs D. Boalch

**BEDROOMS 9 Grade 2 £C** (No dogs)
Eldridge Pope Royal Oak, Dorset IPA; Flowers Original; Guinness; Carling Black Label; Faust Export; Taunton cider. *Real ale*

This handsome gabled inn stands near the sea in a pleasant fishing village once notorious for smugglers. Public rooms include two traditionally furnished bars and a little reception-lounge, and there are nine neat, attractive bedrooms. All have tea-makers and colour TVs and some enjoy lovely sea views. Bathrooms are modern. No children under seven overnight. Accommodation closed 1 week Christmas. Garden. **Family pub**

## Beetham *(Food, B & B)* — *Wheatsheaf Hotel*

Near Milnthorpe · *Cumbria* · Map 3 B2
Milnthorpe (044 82) 2123

*Free House*
*Landlord* Mrs F. Miller

**BEDROOMS 8 Grade 2 £B**
Cottage pie £1.40 Hot pot £1.30 (Last order 10pm)
Slater's Bitter; Stones Bitter, Mild; Guinness; Carlsberg; Taunton cider. *Real ale*

Mrs Miller's welcoming corner pub, just across the road from the church, makes a useful halt for travellers on the A6. The beamed bar is a cosy place to enjoy homely snacks like sweet and savoury pies, freshly made sandwiches, hot pot and appetising cold meat salads. Eight neatly furnished bedrooms all have washbasins and electric blankets and there are four well-kept bathrooms.

## Belsay *(Food)* — *Highlander Inn*

Hygham Dykes · *Northumberland* · Map 4 C1
Belsay (066 181) 220

*Owners* Newcastle Inns
*Landlord* Barrie Dixon

Game pie with salad £2.25 Haggis with potato & turnip £1.70 (Last order 9.30pm)
Younger's No. 3 Ale; Scottish & Newcastle Exhibition, Newcastle Bitter; Guinness; Harp; Carlsberg Hof; Taunton cider. *Real ale*

South of Belsay on the A696, this handsome converted farmhouse attracts the crowds with a good range of hot and cold bar snacks. You can help yourself from the buffet of pies, salads and home-cooked meats, or choose from a menu of daily specials like sweetbreads with rice, a roast, or an excellent steak and kidney pie. Good home-made sweets, too. Courtyard.

## Benenden *(Food)* — *King William IV*

The Street · *Kent* · Map 6 C3
Benenden (0580) 240636

*Brewery* Shepherd Neame
*Landlords* Nigel & Hilary Douglas

Duck liver pâté £1 Supreme of chicken Wellington £3.45 (Last order 9.30pm. No bar food Sun)
Eldridge Pope Master Brew, Mild; Guinness; Hurlimann; Taunton cider. *Real ale*

The Douglases are the affable hosts at this pleasant village pub, whose lounge bar sports oak beams and a fine old fireplace. Snacks are a popular feature, and the blackboard menus offers a good variety, from simple ploughman's or garlic mussels to onion tart, chicken curry and full-flavoured beef and red wine casserole. Leave room for a delicious sweet like our lovely strawberry confection. Garden.

## Berkeley Road *(B & B)* — *Prince of Wales Hotel*

Near Berkeley · *Gloucestershire* · Map 7 D2
Dursley (0453) 810474

*Free House*
*Landlords* David & Jane Taylor

**BEDROOMS 8 Grade 1 £A**
Marston's Pedigree; Theakston's Best Bitter; Whitbread's West Country Pale Ale; Guinness; Harlech Lager; cider. *Real ale*

Housekeeping and maintenance are both excellent at this efficiently run hotel alongside the A38. The bedrooms are comfortable and well equipped, with smart modern furnishings, colour TVs, direct-dial telephones and tea-makers. All rooms have attractively tiled private bathrooms with modern suites. Public areas include a spacious bar and neat reception-lounge, and there's a very pretty garden. Good breakfasts. **Family pub**

## Bewdley *(Food, B & B)* — *Black Boy Hotel*

Kidderminster Road · *Hereford & Worcester*
Map 7 D1
Bewdley (0299) 402119
*Free House*
*Ladlords* Mr A. R. Wilson
**BEDROOMS 28 Grade 2 £B**
Cottage pie £1.15 Braised oxtail & vegetables £1.95 (No bar food eves & all Sun)
Mitchells & Butlers Springfield Bitter, Bitter, Mild; Guinness; Tennent's Pilsner; Carling Black Label. *Real ale*

The club-like bar of this fine old inn is a popular place at lunchtime, when honest, homely fare ranges from rich, nourishing turkey soup to salads, sandwiches and a splendid casserole of lamb's liver and onions. Tangy lemon cheesecake to finish. Bedrooms vary from spacious and handsomely furnished to smaller and simpler. There's a comfortably traditional lounge and a quiet writing room. **Family pub**

## Bexhill *(Food)* — *Wilton Court*

Wilton Road, Marina · *East Sussex* · Map 6 C4
Bexhill (0424) 210208

*Free House*
*Landlord* Mrs Frances M. Burt

Cottage pie £1.50 Sherry trifle 85p
(Last order 10pm)
Courage Directors Bitter; Bass; Fullers London Pride; Whitbreads Tusker; Guinness; cider. *Real ale*

Mrs Burt's seaside pub is just the place to go for a tasty and sustaining lunch. Daily roasts like shoulder of lamb or beef sirloin top the bill, and dressed crab, whether served in a salad or a sandwich, is another popular choice. Home-made soup, steak and kidney pie, and some delicious desserts are also on offer. Evening fare consists of soup and sandwiches only.
**Family pub**

## Bibury *(Food, B & B)* — *Catherine Wheel*

Near Cirencester · *Gloucestershire* · Map 6 A3
Bibury (028 574) 250

*Brewery* Courage
*Landlord* Mr Bill May
**BEDROOMS 2 Grade 2 £C**
Bibury trout £3.50 Olde English sausages £1.80 (Last order 10pm)
Courage Best Bitter, JC; Simonds Bitter; Guinness; Hofmeister; Kronenbourg; Taunton cider. *Real ale*

With its massive walls, oak doors and low beamed ceilings, this Cotswold-stone pub possesses considerable period charm. The menu revolves around simple snacks, well-prepared and generously served; soups and pâté, home-cooked beef, plump, herby bangers, winter casseroles, trout from the farm down the road. The two bedrooms – sturdily furnished and smartly maintained – share a splendidly equipped bathroom. Garden. **Family pub**

## Biddenden *(Food)* ★ — *Three Chimneys*

*Kent* · Map 6 C3
Biddenden (0580) 291472

*Free House*
*Landlords* Christopher & Pippa Sayers

Avocado mousse £1.45 Sherried kidneys £3.50 (Last order 10pm)
Adnams Bitter; Marston's Pedigree; Harvey's Best Bitter; Godson's Black Horse; Guinness; Stella Artois; cider. *Real ale*

Real ale, cosy beamed bars and charming hosts are just some of the assets of this old country pub. There's also an enormous garden for fine weather, and excellent bar food ranging from warming soups to dishes like leek gratin, cheese and onion flan, stuffed shoulder of lamb and home-baked ham. Apple charlotte and date and walnut pudding are among the irresistible desserts. **Family pub**

## Biddestone *(Food)* — *Biddestone Arms*

Near Chippenham · *Wiltshire* · Map 7 D2
Corsham (0249) 714377

*Free House*
*Landlords* Roy and Pam Chippendale

Chilli con carne £1.50 Stilton ploughman's £1.25 (Last order 10pm)
Wadworth's 6X; Usher's Best Bitter, PA; Flowers Best Bitter; Whitbread West Country Bitter; Guinness; cider. *Real ale*

Familiar bar fare is offered in good variety at this attractive stone pub standing at one end of the village. Sandwiches, ploughman's and pâté are popular choices for quick snacks, with other items running the gamut from soup and tasty Cornish pasties to omelettes, seafood and sirloin steak. For Sunday lunch there's a four-course menu or a basket meal. Garden.

## Bidford-on-Avon *(Food, B & B)* — *White Lion Hotel*

High Street · *Warwickshire* · Map 5 A2
Bidford-on-Avon (0789) 773309

*Free House*
*Landlord* Mr John McDonald
**BEDROOMS 15 Grades 1 & 2 £B**
Savoury baked egg with salmon £2.10 Baked cheesecake 85p (No bar food eves or Sun)
Everards Old Original; Newcastle Bitter; Younger's Shire Mild; Tuborg; McEwan's lager; cider. *Real ale*

A riverside terrace is a summertime bonus at this cosy old hostelry by an ancient stone bridge. Lunchtime snacks are simple and satisfying: warming soups, filled jacket potatoes, ploughman's platters, savoury baked eggs, with some old-fashioned puddings to fill any gaps. Good-sized bedrooms (six with well-appointed private bathrooms) range from traditional to modern in style; all have tea-makers and TVs. There's a comfortable residents' lounge.

## Bierton *(Food)* — *Red Lion*

Near Aylesbury · *Buckinghamshire* · Map 5 B2
Aylesbury (0296) 24453

*Brewery* Aylesbury
*Landlords* Mr & Mrs L. Bishop

Chicken & ham pie £1.25 Fillet of plaice £3.60 (Last order 9pm. No bar food Sat & Sun)
ABC Bitter; Benskins Light Mild; Bass; Ben Truman; Guinness; Carlsberg.

Run by the Bishop family for several generations, this friendly pub offers a different menu in each of its bars. The simple public bar is the place for homely snacks like cauliflower cheese, shepherd's pie or lasagne, while the plush lounge bar features more elaborate choices like grilled gammon steak and veal escalope with ginger wine. Try a lemon meringue pie or raspberry flan for dessert. Patio.

## Binfield — *Stag & Hounds*

A historic hunting lodge, from which Elizabeth I watched maypole dancing on the green. In addition to the cosy, characterful lounge bar with sturdy old settles and pews, there are several little beamed snugs in the converted stables. Just outside stands the stump of an ancient elm which marked the centre of Windsor Great Forest.

Forest Road · *Berkshire* · Map 6 B3
Bracknell (0344) 483553
*Brewery* Courage *Landlords* Mr & Mrs B. Howard
Courage Best Bitter, Directors Bitter, John Courage Bitter; Guinness; Hofmeister; Kronenbourg 1664; Taunton cider. *Real ale*

## Bircham *(B & B)* — *Kings Head*

Near King's Lynn · *Norfolk* · Map 5 C1
Syderstone (048 523) 265

*Free House*
*Landlords* Sutton family

**BEDROOMS 5 Grade 1 £C**
Adnams Bitter; Bass; Marston's Owd Rodger (winter only); Stones Bitter; Carling Black Label; Tennent's Extra; Taunton cider. *Real ale*

Guests receive a warm, friendly welcome from the Sutton family at this rambling pub on the edge of the Sandringham estate. The homely lounge bar and traditional public bar are popular with those wanting a tipple; there's also a cosy TV lounge. Sturdily furnished bedrooms with attractive soft furnishings provide excellent comfort; all have tea-coffee making facilities and modern bath/shower rooms. Accommodation closed Christmas week. **Family pub**

## Bishop Wilton *(B & B)* — *Fleece Inn*

Near York · *Humberside* · Map 4 D2
Bishop Wilton (075 96) 251

*Free House*
*Landlords* Allan, Barbara & Irene Hawcroft

**BEDROOMS 4 Grade 2 £C** (No dogs)
Theakston's Best Bitter; John Smith's Bitter; Tetley's Bitter; Guinness; Skol; Carlsberg Hof; Taunton cider. *Real ale*

The red-brick facade of this village pub blends in well with its peaceful surroundings. Darkened beams give a rustic appeal to the pleasant lounge with TV. Tissues and books strike a homely note in the bedrooms, which are cheerful, spotless and beautifully warm; they share a sparkling bathroom. Simple, hearty breakfasts are served in the tiny dining room. No children under 12 overnight. **Family pub**

## Bishop's Lydeard *(B & B)* — *Lethbridge Arms*

Near Taunton · *Somerset* · Map 8 C3
Bishop's Lydeard (0823) 432234

*Brewery* Whitbread
*Landlords* Mr & Mrs A. J. Wilkins

**BEDROOMS 6 Grade 2 £C** (No dogs)
Flowers Original; Whitbread Best Bitter, IPA, Trophy; Bass; Guinness; Heineken; Stella Artois; Taunton cider. *Real ale*

Dating back to the 14th century, this cosy village inn at the foot of the Quantock Hills is a popular place for a drink and a chat. Pub games are a feature, and there is a comfortable TV lounge for residents. Simply furnished bedrooms provide adequate comforts and the public bathrooms are well kept. No children overnight. **Family pub**

## Bishop's Lydeard *(Food)* — *Rose Cottage*

Near Taunton · *Somerset* · Map 8 C3
Bishop's Lydeard (0823) 432394

*Free House*
*Landlords* Mr & Mrs P. Dale-Thomas

Fish & prawn mornay £4.25 Vegetarian moussaka £2.65 (Last order 9.30pm)
Eldridge Pope Dorset IPA, 1880 Ale; Carlsberg Pilsner; cider. *Real ale*

Excellent food is a top priority at this attractive little roadside pub. Mrs Dale-Thomas's bar menu might include fresh vegetable soup, quiche, smoked salmon mousse, sweet and sour chicken with pasta, and some delicious sweets. There's also a formal à la carte menu in the evening. Closed Sun, Mon, 1st two weeks November and 2 weeks from 24 December. Patio.

## Bishop's Waltham *(Food)* — *White Horse*

Beeches Hill · *Hampshire* · Map 6 A4
Bishop's Waltham (048 93) 2532

*Brewery* Whitbread
*Landlords* Arthur & Carol Noot

Rabbit pie £1.60 Tandoori chicken £3 (Last order 10pm. No bar food Mon in winter)
Flower's Original; Wethered's Bitter; Whitbread Strong Country Bitter; Guinness; cider. *Real ale*

Much loved by the locals, this splendid little inn provides wholesome, tasty food in the most convivial and welcoming of surroundings. Carol Noot's homely offerings could include familiar favourites like steak and kidney pie and chilli con carne, with an Indian dish such as lamb biryani to ring the changes. Sandwiches and salads, too, with jam roly-poly for a truly traditional finale. Garden with children's play area.

## Blacko *(Food, B & B)* — *Moorcock Inn*

Gisburn Road, Near Nelson · *Lancashire*
Map 4 C3
Nelson (0282) 64186

*Brewery* Thwaites
*Landlords* Peter & Kathy Brandstatter
**BEDROOMS 3 Grade 2 £C**
Steak & kidney pie & chips £2.20 Savoury pancake & chips £2.20 (Last order 11pm)
Thwaites Bitter, Best Mild; Guinness; Kronenbourg; Stein.

Peter Brandstatter, landlord of this converted farmhouse on the Lancashire fells, comes from Austria and his bar menu includes Continental treats like bratwurst with sauerkraut and rösti potatoes. There's also a good choice of more familiar items such as steak and kidney pie, omelettes, lasagne and steakburger with onion sauce. Overnight guests have three comfortable bedrooms with their own TVs and shower units. **Family pub**

## Blackpool *(Food)* — *Grosvenor Hotel*

Cookson Street · *Lancashire* · Map 3 B3
Blackpool (0253) 25096

*Brewery* Bass
*Landlords* John & Jackie McKeown

Macaroni cheese with ham £1.70 Paella £1.70 (No bar food eves or Sun)
Bass, Dark Mild; Stones Bitter; Guinness; Carling Black Label; Taunton cider. *Real ale*

Welcoming landlords John and Jackie McKeown provide a splendid range of lunchtime food at this large Victorian pub. Besides soup, sandwiches and omelettes for a light bite, you can choose a more filling hot special like breaded haddock, mixed grill or hearty minced beef pie with chips and fresh vegetables. There's also a cold buffet in summer.

## Blakesley *(B & B)* — *Bartholomew Arms*

Near Towcester · *Northamptonshire*
Map 5 B2
Blakesley (0327) 860292

*Free House*
*Landlords* Mr & Mrs C. A. Hackett

**BEDROOMS 5 Grade 1 £C** (No dogs)
Marston's Pedigree; Younger's Scotch Bitter, Tartan; Newcastle Bitter; Guinness; Carlsberg Hof; Taunton cider. *Real ale*

Soap-box racing is a star local attraction and Mr Hackett's delightful little pub is a great favourite with both drivers and spectators. The three rustic bars are cosy drinking places, and there are five comfortable, prettily furnished bedrooms, all with TVs. The public bathroom that they share is tiled and well kept. Garden. **Family pub**

## Bledington *(Food, B & B)* — *King's Head*

The Green, Near Kingham · *Gloucestershire*
Map 5 A2
Kingham (060 871) 365
*Free House*
*Landlords* Rita & Graham Smith
**BEDROOMS 3 Grade 1 £B** (No dogs)
Rack of lamb £5.20 Mushroom & prawn pancake £2.75 (Last order 10.45pm)
Wadsworth's 6X, Devizes Bitter; John Smith's Bitter; Younger's Tartan; Guinness; Löwenbräu; Heineken; cider. *Real ale*

A delightful 16th-century village inn, complete with landscaped gardens and a little stream. In the beamed bars, where the snooker memorabilia are a major talking point, you'll eat heartily and well off traditional English fare like ploughman's platters, home-baked pies and enormous racks of lamb. Pretty bedrooms are comfortable and well equipped, with TVs, teamakers and neat bathrooms. **Family pub**

## Bletchingley *(B & B)* — *Whyte Harte*

High Street · *Surrey* · Map 6 C3
Godstone (0883) 843231

*Brewery* Allied Breweries
*Landlords* Mr & Mrs Derek King

**BEDROOMS 9 Grade 2 £A** (No dogs)
Burton Ale; Friary Meux Bitter; John Bull Bitter; Guinness; Skol; Löwenbräu; cider. *Real ale*

Easy to spot with its striking white-painted exterior, this popular village pub has a history that goes back to the 14th century. The large, convivial bar has a splendid inglenook fireplace where a welcome log fire roars in winter. Bedrooms in the old part have a delightfully cottagy feel, while others are more modern and have their own bathrooms. The beamed bar is large and convivial and there's a tiny TV room. Garden.

## Blickling *(Food, B & B)* — *Buckinghamshire Arms*

Near Aylsham · *Norfolk* · Map 5 D1
Aylsham (026 373) 2133

*Free House*
*Landlord* Mr Nigel Elliott
**BEDROOMS 3 Grade 1 £B**
Smoked salmon salad £3.20 Home-made pâté £2.20 (Last order 10pm)
Adnams Bitter, IPA; Greene King Abbot Ale; Ind Coope Burton Ale, John Bull; Guinness; cider. *Real ale*

Nigel Elliott offers good food and a friendly welcome in this handsome 17th-century hostelry. On the bar menu is simple fare like delicious stockpot soup, a few hors d'oeuvre platters (our seafood one was excellent), plus salads, sandwiches and hot dishes such as toad-in-the-hole. Comfortable bedrooms (one with a four-poster), all with TVs, share an old-fashioned bathroom. Lots of tables for outdoor eating.
**Family pub**

## Bollington *(Food)* — *Church House Inn*

24 Church Street, Nr Macclesfield · *Cheshire*
Map 4 C3
Bollington (0625) 74014
*Free House*
*Landlord* Leonard Boyd
Steak & kidney pie with vegetables £2.60
Crab sandwich 65p (Last order 9.30pm. No bar food Tues eve)
Tetley's Bitter, Mild; Ruddle's County; Saxon Cross Bitter; Carlsberg Export; Guinness; cider. *Real ale*

Tasty home cooking draws the crowds, especially at lunchtime, to this sturdy pub furnished with padded church pews. Soup or mushrooms in garlic butter make an excellent start, and there are satisfying main courses like goulash, lasagne and beef and orange in cider. There are sandwiches (at lunchtime only) and salads, too, as well as delicious sweets like bilberry pie or crisp almond torte.

## Boot *(Food, B & B)* — *Woolpack Inn*

Eskdale · *Cumbria* · Map 3 B2
Eskdale (094 03) 230

*Free House*
*Landlords* Mr & Mrs J. G. Pease

**BEDROOMS 7 Grade 1 £C**
Ploughman's lunch £1.45 Sandwiches 75p (No bar food eves)
Younger's Scotch Bitter; Newcastle Exhibition; McEwan's Lager; Taunton cider.

The Pease family's friendly inn is a welcoming haven for hikers in the Eskdale valley. At lunchtime hearty soups, generously filled sandwiches and ploughman's cater for the hungry in the cosy bar (only sandwiches on Sundays), and there are seven cheerful, roomy bedrooms with tea-makers and a neat public bathroom. Two lounges include one with TV. Rooms closed 1 Nov–31 March, when bar is open Fri and Sat eves only.
**Family pub**

## Boscastle *(B & B)* — *Wellington Hotel*

The Harbour · *Cornwall* · Map 8 B3
Boscastle (084 05) 203

*Free House*
*Landlord* Mr G. J. Stedman

**BEDROOMS 21 Grade 2 £C**
Flowers Original; St Austell Best; Whitbread Best Bitter; Usher's Triple Crown; Guinness; Carlsberg Hof; cider. *Real ale*

This one-time coaching inn close to the little harbour remains a popular stopping place for travellers. Drinkers can choose between the simply furnished lounge bar and the spacious public bar with its rough-stone walls and bar billiards; and there's also a quiet TV lounge. Comfortable, brightly decorated bedrooms with radios have mostly built-in units, and compact bathrooms are up to date. Accommodation closed November–February. **Family pub**

## Boston *(B & B)* — *New England Hotel*

49 Wide Bargate · *Lincolnshire* · Map 5 C1
Boston (0205) 65255

*Owners* Anchor Hotels
*Landlords* Mr & Mrs W. N. Davies

**BEDROOMS 25 Grade 1 £A+** (No dogs)
Old Tom Mild; John Smith's Bitter; Hofmeister. *Real ale*

Accommodation is first class at this well-maintained, brick-built pub in the centre of town. All the bedrooms have been smartly modernised, with fitted units, tea-makers, colour TVs and radio-alarms. There's plenty of writing space, too, and every room has its own compact tiled bathroom. Note the fine plasterwork ceiling in the spacious bar, which is a favourite local meeting place. **Family pub**

## Boston Spa *(B & B)* — *Royal Hotel*

High Street · *West Yorkshire* · Map 4 C3
Boston Spa (0937) 842142

*Owners* Chef & Brewer
*Landlords* Mr & Mrs William Patterson

**BEDROOMS 7 Grade 1 £B**
Webster's Yorkshire Bitter, Green Label Best; Guinness; Carlsberg; Foster's; cider. *Real ale*

About a mile east of the A1 on the A659, this smartly painted inn makes a comfortable overnight stop. Bedrooms have good fitted carpets, duvets, tea-makers and radios, and they share a neatly kept public bathroom. Guests can relax with a drink in the cosy beamed bar or watch TV in the residents' lounge. Excellent breakfasts. Garden. **Family pub**

## Bottesford *(Food)* — *Red Lion*

Grantham Road · *Nottinghamshire* · Map 5 B1
Bottesford (0949) 42218

*Brewery* Kimberley
*Landlords* Mr & Mrs M. Kay

Steak & kidney pie £2.25 Apple crumble 70p (Last order 10.30pm)
Hardy & Hansons Best Mild, Best Bitter; Guinness; Stella Artois; Heineken; cider. *Real ale*

Mick and Jill Kay are friendly, professional hosts at this neat whitewashed pub near Belvoir Castle. The two bars – spacious lounge, snug public – offer a varied menu, from chip butties and cheeseburgers to quiches, salads and tasty pies (cottage, fisherman's, mince with mushrooms and onions). There's often a roast, especially on Sunday. Simple sweets such as apple crumble and cheesecake. Garden. **Family pub**

## Bourton-on-the-Hill *(B & B)* — *Horse & Groom*

Near Moreton-in-Marsh · *Gloucestershire*
Map 5 A2
Blockley (0386) 700413

*Free House*
*Landlord* Mr J. L. Aizpuru

**BEDROOMS 3 Grade 2 £C** No dogs
Bass, Toby Bitter; Worthington 'E'; Tennent's Lager; Carling Black Label. *Real ale*

Pictures of racehorses adorn the rugged bar walls of this handsome sandstone pub with a pretty garden and nice views of the Cotswolds. Simple comforts for an overnight stay (no children) are provided by three spacious, centrally heated bedrooms, all with shower cubicles and washbasins. There's a good public bathroom. Accommodation closed December–January. Garden.

## Bowdon *(Food)* — *Griffin*

Stamford Road, Near Altrincham
*Cheshire* · Map 3 B3
061-928 1211

*Owners* Pennine Host
*Landlords* Tony & June Lee
Prawn & coleslaw barmcake £1.10 Home-cooked ham salad £2.95 (No bar food eves & Sun)
Wilsons Great Northern Bitter, Mild; Guinness; Carlsberg; Foster's. *Real ale*

The Lees are carrying on a tradition of hospitality that dates back to Georgian times at this white-painted pub opposite the parish church. In the bar there's a simple bill of fare consisting of soup, pâté, ploughman's and toasted sandwiches. Or try a traditional barmcake with topside of beef or prawn and coleslaw. The salad bar offers an excellent selection of imaginative salads to accompany the choice from the cold table – perhaps turkey pie or smoked mackerel. Patio.

## Bowes *(B & B)* — *Ancient Unicorn*

Near Barnard Castle · *Co. Durham* · Map 4 C2
Teesdale (0833) 28321

*Free House*
*Landlords* Bob & Jean Saunders

**BEDROOMS 11 Grade 2 £B**
Piper Scotch Bitter; Worthington Pale Ale; Bass Best Mild; Carling Black Label; Taunton cider.

Dating from the early part of the 16th century, this sturdy coaching inn has been brought up to date by Bob and Jean Saunders. Bedrooms in the converted stables provide modest comforts for an overnight stay: all have modern furniture, TVs, tea-makers and private bath or showers rooms. A log fire is a welcoming sight in the convivial beamed bar. Patio.

**Family pub**

## Bowland Bridge *(Food, B & B)* — *Hare & Hounds*

Grange-over-Sands · *Cumbria* · Map 3 B2
Crosthwaite (044 88) 333

*Free House*
*Landlords* Peter & Barbara Thompson

**BEDROOMS 7 Grade 1 £B**
Salmon salad £2.95 Chicken curry £2.50 (Last order 9.30pm)
Tetley's Traditional, Bitter, Mild; Guinness; Skol; Oranjeboom; cider. *Real ale*

Well looked after by its delightful owners, this fine old inn enjoys a quiet position in a pleasant valley. The beamed bar is a comfortable place to enjoy tasty snacks, from sandwiches and salads to pizzas, steak and chilli con carne. Bedrooms in the old building have considerable period charm; the others, with private facilities, are smartly modern. All have colour TVs. Garden.

**Family pub**

## Box *(Food, B & B)* ★ — *Chequers*

Market Place, Near Corsham · *Wiltshire*
Map 7 D2
Box (0225) 742 383
*Brewery* Usher
*Landlords* Ken & Jackie Martin
Beef curry £4 Steaks £4.95 (Last order 10pm)
**BEDROOMS 1 Grade 2 £B** (No dogs)
Usher's PA, Best Bitter, Founder's Ale, Country Bitter; Guinness; Holsten; cider. *Real ale*

Hospitality is a way of life at this charming 17th-century pub, where Malaysian-born Jackie Martin produces some outstanding bar food. Her curries – two days in the making – are renowned locally, and steaks are also very popular. More traditional lunchtime fare – ploughman's and pies – with a summer cold table. Superb apple pie to finish. There's a single attractive bedroom with modern shower room.

**Family pub**

## Boxford *(Food)* — *Fleece*

Near Colchester · *Suffolk* · Map 5 D2
Boxford (0787) 210247

*Brewery* Tollemache & Cobbold
*Landlords* Mr & Mrs F. Crocco

Lasagne £2.50 Fish soup £2.25
(Last order 10pm. No bar food Mon)
Tolly Cobbold Best Bitter, Original; Hansa. *Real ale*

Franco Crocco's Italian specialities add extra appeal to this charming village pub. Seafood looms large on the menu, with dishes like fish soup and garlicky prawns, and there's also expertly prepared pasta, as well as chicken pancakes and lovely fruit tarts to finish. During the shooting season, you might be offered roast partridge or a pheasant casserole. Garden.

## Braintree *(Food)* — *Retreat*

42 Bocking Church Street · *Essex* · Map 5 C2
Braintree (0376) 47947

*Free House*
*Landlords* Mr & Mrs David Locke

Prawn & mushroom puff pie £2.65 Apple crumble 50p (Last order 11pm)
Tolly Cobbold Original Bitter; Trumans Bitter, Best Bitter; Dortmunder Union; Holsten; cider. *Real ale*

Skill and imagination go into the cooking at this fine old inn, whose bars feature beamed ceilings and a huge inglenook fireplace. The blackboard menu changes daily, offering soups, pâté and a wide selection of main courses – from omelettes and grills to salads and our splendid sole with mushrooms and grapes. Desserts are simple and delicious, and there's an impressive cheeseboard. Garden. **Family pub**

## Branscombe *(B & B)* — *Masons Arms*

Near Seaton · *Devon* · Map 8 C3
Branscombe (029 780) 300

*Free House*
*Landlord* Mrs Janet Inglis

**BEDROOMS 22 Grade 1 £A+**
Hall & Woodhouse Badger Best Bitter; Devenish Bitter, Wessex Best Bitter; Whitbread Trophy; Guinness; Heineken; cider. *Real ale*

This 14th-century village inn, with its beamed bar and tables set out on the terrace in summer, makes a delightful place to stay, and Janet Inglis is a welcoming hostess. Bedrooms, including some in nearby cottages, are neat and prettily furnished and bathrooms are well maintained. Residents can relax in the peaceful upstairs lounge or TV room. **Family pub**

## Bratton *(B & B)* — *Duke*

Melbourne Street, Near Westbury · *Wiltshire*
Map 8 D3
Bratton (0380) 830242

*Brewery* Usher
*Landlord* Mr K. H. Stolzenberg

**BEDROOMS 5 Grade 2 £C** (No dogs)
Usher's Founders Ale, Best Bitter, Pale Ale; Guinness; Carlsberg; Holsten Pils; cider. *Real ale*

Standing on the B3098 about halfway between Salisbury and Bath, this smartly renovated pub provides comfortable overnight accommodation for tourists and travellers. Five spacious bedrooms, all with modern fitted units, TVs and tea-makers, are served by two well-equipped bathrooms. The spacious open-plan bar and lounge area retains a characterful air, and housekeeping is excellent throughout. Patio and garden. **Family pub**

## Bray *(Food)* — *Crown at Bray*

High Street · *Berkshire* · Map 6 B3
Maidenhead (0628) 21936

*Brewery* Courage
*Landlords* Mr Ashcroft & Mr Whitton

Pâté £1.75 Honey-roast chicken & vegetables £2.75 (No bar food eves)
Courage Best Bitter; Guinness; Hofmeister; Kronenbourg. *Real ale*

Swift, friendly service at neatly laid tables copes with the crowds who enjoy the combination of an atmospheric setting – plenty of old beams – and tasty lunchtime bar snacks. Popular dishes include tandoori chicken, roast beef and York ham, all with salad, and a minced beef hot pot. A gooey treacle tart is top of the home-made sweets. Saturday and Sunday lunch consists of a barbecue in summer and jacket potatoes in winter. Garden.

## Breage *(B & B)* — *Queen's Arms*

Near Helston · *Cornwall* · Map 8 A4
Helston (032 65) 3485

*Brewery* Devenish
*Landlords* Mr & Mrs V. M. Graves

**BEDROOMS 3 Grade 2 £C** (No dogs)
Devenish Cornish Best Bitter, Bitter; Whitbread Tankard, Mild; Guinness; Grünhalle; cider. *Real ale*

The Graveses make visitors feel most welcome at this tiny village pub dating from 1854. The two bars are very comfortable, and upstairs there are three quite spacious bedrooms with simple modern furnishings and tea-making facilities. The carpeted public bathroom has a shower cubicle. Children not accommodated overnight. Garden.

## Bredwardine *(B & B)* — *Red Lion Hotel*

Near Hereford · *Hereford & Worcester*
Map 7 D1
Moccas (098 17) 303

*Free House*
*Landlords* Mr & Mrs M. J. Taylor

**BEDROOMS 10 Grade 1 £C** (No dogs)
Bass, Allbright; Mitchells & Butlers DPA; Carling Black Label; Taunton cider. *Real ale*

Set in a peaceful village on the B4352 between Hereford and Hay-on-Wye, this old red-brick inn is a great favourite with fishing and shooting folk. Bedrooms in the converted outbuildings have their own bath or shower rooms, and all are spacious and well maintained. Guests can relax in the beamed bar or in the large, comfortable lounge.

## Brendon *(Food, B & B)* — *Stag Hunters Inn*

Near Lynton · *Devon* · Map 8 C3
Brendon (059 87) 222

*Free House*
*Landlords* Mr & Mrs J. Parffrey
**BEDROOMS 22 Grade 2 £B**
Cottage pie £2.50 Apple pie 75p (Last order 9pm)
Flowers Original; Whitbread Trophy, Best Bitter, Poachers; Exmoor Ale; Guinness; Heineken; cider. *Real ale*

This lovely old inn enjoys a setting of great beauty and serenity by the banks of the East Lyn river. The roomy bars and attractive garden are delightful spots for enjoying excellent home-prepared fare like French onion soup, cottage pie, seafood platter and flavour-packed chicken casserole. The spacious, comfortable bedrooms are spotless, and there are two peaceful lounges, one with TV. Accommodation closed January–end March. **Family pub**

## Brendon Hills *(B & B)* — *Ralegh's Cross Inn*

Near Watchet · *Somerset* · Map 8 C3
Washford (0984) 40343

*Free House*
*Landlords* Mr & Mrs P. N. Nash

**BEDROOMS 9 Grade 1 £B** (No dogs)
Golden Hill Exmoor Ale; Flowers Best; Whitbread Best Bitter, Trophy; Guinness; Heineken; cider. *Real ale*

This isolated pub makes an ideal base from which to explore the rugged beauty of Exmoor, and the Nashes welcome visitors to the area. Three traditionally furnished bedrooms in the original building and six extremely comfortable ones in the bungalow annexe have colour TVs and smart carpeted bathrooms. A log fire warms the long, narrow bar when it's chilly outside. Garden. Closed last two weeks November.
**Family pub**

## Bridestowe *(Food)* — *White Hart*

Fore Street · *Devon* · Map 8 B3
Bridestowe (083 786) 318

*Free House*
*Landlords* Owen & Millard families

Local poached trout £2.95 Steak on toast £2.75
(Last order 10pm)
Palmer's IPA; St Austell Extra; Worthington Best Bitter; Guinness; Carling Black Label; cider. *Real ale*

You'll find simple, well-prepared bar food in this 17th-century pub in a village just off the A30. You might start with delicious tomato and vegetable soup or pâté and go on to some home-cooked ham. Steaks and fish are cooked to order: we enjoyed a delicious poached trout with an attractively presented salad. Pasties, pies and gâteaux in summer. The beer garden is useful for children in good weather.

## Bridge Trafford *(Food)* — *Nags Head*

Near Chester · *Cheshire* · Map 3 B4
Chester (0244) 300206

*Brewery* Greenall Whitley
*Landlords* Jim & Vera McPeake

Steak & kidney pie with vegetables £1.90
Toasted ham & pineapple sandwich 90p
(Last order 10pm)
Greenall Whitley Bitter, Festival, Mild; Guinness; Grünhalle; cider. *Real ale*

A good selection of tasty snacks makes this roadside pub a popular spot for lunch. Besides plain and toasted sandwiches, there are flavoursome home-made soups, cold meat salads, steaks and hot specials like lasagne or an excellent chicken casserole. The choice in the evenings and at weekends is mainly sandwiches and basket meals. Swings in the garden.
**Family pub** (till 8pm)

## Bridgnorth *(B & B)* — *Falcon Hotel*

St John Street, Lowtown
*Shropshire* · Map 7 D1
Bridgnorth (074 62) 3134

*Brewery* Mitchells & Butlers
*Landlord* Mr A. R. Owen

**BEDROOMS 16 Grades 1 & 2 £C**
Mitchells & Butlers Mild, Springfield Bitter, Brew XI; Carling Black Label; Taunton cider. *Real ale*

Just across the Severn bridge from the main part of Bridgnorth, this white-painted inn provides comfortable overnight accommodation. Bedrooms in traditional or modern style are pleasantly furnished and bathrooms are well maintained. Relax in the cosy bar with its antique clocks or in the TV lounge. The Owens provide very enjoyable breakfasts. Patio. **Family pub**

## Bridport *(Food, B & B)* — *Bull Hotel*

34 East Street · *Dorset* · Map 8 D3
Bridport (0308) 22878
*Free House*
*Landlords* Terleski family
**BEDROOMS 20 Grades 1 & 2 £C**
Grilled whole plaice £2.25 Beef curry & rice £2.25 (Last order 9.15pm. No bar food Sun lunch)
Eldridge Pope Royal Oak; Hall & Woodhouse Badger Best Bitter; Bass Triangle; Dorchester Bitter; Guinness; Carlsberg. *Real ale*

The Terleski family take good care of this 16th-century coaching inn in the centre of town. An extensive bar menu caters for all tastes, with snacks ranging from grills, omelettes and salads to hot specials like curry, goulash, cauliflower cheese and fresh seafood. Overnight guests will find the simply furnished bedrooms comfortable. Patio. **Family pub**

We neither seek nor accept hospitality, and we pay for all food, drinks and accommodation in full.

## Bridport *(Food, B & B)* — *George Hotel*

4 South Street · *Dorset* · Map 8 D3
Bridport (0308) 23187

*Brewery* Palmer
*Landlords* John & Elizabeth Mander
**BEDROOMS 4 Grade 2 £C**
Moussaka £1.65 Home-made pies £1.65 (Last order 9.30pm. No bar food Thurs eve & Sun lunch, also Sun eve in winter)
Palmer's IPA, Bridport Bitter; Guinness; Shilthorn Lager. *Real ale*

The warmth of the welcome is exceptional at the Manders' appealing stone-built pub, where the bar provides a delightfully traditional setting for wholesome, freshly cooked food. Generously filled omelettes are among the all-time favourites, and other popular items include pies, salads, quiches and the day's fish special. Guests staying overnight in the simple, spacious bedrooms can look forward to a really good breakfast. **Family pub**

## Brightling *(Food)* — *Fullers Arms*

Oxley Green, Near Robertsbridge
*East Sussex* · Map 6 C4
Brightling (042 482) 212

*Free House*
*Landlords* John & Sheila Mitchell-Sadd
Prawn & halibut pie £2.50 Chocolate brandy cake 95p (Last order 10pm)
Wethered's Bitter; Fremlins Bitter; Whitbread Best; Samuel Whitbread; Guinness; Stella Artois; cider. *Real ale*

This simple sandstone pub in the rolling Sussex countryside is a pleasant spot to pause awhile. In the cosy bar or well-kept garden you can enjoy light snacks like quiche or ploughman's, or go for something more substantial – perhaps lasagne or the popular prawn and halibut pie. Be sure to leave room for the gorgeous chocolate brandy cake. Closed Monday. Garden. **Family pub** (lunchtime)

## Brightlingsea *(Food)* — *Cherry Tree*

29 Church Road · *Essex* · Map 5 D2
Brightlingsea (0206 30) 2713

*Brewery* Greene King
*Landlord* Mr A. D. Vowles
Chicken in port sauce £2.95 Omelettes £1.95 (Last order 10pm. No bar food Wed eve & all Sun)
Greene King IPA, Abbot Ale, XX Mild; Guinness; Harp; Taunton cider; Kronenbourg. *Real ale*

Looking very smart after recent renovation, this 19th-century cherry-pink pub has gained a well-earned reputation for its fine home cooking. A blackboard menu offers a daily-changing range of tempting fare, from simple salads and sandwiches to delicious omelettes and flavoursome chicken in port sauce with prawns and tomatoes. To finish, try the excellent fresh fruit pies. Patio.

## Brighton *(B & B)* — *Black Lion Hotel*

London Road · *East Sussex* · Map 6 C4
Brighton (0273) 501220

*Brewery* Beard & Co
*Landlords* Mr & Mrs Colin Patey-Johns

**BEDROOMS 16 Grade 1 £A**
Harveys Bitter, Old Ale, Mild; Guinness; Carlsberg; cider. *Real ale*

This smartly maintained brick, stone and pebbledash pub stands on the A23, providing motorists with easy access to the north and ring roads as well as the town centre. Centrally heated bedrooms are uniform in style, with practical modern furnishings and televisions; all but two have up-to-date private facilities. There are two plush bars, one of which leads on to the spacious garden with plenteous seating.

## Brighton *(Food)* — *Cricketer's*

15 Black Lion Street · *East Sussex* · Map 6 C4
Brighton (0273) 24620

*Brewery* Watneys
*Landlord* Miss W. Sexton

Chicken, ham & mushroom pie £1.35 Crab sandwich £1 (Last order 10.45pm)
Watneys Special, Stag Bitter; Ben Truman; King & Barnes Festive; Guinness; Foster's; Carlsberg; Harp; cider. *Real ale*

Winnie Sexton is a lively, popular hostess at this friendly old pub where locals and visitors like to relax in the plush bar. Delicious home-made savoury pies are a feature of the menu, which also offers sausages, jacket potatoes, and tempting daily specials like chilli con carne or chicken provençale. Wide selection of sandwiches, too.

## Brighton *(Food)* — *The Greys*

103 Southover Street, off Lewes Road
*East Sussex* · Map 6 C4
Brighton (0273) 680734
*Brewery* Whitbread
*Landlords* Alan & Sarah Gray
Avocado & smoked chicken with walnut vinaigrette £1.75 Mediterranean fish stew £2.75 (Last order 9pm. No bar food Sun & Mon)
Whitbread Strong Country Bitter, Flower's Original; Guinness; Stella Artois; cider. *Real ale*

The local fish market provides many of the raw materials for Jackie Fitzgerald's splendid bar food at this friendly modern pub just off the Lewes Road. Fresh sardines, garlic prawns and whole grilled plaice are typical seafood specials on a menu whose delights could also include tortellini served with a rich basil-flavoured tomato sauce. For meat eaters there's game pie, steaks and hearty casseroles.

## Brightwell Baldwin *(Food)* ★ *Lord Nelson*

Near Watlington · *Oxfordshre* · Map 6 B3
Watlington (049 161) 2497

*Free House*
*Landlords* S. A. Johnson & J. K. Jorgensen

Beef Nelson £4.50 Fresh calf's liver £4.25 (Last order 10pm)
Brakspears Pale Ale; Webster's Yorkshire Bitter; Ben Truman Export. *Real ale*

Jack Jorgensen's cooking steals the show at this handsome old pub, where the bars are laid out with carefully set tables. High-quality ingredients are used throughout, and favourites on the interesting menu include creamy-sauced chicken maritime and the superb beef Nelson – prime fillet in a memorable port wine sauce. Good vegetables and lovely sweets, too, such as fruit pies and sorbets. Closed Monday except Bank Holidays.

## Briston *(Food)* *John H. Stracey*

Near Melton Constable · *Norfolk* · Map 5 D1
Melton Constable (0263) 860891

*Free House*
*Landlord* Mr I. Verrando

Lasagne £3 Steak & kidney pie £3.80 (Last order 9pm)
Greene King Abbot Ale; Adnams Bitter; Ind Coope Burton Ale, John Bull; Tetley's Bitter; Guinness; cider. *Real ale*

Isidoro Verrando and his wife are true professionals, who run this welcoming roadside pub with real dedication. In the cosy beamed bar you can tuck into authentic, flavour-packed minestrone, lasagne and cannelloni, as well as English favourites like rich, tender steak and kidney pie, Cromer crab salad and home-cooked ham and chips. At lunchtime there are also French bread sandwiches and several ploughman's. Patio. **Family pub**

## Broad Chalke *(B & B)* *Queen's Head*

*Wiltshire* · Map 6 A4
Salisbury (0722) 780344

*Free House*
*Landlords* Robert & Judith Grier

**BEDROOMS 4 Grade 1 £B**
Courage Directors Bitter; Wadworth's 6X; Ringwood Best Bitter; Salisbury Bitter; Guinness; Hofmeister; Taunton cider. *Real ale*

Beams, rough stone walls and traditional decor sustain a sense of history in the bars of this immaculate village pub, run in friendly fashion by Robert and Judith Grier. To the rear, in a well-designed annexe, are the comfortable, spacious bedrooms, with simple white furniture, tea-makers, telephones and remote-control TVs. Each has its own spotless modern bathroom. Patio.

## Broad Hinton *(B & B)* *Crown Inn*

Near Swindon · *Wiltshire* · Map 6 A3
Broad Hinton (079 373) 302

*Free House*
*Landlords* Mr & Mrs Albert Harris

**BEDROOMS 4 Grade 1 £B**
Eldridge Pope Royal Oak, Dorchester Bitter; Wadworth's 6X; Bass Triangle; Guinness; Carling Black Label; Taunton cider. *Real ale*

The Harrises are conscientious hosts at this pleasant, mustard-coloured inn. The olde-worlde lounge bar opens on to the patio and garden, and there's a simple public bar. Bedrooms are all well equipped with good modern furniture, colour TVs and tea-makers, plus tiled shower cabinets. No under-sixes overnight; accommodation closed during Christmas period.
**Family pub**

## Broad Oak *(Food)* ★ *Broad Oak Inn*

Near Garway · *Hereford & Worcester*
Map 7 D2
St Weonards (098 18) 263

*Free House*
*Landlords* Clive & Angela Russell-Taylor

Wye smoked salmon £4.50 Broad Oak casserole £4.95 (Last order 9pm)
Flower's Original Bitter; Heineken. *Real ale*

Standing in open countryside with only a stately oak for company, this lovely old pub is a marvellous place for a meal. The menu is a delight from beginning to end: stuffed vine leaves with a savoury dip, home-cured pastrami, seafood pancakes, smoked Wye salmon and a sensational hot brandy chocolate cake. Closed Sunday evening and all Monday (except Bank Holidays). Garden.

## Broadwell *(Food, B & B)* *Fox Inn*

Moreton-in-Marsh · *Gloucestershire*
Map 5 A2
Stow-on-the-Wold (0451) 30212
*Brewery* Donnington
*Landlords* Dennis & Debbie Harding
**BEDROOMS 2 Grade 2 £C** (No dogs)
Chicken casserole with mustard sauce £2.65 Caribbean ham £1.80 (Last order 8.45pm. No bar food Tues eve & all Sun)
Donnington's Best Bitter, SPA; Löwenbräu; cider. *Real ale*

Nestling on the village green, this cosy inn has a pleasant beer garden where traditional pub games like Aunt Sally are still played. In the beamed bars robust dishes – casseroles, roasts, seasonal game – are served with a good selection of fresh vegetables. Pâté, salads and ploughman's at Tuesday lunchtime. Two homely bedrooms with TV share the family bathroom. Hearty cooked breakfasts. **Family pub**

## Brockton *(Food)* *Feathers Inn*

Near Much Wenlock · *Shropshire* · Map 7 D1
Brockton (074 636) 202

*Free House*
*Landlords* Robbie & Jackie Robinson
Beef & mushroom casserole £2.55 Risotto with chicken, prawns, crab & peppers £3.95 (Last order 10pm)
Simpkiss Bitter; Shire Mild; Wem Bitter; Younger's Tartan; Guinness; Kestrel; cider. *Real ale*

Two converted Elizabethan cottages make up this charming, heavily beamed pub on the B4378. Robbie and Jackie Robinson's bar menu offers ample choice, from ploughman's jumbo sausages and garlic mushrooms to fish or chicken with chips and daily specials like risotto or spiced lamb's kidneys in wine. Toasted sandwiches, too. Closed Tuesday lunchtime.
**Family pub**

## Brome *(Food)* *Oaksmere*

Near Eye · *Suffolk* · Map 5 D2
Eye (0379) 870326

*Free House*
*Landlords* W. J. & M. P. Hasted

Lowestoft pie £2.95 Prawns provençale £2.25 (Last order 10pm)
Courage Directors Bitter, Best Bitter, Mild; Guinness; Kronenbourg; Hofmeister; Taunton cider. *Real ale*

Built in 1550 and altered in Victorian times, this fine country mansion stands in 200 acres of parkland and formal gardens. Tasty snacks served in the beamed bar range from soup, sandwiches and ploughman's to herby garlic sausage, chargrilled Vienna steak and potato-topped fish pie. Super sweets, excellent cheeseboard. *For accommodation see Egon Ronay's Lucas Hotel & Restaurant Guide 1985.* **Family pub**

## Bromeswell *(Food)* — *Cherry Tree*

Near Woodbridge · *Suffolk* · Map 5 D2
Eyke (039 47) 310

*Brewery* Tollemache & Cobbold
*Landlords* Mr & Mrs Cheek

Shepherd's pie £1.90 Apple pie 60p (Last order 10.30pm)
Tolly Cobbold Bitter, Mild; Guinness; Hansa Lager; Dortmunder; Taunton cider. *Real ale*

Mrs Cheek's cooking is a popular attraction at this former hunting lodge, where on fine days the customers make good use of the little garden. Tasty quiches are the centrepiece of the lunchtime cold buffet, which also features serve-yourself salads and various sweets. There are filled rolls, too, and hot dishes include individual cottage pies and chilli con carne. Garden.

**Family pub**

## Bromham *(Food)* — *Greyhound Inn*

High Street, Near Chippenham · *Wiltshire*
Map 6 A3
Bromham (0380) 850241

*Free House*
*Landlords* George & Mo Todd
Taramasalata £1.15 Chicken Verluccio £2.70 (Last order 10pm)
Wadworth's IPA, 6X; Bass Special; Younger's Tartan; Guinness; Carlsberg Hof; Carling Black Label; Taunton cider. *Real ale*

Jugs and chamber pots hanging from the ceiling are a trademark of this friendly pub where George Todd's tasty, generously served bar meals are sure to satisfy the hungriest customer. Sauced dishes like beef with tomato, garlic and red wine are a speciality, and there are also simpler items such as soup, ploughman's and curry. Sweets are good, too.

## Bromyard *(Food)* — *Hop Pole Hotel*

The Square · *Hereford & Worcester* · Map 7 D1
Bromyard (088 58) 82449

*Brewery* Marston, Thompson & Evershed

*Landlords* Peter & Anne Robinson
Pasta in walnut sauce £1.50 Honey roast duckling £4.50 (Last order 9pm. No bar food Sun eve for non-residents)
Marston's Pedigree, Lager; Guinness; cider. *Real ale*

The Robinsons provide a good choice of enjoyable bar food in this imposing old coaching inn. Lunch brings simple offerings like hearty vegetable soup, burgers and tasty steak, kidney and mushroom pie along with salads and ploughman's. In the evening there are more interesting dishes such as Greek-style sardines and lamb's kidneys casseroled in champagne cider with mushrooms.

**Family pub**

## Buckler's Hard — *Master Builders House Hotel*

The beamed bars were once part of the home of Henry Adams, a renowned 18th-century shipbuilder. A miniature cannon has pride of place on a mantelpiece, and the walls are festooned with photographs of sailing ships old and new. Note, too, the list of over 50 ships built here on the Beaulieu River between 1698 and 1822. Garden.

**Family pub**

Near Beaulieu · *Hampshire* · Map 6 A4
Buckler's Hard (059 063) 253
*Brewery* Allied-Lyons *Landlord* Mr R. Dinnage
Halls Harvest Bitter, Burton Bitter; John Bull Bitter; Tetley Bitter; Guinness; Skol; Löwenbräu; cider. *Real ale*

## Bungay — *Fleece Hotel*

In the centre of a medieval market town near the Norfolk border, the Fleece, originally a coaching house, retains a good deal of atmosphere and charm. Low ceilings, heavy beams and a large inglenook fireplace characterise the bar, which also features delightful touches like the wrought-iron Fleece motif in the partitions. Patio.

8 St Mary's Street · *Suffolk* · Map 5 D1
Bungay (0986) 2192
*Brewery* Adnams *Landlord* Mrs G. Haynes
Adnams Bitter, Old Ale (winter only); Courage Best Bitter; Guinness; Skol; Löwenbräu; cider. *Real ale*

## Burcot *(Food)* — *Chequers Inn*

Near Abingdon · *Oxfordshire* · Map 6 B3
Clifton Hampden (086 730) 7771

*Brewery* Usher
*Landlords* Mary & Michael Weeks

Hot pot £2.35 Apple & raspberry pancake £1.35 (No bar food eves)
Usher's Founder's Ale, PA; Guinness; Carlsberg; Holsten. *Real ale*

A blackboard displays the day's offerings at this recently extended thatched pub dating from 1500. And excellent fare it is, too, from sweetcorn and watercress soup to smoked ham salad, beef Stroganoff and flavoursome creamy fish pie. Also ploughman's and farmer's platters, and, to finish, Mary Weeks' popular chocolaty 'Disaster Cake' with a crunchy biscuit centre. Roast on Sunday. Garden.

## Burham *(Food)* ★ — *Golden Eagle*

80 Church Street · *Kent* · Map 6 C3
Medway (0634) 668975

*Free House*
*Landlords* Chris & Chiu Blackmore

Nasi goreng £2.25 Beef & chilli £2.50 (Last order 10.30pm. No Malaysian food Mon eve)
Wadworth's 6X; Goachers Maidstone Ale; Shepherd Neame Master Brew; Guinness; Hurlimann; cider. *Real ale*

The fresh spicy flavours of Malaysian cooking are the unexpected attraction at this friendly pub. Nasi goreng and creamy chicken curry are popular items in Chiu Blackmore's repertoire, and our beef and peppers with chilli in black bean sauce was as good as you'll find anywhere. The number of locals eating in the beamed bar tells you just how much it's all appreciated. More familiar bar fare also available.

## Burnham-on-Crouch *(B & B)* — *Ye Olde White Harte*

The Quay · *Essex* · Map 6 D3
Maldon (0621) 782106

*Free House*
*Landlords* Mr & Mrs G. J. Lewis

**BEDROOMS 15 Grade 2 £C**
Tolly Cobbold Bitter; Charrington's IPA; Stones Bitter; Guinness; Carling Black Label; Foster's. *Real ale*

The talk is mainly of yachts and yachting in this delightful riverside pub, where the Lewises are charming and attentive hosts. The panelled bar features some nautical instruments, and there's a TV lounge with a collection of china. Cheerful bedrooms are smaller on the top floor (dormer windows, lovely views), larger downstairs (some with private facilities) and more modern in the annexe. Sit on the jetty in fine weather.

Imagine the flavour of the French countryside, in a wine glass. Vin de Pays. The everyday wine of France.
Make friends with the wines of France.

LOW TO MIDDLE TA
DANGER: Government Health WARNING: CIGARETTE

s defined by H.M.Government

AN SERIOUSLY DAMAGE YOUR HEALTH

**Whether on business or vacation in Great Britain & Ireland, consult *Egon Ronay's Lucas Guide 1985* to Hotels, Restaurants & Inns**

It recommends the 2,500 best UK hotels and restaurants, spotlighting de luxe, country house and executive hotels as well as those with sporting and leisure facilities. Restaurants with above average food are starred. There is also an extensive economy section including hundreds of bargain weekend breaks and inexpensive evening meals in London.

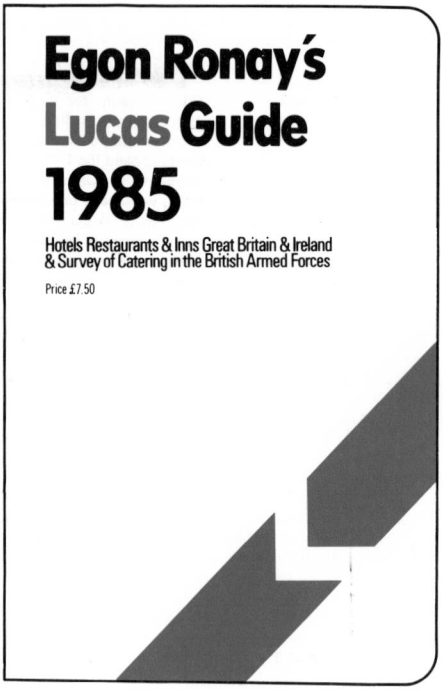


Contains 832 pages including 56 pages of maps

£7.50 from bookshops everywhere or £8.60 including postage and packing from:

Egon Ronay Organisation Ltd, Greencoat House,
Francis Street, London SW1P 1DH

*See colour pages and page 14 for news about Egon Ronay's other 1985 guides.*

## Burnt Hill *(Food)* — *Nut & Bolt*

Near Yattendon · *Berkshire* · Map 6 A3
Hermitage (0635) 201496

*Free House*
*Landlords* Gerry & Jane Campkin

Filled jacket potatoes from £1.20 Curry & rice £1.50 (Last order 10pm)
Morland's Best Bitter, Bitter; Ruddle's Bitter, County; Fuller's ESB, London Pride; Guinness; Taunton cider. *Real ale*

Outside Yattendon just off the Pangbourne road, this friendly, red-brick pub is popular for its tasty and generously served bar snacks. A regularly changing menu offers hot specials like moussaka, haddock and prawn pie and various curries, and there's always a good choice of sandwiches and filled jacket potatoes for those in search of a quick bite. Garden.

## Burpham *(Food)* — *George & Dragon*

Near Arundel · *West Sussex* · Map 6 B4
Arundel (0903) 883131

*Free House*
*Landlord* Mr Eric Brookfield

Ham salad £1.60 Plaice, chips & peas £1.95 (Last order 10pm)
Bass, Toby Bitter; Charrington's IPA, Mild; Guinness; Löwenbräu; Taunton cider. *Real ale*

Once a haunt for local smugglers, this 16th-century pub offers a cheerful welcome to present-day customers in search of tasty, home-cooked food. There's always a daily special to supplement sandwiches, soup, steak, well-made omelettes and salads. Or you may choose a jacket potato filled with chicken livers or perhaps curried prawns. There are tempting sweets from the trolley as well. Patio. **Family pub**

## Burslem *(Food)* — *Traveller's Rest*

239 Newcastle Street · *Staffordshire*
Map 4 C4
Stoke-on-Trent (0782) 810418
*Free House*
*Landlords* John & Janet Pazio
Tourte aux champignons with vegetables £1.50 Old English hot pot & vegetables £1.80 (Last order 10.30pm. No bar food Sun & Mon eves)
Ind Coope Burton Ale, Bitter; Ansells Mild; ABC Bitter; Guinness; Skol; Löwenbräu; cider. *Real ale*

Former musicians John and Janet Pazio deserve applause for the excellent food served in their modern roadside pub. Lunchtime brings an appetising buffet of home-cooked meats and colourful salads, as well as hot dishes like braised beef with beans or leek and fish pie. There are sandwiches, too, and perhaps a satisfying bread and butter pudding to finish. Less choice in the evening. Garden.

## Burtle *(Food)* — *Ye Olde Burtle Inn*

Near Bridgwater · *Somerset* · Map 8 D3
Bridgwater (0278) 722269

*Free House*
*Landlords* Stuart & Valerie Boulton

Steak & kidney pie £1.95 Special mixed grill £4.30 (Last order 10pm)
Golden Hill Exmoor Ale; Wadworth's 6X; Whitbread Trophy; Newcastle Bitter; Guinness; Heineken; cider. *Real ale*

There's a friendly welcome and a good choice of bar food at this old whitewashed pub. Chicken, sausages or scampi with chips are featured on the menu, along with more elaborate items like coq au vin or prawn-stuffed fillets of plaice with mushrooms. The huge Barnsley chop is a great favourite, and there are baked potatoes and salads too. Traditional roast on Sundays (book). Garden. **Family pub**

## Burton *(Food)* ★ *Plume of Feathers*

Near Chippenham · *Wiltshire* · Map 7 D2
Badminton (045 421) 251

*Brewery* Usher
*Landlords* Peter & June Bolin

Beef & venison pie £3.25 Curries £2.30 (Last order 10.30pm)
Usher's Best Bitter, Founder's Ale, Triple Crown; Ben Truman; Guinness; Carlsberg; Taunton cider. *Real ale*

East meets West on the enticing menu of this 16th-century village pub, whose stone-walled bars have a cosy, rustic charm. The landlords spent many years in the Far East, and deliciously authentic dishes like Sinhalese chicken curry and Indonesian beef rendang are real winners. Occidental options range from American-style hamburgers to seafood provençale and a crispy apple and sultana pancake. Garden

**Family pub**

## Burtonwood *(Food)* *Fiddle i'th Bag Inn*

Alder Lane, Near Warrington · *Cheshire*
Map 3 B3
Newton-le-Willows (092 52) 5442

*Brewery* Greenall Whitley
*Landlords* Don & Jean Roy
Assorted cold platter with salads £2.95 Chicken hongroise with lyonnaise potatoes £2.35 (Last order 10.30pm)
Greenall Whitley Bitter, Mild, Festival; Guinness; Grünhalle; cider. *Real ale*

A wide-ranging menu caters for all tastes at this smart country pub. Hot dishes might include beef kebab with chilli sauce or chicken chasseur, and there are also soups, filled baps, a variety of ploughman's and an excellent beef pie. Weekday lunchtimes you can also help yourself to salads from the cold buffet. Patio and garden.

**Family pub**

## Burwash *(B & B)* *Bell Inn*

High Street · *East Sussex* · Map 6 C4
Burwash (0435) 882304

*Brewery* Beard
*Landlord* Mr & Mrs P. Ingham

**BEDROOMS 5 Grade 2 £C**
Beard's Best Bitter, Old Ale (winter only); Guinness; Carlsberg Hof, Pilsner; cider. *Real ale*

Hanging baskets in summer add extra appeal to this pretty pub, which has a delightful beer garden at the back. The beamed bar is a friendly place for a drink, and you can listen to live jazz on Tuesday evenings. Simple, charming bedrooms provide good comfort and all have tea-makers. Guests share the family bathroom.

**Family pub**

## Byworth *(Food)* *Black Horse*

Near Petworth · *West Sussex* · Map 6 B4
Petworth (0798) 42424

*Free House*
*Landlord* Harry King

Mussels in garlic sauce £1.55 French apricot tart 75p (Last order 9.30pm)
Young's Bitter; Eldridge Pope Dorset IPA; Guinness; Heineken; cider. *Real ale*

It's best to arrive early at this busy pub, widely known for an enterprising choice of bar food. Blackboard specials might range from gravad lax and mushrooms in garlic sauce to crab salad, Peking duck or chicken in cider. For those in a conservative mood, there are also more familiar items like burgers and fry-ups. Delicious desserts, too. The terraced garden has lovely views.

## Calderbridge *(B & B)* — *Stanley Arms*

Near Egremont · *Cumbria* · Map 3 B2
Beckermet (094 684) 235

*Brewery* Younger
*Landlord* Mr I. W. Robinson·

**BEDROOMS 9 Grade 2 £C**
Younger's XXPS Scotch, Bitter, Lager; Taunton cider. *Real ale*

This modernised 18th-century roadside pub stands in extensive grounds reaching to the river Calder, on which it has fishing rights. The garden is a popular spot in summer, while in cooler weather the spacious panelled bar comes into its own. Decently furnished bedrooms offer simple comforts for an overnight stay, and there's a modest little TV room. **Family pub**

## Callington *(B & B)* — *Coachmakers Arms*

Newport Square · *Cornwall* · Map 8 B4
Liskeard (0579) 82567

*Free House*
*Landlords* Ken & Sheila Hadfield

**BEDROOMS 4 Grade 1 £B** (No dogs)
Bass; Stones Bitter; Worthington Best Bitter, 'E'; Tennents Pilsner; Carling Black Lager; Taunton cider. *Real ale*

Friendly landlords and staff make visitors very welcome at this characterful old pub in a part of the world once closely linked with coachmaking. Oak beams and horse brasses provide period atmosphere in the bar, while the bedrooms are smartly contemporary. All have private facilities and one boasts its own sun terrace. No under-eights overnight. Accommodation closed 2 weeks Christmas.

## Calstock *(B & B)* — *Boot Inn*

Fore Street · *Cornwall* · Map 8 B4
Tavistock (0822) 832331

*Free House*
*Landlords* Mr & Mrs Bob Slack

**BEDROOMS 2 Grade 2 £C** (No dogs)
Flowers Original, IPA; Whitbread Best Bitter, Best Mild; Poacher Bitter; Guinness; Stella Artois; Taunton cider. *Real ale*

Hobnail boots as a decorative theme recall the name of this charming village inn perched on a hillside above the river Tamar. Liz and Bob Slack are very welcoming hosts, and traditional pub games add to the friendly atmosphere in the stone-walled bar. The two bedrooms, each with a shower cubicle, are prettily furnished and have tea-makers. Patio.

## Carey *(Food, B & B)* — *Cottage of Content*

*Hereford & Worcester* · Map 7 D2
Carey (043 270) 242

*Free House*
*Landlord* Peter Nash
**BEDROOMS 3 Grade 2 £C**
Rabbit casserole £4.25 Lamb curry £4.25 (Last order 10pm)
Hook Norton Best Bitter, Old Hookey; Worthington Best Bitter; Flower's Original; Guinness; cider. *Real ale*

Landlord Peter Nash is celebrating the 500th birthday of this delightfully rustic little inn by providing private facilities for all three bedrooms, which are centrally heated and have sturdy furniture, good carpets and tea-makers. The bar menu changes frequently, offering tasty home-cooked dishes like ham and eggs, chilli con carne and rabbit casserole. Soup and sandwiches, too, plus a summer cold table and nice sweets. Garden. **Family pub**

## Cartmel Fell *(Food)* — *Mason's Arms*

Strawberry Bank, Near Grange-over-Sands
*Cumbria* · Map 3 B2
Crosthwaite (044 88) 486

*Free House*
*Landlord* Mrs Helen Stevenson
Coachman's casserole with vegetables £3.50
Lasagne £2.50 (Last order 9pm)
Thwaites Mild, Bitter; Guinness; McEwans Export; Beck's Bier; Kronenbourg; cider.

There are splendid views from this fine old converted farmhouse, and Helen Stevenson's sustaining bar food makes the trip doubly worthwhile. Sandwiches and ploughman's are made to order, and weightier dishes include home-cooked pies and casseroles. In summer, the blackboard menu might offer a Morecambe crab or shrimp salad. Lovely desserts, too. Terrace.
**Family pub**

## Casterton *(Food, B & B)* — *Pheasant Inn*

Near Kirkby Lonsdale · *Cumbria* · Map 3 B2
Kirkby Lonsdale (0468) 71230

*Free House*
*Landlord* Mr D. Hesmondhalgh
**BEDROOMS 16 Grade 1 £B**
Pork pie with mushy peas 75p Battered haddock £2.25 (Last order 9.30pm)
Younger's Scotch Bitter; Tetley's Bitter, Mild; Kronenbourg; Oranjeboom; cider. *Real ale*

Food and accommodation are both excellent at this immaculate white-painted inn. Bedrooms are attractively decorated and comfortably furnished; TVs are standard, and most rooms have private facilities. The lounges are cosy and chintzy and there's a homely beamed bar, where the long menu of tasty snacks ranges from pâté and plated salads to steak and kidney pie and roast chicken. Terrace.
**Family pub**

## Castle Combe *(B & B)* — *Castle Hotel*

Near Chippenham · *Wiltshire* · Map 7 D2
Castle Combe (0249) 782461

*Free House*
*Landlords* Mr & Mrs D. Packer & Mrs A. J. Randle

**BEDROOMS 9 Grade 1 £A**
Whitbread Best Bitter; Wadworth's 6X; Flower's Original; Guinness; Heineken; Tuborg; cider. *Real ale*

Right in the centre of a picture postcard village, this fine 14th-century hostelry is rich in period atmosphere. Exposed timbers, steep staircases and low ceilings are all part of the charm, and there are even secret passages and a tunnel leading to the village church. First-class bedrooms of various sizes have freestanding furniture, TVs, radio-alarms and good modern bathrooms. Garden.
**Family pub**

## Castleton *(Food, B & B)* — *Castle Hotel*

Castle Street · *Derbyshire* · Map 4 C3
Hope Valley (0433) 20578

*Brewery* Bass
*Landlords* Mr & Mrs G. Walker

**BEDROOMS 5 Grade 1 £B** (No dogs)
Steak & kidney pie £2.50 Sweets 85p (Last order 10.15pm)
Stones Bitter; Worthington 'E'; Guinness; Carling Black Label; Hemeling; cider. *Real ale*

Close to Peveril Castle, this fine old pub makes an excellent haven in the heart of the Peak District. Tasty snacks served in the cosy beamed bars range from soup and sandwiches to lasagne, grilled fish and a daily roast. Luxuriously furnished bedrooms (including two with four-posters) all have fitted carpets, TVs, tea-makers and up-to-date bath or shower rooms.

## Castleton *(B & B)* — *Ye Olde Cheshire Cheese*

How Lane · *Derbyshire* · Map 4 C3
Hope Valley (0433) 20330

*Free House*
*Landlords* Mr & Mrs J. A. Nuttall

**BEDROOMS 6 Grade 1 £C**
Webster's Yorkshire Bitter, Pennine, Mild; Guinness; Foster's; Carlsberg; cider. *Real ale*

Hikers, holiday-makers and locals are all made to feel at home in the Nuttalls' friendly pub in the heart of the Peak District National Park. There are two pleasant bars, both fitted out in traditional rustic style. Compact bedrooms with pretty wallpaper and attractive modern whitewood units are equipped with duvets and tea-making facilities; all have neatly designed shower rooms.

## Castleton *(Food, B & B)* — *Ye Olde Nag's Head*

Cross Street · *Derbyshire* · Map 4 C3
Hope Valley (0433) 20248

*Free House*
*Landlords* Mr & Mrs G. Walker

**BEDROOMS 8 Grade 2 £C**
Taramasalata £1.95 Prawns on rye £2.50 (Last order 10.15)
Stones Bitter, Mild; Tennent's Lager; Carling Black Label; Taunton cider. *Real ale*

Dazzling flower displays are a feature throughout this well-kept former coaching inn, where the beamed bar has bags of charm and atmosphere. A good variety of snacks is available, from soup and sandwiches to salads, lasagne and steak and kidney pie. Cheerfully decorated bedrooms have whitewood furniture and tea-makers and, like the bathrooms, are spotlessly clean. There's a cosy residents' lounge.

## Castleton *(Food, B & B)* — *Moorlands Hotel*

Near Whitby · *North Yorkshire* · Map 4 D2
Castleton (0287) 60206

*Free House*
*Landlords* Mr & Mrs J. E. Aubertin

**BEDROOMS 10 Grade 1 £B**
Paella £3 Home-baked ham & salad £3.20 (Last order 9.30pm)
Tetley's Bitter, Imperial, Falstaff; Skol.

Fresh flowers and plants are a charming feature in this pleasant moorland pub, where ten smartly kept bedrooms with pretty floral curtains and fitted furniture provide homely overnight accommodation. There's also a comfortable residents' lounge and a separate TV room. Bar snacks include home-baked ham, tasty steak and kidney pie, spaghetti, curries and lots of moreish sweets. Closed end October–Easter.

## Cavendish *(Food, B & B)* — *Bull*

High Street, Near Sudbury · *Suffolk* · Map 5 C2
Glemsford (0787) 280245

*Brewery* Adnams
*Landlords* Laura & Michael Sansome

**BEDROOMS 3 Grade 2 £C** (No dogs)
Chicken casserole £2 Cheesecake 65p
(Last order 9pm. No bar food Sun–Thurs eves)
Adnams Bitter, Old (winter only); Carling Black Label; cider. *Real ale*

Visitors are greeted like old friends at this convivial red-brick pub, where Mrs Sansome prepares super snacks from fresh local produce. A savoury pie, quiche and roast may be among the tempting offerings, along with salads, evening grills and some delicious sweets. Comfortably furnished bedrooms share two spotless bathrooms, and residents can watch TV in the Sansomes' lounge. No under-12s overnight. Garden.

## Cavendish *(B & B)* — *George*

The Green, Near Sudbury · *Suffolk* · Map 5 C2
Glemsford (0787) 280248

*Brewery* Truman
*Landlords* Mr & Mrs M. Vincent

**BEDROOMS 3 Grade 2 £C** (No dogs)
Truman's Bitter, Special, Prizebrew, Ben Truman; Carlsberg; Foster's; cider. *Real ale*

Mr and Mrs Vincent are welcoming landlords at this white-painted pub on the village green and the cosy, friendly bars are perfect for a relaxing pint. Bedrooms are neatly furnished and all have TVs; one has its own shower cabinet, the rest share a spotless bathroom. No children under five overnight. **Family pub**

## Cerne Abbas *(B & B)* — *New Inn*

14 Long Street · *Dorset* · Map 8 D3
Cerne Abbas (03003) 274

*Brewery* Eldridge Pope
*Landlords* Mr & Mrs M. W. Austin

**BEDROOMS 4 Grade 2 £C**
Eldridge Pope Royal Oak, Dorchester Bitter, Dorset IPA; Guinness; Faust; Taunton cider. *Real ale*

This fine stone-roofed pub in a showpiece Dorset village has an interesting history that traces back to the 16th century. Public rooms include a cheerful bar (note the collection of horse tackle and farm implements), a children's room and a large garden. Bedrooms, all with TVs and tea-makers, are neat and simple; they share two public bathrooms. Good breakfasts. **Family pub**

## Chaddesley Corbett *(Food)* — *Talbot Inn*

Near Kidderminster · *Hereford & Worcester*
Map 7 D1
Chaddesley Corbett (056 283) 388

*Brewery* Wolverhampton & Dudley
*Landlord* Mr P. B. Cartwright

Steak & mushroom pie £2 Cold buffet £2 (Last order 9.30pm. No bar food Sun & Mon eves)
Banks's Best Bitter, Mild; Kronenbourg. *Real ale*

The cold table offers an extensive choice and good value for money at this fine old part-timbered inn. The salads are fresh and colourful, ideal accompaniments for succulent cooked meats, savoury pies and quiches. A blackboard lists daily specials like plaice, liver and bacon, casseroles and hot pots, plus a few home-made sweets. Table service in the attractive bar is friendly and efficient. Patio. **Family pub**

## Chaddleworth *(Food)* — *Ibex*

Near Newbury · *Berkshire* · Map 6 A3
Chaddleworth (048 82) 311

*Brewery* Courage
*Landlord* Sheila Cunningham
Steak, kidney & mushroom pie with vegetables £2.95 Prawns in garlic butter with crusty bread £2.60 (Last order 9.30pm. No bar food Sun eve)
Courage Best Bitter; Guinness; Hofmeister; cider. *Real ale*

Set among the Newbury Downs, this cosy litle pub is very popular with the racing fraternity, who are happy to put their money on the highly commendable bar snacks. As well as salads and sandwiches made with lovely crusty bread, the wide-ranging menu features items like country pâté, Cumberland sausage, pizza and tender steak and kidney pie, plus spicy specials such as South African bobotie and Mexican goulash. **Family pub**

## Chagford *(B & B)* — *Globe Hotel*

High Street · *Devon* · Map 8 C3
Chagford (064 73) 3485

*Free House*
*Landlord* Mrs B. Abson

**BEDROOMS 5 Grade 1 £C**
Bass; Harvest; Whitbread Trophy, Best; Ansells Mild; Guinness; Harp; Carlsberg. *Real ale*

Pleasant staff and excellent housekeeping contribute to the delights of a stay at this 18th-century coaching house in the heart of Dartmoor. Locally made pine units are fitted in the spacious bedrooms, which are all supplied with fridges and tea-makers. Public rooms include a residents' lounge, lounge bar and a splendid public bar with authentic Victorian decor. Good breakfasts.
**Family pub**

## Chale *(B & B)* — *Clarendon Hotel*

Newport Road · *Isle of Wight* · Map 6 A4
Niton (0983) 730431

*Free House*
*Landlords* John & Jean Bradshaw

**BEDROOMS 13 Grade 1 £A**
Burt's Bitter; Whitbread Strong Country Bitter, Best Bitter, Trophy; Flowers Original; Guinness; Stella Artois; cider. *Real ale*

Lovely views out over the sea towards the Needles make this 17th-century coaching inn a delightful place to stay. Charming, individually decorated bedrooms (several are family-size) have duvets, and bathrooms are well equipped. There's a homely TV lounge, and the hotel's own pub – the characterful Wight Mouse Inn – is a popular meeting place with a collection of some 150 malt whiskies. Pleasant garden for fine weather.
**Family pub**

## Chappel *(Food)* — *Swan Inn*

The Street, Nr Colchester · *Essex* · Map 5 C2
Earls Colne (078 75) 2353

*Free House*
*Landlords* Terence & Frances Martin

Jumbo peeled scampi £4.75 Grilled fresh sardines £1.95 (Last order 10.30pm)
Greene King IPA, Abbot Ale, Mild XX; Guinness; Harp; Dörtmunder; Kronenbourg; Taunton cider. *Real ale*

The garden of this 500-year-old pub runs right down to the river Colne, and the heavily beamed lounge bar is very welcoming in cooler weather. Terence Martin makes weekly shopping trips to London for the ingredients of his excellent bar snacks, which range from home-made soups and succulent grills to a variety of seafood dishes including a delicious assortment of crisply battered fish. Sandwiches and salads cater for light appetites

## Charlbury *(Food, B & B)* — *Bell at Charlbury*

Church Street · *Oxfordshire* · Map 5 A2
Charlbury (0608) 810278

*Free House*
*Landlords* Carlos & Dorothy da Cruz

**BEDROOMS 13 Grade 1 £A**
Guinness & steak pie & vegetables £2.25 Lasagne £1.95 (No bar food eves or Sun)
Wadworth's 6X, IPA; Whitbread Trophy; Guinness; Heineken; Grünhalle. *Real ale*

Tasty lunchtime fare adds to the popularity of this handsome 18th-century Cotswold inn. The blackboard menu might offer onion soup to start, followed by tempting main courses such as chilli con carne, hot smoked mackerel with Biscay sauce, and roast stuffed venison. Elegant bedrooms combine antique furniture with modern comforts like TVs and telephones.
**Family pub**

## Charlton Village *(Food)* — *Harrow*

142 Charlton Road, Shepperton · *Middlesex* · Map 6 B3
Sunbury (76) 83122
*Brewery* Watney
*Landlord* Ralph John
Shepherd's pie £1.85 Roast beef, Yorkshire pudding & vegetables £3 (No bar food Sun or eves)
Watney's Stag Bitter; Ben Truman; Wilson Great Northern Bitter; Guinness; Foster's; Carlsberg. *Real ale*

Generous portions of tasty home-cooked fare are served at lunchtime in this attractive thatched cottage, reputedly the oldest inhabited building in Middlesex. In the two low-beamed bars you can make your choice from the blackboard menu – perhaps a jacket potato with savoury mince, stuffed pancakes, roast lamb or ham and eggs with bubble and squeak. Also sandwiches (the only Saturday choice), ploughman's and simple puds. Garden.

## Cheddington *(Food)* — *Rosebery Arms*

Station Road, Near Leighton Buzzard, Beds
*Buckinghamshire* · Map 5 B2
Cheddington (0296) 668222

*Brewery* Wells
*Landlord* Mr Len Large

Steak & game pie 65p Treacle tart with ice cream 50p (Last order 10pm)
Wells Bitter, Noggin; Guinness; Kellerbräu.

Len Large's efforts in the kitchen are well rewarded at this friendly, red-brick pub. Home-cooked savoury pies – perhaps chicken and mushroom or steak and game – are a speciality and go nicely with a crisp side salad. You can also enjoy flavoursome soups, salmon mousse and an excellent pork and parsley brawn. Don't miss the gooey treacle tart. Cheese and sandwiches in the evening and on Sunday. **Family pub**

## Chedworth *(Food)* — *Seven Tuns*

Near Cheltenham · *Gloucestershire* · Map 5 A2
Fossebridge (028 572) 242

*Brewery* Courage
*Landlords* Brian & Barbara Eacott

Ploughman's £1.50 Chilli con carne £1.50 (Last order 9pm)
Courage Best Bitter, Directors Bitter, JC; Guinness; Hofmeister; Taunton cider. *Real ale*

Barbara Eacott's simple, wholesome snacks are among the attractions of this cosy old stone pub, which also boasts a children's games room and an upstairs skittle alley. There's a good choice of pâtés and ploughman's, as well as tasty, home-cooked ham. More elaborate items include a delicious turkey loaf or perhaps chilli con carne, and cinnamon-flavoured apple pie makes an excellent finish. **Family pub**

## Chelsfield *(Food)* — *Bo-Peep*

Hewitts Road · *Kent* · Map 6 C3
Knockholt (0959) 34457

*Brewery* Courage
*Landlord* Mr & Mrs A. Peel

Devilled kidneys & vegetables £1.65 Treacle sponge 65p (No bar food eves or Sun)
Courage Directors Bitter, Best Bitter; JC; Guinness; Hofmeister; Kronenbourg. *Real ale*

Check directions, or you could go astray while heading for this fine old country pub, where crowds flock to enjoy hearty, well-prepared bar fare. Smoked mackerel fillet and chicken liver pâté make tasty snacks or starters, and main courses – the menu changes frequently – could include chicken Kiev, chilli beef or devilled kidneys. Before leaving the fold try a nice fruit pie or steamed pudding. Garden.

## Chelsworth *(Food, B & B)* — *Peacock Inn*

The Street, Near Ipswich · *Suffolk* · Map 5 D2
Bildeston (0449) 740758

*Free House*
*Landlords* Anthony & Lorna Marsh
**BEDROOMS 5 Grade 1 £B** (No dogs)
Game pie £3.25 Quiche £2.50
(Last order 10.30pm)
Adnams Bitter; Greene King IPA, Abbot Ale; Mauldon's Bitter, Porter (winter only); Guinness; cider. *Real ale*

Visitors will find wholesome food and comfortable accommodation at this friendly old village pub. Besides sandwiches and quiches, tasty bar snacks include local game, plus a cold buffet in summer and spit-roast rib of beef for lunch on Sundays in winter. The five bedrooms are solidly furnished and share a neat modern bathroom. Good breakfasts. No children under five overnight. Garden.

## Chenies *(Food)* ★ *Bedford Arms Thistle Hotel*

Near Rickmansworth · *Hertfordshire* · Map 6 B3
Chorleywood (092 78) 3301

*Owners* Thistle Hotels
*Landlord* Mr C. Freybourger

Baked avocado with mushrooms £3.90
Salmon trout £4.90 (Last order 10pm)
Younger's No. 3 Ale, Scotch Bitter, Tartan; McEwan's Export; Guinness; Kestrel; McEwan's Lager. *Real ale*

The bar snacks served at this handsome hotel are a delight to both eye and palate. A long and varied lunchtime menu offers sandwiches, superb country pâté, bangers and mash, ravioli, plated salads. . . and, widening the choice still further, daily specials like soft herring roes and perfectly prepared calf's sweetbreads. Scrumptious sweets, too. Sandwiches only evenings and Sunday. *For accommodation see Egon Ronay's Lucas Hotel & Restaurant Guide 1985.* **Family pub**

## Cherington *(Food)* — *The Cherrington*

Near Tetbury · *Gloucestershire* · Map 7 D2
Rodmarton (028 584) 255

*Free House*
*Landlord* Mr B. Nunn
Italian hamburger £1.95 Chicken Caribbean £3.45 (Last order 10pm)
Wadworth's 6X; Flowers Original; Whitbread Best Bitter; Hook Norton; Guinness; Heineken; Hofmeister; cider. *Real ale*

A narrow winding lane leads to this welcoming pub, where you will find a splendid choice of well-prepared food which ranges from French onion soup and lasagne to chicken casserole and an excellent beef burgundy. There's also a tempting cold buffet featuring honey-roast ham and various quiches, and delicious puddings and ice creams round things off nicely. Garden. **Family pub**

## Chester *(B & B)* — *Ye Olde King's Head*

48 Lower Bridge Street · *Cheshire* · Map 3 B4
Chester (0244) 24855

*Brewery* Greenall Whitley
*Landlords* Mr & Mrs R. Musker

**BEDROOMS 11 Grade 2 £B**
Greenall Whitley Local Bitter, Festival; Grünhalle. *Real ale*

Dating back to the 16th century, this splendid old half-timbered inn is a great favourite with foreign visitors. Oak-beamed bedrooms offer comfortable accommodation, with solid furnishings and modern amenities like radios. Bath and shower rooms are well kept. Guests can relax in the TV lounge, or admire the relief map of Civil War battles in the open-plan bar.

## Chichester *(Food, B & B)* — *The Nags*

3 St Pancras · *West Sussex* · Map 6 B4
Chichester (0243) 785823

*Brewery* Whitbread
*Landlords* Brian & June Kirby & son
**BEDROOMS 10 Grade 1 & 2 £B** (No dogs)
Carvery meal £5.50 Toasted sandwich £1.20 (Last order 9.15)
Flower's Original, Strong Country Bitter; Whitbread Bitter; Guinness; Heineken; Stella Artois; cider. *Real ale*

Food is a strong point at this handsome town pub, where each weekday lunchtime there's a good buffet selection that includes cold meats, salads and tasty specials like shepherd's pie. A hot carvery takes over in the evening (Sunday lunchtime too), and sandwiches are always available. Ten bedrooms with washbasins and colour TVs are in period style and offer traditional comforts (no children overnight). Patio and garden.

## Chickerell *(B & B)* — *Turks Head Inn*

6 East Street, Near Weymouth · *Dorset*
Map 8 D4
Weymouth (0305) 783093

*Brewery* Devenish
*Landlords* Williams family

**BEDROOMS 4 Grade 1 £C**
Devenish Bitter, Wessex Bitter, Weymouth Bitter, Mild; Guinness; Heineken; Grünhalle; cider. *Real ale*

A delightful, stone-built pub in a peaceful location. Overnight guests (no under-threes) will find plenty of space and comfort in the well-furnished bedrooms, which all have TVs, tea-makers and spotless modern bathrooms. Good breakfasts, too. There's a large, cheerful public bar, and the skittle alley is a popular attraction. Accommodation closed 1 week Christmas. Patio.
**Family pub**

## Chiddingfold *(B & B)* — *Crown Inn*

The Green · *Surrey* · Map 6 B3
Wormley (042 879) 2255

*Free House*
*Landlord* Mr K. Playter

**BEDROOMS 5 Grade 1 £A+** (No dogs)
Gales HSB; Badgers Best Bitter; Young's Special; Charrington IPA; Guinness; cider. *Real ale*

The handsome half-timbered facade testifies to the great age of this splendid village inn, originally a stopping place for pilgrim monks and a hostelry for 600 years. Solid oak beams, a great inglenook fireplace and fine linenfold panelling characterise the lounge bar, and there's a wealth of period charm in the comfortable bedrooms, which have TVs, tea-makers and private bathrooms. Courtyard.
**Family pub**

## Chiddingfold *(Food)* — *Swan*

Petworth Road · *Surrey* · Map 6 B3
Wormley (042 879) 2073

*Brewery* Friary Meux
*Landlords* Mr & Mrs N. I. G. Bradford

Pigeon breast in port £5.10 Steak & kidney pie & vegetables £1.85 (Last order 10pm)
Friary Meux Bitter; Ind Coope Burton Ale, Mild, John Bull; Guinness; Löwenbräu; cider. *Real ale*

The landlord of this friendly village pub is an enthusiastic angler, and fish features strongly on the menu – whether caught by himself or bought fresh from the market. Local trout, prawns in garlic and grilled sardines are popular choices, and you can also have a home-made soup or meat pie, a jacket potato or a crusty French bread sandwich. Tables are set out in the garden across the road in summer.

## Chilgrove *(Food)* — *White Horse Inn*

Near Chichester · *West Sussex* · Map 6 B4
East Marden (024 359) 219

*Free House*
*Landlords* Barry & Dorothea Phillips

White Horse prawns £3.45 Home-made dessert 95p (No bar food eves)
Ben Truman; Antelope Ale; Guinness; Carlsberg. *Real ale*

Nestling peacefully below the South Downs, this fine old country pub is a favourite spot to pause for a lunchtime snack. The little bar soon fills up with customers enjoying Adrian Congdon's excellent fare, which ranges from smoked salmon sandwiches and a summertime cold buffet to crab gratin, coq au vin and delectable puds like gooey treacle tart. Garden. Closed Monday, all January & last week October.

## Chilham *(Food, B & B)* — *Woolpack*

High Street · *Kent* · Map 6 D3
Canterbury (0227) 730208

*Brewery* Shepherd Neame
*Landlord* Mr John Durcan
**BEDROOMS 13 Grade 1 £A**
Prawns in oil & garlic £1.85 Grilled lemon sole £3.45 (Last order 10pm)
Shepherd Neame Master Brew, Invicta Bitter; Guinness; Hürlimann. *Real ale*

Once an overnight stop on the London–Dover coaching route, this handsome whitewashed pub is equally welcoming to today's travellers, offering comfortable accommodation and good, simple fare. Well-carpeted bedrooms, most with private facilities, have neat modern furniture, tea-makers and colour TVs. Snacks served in the oak-beamed bar include sandwiches and salads based on cold meats, plus a few hot dishes like chilli. **Family pub**

## Chipping *(Food)* — *Dog & Partridge*

Hesketh Lane, Near Preston · *Lancashire*
Map 3 B3
Chipping (099 56) 201

*Free House*
*Landlords* John & Mary Barr

Roast duckling £4 Pâté with toast £1.25 (Last order 9.45pm. No bar food Sat eve & Sun lunch)
Tetley's Bitter, Mild; Skol.

Stop at this sturdy white-painted inn for a very friendly welcome and some wholesome, enjoyable snacks. John and Mary Barr's short menu offers simple treats like a delicious chicken liver pâté with toast, home-made vegetable soup, roast chicken or duckling, scampi and a hearty ploughman's. You can eat in the cosy bar or out on the cobbled terrace in fine weather.

## Chipping Camden *(Food)* — *King's Arms Hotel*

The Square · *Gloucestershire* · Map 5 A2
Evesham (0386) 840256

*Free House*
*Landlord* Mr A. S. Guthrie

Lamb cutlets café de Paris £2.70 Samosa with apple chutney £2.10 (No bar food eves & all Sun)
Hook Norton Bitter; Carlsberg Hof. *Real ale*

New owner Mr Guthrie has retained the excellent team that runs this fine old market-square inn. Lunchtime bar snacks put the emphasis on seafood, with moules marinière, baked smelts and tasty salmon pancakes among the favourites. Also available are soup, garlicky chicken livers and savoury pies, with a yummy strawberry fool to finish. Garden. *For accommodation see Egon Ronay's Lucas Hotel & Restaurant Guide 1985.* **Family pub**

## Chipping Norton *(B & B)* — *Crown & Cushion*

High Street · *Oxfordshire* · Map 5 A2
Chipping Norton (0608) 2533

*Free House*
*Landlord* Mr J. M. Fraser

**BEDROOMS 14 Grades 1 & 2 £B**
Wadworth's 6X, IPA; Hook Norton Best Bitter; McEwan's Export; Guinness; Kronenbourg. *Real ale*

This well-maintained inn opened its doors in 1497 and has been providing good hospitality ever since. The past looms large in the popular beamed bar with its fine old fireplace shining with brass ornaments; there's also a cosy TV room and a spacious residents' lounge. Nicely coordinated bedrooms are thoroughly up to date with simple contemporary furniture, TVs, telephones and good modern bathrooms. Patio. **Family pub**

## Chipping Norton *(B & B)* — *Fox Hotel*

Market Place · *Oxfordshire* · Map 5 A2
Chipping Norton (0608) 2658

*Brewery* Hall
*Landlord* Mr & Mrs J. D. Philp

**BEDROOMS 6 Grade 2 £C**
Hall's Harvest Bitter; Tetley's Bitter; Ind Coope John Bull Bitter, Double Diamond; Guinness; Löwenbräu; cider. *Real ale*

New managers the Philps make visitors feel very much at home in this comfortable hotel facing the town hall. The bedrooms, all with televisions and tea-makers, are furnished in a variety of styles and share two carpeted bathrooms. There are two bars (the main one quite large, with dark-wood panelling and copper ornaments) and a pleasant little lounge. **Family pub**

## Chiseldon *(B & B)* — *Patriots Arms*

New Road · *Wiltshire* · Map 6 A3
Swindon (0793) 740331

*Brewery* Courage
*Landlords* Mr & Mrs D. Day

**BEDROOMS 3 Grade 2 £C** (No dogs)
Courage Directors Bitter, Best Bitter, Mild; Simonds Bitter; Guinness; John Smith's Lager; Taunton cider. *Real ale*

A family room and patio are part of the plans that have recently been taking shape at this unpretentious, white-painted pub. Overnight accommodation is modest but comfortable in three centrally heated bedrooms with simple furnishings and coordinated fabrics. The bathroom they share is practical, modern and well-maintained. The lounge and bar areas are also part of the improvement scheme. Garden. **Family pub**

## Christow *(B & B)* — *Artichoke Inn*

Village Road, Near Exeter · *Devon* · Map 8 C4
Christow (0647) 52387

*Brewery* Heavitree
*Landlords* Mr & Mrs M. H. Fox

**BEDROOMS 3 Grade 2 £C**
Flower's IPA, Original; Whitbread Trophy; Poachers; Guinness; Heineken; cider. *Real ale*

Flagstone floors, low beams, horse brasses and an inglenook fireplace are familiar features in a traditional English pub, and you'll find them all in the bar of this ancient thatched inn not far from Exeter. Steep, narrow stairs lead to the pretty bedrooms (one family size, all with TVs and tea-makers), which share a well-equipped bathroom. A cosy breakfast room overlooks the garden. **Family pub**

## Church Stretton *(B & B)* — *Kings Arms*

High Street · *Shropshire* · Map 7 D1
Church Stretton (0694) 722807

*Brewery* Shrewsbury & Wem
*Landlords* Ken & Jean MacKechnie

**BEDROOMS 2 Grade 2 £C**
Wem Best Bitter, Best Mild; Guinness; Grünhalle. *Real ale*

Long-serving landlords Ken and Jean MacKechnie keep everything really spick and span at their popular late-Tudor pub on the main street of an ancient market town. Behind a white pebbledash facade, solid oak beams give a homely old-world appeal, and the two little bedrooms provide simple comforts for an overnight stay. They share a well-fitted modern bathroom.

## Churchstow *(Food)* — *Church House Inn*

Near Kingsbridge · *Devon* · Map 8 C4
Kingsbridge (0548) 2237

*Free House*
*Landlords* Messrs Nicholson & Tucker

Devilled chicken £1.95 Speciality fish pie £1.85 (Last order 9pm)
Usher's Best Bitter; Founder's Ale; Bass; Carlsberg; Guinness; cider. *Real ale*

You'll find this cosy, beamed 15th-century inn right opposite the church. Wholesome, enjoyable bar snacks range from simple salads and sandwiches to warming soups in winter, a tasty fish pie, spicy devilled chicken and cold meats served with delicious bubble and squeak. Lemon meringue pie is a favourite among the lovely homely sweets. Patio.

## Clanfield *(Food, B & B)* — *Clanfield Tavern*

Near Witney · *Oxfordshire* · Map 6 A3
Clanfield (036 781) 223

*Free House*
*Landlords* Mr & Mrs K. Nadin
**BEDROOMS 3 Grade 2 £B**
Spiced pork pancake £2.95 Steak & mushroom kebab £3 (Last order 9.45pm)
Morland's Bitter; Hook Norton Best Bitter; Arkell's BBB; Greenall Whitley Festival; Guinness; Carlsberg; cider. *Real ale*

An attractive old stone tavern with thick walls, heavy beams and well-worn flagstone floors. Mrs Nadin's bar snacks are a popular feature: try her flavoursome smoked mackerel pâté, followed perhaps by a burger, steak or chicken and ham vol-au-vent. Nice sweets, too. The bedrooms have good carpets and comfortable beds; they share an up-to-date bathroom. Garden. **Family pub**

## Clare *(Food, B & B)* — *Bell Hotel*

Near Sudbury · *Suffolk* · Map 5 C2
Clare (0787) 277741

*Free House*
*Landlords* H. Jones & M. Jones
**BEDROOMS 21 Grades 1 & 2 £B**
Suffolk sausages £1.95 Fruit pie 95p (Last order 9.30pm)
Greene King IPA; Adnams Bitter, Old (winter only); Mauldon's Bitter; Guinness. *Real ale*

This fine old half-timbered inn serves very good snacks in its rustic bar. Starters like soup or pâté could be followed by a richly flavoured steak and onion pie, and there's plenty of variety among the sandwiches, salads and homely puds. Courtyard bedrooms have lovely period furnishings, colour TVs and private bathrooms. Rooms in the original building are generally simpler. Garden. **Family pub**

## Clare *(Food)* — *Seafarer Inn*

Nethergate Street · *Suffolk* · Map 5 C2
Clare (0787) 277449

*Free House*
*Landlords* John & Celia Blanshard

Seafood bake £4.50 Pork fillet Celia £3.50 (Last order 10pm. No bar food Mon eve)
Adnams Bitter, Mild, Old Ale; Double Diamond; Hurlimann; cider. *Real ale*

Fish and shellfish are the speciality of this aptly named pub that prides itself on good fresh produce. Try the king prawns, ceviche or fish soup to start, with perhaps a seafood bake to follow. Meat lovers are catered for with dishes like pork fillet or hunter's chicken. There are salads and sandwiches for light eaters, and a selection of simple sweets. Garden.

## Clare *(Food)* — *Swan Inn*

4 High Street, Near Sudbury · *Suffolk*
Map 5 C2
Clare (0787) 278030
*Brewery* Greene King
*Landlords* Mr & Mrs R. Greybrook
Cheese-topped cottage pie £1.50 Beefsteak, kidney & mushroom pie £2.40 (Last order 10pm. No bar food Mon eve)
Greene King Abbot Ale, IPA, Dark Mild; Guinness; Harp; Kronenbourg; Taunton cider. *Real ale*

An imposing carved swan, reputedly the oldest inn sign in Europe, stands above the portal of this ancient hostelry. In the cosy bars they serve a good variety of fare: hot potted shrimps, Camembert fritters or garlicky tsatsiki makes a tasty light snack, and more hearty main courses might include saucy porterhouse steak, baked trout and the ever-popular beefsteak, kidney and mushroom pie enriched with ale. Daily specials too. Garden.

## Clayton *(B & B)* — *Jack & Jill Inn*

Brighton Road · *West Sussex* · Map 6 C4
Hassocks (079 18) 3595

*Brewery* Watneys
*Landlords* Mike & Joan Harman

**BEDROOMS 4 Grade 2 £C** (No dogs)
Watneys Stag Bitter; Tamplins Bitter; Webster's Yorkshire Bitter; Guinness; Holsten; Foster's; cider. *Real ale*

About seven miles north of Brighton on the A273, this friendly roadside inn has a playground and special children's room that make it especially useful for families. The cosy bar is a relaxing spot for a drink and the bedrooms are clean and cheerful, with whitewood furniture, tea-makers and washbasins. There are two well-fitted shower rooms. **Family pub**

## Clearwell *(Food, B & B)* — *Wyndham Arms*

Near Coleford · *Gloucestershire* · Map 7 D2
Dean (0594) 33666

*Free House*
*Landlords* Mr & Mrs J. Stanford
**BEDROOMS 5 Grade 1 £A+**
Grilled Portuguese sardines £2.75 Chicken liver pâté £2.15 (Last order 10pm)
Flower's Best Bitter, Original, West Country Pale Ale; Guinness; Heineken; Stella Artois; cider. *Real ale*

Two new bedrooms have recently increased the accommodation at this spick and span 14th-century pub; all rooms have central heating, TVs, tea-makers and private bathrooms. The bar menu offers a good choice of simple, tasty snacks, from soup and sandwiches to grilled rainbow trout, prawn curry and chilli con carne. Snack service may be suspended when the restaurant is busy. Closed 2 weeks end October. Garden.

## Clifton Hampden *(Food, B & B)* — *Barley Mow*

Near Abingdon · *Oxfordshire* · Map 6 A3
Clifton Hampden (086 730) 7847

*Owners* Thames Hosts
*Landlords* Mr & Mrs Paul Turner
**BEDROOMS 4 Grade 2 £C**
Beef, lamb & mussel pie £2.60 Beef curry £2.10 (Last order 10pm. No bar food Sun eve)
Usher's Founder's Ale, Best Bitter, Pale Ale; Webster's Yorkshire Bitter; Guinness; Carlsberg. *Real ale*

Tasty bar snacks bring a cheerful clientele to this delightful old thatched pub, which enjoys a pleasant setting near the Thames. Hand-raised pies and home-baked ham make popular salad platters, and other choices include roast beef (hot and cold), spare ribs and turkey drumsticks. Well-kept bedrooms with TVs and tea-makers share a modern bathroom. Good breakfasts. Garden. **Family pub**

## Clun *(Food, B & B)* — *Sun Inn*

High Street, Near Craven Arms · *Shropshire*
Map 7 C1
Clun (058 84) 559
*Free House*
*Landlords* Rodney & Beryl Marsden
**BEDROOMS 7 Grade 2 £C** (No dogs)
Vegetable soup 80p Escalope of pork with apple sauce £3.25 (Last order 9.30pm)
Wood's Parish Bitter; Mitchells & Butlers Springfield Bitter; Ansells Mild; Bass; Guinness; Tennent's Extra; cider. *Real ale*

A 15th-century village pub of cruck construction abounding in rustic charm. Snacks served in the little beamed bars are simple and delicious – flavoursome vegetable soup, home-cooked ham for sandwiches or salads, escalope of pork, fresh plum tart. Bedrooms range from homely and old-fashioned in the main building to more modern, with tea-makers and shower facilities, in the annexe. There are two cosy lounges, one with TV. Patio.

## Clyst Hydon *(Food)* — *Five Bells*

Cullompton · *Devon* · Map 8 C3
Plymtree (088 47) 288

*Free House*
*Landlords* Mr & Mrs J. A. Hayward
Mushroom omelette with chips & salad £1.70 Steak & kidney pie & vegetables £2.50 (Last order 9.45pm)
Hall & Woodhouse Badger Best Bitter; Bass; Worthington Best Bitter; Carlsberg Pils; Taunton cider. *Real ale*

Tasty snacks are available both at lunchtime and in the evening in the handsome beamed bar of this secluded farmhouse inn. Omelettes, served nicely soft with fillings of ham, cheese or mushroom are a house speciality, and other favourites range from fresh-flavoured vegetable soup to sandwiches, ploughman's platters, home-made pies and basket meals. Apple crumble rounds things off nicely. Closed Mon evenings in winter. Garden.

## Cobham *(Food)* — *Plough*

Plough Lane · *Surrey* · Map 6 B3
Cobham (093 26) 2514

*Brewery* Courage
*Landlords* John & Irene Huetson

Ploughman's lunch £1.10 Prawn salad £2.75 (Last order 9.30pm)
Courage Directors Bitter, Best Bitter; John Smith's Bitter; Guinness; Hofmeister; Kronenbourg; cider. *Real ale*

Goats, bantams and a donkey make this friendly little red-brick pub near Downside Bridge especially popular with children. A cold cabinet in the lounge features an appetising display of succulent beef, fresh crab, smoked salmon and salads, and you can also choose hot dishes like a prawn-filled baked potato, tasty shepherd's pie or a toasted sandwich. **Family pub**

## Cockwood *(Food)* — *Ship Inn*

Starcross, Near Exeter · *Devon* · Map 8 C4
Starcross (0626) 890373

*Brewery* Courage
*Landlord* Mr B. Hoyle
Cockwood special £4.95 Moules marinière £1.75 (Last order 10.15pm)
Courage Directors Bitter, Best Bitter, JC; John Smith's Yorkshire; Simmonds Mild; Guinness; Hofmeister; Kronenbourg; Taunton cider. *Real ale*

This unassuming old pub stands just a short walk from Cockwood harbour, so it's not surprising that seafood is a speciality. Crab, lobster, mussels and monkfish are carefully prepared and prettily presented, and you can push the boat out with a splendid mixed platter. Also sandwiches and salads, excellent chicken liver pâté and steaks, plus nice home-made sweets. Garden. **Family pub**

## Coggeshall *(Food)* — *White Hart Hotel*

Market End · *Essex* · Map 5 C2
Coggeshall (0376) 61654

*Free House*
*Landlords* Mr & Mrs R. Pluck

Scallop & prawn Mornay £2.50 Rack of lamb £5.25 (No bar food eves & Sun)
Ansells Best Bitter; Stella Artois. *Real ale*

History abounds at this 500-year-old hostelry, whose public rooms feature some marvellous timbers. The bar menu ranges from sandwiches and pâté to steak and kidney pie, smoked trout and savoury pancakes. There's also a wide selection of charcoal grills from calf's liver to steaks. Closed August and 1 week Christmas. Patio. *For accommodation see Egon Ronay's Lucas Hotel & Restaurant Guide 1985.* **Family pub**

## Coggeshall *(Food, B & B)* — *Woolpack Inn*

91 Church Street · *Essex* · Map 5 C2
Coggeshall (0376) 61235
*Brewery* Ind Coope
*Landlords* Mr & Mrs W. T. Hutchinson
**BEDROOMS 2 Grade 2 £B** (No dogs)
Fresh Dover sole £2.95 Game pie £2.50 (Last order 9.30pm. No bar food Sun–Tues eves)
Ind Coope Bitter, Friary Meux Bitter; Benskins Bitter; Taylor Walker Bitter; Löwenbräu; Skol; cider. *Real ale*

Built for a wool merchant in the 15th century, this splendid pub still boasts fine beams, panelling and lattice windows. Mrs Hutchinson's excellent bar snacks are an additional attraction, ranging from soup with garlic bread to smoked mackerel pâté, fresh fish, game pie or a cold meat salad, with perhaps a treacle tart to finish. Bedrooms are homely and comfortable. No children overnight. Garden.

## Colesbourne *(Food)* — *Colesbourne Inn*

Nr Cheltenham · *Gloucestershire* · Map 5 A2
Coberley (024 287) 376

*Brewery* Wadworth
*Landlords* Mr & Mrs M. J. Pringle

Herby beef £2.50 Turkey & ham pie salad £3.50 (Last order 10pm)
Wadworth's IPA, 6X, Old Timer (winter only), Northgate Bitter, Löwenbräu; Heineken. *Real ale*

Appetising salads featuring home-cooked meats and locally made pies are a popular choice at this comfortable roadside pub, and spare ribs and lamb hot pot are typical hot specials at lunchtime. You can also get a sandwich, and there are delicious fruit pies for dessert. Grills are a staple of the more extensive evening menu. Garden.

## Coleshill *(B & B)* — *Coleshill Hotel*

152 High Street · *Warwickshire* · Map 5 A2
Coleshill (0675) 65527

*Free House*
*Landlord* Mr T. J. Lock

**BEDROOMS 15 Grade 1 £B**
Mitchells & Butlers Mild, Bitter; Ansells Bitter; Banks's Mild; Carling Black Label; cider.

Conveniently situated close to junction 4 of the M6, this comfortably refurbished hostelry is a welcome stopping place for tired motorists. Visitors can relax in the attractive beamed lounge or enjoy a drink in the pleasant bar. Spotlessly clean bedrooms (including a bridal suite with a four-poster) have plenty of wardrobe space, radios, TVs and tea-makers, plus prettily tiled bath or shower rooms. Patio.
**Family pub**

## Coleshill *(B & B)* — *Swan Hotel*

High Street · *Warwickshire* · Map 5 A2
Coleshill (0675) 62212

*Brewery* Ansells
*Landlords* P. J. Stubbins & G. C. Donovan

**BEDROOMS 35 Grade 1 £B**
Ansells Bitter, Mild; Tetley's Bitter; Guinness; Skol; cider. *Real ale*

Smartly updated behind its 17th-century façade, this former coaching inn appeals to modern travellers with its excellent accommodation and handy position (it's very near the M6 and National Exhibition Centre). Bedrooms (all with extras such as hairdryers) have practical built-in units, TVs and trouser presses, and the 20 annexe rooms have shower rooms. There's a spacious public bar and an intimate cocktail lounge.
**Family pub**

## Collyweston *(Food, B & B)* — *Cavalier*

Near Stamford · *Northamptonshire* · Map 5 B1
Duddington (078 083) 288
*Free House*
*Landlords* A. B., N. A. & E. J. Haigh
**BEDROOMS 5 Grade 2 £C**
Steak & kidney pie £2.95 Salmon steak trouvillaise £4.25 (Last order 9.30pm)
Bateman's XXXB; Greene King IPA; Webster's Yorkshire Bitter; Ruddle's County; Younger's Tartan; Guinness; Taunton cider. *Real ale*

A varied menu caters for all tastes at this welcoming village pub just off the A43. Besides sandwiches and pizzas, there's garlicky pâté plus a selection of hot dishes like curry, steak and sweet and sour chicken. The traditional Sunday roast is a popular feature. Prettily decorated bedrooms (three with smart modern bathrooms) have TVs and tea-makers.
**Family pub**

## Coln St Aldwyns *(B & B)* — *New Inn*

Near Cirencester · *Gloucestershire* · Map 6 A3
Coln St Aldwyns (028 575) 202

*Free House*
*Landlords* Mr & Mrs R. Warren

**BEDROOMS 5 Grade 2 £B**
Morland's Bitter; Wadworth's 6X; Mitchells & Butlers Brew X1; Guinness; Carling Black Label. *Real ale*

Far from being new, this Cotswold-stone inn actually dates back to the 16th century! The public bar is the social centre of village life, and there's a comfortable lounge bar with oak beams and an inglenook fireplace. Homely bedrooms in the main building share a well-maintained bathroom, while those in the annexe have their own facilities. There's a TV lounge for residents. Terrace.
**Family pub**

## Compton *(Food)* — *Harrow Inn*

Guildford · *Surrey* · Map 6 B3
Guildford (0483) 810379

*Brewery* Friary Meux
*Landlords* Roger & Sue Seaman

Seafood special £3.75 Lasagne with salad £2.50 (Last order 10pm)
Friary Meux Bitter; Ind Coope Burton Ale; Guinness, Skol; Löwenbräu; cider. *Real ale*

Racing pictures line the walls of this comfortable pub but the lavish cold counter is the real winner. Seafood lovers can choose between mussels, prawns, trout and smoked mackerel, while meat eaters have juicy roast beef, chicken and ham pie or lasagne to go with a selection of fresh, colourful salads. Pizzas and toasted sandwiches too. Garden.

## Congleton *(Food, B & B)* — *Lion & Swan Hotel*

West Street · *Cheshire* · Map 4 C4
Congleton (026 02) 3115

*Free House*
*Landlords* Messrs T. R. & B. Harrison
**BEDROOMS 13 Grade 1 £A** (No dogs)
Quiche & salad £1.85 Steak & kidney pie £2.25 (Last order 9.30pm. No bar food Sun eve)
Marston's Bitter, Pedigree; Burtonwood Bitter, Mild; Guinness; Tuborg; Löwenbräu; cider. *Real ale*

Many original features survive in this 16th-century timbered coaching inn, whose entrance is flanked by Doric columns and stone lions. Snacks served in the characterful bars include sandwiches and salads, well-made quiches and the ever-popular steak & kidney pie. Smartly refurbished bedrooms with whitewood furniture, tea-makers, TVs and direct-dial telephones provide good comforts. There's a cosy lounge. **Family pub**

## Congresbury *(Food)* — *White Hart & Inwood*

Wrington Road, Near Bristol · *Avon* · Map 8 D3
Yatton (0272) 833303

*Free House*
*Landlords* Mellor family

Chicken & almond soup 70p Garlic beef £2.75 (No bar food Sun or eves)
Wadworth's 6X; Butcombe Bitter; Flower's Original; Guinness; Heineken; Stella Artois; Taunton cider. *Real ale*

Lunchtime sees a wide selection of hot and cold fare in the cosy, characterful bars of the timbered White Hart and its neighbour just across the car park. Ploughman's platters and toasted sandwiches are popular choices for quick snacks, and other favourites from a daily-changing selection range from hearty soups and jacket potatoes to baked ham, quiches, curries and casseroles. Garden. **Family pub**

## Constable Burton *(Food)* — *Wyvill Arms*

Near Leyburn · *North Yorkshire* · Map 4 C2
Bedale (0677) 50581

*Free House*
*Landlord* Mr S Dean

Steak & kidney pie £2.50 Madras beef curry £2.60 (Last order 9.30pm)
Theakston's Best Bitter; John Smith's Bitter, Magnet; Hofmeister; Carlsberg Hof; Taunton cider. *Real ale*

Bar snacks are varied and satisfying at this handsome converted farmhouse. The choice ranges from soup or a sandwich for a quick bite to grilled trout, braised chicken, beef curry, juicy steaks and huge cold meat platters. There are also some delicious sweets and fine English cheeses. Lunch on Sunday is a traditional roast. Garden.
**Family pub**

## Cornhill-on-Tweed *(B & B)* — *Collingwood Arms Hotel*

*Northumberland* · Map 2 D4
Coldstream (0890) 2424

*Free House*
*Landlords* Mr & Mrs Scott

**BEDROOMS 18 Grade 1 £B**
Drybrough's Heavy, Best Scotch; Burns Special; Guinness; Carlsberg; Foster's. *Real ale*

Just a few miles from the Scottish border this fine old creeper-covered inn on the A697 is a good place for an overnight stop. A blazing winter fire provides a welcome in the entrance hall, and there are two pleasant bars. Bright, well-kept bedrooms are furnished mainly in traditional style. Seven have TVs and nicely decorated bath or shower rooms. Garden. **Family pub**

## Corsham *(B & B)* — *Methuen Arms*

High Street · *Wiltshire* · Map 7 D2
Corsham (0249) 714867

*Brewery* Gibbs Mew
*Landlord* Mr Tom Stewart

**BEDROOMS 23 Grades 1 & 2 £A+**
Gibbs Anchor Best Bitter, SPA; Bass; Guinness; Harp; cider. *Real ale*

The Georgian façade of this fine old inn hides a history that goes back to the 15th century. The aptly named Long Bar in the oldest part features splendid beams, exposed stone walls and a popular skittle alley. Good-sized bedrooms vary from basic to very comfortable; all have darkwood furniture, tea-makers and direct-dial telephones and many have televisions. Good modern bathrooms. **Family pub**

## Corton *(Food)* — *Dove*

Near Warminster · *Wiltshire* · Map 8 D3
Warminster (0985) 50378

*Free House*
*Landlords* Jane & Michael Rowse

Steak, kidney & oyster pie £3 Tipsy cake £1.20 (Last order 9.30pm)
Usher's Best Bitter, Triple Crown, Country; Carlsberg. *Real ale*

This charming Victorian pub is well worth a visit for its excellent snacks. In the cosy, attractive bar you can enjoy really tasty home-prepared fare, from gazpacho and smoked trout to salads, savoury pies and well-seasoned salmon and sweetcorn bake. More hot choices in winter, and always some delectable desserts. Closed Sunday evening, Monday (except Bank Holidays) & 2 weeks mid Jan. Garden.

## Cottesmore *(Food)* — *Sun Inn*

Rutland · *Leicestershire* · Map 5 B1
Oakham (0572) 812321

*Brewery* Everards
*Landlord* Mr Allan Plummer

Steak & kidney pie with vegetables £2.30
Seafood pie £4.50 (Last order 10.30pm)
Everards Tiger, Beacon, Old Original, Mild; Guinness; cider. *Real ale*

Pull in at this attractive, white-painted village pub to enjoy a sunny welcome from Allan Plummer and some tasty, wholesome home cooking by his wife Gillian. The lunchtime menu changes daily, offering soup, salads, a very good roast with all the trimmings and another hot choice like liver and onions, while evening options might include steaks, seafood pie and smoked gammon. Excellent English cheeseboard. Terrace. **Family pub**

## Cousley Wood *(Food)* — *Old Vine*

Near Wadhurst · *East Sussex* · Map 6 C3
Wadhurst (089 288) 2271

*Brewery* Whitbread
*Landlords* Mr & Mrs A. Peel
Steak, kidney & mushroom pie £1.95 Chicken breast in cream sauce £2.75 (Last order 9.30pm. No bar food Sun eve)
Fremlins Tusker; Whitbread Best Bitter; Guinness; Stella Artois; Heineken; cider. *Real ale*

Good food is a major attraction at this charming and bustling village pub. The blackboard menu in the low-ceilinged bar advertises interesting daily specials like pork chop with mushrooms, chicken in red wine and lamb provençale. There are salads, sandwiches and ploughman's, too, as well as some delicious sweets from the trolley. Garden.

## Coxwold *(Food, B & B)* — *Fauconberg Arms*

*North Yorkshire* · Map 4 C2
Coxwold (034 76) 214

*Free House*
*Landlords* Mr & Mrs R. Goodall
**BEDROOMS 4 Grade 2 £B** (No dogs)
Soup 80p Sandwich 80p (No bar food eves)
Younger's Scotch Bitter; Tetley's Bitter; Theakston's Best Bitter; Guinness; Harp; Carlsberg. *Real ale*

Lunchtime visitors are assured of an excellent snack at this nicely kept 17th-century stone inn. Home-made soups like cream of cauliflower or fennel and mushroom make a most enjoyable prelude to freshly cut sandwiches such as the Fauconberg special – filled with cottage cheese, fruit and nuts. Simple sweets and cheese, too. Prettily decorated bedrooms include one with TV and a private bathroom.

**Family pub**

## Cranborne *(Food, B & B)* — *Fleur de Lys Hotel*

Near Wimborne · *Dorset* · Map 6 A4
Cranborne (072 54) 282
*Brewery* Hall & Woodhouse
*Landlords* Mr & Mrs C. T. Hancock
**BEDROOMS 4 Grade 2 £C**
Steak pie with vegetables £1.95 Smoked trout £2.85 (Last order 9.45)
Hall & Woodhouse Badger Best Bitter, Hector's Bitter, Tanglefoot; Mitchells & Butlers Mild; Guinness; Stella Artois; Taunton cider. *Real ale*

Mrs Hancock is justly proud of the flowers that provide a splash of colour outside this historic, centuries-old inn, while in the beamed bar there's an atmosphere of rustic charm and character. Here you can enjoy traditional fare like rich Dorset pâté, home-made soup, salads and savoury pies, as well as grills and basket meals. Bedrooms are sturdily furnished, and the public bathroom is adequate. Accommodation closed 1 week Christmas. Garden. **Family pub**

## Crawley *(Food)* — *Fox & Hounds*

Near Winchester · *Hampshire* · Map 6 A3
Sparsholt (096 272) 285
*Free House*
*Landlords* Mr & Mrs Dodge & Mr & Mrs Silsbury
Sparsholt smokie £1.20 Bacon & mushroom open toasted sandwich £1.70 (Last order 9pm. No bar food Sun eve)
Whitbread Best Bitter; Flowers Original Bitter; McEwan's Export; Wadworth's 6X; Guinness; Stella Artois; cider. *Real ale*

The cosy bars of this fine old red-brick village inn are very welcoming, and there's always an enjoyable snack, whether at lunchtime or in the evening. Nourishing soups, pâtés, varied sandwiches and ploughman's are the staples of the menu, which also features tempting daily specials like gammon with sauté potatoes, courgette quiche and tongue and ham mousse. Patio.

## Crazies Hill *(Food)* — *Horns*

Near Wargrave · *Berkshire* · Map 6 B3
Wargrave (073 522) 3226

*Brewery* Brakspear
*Landlords* Mr & Mrs A. Wheeler

Thai noodles £1.40 Lasagne verdi £1.70
Brakspear's Bitter, XXXX; Heineken. *Real ale*

There's always a south-east Asian dish on Mrs Wheeler's daily menu at this pleasant old black and white pub. Chicken satay or Thai noodles might be the day's spicy special, joining more familiar pub fare like flavoursome soup, lasagne and robust lamb hot pot. Curries make a popular appearance on Tuesday evenings and Saturday lunchtime; limited menu Sunday and Monday evenings.

## Croscombe *(Food)* — *Bull Terrier*

Near Wells · *Somerset* · Map 8 D3
Shepton Mallet (0749) 3658

*Free House*
*Landlords* Mr & Mrs S. A. Lea & Mrs J. Preston
Turkey, ham & mushroom pie £2.05 Pork in cider £2.30 (Last order 9.30pm, 9pm in winter. No bar food Sun & Mon eves Oct–April)
Bull Terrier Bitter; Butcombe Bitter; Wadworth's 6X; Guinness; Holsten; Stella Artois; Taunton cider. *Real ale*

A refuge for pilgrims in medieval times, this fine old pub still has plenty of character with its stone-flagged floor, beams and handsome oak furniture. Bar food also holds a lot of interest, with a choice ranging from tasty pâtés, pies and soups to well-prepared dishes like cannelloni or chicken Maryland. Salads, too, and delicious sweets such as chocolate profiteroles.
**Family pub**

## Croyde *(Food, B & B)* — *Thatched Barn Inn*

Braunton · *Devon* · Map 8 B3
Croyde (0271) 890349

*Free House*
*Landlords* Bruce & Pat Jefford
**BEDROOMS 4 Grades 1 & 2 £C**
Salmon mayonnaise £1.95 Stuffed chicken breast £4.25 (Last order 10pm)
Flower's Original; Bass; Whitbread Best Bitter; Guinness; Stella Artois; Heineken; Taunton cider. *Real ale*

Charming hosts and friendly, efficient staff make it a real pleasure to visit this attractive thatched inn, skilfully converted from a 16th-century barn. An extensive menu is offered in the characterful bars, including sandwiches, salads, poultry and charcoal-grilled steaks. Overnight accommodation comprises three simple, spotless bedrooms and a splendid suite, the latter with colour TV and a smart modern bathroom. Patio.
**Family pub**

## Croydon *(B & B)* — *Windsor Castle*

415 Brighton Road · *Surrey* · Map 6 C3
01-680 4559

*Brewery* Bass
*Landlords* Mr & Mrs G. R. Wenham

**BEDROOMS 30 Grade 1 £A** (No dogs)
Charrington's IPA, Stones Bitter; Bass; Guinness; Tennent's; Carling Black Label; Taunton cider. *Real ale*

Situated on the A235 Brighton Road, this former coaching inn provides accommodation of hotel standard in a purpose-built modern extension. All bedrooms have good carpets and practical built-in furniture, and TVs, tea-makers and radio-alarms are standard features, along with compact tiled bathrooms. There are three pleasant bars, one for residents only. Staff are young and friendly. Garden.

## Cumnor *(Food)* — *Bear & Ragged Staff*

Appleton Road · *Oxfordshire* · Map 6 A3
Cumnor (0865) 862329

*Owners* Sun Taverns Ltd
*Landlord* Mr Howard Hill-Lines

Pork & Calvados casserole £3.25 Fresh Scotch salmon in pastry parcel with herb sauce £3.75 (Last order 10pm)
Morrell's Bitter, Varsity; Guinness; Harp; Kronenbourg; cider. *Real ale*

Enterprising, carefully prepared food is the trademark of this charming Cotswold-stone pub. The menu in the rustic bar might offer dishes like veal escalope with herbs, casseroled pork with Calvados or duckling with Dubonnet and orange. Equally tempting is the cold buffet display of pies, cold meats and salads, and there are some delicious sweets and well-kept cheeses.
**Family pub**

## Damerham *(Food, B & B)* — *Compasses Inn*

Near Fordingbridge · *Hampshire* · Map 6 A4
Rockbourne (072 53) 231

*Free House*
*Landlords* Mr & Mrs Reilly
**BEDROOMS 4 Grade 2 £C** (No dogs)
Damerham trout £4.50 Liver & bacon casserole £2.50 (Last order 9.30pm)
Courage Best Bitter, Directors Bitter; John Smith's Yorkshire Bitter, lager; Guinness; Hofmeister; Taunton cider. *Real ale*

There's an unspoilt charm about this friendly old pub, a popular spot with fishermen and a favourite village meeting place. June Reilly's snacks will delight all lovers of good, flavoursome cooking: try her homely soups, superfresh local trout, liver and bacon casserole, delicious summer pudding. Simple bedrooms with pretty floral bedspreads and well-polished period furnishings share a spotless old-fashioned bathroom.
**Family pub**

## Darrington *(B & B)* — *Darrington Hotel*

Great North Road, Near Pontefract
*West Yorkshire* · Map 4 C3
Pontefract (0977) 791458

*Brewery* Younger
*Landlord* Mr James Weatherhead
**BEDROOMS 30 Grade 1 £A**
Younger's Scotch Bitter; Newcastle Bitter; Kestrel; Harp; Becks Bier; Taunton cider. *Real ale*

Just off the A1 and conveniently near the M62, this unassuming red-brick pub is a comfortable, characterful stopping place for the motorist. The spacious L-shaped bar has a cosy Victorian atmosphere, with buttoned velour banquettes, and there's also a small cocktail bar. Spacious bedrooms, most with shower/bathrooms, have neat fitted units, telephones and tea-makers. Guests can bask in the sauna and solarium. Garden.
**Family pub**

## Dartington *(Food, B & B)* — *Cott Inn*

*Devon* · Map 8 C4
Totnes (0803) 863777
*Free House*
*Landlords* Mr & Mrs Yeadon & Mr & Mrs Shortman
**BEDROOMS 6 Grade 2 £A**
Suprême of chicken with mushroom sauce £4.25 Cheese & onion flan £2.95 (Last order 10pm)
Ansells Bitter, Mild; Worthington 'E'; Bass; Guinness; Carlsberg Export; cider.

Dating back to the 14th century, this rambling thatched inn offers enjoyable, homely fare in its heavily beamed bar. Most appealing of all is the elaborate cold buffet, with its flans, pies and treats like salmon coulibiac, and there are always some hot dishes too. Leave room for delicious traditional sweets like Bakewell tart. Six cottagy bedrooms and a comfortable TV lounge cater for overnight guests. Patio.

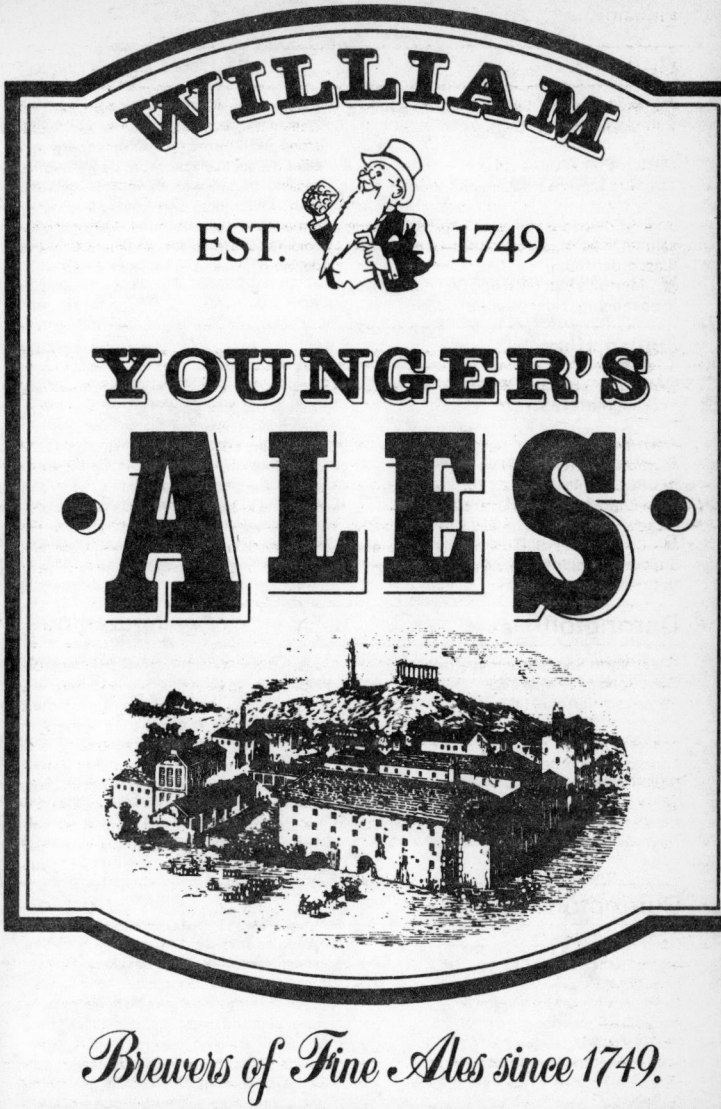
WILLIAM
EST. 1749
YOUNGER'S
ALES
Brewers of Fine Ales since 1749.

## Dedham *(Food, B & B)* — *Marlborough Head*

Mill Lane · *Essex* · Map 5 D2
Colchester (0206) 323124

*Brewery* Ind Coope
*Landlord* Mr Brian Wills
**BEDROOMS 4 Grade 2 £B** (No dogs)
Marlborough soup 70p Poached halibut £4 (Last order 9.30pm)
Ind Coope Bitter, John Bull, Double Diamond, Mild; Skol; Löwenbräu; cider. *Real ale*

A fine 15th-century inn, with sturdy beams, carved wooden fireplaces and few right angles. Its bar snacks are a popular feature, ranging extensively from sandwiches and delicious vegetable soup to cottage pie, poached halibut and beef curry. Four traditionally furnished bedrooms with washbasins and colour TVs make for a comfortable overnight stay (no children). Accommodation closed 2 weeks Christmas. Garden. **Family pub**

## Derry Hill *(Food)* — *Lansdowne Arms*

Near Calne · *Wiltshire* · Map 6 A3
Calne (0249) 812422

*Brewery* Wadworth
*Landlord* Mrs Evelyn Jones & family

Steak & kidney pie £1.60 Wiltshire faggots £1.40 (Last order 10pm)
Wadworth's Old Timer, 6X, Farmer's Glory; Guinness; Löwenbräu; Heineken; cider. *Real ale*

Evelyn Jones and her family run this handsome Victorian pub, where good food is served in pleasant surroundings. Sandwiches, ploughman's and coarse liver pâté are popular quick snacks, while more substantial items include basket meals and tasty home-made pies – pheasant, steak and kidney, chicken with mushrooms. To finish, try the delicious mint and chocolate gâteau served with lashings of whipped cream. Garden.

## Dersingham *(B & B)* — *Feathers Hotel*

Manor Road · *Norfolk* · Map 5 C1
Dersingham (0485) 40207

*Brewery* Charrington
*Landlord* Mr A. P. Martin

**BEDROOMS 6 Grade 2 £B**
Springfield Bitter; Adnams Bitter; Worthington 'E'; Carling Black Label; Tennent's Export; Taunton cider. *Real ale*

The Prince of Wales' feathers are depicted on an old stable wall at this welcoming stone inn, which stands in attractive countryside on the fringe of the Sandringham Estate. The comfortable bedrooms are quite simple in style, with modern furniture, colour TVs and washbasins; they share a large public bathroom. There are two inviting bars, one of which overlooks the well-tended gardens.

We have raised our standards considerably since last year. The omission of some houses that appeared in last year's Guide is no reflection on their standing.

## Devizes *(Food, B & B)* — *Bear Hotel*

Market Place · *Wiltshire* · Map 6 A3
Devizes (0380) 2444

*Brewery* Wadworth
*Landlords* Mr & Mrs W. K. Dickenson
**BEDROOMS 26 Grade 2 £B**
Wiltshire ham salad £2.95 Devizes pie £3.25 (Last order 10pm)
Wadworth's IPA, 6X, Old Timer (winter only); Guinness; Harp; Heineken; Taunton cider. *Real ale*

This prominent 400-year-old inn is steeped in history, and it still exudes a richly traditional atmosphere. Wholesome bar snacks range from beefsteak butties and the hearty 'Bear Bait' (plump sausages stuffed with cheese and wrapped in bacon) to Devizes pie, a roast and salads, which include slimmer's and vegetarian. Cheerful bedrooms have sturdy furniture, TVs and tea-makers; most also have simple, well-fitted bathrooms. Patio. **Family pub**

## Devizes *(B & B)* — *Moonrakers*

29 Nursteed Road · *Wiltshire* · Map 6 A3
Devizes (0380) 2909

*Brewery* Wadworth
*Landlords* Mr & Mrs V. Gafney

**BEDROOMS 5 Grade 2 £C** (No dogs)
Wadworth's IPA, 6X, Northgate Bitter; Guinness; Heineken; Löwenbräu. *Real ale*

Rose and Vic Gafney make guests feel thoroughly welcome at this 50-year-old red-brick pub. Five spacious bedrooms are comfortably furnished, with good carpeting, TVs, tea-makers and their own shower cubicles. There's also a well-kept public bathroom. Relax with a drink in the pleasant lounge bar or join the locals for darts and pool in the public bar. Garden.

## Disley *(Food)* — *Dandy Cock Inn*

Market Street · *Cheshire* · Map 4 C3
Disley (066 32) 3712

*Brewery* Robinson
*Landlord* Mr D. A. Booth

Steak & kidney pie £1.95 Pancakes £1.85 (Last order 10pm)
Robinson's Best Bitter, Mild; Einhorn. *Real ale*

Simple, enjoyable snacks are served at neatly laid tables in this cosy little pub. Daily hot specials might include tomato and basil soup, cannelloni, and a flavoursome home-made pie. Savoury pancakes are always popular, and there are freshly prepared sandwiches and salads. You might finish with a fruit crumble or blackcurrant pie. **Family pub**

## Doddiscombsleigh *(B & B)* — *Nobody Inn*

Near Exeter · *Devon* · Map 8 C3
Christow (0647) 52394

*Free House*
*Landlords* Mr P. W. Bolton, Mrs K. J. Bolton & Mr N. F. Borst-Smith

**BEDROOMS 4 Grade 2 £C** (No dogs)
Bass; Hall & Woodhouse Badger Bitter; Bates Bitter; Hancock's Ale; Stones Best Bitter; Guinness; Taunton cider. *Real ale*

Travellers long ago, getting no answer from an inhospitable tenant, concluded that there was nobody in. The name stuck, but not the way of dealing with customers, as today's visitors can look forward to a friendly welcome in the beamed bar. Individually styled bedrooms with tea-making facilities are cosy and comfortable; two have shower rooms, the others shower cubicles. Good breakfasts. No under-14s overnight. Patio.

## Dorchester *(B & B)* — *Exhibition Hotel*

London Road · *Dorset* · Map 8 D3
Dorchester (0305) 63160

*Brewery* Eldridge Pope
*Landlords* Mr & Mrs A. C. Ripley

**BEDROOMS 5 Grade 2 £C** (No dogs)
Eldridge Pope Dorchester Bitter, 1880 Ale, Dorset IPA; Faust; Taunton cider. *Real ale*

A friendly, down-to-earth pub on Dorchester's busy main street, with a swinging sign depicting Crystal Palace at the time of the Great Exhibition. Darts and bar billiards are popular pastimes in the simple, cheerful bar, a favourite local meeting place. Overnight accommodation comprises five bright, airy bedrooms (all with tea-makers), which share a well-equipped bathroom with shower. Patio.

## Dorchester *(B & B)* — *King's Arms*

30 High East Street · *Dorset* · Map 8 D3
Dorchester (0305) 65353

*Brewery* Devenish
*Landlord* Mr Robin Charlton

**BEDROOMS 27 Grade 1 £A+**
Devenish Wessex Best Bitter, Ordinary Bitter; John Grove's Weymouth Bitter; Guinness; Grünhalle. *Real ale*

The old and the new blend happily in this popular high-street inn, where Thomas Hardy set some scenes in *The Mayor of Casterbridge.* The hall and lofty lounge afford elegant glimpses of the past, while the bedrooms (apart from two with four-posters) have practical modern appeal. All have TVs, telephones and tea-makers, the majority spacious private bathrooms. There are two relaxing bars. **Family pub**

## Dorchester-on-Thames *(Food, B & B)* — *George Hotel*

High Street · *Oxfordshire* · Map 6 A3
Oxford (0865) 340404

*Free House*
*Landlord* Mr Brian Griffin
**BEDROOMS 16 Grade 1 £A**
Ploughman's lunch £1.50 Prawn & pineapple salad £2.25 (Last order 9.45pm)
Brakspear's Bitter; Morland's Best Bitter; Wadworth's 6X; Guinness; Heineken; Stella Artois. *Real ale*

Although now boasting the best of 20th-century comforts, this medieval hostelry has lost none of its original charm. Most bedrooms are in fine traditional style, compact ones in the annexe being more modern. All have tea-makers, TVs, telephones, and most have good bathrooms. Simple, enjoyable bar snacks consist of pâté, salads, sandwiches, plus a daily special like gammon and peach or kidneys Turbigo. **Family pub**

## Dorking *(Food, B & B)* — *Pilgrim*

Station Road · *Surrey* · Map 6 B3
Dorking (0306) 889951

*Brewery* Friary Meux
*Landlord* Mr A. Stappard
**BEDROOMS 4 Grade 2 £C** (No dogs)
Ham omelette soufflé £1.30 Steak & kidney pie £2.25 (Last order 9.45pm. No bar food Sun eve)
Ind Coope Burton Ale; Friary Meux Bitter; Romford John Bull Bitter; Guinness; Löwenbräu; Skol; cider. *Real ale*

This handsome old coaching inn on the outskirts of town has two busy bars and a pleasant beer garden. The food is a major feature with dishes like ham omelette soufflé showing real skill and flair. Pies, both savoury and sweet, are popular orders, along with sandwiches (the only Sunday lunchtime choice) and salads. Well-carpeted bedrooms, all with colour TVs and washbasins, share a bathroom. Accommodation closed Christmas–New Year.

## Downside *(Food)* — *Cricketers*

Near Cobham · *Surrey* · Map 6 B3
Cobham (0932) 62105

*Brewery* Watneys
*Landlords* Brian & Wendy Luxford

Beef salad £2.90 Calf's liver £2.15 (Last order 10.30pm)
Watneys Special; Combes Bitter; Webster's Yorkshire Bitter; Guinness; Carlsberg; Foster's. *Real ale*

Sixteenth-century with harmonious later additions, this characterful, white-painted inn stands in a little lane on the edge of the common. The rustic beamed bar is the scene of a popular lunchtime buffet featuring cold meats, seafood and simple salads. Other home-made dishes include sandwiches, ploughman's and specials like pork chops or a good meaty oxtail casserole. Less evening choice. Garden.

**Family pub**

## Dragons Green — *George & Dragon*

Set in peaceful Sussex countryside, this delightful 17th-century pub is small, cosy and full of old-world charm. It's looked after with great pride by landlord John Jenner, and everything gleams in the low-beamed bar. The local beer is excellent, and in summer you can enjoy it in the garden under the shade of the fruit trees.

Near Shipley, Horsham · *West Sussex* · Map 6 B4
Coolham (040 387) 320
*Brewery* King & Barnes *Landlord* Mr John Jenner
King & Barnes Sussex Bitter, Festive, Old Ale; Guinness; Holsten; Carling Black Label. *Real ale*

## Driffield *(Food, B & B)* — *Bell Hotel*

Market Place · *Humberside* · Map 4 D2
Driffield (0377) 46661

*Free House*
*Landlords* Mr & Mrs Riggs
**BEDROOMS 14 Grade 1 £A** (No dogs)
Beef in beer £1.75 Steak & kidney pie £2.25 (Last order 9.30pm)
North Country Old Traditional, Mild; Theakston's Old Peculier; Guinness; Harp; cider. *Real ale*

A lovely glass-covered courtyard is a feature of this welcoming old coaching inn which also offers tasty food and comfortable accommodation. Sandwiches and salads are supplemented by farmhouse soup and hot specials like beef in beer, fried haddock and a roast for Sunday lunch. Excellent bedrooms have TVs, trouser presses, hairdryers and carpeted private bathrooms. No under-12s overnight.

**Family pub**

## Dunchurch *(B & B)* — *Dun Cow Hotel*

The Green · *Warwickshire* · Map 5 A2
Rugby (0788) 810233

*Free House*
*Landlord* Bruno Carouche

**BEDROOMS 24 Grade 1 £A** (No dogs)
Bass; Mitchells & Butlers Brew XI, Springfield Bitter; Highgate Mild; Guinness; Carling Black Label; Taunton cider. *Real ale*

Once the haunt of Dick Turpin, this fine old coaching inn boasts many period features, including heavy beams, oak panelling and handsome antiques. The traditionally furnished bedrooms are warm and comfortable, those in the annexe being particularly roomy. All have TVs and radios, and most are provided with private facilities. There are two mellow bars and a pleasant courtyard.

**Family pub**

## Duns Tew *(Food)* — *White Horse Inn*

Near Oxford · *Oxfordshire* · Map 5 A2
Steeple Aston (0869) 40272

*Free House*
*Landlords* Mr & Mrs Peter Smith
Avocado with prawn mayonnaise & salad £1.95 Whitebait with salad or chips £1.75 (No bar food eves)
Courage Directors Bitter, Mild; John Smith's Bitter; Guinness; Hofmeister; Taunton cider. *Real ale*

Exposed stone walls and sloping floors give the bar plenty of character at this quaint old pub in the centre of the village. Landlord Peter Smith's enjoyable lunchtime snacks range from soup and freshly cut sandwiches to pâté, quiche lorraine and grilled trout or steak. Chocolate mousse and an excellent crème brûlée are among the delicious sweets. Traditional roast on Sunday. Closed Monday. **Family pub**

## Durham *(Food)* — *Traveller's Rest*

72 Claypath · *Co. Durham* · Map 4 C1
Durham (0385) 65370

*Free House*
*Landlord* Mr J. Brown

Ham & pease pudding sandwich 50p Beef & mushroom pie £1.65 (Last order 10pm)
Joshua Tetley's Bitter, Falstaff Best; Archibald Arrol's 70/-; Skol; Löwenbräu; cider. *Real ale*

Honest, wholesome bar snacks are advertised on a blackboard menu at this unpretentious pub in the city centre. Savoury pies – leek and ham, ever-popular beef and mushroom – cater admirably for hearty appetites, and there's a good range of sandwiches as well as filling soup and a summer cold buffet. The fruit crumble of the day is a nice way to round off a meal.
**Family pub**

## Duxford *(Food)* — *John Barleycorn*

Moorfield Road · *Cambridgeshire* · Map 5 C2
Cambridge (0223) 832699

*Brewery* Greene King
*Landlords* Henry & Chris Sewell

Toasted sandwich 86p Grilled sirloin & salad £5.70 (Last order 10pm)
Greene King IPA, Abbot Ale, Mild; Guinness; Kronenbourg; Harp; Taunton cider. *Real ale*

Rustic bars with heavy beams and ancient farm implements displayed on exposed stone walls make a delightful setting for Christine Sewell's homely fare. You might start with soup or tasty chicken liver pâté, and go on to steak and kidney pie, chilli con carne or spicy Turkish lamb with apricots and nuts. There are also grills in the evening except Sunday.

## Eartham *(Food)* — *George Inn*

Near Chichester · *West Sussex* · Map 6 B4
Slindon (024 365) 340

*Free House*
*Landlord* Mr R. J. Colman
Loin of pork with prunes & apples £2.95
Leek & ham au gratin £1.95 (Last order 10pm)
Hall & Woodhouse Badger Best Bitter; Fuller's ESB; Harvey's Bitter; Gale's HSB; Guinness; Stella Artois; Heineken; cider. *Real ale*

There's no lack of choice on the bar menu of this popular, lively pub. Filled jacket potatoes are a perennial favourite. You can also get home-made soup, sandwiches, salads, steak, as well as hot dishes like curry, lasagne and even daily specials – perhaps chicken provençale or pork in cider. Finish with a slice of chocolate gâteau or apple pie. Garden.

## East Dean — *Tiger Inn*

This delightful whitewashed pub is part of a cluster of little flint cottages set around the green in a pretty village. It has a great deal of old-world charm, with old beams, mellow paintwork and a gleaming copper canopy over the fireplace. Rustic furniture, pastoral prints and an assortment of homely knick-knacks complete the cosy scene.

*East Sussex* · Map 6 C4
East Dean (032 15) 3209
*Brewery* Courage *Landlord* Mr James Conroy
Courage Directors Bitter, Best Bitter; Guinness; Hofmeister; Kronenbourg. *Real ale*

## East Dereham *(B & B)* — *King's Head Hotel*

42 Norwich Street · *Norfolk* · Map 5 D1
Dereham (0362) 3842

*Brewery* Norwich
*Landlords* Mr & Mrs R. Black

**BEDROOMS 15 Grade 1 £B**
Norwich Bitter; Ben Truman; Guinness; Carlsberg; Holsten; cider. *Real ale*

Maintenance and housekeeping both score high marks at the Blacks' smartly modernised 17th-century pub in the town centre. Overnight accommodation is excellent, rooms in the converted stable block being particularly desirable. Central heating, TVs and radios are standard throughout, and most rooms have up-to-date private facilities. A comfortably furnished bar overlooks the terrace and popular bowling green.

## East End *(Food)* — *Plough & Sail*

Paglesham, Near Rochford · *Essex* · Map 6 D3
Canewdon (037 06) 242

*Brewery* Watney Combe Reid
*Landlords* Oliver family

Prawn omelette £2.80 Cheesecake 95p (Last order 9pm)
Watneys IPA, Stag; Webster's Yorkshire Bitter; Guinness; Foster's; Carlsberg; cider. *Real ale*

With fields close by and the river Roach just down the lane, this popular old inn is aptly named. Two beamed bars with masses of gleaming copper and brass are the setting for the very good snacks, which feature local seafood including oysters, mussels and plaice. Steaks and chops for the red-blooded, plus sandwiches, salads, omelettes and delicious sweets. Well-equipped children's play area in the garden.

## East Haddon *(Food, B & B)* — *Red Lion*

Near Northampton · *Northamptonshire*
Map 5 B2
Northampton (0604) 770223

*Brewery* Wells
*Landlords* Mr & Mrs Kennedy
**BEDROOMS 6 Grade 1 £A** (No dogs)
Steak & kidney pie £3 Quiche with salad £2.75 (No bar food eves or Sun)
Wells Eagle Bitter, Noggin; Red Stripe. *Real ale*

Pretty gardens make this fine old stone pub particularly pleasant in summer, and the bar with its gleaming copper and brass is both elegant and cosy. Enjoyable lunch-time fare includes soup, pâte, salmon fish-cakes, home-cooked meats and excellent sweet and savoury pies. Overnight guests have six comfortably furnished bedrooms and a smart TV lounge.

## East Layton *(B & B)* — *Fox Hall Inn*

Near Richmond · *North Yorkshire* · Map 4 C2
Darlington (0325) 718262

*Free House*
*Landlord* Mr John Jackson

**BEDROOMS 14 Grade 2 £C**
Theakston's Best Bitter, Old Peculier; John Smith's Bitter; Guinness; Carlsberg Hof; cider.

Standing on the A66 just outside the village, this old stone inn has been nicely modernised by landlord John Jackson. Homely bedrooms feature some fine Victorian wardrobes, and eight rooms have their own neat bath or shower rooms. The bar with its dark panelling and flagstone floor is a relaxing place for a drink.
**Family pub**

## Eastbourne *(Food)* — *Beachy Head Hotel*

Beachy Head · *East Sussex* · Map 6 C4
Eastbourne (0323) 28060

*Brewery* Charrington
*Landlords* Phyllis & David Coe

Ploughman's £1.40 Carvery £4.95 (No bar food eves)
Bass IPA; Carling Black Label; Toby Bitter; Stones Bitter; Guinness; Tennent's Lager; cider. *Real ale*

The surroundings are pleasant and the views spectacular at this large, brick-built pub on top of Beachy Head. A two-course meal at the lunchtime carvery offers decent roast meats (beef, leg of pork, best end of lamb) with well-cooked vegetables, and a simple sweet to follow. There's also a cold buffet in summer, plus sandwiches and ploughman's for a lighter bite. **Family pub**

## Eastergate *(Food)* — *Wilkes Head*

Near Chichester · *West Sussex* · Map 6 B4
Eastergate (024 368) 3380

*Brewery* Friary Meux
*Landlords* Brian & Kathy Goldsmith

Burger £1.90 Moussaka £2 (Last order 10.30pm. No bar food Sun eve)
Friary Meux Bitter, Mild; Ind Coope Burton Ale; Guinness; Löwenbräu; Skol; cider. *Real ale*

The homely bar of this modest little pub between the downs and the sea provides a cosy setting for Kathy Goldsmith's simple, wholesome fare. Dishes on her blackboard menu range from country-style pâté and jumbo sausages to fisherman's pie, casseroles and splendid moussaka. Sweets like rum and raisin truffle pudding or apple and blackberry pie make the perfect finish. Less choice Sunday lunch. Garden.

## Easthorpe — *House Without a Name*

Without a name it may be, but this cottagy village pub dating from the 16th century is certainly not without a good deal of rustic charm. A large inglenook fireplace separates the bar areas, two snug rooms with heavy beams, velvet-covered banquettes and a variety of old photographs on the walls. **Family pub**

Near Kelvedon, Colchester · *Essex* · Map 5 C2
Colchester (0206) 210455
*Free House* *Landlord* Mr B. Medcalf
Mauldon's Bitter; Adnams Bitter; Greene King IPA, Abbot Ale; Guinness; Foster's; Carlsberg; cider. *Real ale*

## Eastling *(Food, B & B)* — *Carpenter's Arms*

Near Faversham · *Kent* · Map 6 D3
Eastling (079 589) 234

*Brewery* Shepherd Neame
*Landlord* Mrs M. J. Wright
**BEDROOMS 2 Grade 2 £C**
Carpenter's lunch £1.75 Beef in ale £3.95 (Last order 10pm)
Shepherd Neame Bitter, Mild, Stock Ale (winter only), Abbey; Hurlimann Sternbräu; Taunton cider. *Real ale*

Winding lanes lead through Kentish orchards to this charming old village pub, a delightful spot for a tasty bar meal. Fresh mushroom or tomato salad makes a simple, appetising starter, perfect before a hearty beef casserole, pan-fried trout or a plate of ham and eggs. Sandwiches for a lighter snack. Puddings include treacle tart and a splendid apple flan. Limited Sunday choice. Two simple bedrooms share a spacious bathroom.

## Easton *(Food)* — *White Horse*

Near Wickham Market · *Suffolk* · Map 5 D2
Wickham Market (0728) 746456

*Brewery* Tollemache & Cobbold
*Landlords* David & Sharon Grimwood
Fisherman's pie £2.50 Wild duck casserole £2.50 (Last order 9pm. No bar food Sun & Mon eves)
Tolly Cobbold Bitter, Mild, Old Strong (winter only); Guinness; Hansa; Taunton cider. *Real ale*

David Grimwood provides an enterprising choice of well-prepared food at this charming old village pub. Specials on the blackboard menu might range from mussels in garlic butter to moussaka, seasonal game and an excellent fisherman's pie. You could also choose soup or a French bread sandwich, and perhaps a slice of home-made gâteau for dessert. Garden.

## Edge *(Food)* — *Edgemoor Inn*

Near Stroud · *Gloucestershire* · Map 7 D2
Painswick (0452) 813576

*Free House*
*Landlords* Mr & Mrs M. E. H. Smith

Steak & kidney pie £2.75 Sherry trifle 85p (Last order 10pm. No bar food Sun eve)
Flowers Original, IPA, Best Bitter; West Country Pale Ale; Younger's Tartan; Worthington Best Bitter; Guinness; cider.

There are splendid views from the terrace of this large roadside inn, and Mrs Smith's enjoyable food adds to its popularity. If you're hungry, go for the special lunch, consisting of a daily special followed by home-made fruit pie – excellent value at £2.35. Otherwise, you could choose soup, pâté, an omelette or a grill. Salads and sandwiches, too, and simple sweets to finish.

## Eggesford *(Food)* — *Fox & Hounds Hotel*

Near Chulmleigh · *Devon* · Map 8 C3
Chulmleigh (0769) 80345

*Free House*
*Landlord* Mr A. Chappell

Rump steak with vegetables £5.20 Fresh local salmon £6.20 (Last order 9.30pm)
Usher's Best Bitter, Triple Crown; Ben Truman; Carlsberg; Holsten; cider. *Real ale*

The bill of fare is long and varied at this pleasant old fishing pub, whose rustic bar features prints of the Devon hunts. Tender, well-flavoured steaks are a speciality, and other popular choices range from sandwiches and richly flavoured game soup to savoury pies and sautéed chicken. Nice sweets too. Closed all Monday and Tuesday lunchtime in winter. Garden.

**Family pub**

## Eggleston *(Food)* — *Three Tuns Inn*

Near Barnard Castle · *Co. Durham* · Map 4 C2
Teesdale (0833) 50289

*Free House*
*Landlords* James & Christine Dykes

Cottage pie £1.75 8oz. sirloin steak £4.75 (Last order 9.45pm. No bar food Sun eve)
Whitbread Trophy; Guinness; Heineken; cider.

James and Christine Dykes are welcoming landlords at this appealing village pub where guests are sure of a nourishing, tasty snack. There's always a home-made soup, and you can go on to wholesome cottage pie, duck with orange sauce or a beefburger and egg. Ploughman's and salads, too, and tempting sweets like fresh fruit salad or treacle lick. The large garden is popular in summer. Closed Monday. **Family pub**

## Elkstone *(Food)* — *Highwayman*

Near Cheltenham · *Gloucestershire* · Map 7 D2
Miserden (028 582) 221

*Brewery* Arkell
*Landlords* David & Heather Bucher

Steak & mushroom pie (winter only) £2.95 Lasagne £2.50 (Last order 10.15pm)
Arkell's BBB; BB, Kingsdown Ale; Guinness; 1843 Premium Lager. *Real ale*

A splendidly restored black and yellow stagecoach stands in the car park of this very popular pub, which caters admirably for all ages. Families are very much in evidence in the beamed bars, tucking into snacks that range from bumper toasted sandwiches and filled potatoes to jumbo sausages and a spicy chilli con carne. Sweets include fruit crumbles and treacle tart. Garden. **Family pub**

## Elslack *(Food)* — *Tempest Arms*

Near Skipton · *North Yorkshire* · Map 4 C3
Earby (0282) 842450

*Free House*
*Landlord* Francis Pierre Boulongne

Turkey pie & chips £1.20 Fillets of sole in white wine £2 (Last order 10pm)
Thwaites Bitter, Mild; Webster's Green Label; Guinness; Carlsberg Hof; Harp; Taunton cider. *Real ale*

In a peaceful location near the junction of the A56 and A59, this comfortable pub is well worth a visit for its excellent bar fare. Soup of the day could be game or flavoursome celery and Stilton, and other choices include potted shrimps, filled baked potatoes, steak sandwiches and lunchtime specials like baked ham in Madeira. Also available at lunchtime is a help-yourself salad bar. Garden. **Family pub**

## Elsted *(Food)* — *Three Horseshoes*

Near Midhurst · *West Sussex* · Map 6 B4
Harting (073 085) 746

*Free House*
*Landlord* Benjamin Heath

Peppered chicken £4.25 Courgette & smoked haddock pie £2.95 (Last order 10pm)
Fuller's London Pride; Ballard's Wassail; Everards Tiger; Guinness; Harp; Foster's; cider. *Real ale*

A fine selection of real ales and enjoyable bar food add to the appeal of this delightfully beamed and cosy pub. Filled jacket potatoes and various ploughman's are popular choices, and for a heartier meal you could have tasty rabbit in red wine, peppered chicken, lasagne or moussaka. Sweets like lemon soufflé or treacle tart are equally tempting. Garden.

## Elsworth *(Food)* — *George & Dragon*

41 Boxworth Rd · *Cambridgeshire* · Map 5 C2
Elsworth (095 47) 236

*Brewery* Tollemache & Cobbold
*Landlords* Mr & Mrs M. Brownlie

Steak & kidney pie £2.75 Lasagne & salad £2.45 (Last order 10pm)
Tolly Cobbold Original Bitter, Bitter, Old Strong (winter only); Worthington 'E'; Guinness; Hansa; Taunton cider. *Real ale*

Heavy beams, huge fireplaces and gleaming copperware lend a great deal of charm to this old village pub. Home-made soup, open sandwiches, salads and steaks are all featured on the menu, along with varied daily specials like fresh fish, pizza, moussaka and Southern fried chicken. Homely, tempting sweets include a delicious apple pie. **Family pub**

## Elterwater *(B & B)* — *Britannia Inn*

Near Ambleside · *Cumbria* · Map 3 B2
Langdale (096 67) 210

*Free House*
*Landlords* Margaret & David Fry

**BEDROOMS 10 Grade 2 £B**
Tetley's Bitter; Bass; Hartley's Bitter; Guinness; Carling Black Label; cider. *Real ale*

Adjoining the village green, this welcoming inn with its cosy little beamed bar is as popular with locals as it is with Lakeland walkers. Bedrooms are cheerfully furnished in a mixture of old and new styles, and there's a comfortable lounge in which to browse through the good supply of books. The two bathrooms are well kept. Super breakfasts. Accommodation closed Christmas week. **Family pub**

## Eltisley *(B & B)* — *Leeds Arms*

The Green · *Cambridgeshire* · Map 5 C2
Croxton (048 087) 283

*Free House*
*Landlords* Mr & Mrs G. W. Cottrell

**BEDROOMS 8 Grade 1 £B** (No dogs)
Greene King IPA; Stones Bitter; Whitbread Best Mild; Paine's St Neots Bitter; Guinness; Carlsberg; Harp.

Though altered and modernised over the years, this whitewashed 18th-century coaching house retains much period character, with old beams and an inglenook fireplace in the lounge bar. The bedrooms, in contrast, are in modern motel style, with laminated furniture, colour TVs, tea-makers and neat bath or shower rooms. Maintenance and housekeeping are commendable. There's a large garden with a children's play area.

## Empingham *(Food, B & B)* — *White Horse*

2 Main Street · *Leicestershire* · Map 5 B1
Empingham (078 086) 221
*Brewery* John Smith
*Landlord* Mr Robert Reid
**BEDROOMS 3 Grade 2 £B**
Baked sugared ham with parsley sauce £2.45 Steak, kidney & mushroom pie & vegetables £3.25 (Last order 10pm)
Courage Best Bitter; John Smith's Bitter; Guinness; Hofmeister; John Smith's lager; Taunton cider. *Real ale*

Good bar food and comfortable accommodation make this low-built inn a useful stopping place. A comprehensive menu ranges from sandwiches to lasagne, curries, steak and kidney pie and baked ham with parsley sauce; there's also a cold buffet at lunchtime. Three large double bedrooms all have TVs and share a shower room and bathroom. Garden.
**Family pub**

## Enfield *(Food)* — *Robin Hood*

Botany Bay, The Ridgeway · *Middlesex*
Map 6 C3
01-363 3781

*Brewery* McMullen
*Landlords* John & Pearl Heard

Shepherd's pie £2.50 Ploughman's lunch £1.25
(Last order 10.30pm)
McMullen's AK Mild, Country Bitter; Guinness; Steingold.

The lovely garden at the back of this pub just beyond the outer reaches of London is a popular place to enjoy a pint and a tasty bite. Mornings and evenings, there is a wide choice of plain and toasted sandwiches, along with soup, hot pasties and pizzas. At lunchtime (Mon–Sat) there's also a tempting cold buffet of roast joints and plenteously served salads.

## Enstone *(Food)* — *Harrow Inn*

Main Road · *Oxfordshire* · Map 5 A2
Enstone (060 872) 366

*Brewery* Morrell's
*Landlord* Mr R. E. Parker

Home-made soup 40p Beef casserole £2.50
(Last order 10pm)
Morrell's Varsity, Bitter, Mild; Guinness; Kronenbourg; Harp; Taunton cider. *Real ale*

Food's the name of the game at this unpretentious little pub, where the lunchtime focus is an excellent spread of cold meats, robustly flavoured pâté, well-baked quiches and good fresh salads. This buffet is supplemented by hot specials – lasagne, cannelloni, beef casserole – while in the evening the scene shifts to local trout, steaks, salads and the like. The dining area in the stone-walled lounge bar is attractively traditional in style. Beer garden.

## Eskdale *(Food, B & B)* — *Bower House Inn*

Near Holmbrook · *Cumbria* · Map 3 B2
Eskdale (094 03) 244

*Free House*
*Landlords* Smith family
**BEDROOMS 14 Grade 2 £B**
Fillet steak £5.50 Gammon, eggs & chips £2.50
(Last order 9pm)
Hartley's Best Bitter; Younger's Best Bitter; Guinness; Carlsberg; Slalom; cider. *Real ale*

Peacefully situated in beautiful Eskdale, this fine old inn is a pleasant base for tourists. A good range of enjoyable food is served in the beamed bar, from soup and pâté to salads, steaks and seafood risotto. Six simply furnished bedrooms are in the original building, the rest (with private bath and TV) in the modern annexe. All have tea-makers. Garden.

## Eton *(B & B)* — *Christopher Hotel*

110 High Street, Near Windsor · *Berkshire* · Map 6 B3
Windsor (075 35) 52359

*Free House*
*Landlords* Ron & Barbara France

**BEDROOMS 21 Grade 1 £B**
Brakspear's Bitter; Younger's Tartan; John Smith's Bitter; Guinness; Kronenbourg; Taunton cider. *Real ale*

Well - appointed chalet - style bedrooms provide excellent overnight accommodation at this former coaching inn. Colour televisions, trouser presses and hairdryers are standard equipment, along with small fridges and the ingredients for producing continental breakfast. All have carpeted shower rooms, many with bidets. There are two well-patronised bars, one with a Victorian feel, the other more contemporary in style. Patio.

## Etton *(Food)* — *Golden Pheasant*

Near Peterborough · *Cambridgeshire*
Map 5 B1
Peterborough (0733) 252387
*Free House*
*Landlords* Mr & Mrs B. Loasby
Catalan swordfish £3.15 Niw goo yok £2.65 (Last order 10pm. No bar food Sun eve)
Ruddle's County; Greene King IPA; Adnams Southwold Bitter; Kronenbourg; Taunton cider. *Real ale*

Smoked salmon mousse, swordfish Catalan, Lancashire hot pot and chicken in cider are among the tasty, enterprising dishes which help to make this converted Georgian mansion so popular. There's also an appetising cold buffet for summer lunches, as well as a large garden in which to enjoy it all. Good sweets and cheeses, too. Closed Monday.

## Evercreech Junction *(Food)* — *Natterjack*

Near Shepton Mallet · *Somerset* · Map 8 D3
Ditcheat (074 986) 253

*Free House*
*Landlords* Mr & Mrs G. Hickley

Beef in red wine £2.80 Fresh fruit Pavlova 90p (Last order 10pm)
Butcombe Bitter; Courage Best Bitter; Webster's Yorkshire Bitter; Guinness; Skol; Kronenbourg; Löwenbräu; cider. *Real ale*

Situated on the A371 between Shepton Mallet and Castle Cary, this stone pub with colourful window boxes is well worth a stop. June Hickley serves delicious quiches and a superb seafood platter, as well as blackboard specials like beef in red wine or ham and mushroom pizza. Mouthwatering sweets might include raspberry cheesecake or a fresh fruit Pavlova. Sandwiches and salads, too. Garden.

## Ewhurst *(Food)* — *Windmill Inn*

Pitch Hill, Near Cranleigh · *Surrey* · Map 6 B3
Cranleigh (0483) 277566

*Free House*
*Landlords* Dutch & Ann Holland

Salmon & prawn kedgeree £2.50 Chicken casserole £3.75 (Last order 10pm)
King & Barnes Sussex Bitter; Whitbread Trophy; Youngs Special; Guinness; Carlsberg; Löwenbräu; cider. *Real ale*

Take the Shere road out of Ewhurst to find Dutch and Ann Holland's neat pub, where in summer you can sit in the garden and admire the hilltop view. Appetising snacks range from sandwiches and salads to hot dishes like chicken casserole or salmon and prawn kedgeree. Depending on the season, you might also get delicious fresh crab and lobster, or perhaps a pheasant casserole.

## Ewhurst Green *(B & B)* — *White Dog Inn*

Near Robertsbridge · *East Sussex* · Map 6 C4
Staplecross (058 083) 264

*Free House*
*Landlord* Tim Knowland

**BEDROOMS 6 Grade 2 £B** (No dogs)
Harvey's Bitter; Whitbread Best Bitter; Guinness; Heineken; Stella Artois; cider. *Real ale*

Residents will find plenty to amuse them at this welcoming village pub. There's a colour TV in the comfortable lounge, while more active guests can make use of the swimming pool or the full-size snooker table. Bedrooms – three with their own bathrooms – have simple modern furniture and tea-makers, plus flowers, fresh fruit and plenty of magazines. No children under ten overnight. **Family pub**

## Exford *(Food)* — *Crown Hotel*

Near Minehead · *Somerset* · Map 8 C3
Exford (064 383) 554

*Brewery* Usher
*Landlords* J. E. & M. E. Millward

Local trout £3.40 Spaghetti bolognese £1.50 (Last order 10pm)
Usher's Founders Ale, Country Bitter, Triple Crown; Carlsberg; Taunton cider. *Real ale*

Popular with tourists and the hunting fraternity, this delightful 17th-century coaching inn stands opposite the village green. In the rustic pine-panelled bar the menu offers a selection of tasty home-produced fare: local trout is a regular favourite, and other choices include lasagne, spaghetti bolognese and chilli con carne. Garden. *For accommodation see Egon Ronay's Lucas Hotel & Restaurant Guide 1985.* **Family pub**

## Eyam *(Food, B & B)* — *Miners Arms*

Water Lane · *Derbyshire* · Map 4 C3
Hope Valley (0433) 30853

*Free House*
*Landlords* Mr & Mrs P. B. Cooke

**BEDROOMS 4 Grade 2 £C** (No dogs)
Ocean salad £1.85 Brunch menu of the day £3.75 (No bar food eves)
Ward's Sheffield Bitter; Stones Bitter; Vaux Mild; Carling Black Label. *Real ale*

Run for more than two decades by jovial Peter Cooke, this agreeable old pub is known for its tasty lunchtime fare. Snacks include soup and sandwiches, salads, fresh fish and good roast beef, and there's a daily-changing three-course brunch. For overnight guests (no children) there are four well-kept bedrooms that share the family bathroom. Pub closed Monday lunchtime except Bank Holidays. Patio.

## Eyam *(B & B)* — *Rose & Crown*

Main Road, Near Sheffield · *Derbyshire*
Map 4 C3
Hope Valley (0433) 30858

*Free House*
*Landlords* Brian & Val Wharton

**BEDROOMS 3 Grade 2 £C** (No dogs)
Tetley's Bitter; Stones Bitter; Bass Mild; Skol; Carling Black Label; cider. *Real ale*

Brian and Val Wharton are the friendly hosts at this neat little stone pub in a famous Peak District village. Pleasantly furnished bedrooms with shower cubicles, TVs and tea-makers offer homely overnight accommodation, and guests can look forward to a hearty English breakfast. There's a cosy bar with plush red banquettes, an intimate snug and a games room. Patio.

## Fairbourne Heath *(Food)* — *Pepper Box*

Near Ulcombe · *Kent* · Map 6 C3
Maidstone (0622) 842558

*Brewery* Shepherd Neame
*Landlords* Betty & Jack Wood

Fish specials £1.95 Bobotie with saffron rice £1.95 (Last order 10pm)
Shepherd Neame Masterbrew, Bitter; Hurlimann Sternbräu. *Real ale*

The speciality of this friendly little pub off the Ulcombe–Lenham road is superb fresh fish from Dungeness. Betty Wood's menu might offer monkfish provençale or plaice with beautifully crisp chips. Alternative choices include home-made soup, sandwiches, casseroles and excellent locally made herb sausages known as Kent Korkers. In summer, the rose garden is an additional attraction. **Family pub**

## Fairford *(B & B)* — *Bull Hotel*

Market Place · *Gloucestershire* · Map 6 A3
Cirencester (0285) 712535

*Brewery* Arkells
*Landlord* Mrs C. E. Smith

**BEDROOMS 18 Grade 1 £A**
Arkell's BBB, Kingsdown Ale, John Arkell's Bitter, 1843 Lager; Guinness; Carling Black Label. *Real ale*

An attractive stone inn right on the market place. The oldest part (15th century) used to be a monk's chantry, the rest a wool market, and the atmosphere in the beamed bar and well-furnished residents' lounge is warm and traditional. Bedrooms of various shapes and sizes are pleasant and comfortable, with black beams, pretty fabrics, darkwood fitted units and televisions. Most have modern private facilities. Patio.
**Family pub**

## Faringdon *(Food, B & B)* — *Bell Hotel*

Market Place · *Oxfordshire* · Map 6 A3
Faringdon (0367) 20534

*Brewery* Wadworth
*Landlord* Mr W. Dreyer

**BEDROOMS 11 Grade 1 £B**
Lancashire hot pot £2.15 Watercress soup 90p (Last order 9.30pm)
Wadworth's 6X, Farmer's Glory, Old Timer (winter); Guinness; Harp. *Real ale*

Bar snacks are served in delightfully traditional surroundings at this old coaching inn. The daily special – perhaps cottage pie or tasty Lancashire hot pot – is a popular choice, and other goodies range from delicious cream of watercress soup to French bread sandwiches, plated salads and prawn pancakes. Bedrooms are attractively decorated. Seven have TVs and private facilities, and there's a pleasant lounge with TV. **Family pub**

## Farnham *(Food)* — *Spotted Cow*

3 Bourne Grove · *Surrey* · Map 6 B3
Farnham (0252) 726541

*Brewery* Courage
*Landlords* Mr & Mrs B. R. Soulsby

Game pie salad £2.50 Lasagne & salad £2 (Last order 10pm)
Courage Best Bitter, Directors Bitter, JC; Guinness; Hofmeister; Kronenbourg; Taunton cider. *Real ale*

A large beer garden surrounded by trees and a special children's room make this pub a popular spot with families. Enjoyable snacks served in the bar include salads and ploughman's, as well as grills and other hot dishes like chicken and chips, lasagne and tasty moussaka. The pub lies just south of Farnham off the Tilford road. **Family pub**

## Faugh *(Food)* — *String of Horses Inn*

Heads Hook · *Cumbria* · Map 3 B1
Hayton (022870) 297

*Free House*
*Landlords* Mr & Mrs Eric Tasker

Mexican chicken £2.95 Cold table £3.75 (Last order 10.15pm)
Theakstone's Best Bitter, Old Peculier; John Smith's Bitter; Younger's Tartan; Guinness; Carlsberg; Holt. *Real ale*

Open fires and handsome oak furniture create a warm, traditional atmosphere in this fine old village inn. The cold table, with excellent cooked meats, salmon and salads, is a lunchtime favourite and hot dishes include Cumberland sausage, chicken curry and grilled lamb cutlets. Very nice chocolate gâteau to finish. Patio. *For accommodation see Egon Ronay's Lucas Hotel & Restaurant Guide 1985.* **Family pub**

## Fawley *(Food)* ★ *Walnut Tree*

Near Henley-on-Thames, Oxfordshire
*Buckinghamshire* · Map 6 B3
Turville Heath (049 163) 360

*Brewery* Brakspear
*Landlords* Mr & Mrs F. Harding
Chicken suprême Walnut Tree £4.95 Scallops baked in cream & herbs £5.50 (Last order 9.55pm)
Brakspear's Mild, Ordinary, Special Bitter; Stella Artois; Heineken. *Real ale*

Unusually imaginative and skilfully prepared food brings the crowds flocking to this modern red-brick pub down a narrow lane. Regular offerings include deep-fried squid and superb hamburgers, and there are also blackboard specials like quails in white grape sauce or scallops baked in cream. Try the delicious treacle tart with whole walnuts for dessert. Garden and terrace. **Family pub**

## Felixstowe *(B & B)* *Fludyer Arms Hotel*

Undercliff Road East · *Suffolk* · Map 5 D2
Felixstowe (0394) 283279

*Brewery* Tollemache & Cobbold
*Landlord* Mr John Nash

**BEDROOMS 10 Grade 2 £C**
Tolly Cobbold Bitter, Original; Guinness; Hansa; cider. *Real ale*

Splendid sea views are a great asset of this Edwardian pub right on the front. Spacious, traditionally furnished bedrooms are well kept and all have TVs and tea-makers. They share two large, old-fashioned bathrooms. Guests can relax in the smart modern lounge or in the public bar with its little patio area. **Family pub**

## Felixstowe *(Food, B & B)* *Ordnance Hotel*

1 Undercliff Road West · *Suffolk* · Map 5 D2
Felixstowe (0394) 273427

*Brewery* Tollemache & Cobbold
*Landlords* Mr & Mrs D. C. Yeo
**BEDROOMS 11 Grade 1 £B** (No dogs)
Chilli con carne £1.45 Beef bobotie £3.25 (Last order 10.30pm. No bar food Sun eve)
Tolly Cobbold Original, Bitter, Mild, Old Strong (winter only); Guinness; Harp; Hansa. *Real ale*

The Yeo family preside over this comfortable haven offering friendly, efficient service, excellent overnight accommodation and very enjoyable food. Spacious bedrooms with period furnishings have TVs, tea-makers and direct-dial phones. Lunchtime bar fare is carefully prepared and nicely presented, from simple vegetable soup or a sandwich to savoury pancakes and a tasty turkey curry. Evening snacks can be obtained in YoYo's Bistro.

## Fen Drayton *(Food)* *Three Tuns*

High Street · *Cambridgeshire* · Map 5 C2
Swavesey (0954) 30242

*Brewery* Greene King
*Landlords* Mr & Mrs D. Threadgold

Sweet & sour pork with rice £1.85 Lasagne with chips & rice £1.85 (Last order 10pm. No bar food Sun eve)
Greene King IPA, Abbot Ale, Mild; Guinness; Kronenbourg; Harp; cider. *Real ale*

Beams, inglenook fireplaces and an old baker's oven make this 15th-century thatched pub a delightfully cosy place for a drink and a snack. Enjoyable home-made dishes on the menu might include shepherd's pie, mushroom fritters, sweet and sour pork and chicken curry. Grills, salads and sandwiches are other choices, with perhaps a lemon meringue pie for dessert. Garden.

## Fenay Bridge *(Food)* — *Star*

1 Penistone Road, Near Huddersfield
*West Yorkshire* · Map 4 C3
Huddersfield (0484) 602049

*Brewery* Bass
*Landlords* Mr & Mrs Robert G. Lee

Businessman's lunch £4.75 Steak & kidney pie £2.75 (Last order 10pm)
Bass Extra Light, Dark Mild; Stones Bitter; Carling Black Label; Hemeling.

Bob Lee's enjoyable lunchtime fare lures crowds of visitors to this large stone pub by the side of the road. The choice ranges from salads and sandwiches to a hearty steak and kidney pie, grilled gammon and eggs, sirloin steak and beef curry. Gâteaux and pies from an impressive sweet trolley make a fine finish. Traditional set lunch on Sundays. Sandwiches only in the evening.

## Fenny Bentley *(Food, B & B)* — *Bentley Brook Inn*

Near Ashbourne · *Derbyshire* · Map 4 C4
Thorpe Cloud (033 529) 278

*Free House*
*Landlords* David & Jeanne Allingham

**BEDROOMS 8 Grade 1 & 2 £B**
Derbyshire hot pot £2.25 Beef & vegetable stew £2.25 (No bar food eves & Sun lunch)
Marston's Pedigree Bitter, Lager; Guinness; Carlsberg; cider. *Real ale*

Standing in well-kept grounds north of Ashbourne, this pleasant, half-timbered inn has delightful hosts in David and Jeanne Allingham. Lunchtime bar snacks include home-made soup, filled baps and ploughman's, plus robust hot dishes like liver and onions or Derbyshire lamb hot pot and a splendid trifle. Characterful bedrooms, three with private bath, have tea-makers and colour TVs. Garden.
**Family pub**

## Fiddleford *(B & B)* — *Fiddleford Inn*

Sturminster Newton · *Dorset* · Map 8 D3
Sturminster Newton (0258) 72489

*Free House*
*Landlords* Philip, Valerie & Joyce Wilson

**BEDROOMS 4 Grade 1 £C**
Fiddleford Ale; Wadworth's 6X; Gale's HSB; Holsten; Carlsberg; Taunton cider. *Real ale*

Philip Wilson keeps a really excellent selection of real ales at this attractive creeper-clad pub on the Sturminster Newton–Blandford road. There are two characterful bars – one with flagstones and exposed brickwork – and a garden with swings and boules. Prettily decorated bedrooms with a patchwork theme are kept in apple-pie order; one has its own private facilities, the others share two spotless public bathrooms.
**Family pub**

## Fifield *(Food, B & B)* — *Merrymouth Inn*

Stow Road · *Oxfordshire* · Map 5 A2
Shipton-under-Wychwood (0993) 830759

*Brewery* Donnington
*Landlord* Philip Waller

**BEDROOMS 3 Grade 2 £C**
Steak & Guinness pie £2.50 Fish hot pot £1.95 (Last order 10pm)
Donnington Best Bitter, SBA, 3X Mild; Carlsberg; Löwenbräu; cider. *Real ale*

Blackboard specials combine with the standard menu to provide a fine selection of tasty bar food at this ancient roadside inn. Salads, ploughman's platters and potato-topped fish hot pot are among the regular favourites, while dishes of the day could include anything from snails to roast lamb with sage and onion stuffing. Three homely bedrooms share a bright modern bathroom.
**Family pub**

## Fingest *(Food)* — *Chequers Inn*

Near Henley-on-Thames · *Buckinghamshire*
Map 6 B3
Turville Heath (049 163) 335

*Brewery* Brakspears
*Landlords* Bryan & Christine Heasman

Steak & kidney pie £2.95 Paté £1.50 (Last order 9.30pm)
Brakspear's Ordinary, Special, Old; Heineken. *Real ale*

This 12th-century hostelry stands in a large garden opposite the Norman church in a sleepy village. There are two bars, one featuring a buffet laden with succulent cold meats and well-dressed salads. Other items, listed on a blackboard, range from soup and quiche to cool-weather curries and steak and kidney pie. Vegetables are especially nice. **Family pub**

**Prices given are as at the time of our research and are comparative indications rather than firm quotes.**

## Fiskerton *(Food)* — *Bromley Arms*

Near Southwell · *Nottinghamshire* · Map 5 B1
Newark (0636) 830789

*Brewery* Hardys & Hansons
*Landlords* Mr & Mrs H. Taylor

Poacher's pie with chips & peas £2.10
Ploughman's lunch with chips £1.40
(Last order 10pm)
Hardys & Hansons Bitter, Mild; Guinness; Heineken; cider. *Real ale*

Boating enthusiasts favour this 200-year-old inn right beside the river. Harold Taylor presides over the bars, while his wife Sheila takes care of tasty lunchtime specials like poacher's pie, veal à la crème and delicious fruit pies. Evening and Sunday fare consists mainly of salads and well-filled sandwiches and ploughman's. The terrace is a delightful spot for summer drinking.

## Fittleworth *(B & B)* — *Swan*

Lower Street · *West Sussex* · Map 6 B4
Fittleworth (079 882) 429

*Owners* Gateway Hosts
*Landlord* Mr C. Rodriguez

**BEDROOMS 8 Grade 2 £B**
Tamplins Bitter; Webster's Yorkshire Bitter; Guinness; Foster's; Carlsberg; cider. *Real ale*

A fine collection of truncheons and bottle-openers adds extra interest to the beamed lounge bar of this charming old village inn. Comfortable bedrooms have simple, cottagy furnishings, and all are equipped with tea-makers. One room has a private bathroom, the rest shower cubicles, and there are also three public bathrooms. Guests have a small TV lounge. Garden.

**Family pub**

## Flamstead *(Food)* — *Three Blackbirds*

2 High Street · *Hertfordshire* · Map 5 B2
Luton (0582) 840330

*Brewery* Watneys
*Landlord* Mr Mike Byrne

Steak sandwich £1.75 Speciality sausages £1.40
Webster's Yorkshire Bitter; Combes Bitter; Ruddle's County; Hammerton's Porter; Guinness; cider. *Real ale*

Window boxes and hanging baskets make this red-brick pub not far from junction 9 of the M1 a cheerful sight in summer. Jumbo sausages in a variety of flavours (herb, apple, curry) top the bill among bar snacks, which also include well-filled sandwiches, ploughman's and tasty charcoal-grilled hamburgers. In summer, you can take your pick from the cold table. Garden.
**Family pub**

## Fonthill Bishop *(B & B)* — *Kings Arms*

Near Salisbury · *Wiltshire* · Map 8 D3
Hindon (074 789) 523

*Free House*
*Landlords* D. M. Reynolds & C. J. Nell

**BEDROOMS 3 Grade 2 £C**
Wadworth's 6X, IPA, Farmers Glory, Northgate Bitter; Younger's Newcastle Bitter; Guinness; Taunton cider. *Real ale*

Built in 1846 as an agricultural building, this spotless little roadside pub is run with great charm and efficiency by Mark and Hilary Reynolds. Spacious bedrooms with pretty floral wallpapers and matching curtains have neat white furniture and very comfortable beds, and the two public bathrooms are bright and modern. There's a cheerfully decorated bar and a tiny TV lounge. Garden. **Family pub**

## Ford *(B & B)* — *White Hart*

Near Chippenham · *Wiltshire* · Map 7 D2
Castle Combe (0249) 782213

*Free House*
*Landlords* Gardner family

**BEDROOMS 8 Grade 1 £A** (No dogs)
Wadworth's 6X; Archer's Village Bitter; Hall & Woodhouse Badger Bitter; Ruddles County; Fuller's ESB, London Pride; Taunton cider. *Real ale*

A terrace overlooking a trout stream and a swimming pool are among the attractions of this fine old country inn where a collection of armour adds extra interest to the beamed main bar. Bedrooms are most attractive, with pine furnishings and pretty fabrics. Six even have four-poster beds, and all boast tea-makers, TVs and carpeted private bathrooms. No children under three overnight. **Family pub**

## Forton *(B & B)* — *New Holly Hotel*

Near Preston · *Lancashire* · Map 3 B2
Forton (0524) 791568

*Brewery* Thwaites
*Landlords* Monica & Eric Turner

**BEDROOMS 5 Grade 2 £C**
Thwaites Bitter, Mild; Kronenbourg; Stein. *Real ale*

The atmosphere is pleasant and welcoming at this pink-washed roadside pub, which has a terrace where customers can take the summer sunshine. The bar is spacious and convivial, and for guests staying overnight there are five bedrooms with homely furnishings, tea-makers and shower cubicles. Morning brings a hearty traditional English breakfast. **Family pub**

## Forty Green — *Royal Standard of England*

This renowned 11th-century tavern owes its present name to Charles II, who sheltered here after the Battle of Worcester. The feeling of history is everywhere – blackened timbers, uneven floors, a fireplace from the house of Edmund Burke. Note, too, the lovely stained-glass created from the windows of blitzed London churches. **Family pub**

Beaconsfield · *Buckinghamshire* · Map 6 B3
Beaconsfield (049 46) 3382
*Free House* *Landlord* Mr Philip Eldridge
Marston's Pedigree, Owd Rodger; Samuel Smiths Old Brewery Bitter; Carlsberg; Foster's; cider. *Real ale*

## Fossebridge *(Food, B & B)* — *Fossebridge Inn*

Near Northleach · *Gloucestershire* · Map 5 A2
Fossebridge (028 572) 310
*Free House*
*Landlords* Mr & Mrs A. Prior
**BEDROOMS 10 Grades 1 & 2 £B**
(No dogs)
Steak & kidney pie £4.50 Treacle tart £1 (Last order 9.30pm)
Usher's Best Bitter, Founder's Ale; Eldridge Pope Dorchester Bitter; Carlsberg; Taunton cider. *Real ale*

Well-tried favourites ranging from soup and sandwiches to cottage pie and old-fashioned puddings are served in this fine old riverside inn. Bedrooms in the main (early Georgian) house are quite spacious, with antique furniture and smartly modernised bathrooms; those in the annexe are more functional in style. There's a comfortable TV lounge and a peaceful garden. No under-tens overnight. **Family pub**

## Fotheringhay *(Food)* — *Falcon Inn*

Near Peterborough, Cambridgeshire
*Northamptonshire · Map 5 B1*
*Cotterstock (083 26) 254*
*Free House*
*Landlords* Alan & Jill Stewart
Moussaka £2.70 Roast duckling with apple & rosemary stuffing £4 (Last order 9.45pm. No bar food Mon)
Greene King IPA, Abbot Ale; Elgood's Ordinary; Hereward Bitter; Litchborough; Guinness; Harp; cider. *Real ale*

Best known as the place where Mary Queen of Scots was last imprisoned, Fotheringhay is also noteworthy for this charming little stone pub whose tempting bar menu keeps it constantly busy (booking advisable). There's always a delicious home-made soup, and you could follow with a super pigeon or turkey pot pie, seasonal game or roast duckling. Leave room for one of the lovely sweets. Less choice weekend lunch-times. **Family pub**

## Fovant *(B & B)* — *Cross Keys Inn*

*Wiltshire* · Map 6 A4
Fovant (072 270) 284

*Free House*
*Landlord* Mrs P. Story

**BEDROOMS 4 Grade 2 £C**
Gibbs Mew Wiltshire Special, Traditional; Tisbury Local Bitter; Wadworth's 6X, Northgate; Carlsberg Hof; Heineken. *Real ale*

Travellers on the A30 will find a warm welcome at this fine old coaching inn halfway between Salisbury and Shaftesbury. Four simple, cottagy bedrooms provide good comfort and share a well-kept public bathroom. The beamed bar with its grandfather clock and sturdy leather armchairs is very relaxing, and there's also a cosy residents' lounge. Garden. **Family pub**

## Fowlmere *(Food)* ★ *Chequers Inn*

Near Royston · *Cambridgeshire* · Map 5 C2
Fowlmere (076 382) 369

*Brewery* Tollemache & Cobbold
*Landlord* Mr Norman Rushton

Chicken & marjoram soup £1.60 Terrine of wild rabbit £2.40 (Last order 10pm)
Tolly Cobbold Bitter, Original; Guinness; Hansa; Taunton cider. *Real ale*

Samuel Pepys, a regular former patron, would not be disappointed if he returned to this quaint old village pub today. Skilfully prepared dishes on an adventurous menu range from chicken and marjoram soup or superb champagne pâté to Cromer crab gratin, moules marinière, pork chop with mustard sauce and tender lamb with tomato and basil sauce. Some delicious sweets to follow. **Family pub**

## Fownhope *(Food, B & B)* *Green Man Inn*

Near Hereford · *Hereford & Worcester*
Map 7 D2
Fownhope (043 277) 243
*Free House*
*Landlords* Mr & Mrs R. F. Williams
**BEDROOMS 8 Grade 1 £B**
Steak & kidney pie £2.95 Steak sandwich £2.10 (Last order 10.30pm)
Hook Norton Best Bitter; Wadworth 6X; Samuel Smith's Old Brewery Bitter; Flower's Best Bitter; Guinness; cider. *Real ale*

Five centuries of history attach to this fine old inn, once a coaching house and petty sessions court. The beamed bar is a cosy setting for enjoying a variety of well-prepared snacks – sandwiches, salads and hot dishes like grilled trout and roast chicken. Bedrooms are bright and pleasant, with good carpets and tasteful furnishings. Planned improvements include additional bedrooms, along with private bathrooms and TVs throughout. Garden. **Family pub**

## Framfield *(Food)* *Barley Mow*

Eastbourne Road · *East Sussex* · Map 6 C4
Framfield (082 582) 234

*Brewery* Phoenix
*Landlords* Derek & Val Gilbert

Stilton ploughman's £1.35 Lasagne £2.50 (Last order 9.45pm. No bar food Mon eve)
Watney's Special; Webster's Yorkshire Bitter, King & Barnes Draught Festive; Usher's Triple Crown; Guinness; cider. *Real ale*

The Gilberts have built up a large following at their little whitewashed pub, Derek the friendliest of hosts and Val a very capable cook. Everything on the varied menu is fresh and tasty, from vegetable broth and succulent home-cooked ham to omelettes, pies and chilli con carne. Bubble and squeak is a treat not to miss, and there are some nice sweets. Garden. **Family pub**

## Framlingham *(Food)* *Crown & Anchor*

Church Street · *Suffolk* · Map 5 D2
Framlingham (0728) 723611

*Brewery* Tollemache & Cobbold
*Landlords* Mr & Mrs J. M. Benhassoune

Special of the day £1.60 Steak with garlic & oregano £4.80 (Last order 9.30pm)
Tolly Cobbold Mild, Bitter, Original; Hansa. *Real ale*

At lunchtime, the cosy bar of this attractive high street pub is crowded with customers seeking simple, tasty snacks like chicken liver pâté, sausage and onion pie, a ploughman's or a hot daily special like beef casserole. The more elaborate evening menu might offer tournedos Rossini or rich steak and pigeon pie. Excellent home-made sweets, too.

## Frampton Mansell *(Food)* — *Crown Inn*

Near Stroud · *Gloucestershire* · Map 7 D2
Frampton Mansell (028 576) 218

*Free House*
*Landlord* Mrs. E. Coley

Home-made soup 75p Cold platter with salads £3.50 (No bar food eves)
Wadworth's 6X; Worthington 'E'; Ben Truman; Younger's Tartan; Guinness; Carlsberg; cider. *Real ale*

The three low-ceilinged, beamed bars of this old Cotswold-stone inn make a cosy setting for Elizabeth Coley's simple, tasty lunchtime snacks. Soup is served with fresh home-baked bread, and there are succulent home-cooked joints to go with a crisp salad. You can have a ploughman's too, and in winter hot dishes can be enjoyed by the open fire. The terrace has splendid views over hills and valleys.
**Family pub**

## Frilford Heath *(B & B)* — *Dog House Hotel*

Near Abingdon · *Oxfordshire* · Map 6 A3
Frilford Heath (0865) 390830

*Brewery* Morland
*Landlords* Mr & Mrs Morgan

**BEDROOMS 10 Grade 2 £A**
Morland's Bitter, Best Bitter, Mild, Artist; Guinness; Heineken; Stella Artois. *Real ale*

Comfortable overnight accommodation is a feature of this well-kept hostelry, a modernised 17th-century building with a tile-hung first storey. All the bedrooms have central heating and practical modern furnishings, and colour TVs and tea-makers are standard equipment. Some rooms have compact shower cabinets. Drinkers can choose between the relaxing bar and the pleasant garden. **Family pub** (lunchtime)

## Friskney *(B & B)* — *Barley Mow*

Sea Lane, Near Boston · *Lincolnshire*
Map 4 D4
Friskney (075 484) 483

*Brewery* Bateman
*Landlord* Mr T. A. Makemson

**BEDROOMS 2 Grade 2 £C** (No dogs)
Bateman's Bitter, XXXB, Mild; Guinness; Heineken; cider. *Real ale*

Reclamation has pushed the coastline about a mile from this attractive old pub, which stands on the A52 between Boston and Skegness. It's a comfortable place for an overnight stay, and there are plenty of homely touches in the prettily decorated bedrooms. They have practical modern furniture, portable TVs and share the landlord's well-equipped bathroom. There are two bars, plus outside drinking in fine weather.

## Frogmore *(B & B)* — *Globe Inn*

Near Kingsbridge · *Devon* · Map 8 C4
Frogmore (054 853) 351

*Free House*
*Landlord* Mrs J. Wilding

**BEDROOMS 7 Grade 2 £C**
Usher's Best Bitter, Founders Ale, Country Ale; Ben Truman; Guinness; Holsten; cider. *Real ale*

In the centre of a small village some three miles south-east of Kingsbridge on the A379, this friendly pub has a nautically themed bar that's a pleasant spot to drop anchor for a while. Non-mariners may prefer a game of darts in the lively public bar before retiring to one of the comfortable, simply furnished bedrooms, which have tea/coffee-making facilities. Bathrooms are up to date. **Family pub**

## Fulking *(Food)* ★ *Shepherd & Dog*

Near Henfield · *West Sussex* · Map 6 C4
Poynings (079 156) 382
*Brewery* Phoenix
*Landlord* Mr H. A. Bradley-Hole
Mermaid's lunch £1.75 Scrumpy chicken £3.75 (Last order 9.30pm. No bar food Sun & Mon eves)
King & Barnes Festive; Usher's Best Bitter; Webster's Yorkshire Bitter; Tamplins Stag; Guinness; Foster's; Carlsberg; cider. *Real ale*

Locally smoked salmon is just one of the many delights that keep this splendid old village inn packed to the gills. Lunchtime brings a tempting range of platters – mermaid's with prawns, farmer's with pork sausages, ploughman's with farmhouse Cheddar – plus hot specials like sweet and sour chicken. More hot dishes in the evening, including a marvellous beef and Guinness pie. Also salads and lovely sweets. Garden.

## Fyfield *(Food)* *White Hart*

Near Abingdon · *Oxfordshire* · Map 6 A3
Frilford Heath (0865) 390585

*Free House*
*Landlord* Mr E. Howard

Steak & kidney pie £2.65 Lamb kebabs £2.95 (Last order 10pm)
Morland's Bitter; Wadworth's 6X; Theakston's Old Peculier; Ruddle's County; Guinness; Foster's; cider. *Real ale*

There's a wide-ranging menu at this fine old pub with an impressive 15th-century gallery in its flagstoned bar. The choice might include duck or venison and claret pâté, whole pigeon braised in beer, spicy lamb kebabs and even frogs' legs or fried sardines. Chocolate fudge cake and sherry trifle are among the appealing desserts. Garden. **Family pub**

## Ganton *(B & B)* *Greyhound*

Near Scarborough · *North Yorkshire*
Map 4 D2
Sherburn (0944) 70242

*Brewery* Tetley
*Landlords* Mr & Mrs R. Mackinlay

**BEDROOMS 4 Grade 2 £C** (No dogs)
Tetley's Mild, Bitter; Guinness; Skol; cider.

Players and spectators at the nearby championship golf course favour this modest village inn beside the A64. Four bedrooms offer sturdy, old-fashioned comfort and share a single public bathroom. Guests can relax amid the polished brassware in the lounge bar or play dominoes in the simple public bar. Accommodation closed December–January. Garden.

## Gargrave *(B & B)* *Anchor Inn*

Near Skipton · *North Yorkshire* · Map 4 C2
Gargrave (0756) 78666

*Free House*
*Landlords* Mr & Mrs E. R. Feather

**BEDROOMS 8 Grade 1 £B**
Theakston's Bitter, Old Peculier; Younger's Scotch Bitter No. 3; Timothy Taylors Bitter; Guinness; Carlsberg Pils; cider. *Real ale*

A sturdy converted farmhouse, with the busy A65 at the front and the Leeds–Liverpool Canal providing a contrastingly serene setting at the rear. Centrally heated bedrooms are comfortable and well equipped, with practical modern furniture, TVs, radio-alarms and tea-makers. Each has its own bath/shower room. There's a roomy bar and lounge, plus a children's play area in the garden. **Family pub**

## Georgeham — *Rock Inn*

This attractive whitewashed inn, built in the 17th century, stands in a narrow street above the village. Old framed photographs are an interesting feature in the beamed bar, which has a terra-cotta tiled floor and ample pew-style seating. There's also a family-cum-games room, and the garden is popular in summer. **Family pub**

Rock Hill · *Devon* · Map 8 B3
Croyde (0271) 890322
*Free House* *Landlord* Mrs Lesley Ashford
Ushers Best Bitter, Country Bitter; Ben Truman; Guinness; Carlsberg; Foster's; Taunton cider. *Real ale*

## Gestingthorpe *(Food)* — *Pheasant*

Halstead · *Essex* · Map 5 C2
Hedingham (0787) 61196

*Free House*
*Landlords* Mr & Mrs Paul Ruth
Smoked trout £1.90 Beef in red wine £4 (Last order 9.30pm)
Pheasant Bitter; Wethered's Bitter; Greene King IPA, Abbot Ale; Guinness; Kronenbourg; cider. *Real ale*

Seasonal game, including jugged hare, venison and pheasant casserole, is a feature of the menu at this delightful old country pub. Excellent pork and liver pâté, steak and grilled trout are also on offer, along with sandwiches and cheese to accompany a selection of real ales. If you're still hungry, there are also lovely sweets like elderberry and apple tart. **Family pub**

## Gibraltar *(Food)* — *Bottle & Glass*

Near Aylesbury · *Buckinghamshire* · Map 5 B2
Aylesbury (0296) 748488

*Brewery* Aylesbury
*Landlords* John & Eileen Gomersall

Smoked mackerel pâté £1.25 Mixed meat salad £3.50 (Last order 10pm)
ABC Bitter; Tetley's Bitter; Guinness; Skol. *Real ale*

The cold table is a popular feature at this attractive 15th-century thatched inn, which stands on the A418 between Aylesbury and Thame. Beef, ham and pork are carved to order and served with simple fresh salads; there are also home-made pâtés, ploughman's platters, winter soups and a weekday lunchtime hot special. Only sandwiches and pâtés Saturday and Sunday evenings, pâtés Sunday lunchtime. Patio.

## Glastonbury *(Food, B & B)* — *George & Pilgrims Hotel*

1 High Street · *Somerset* · Map 8 D3
Glastonbury (0458) 31146

*Free House*
*Landlords* Jack & Elzebie Richardson
**BEDROOMS 14 Grade 1 £B**
Somerset bacon bake £1.85 Cold steak & kidney pie & salad £1.85 (Last order 9pm)
Bass, Toby; Worthington Best Bitter; Guinness; Carling Black Label; Tennents Pilsner; Taunton cider. *Real ale*

Food and accommodation live up to the promise of the splendid stone façade of this 500-year-old inn at the centre of the town. Snacks range from well-filled sandwiches, local cheese and soup with home-baked bread to a tempting cold buffet (lunchtime) and a hot dish of the day. Bedrooms are comfortably furnished in traditional style and there is a relaxing residents' TV lounge. **Family pub**

## Goldsborough *(B & B)* — *Bay Horse Inn*

Near Knaresborough · *North Yorkshire*
Map 4 C2
Harrogate (0423) 862212

*Brewery* Whitbread
*Landlord* Mrs June Manks

**BEDROOMS 5 Grade 2 £C** (No dogs)
Whitbread Trophy, Castle Eden Ale, Dark Mild; Guinness; Stella Artois; cider. *Real ale*

In the centre of a peaceful village just off the A59, this handsome hostelry offers comfortable overnight accommodation in a rear extension. The five bedrooms are neat and compact, the single bathroom well equipped and spotlessly maintained. Darts are played in the public bar, while in the beamed lounge bar there's an interesting collection of more lethal weapons! Garden.

## Gomshall *(B & B)* — *Black Horse*

Station Road · *Surrey* · Map 6 B3
Shere (048 641) 2242

*Brewery* Young
*Landlord* Anne & Andrew Brown

**BEDROOMS 6 Grade 2 £B** (No dogs)
Young's Special, Ordinary, London Lager; Taunton cider. *Real ale*

Dating from 1690, this solidly built pub stands on the A25 between Dorking and Guildford. The lounge bar with its oak panelling and burnished brass has a comfortable period appeal. Simply furnished, good-sized bedrooms, all with tea-makers and washbasins, share two bathrooms, and there's a large TV room. Under-12s not accommodated overnight. Garden. **Family pub**

## Goostrey *(Food)* — *Olde Red Lion Inn*

Main Road · *Cheshire* · Map 3 B4
Holmes Chapel (0477) 32033

*Brewery* Tetley
*Landlords* Mary & Peter Yorke

Deep-fried stuffed mushrooms £1.75 Seafood open sandwich £2.25 (Last order 10.15pm)
Tetley's Bitter, Mild; Walker's Bitter; Falstaff Bitter; Guinness; Löwenbräu; cider. *Real ale*

Head for the Jodrell Bank radio telescopes to find this friendly, rambling pub with its excellent range of bar snacks. You could start with home-made vegetable soup or deep-fried stuffed mushrooms and go on to a rump steak or cold meat salad. Tasty sandwiches include a delicious open seafood one, and there are some tempting sweets to round things off. Garden.
**Family pub**

## Goudhurst *(B & B)* — *Star & Eagle*

High Street · *Kent* · Map 6 C3
Goudhurst (0580) 211512

*Brewery* Whitbread
*Landlord* Mr Christopher J. Satchell

**BEDROOMS 11 Grade 1 £A**
Fremlins Bitter; Whitbread Best Bitter; Stella Artois; Heineken; cider. *Real ale*

The appeal of the beamed, flagstoned bar and lovely views of the Weald lure visitors to this one-time monastery built in the 14th century. Comfortably furnished bedrooms are in tasteful modern style, except for one which has antiques and a fine four-poster bed. All have TVs and tea-makers, and nine have neat, well-kept private bathrooms.

## Grantchester *(Food)* — *Green Man*

High Street · *Cambridgeshire* · Map 5 C2
Cambridge (0223) 841178

*Brewery* Tollemache & Cobbold
*Landlord* Mr Norman Adamson

Turkey fricassee £2.75 Fresh salmon salad £6.95 (Last order 10pm)
Tolly Cobbold Bitter, Tolly Original, Old Strong (winter only); Guinness; Hansa; Taunton cider. *Real ale*

A popular haunt of Cambridge dons and undergraduates, this welcoming, beamed village pub offers a good choice of tasty, well-prepared snacks. Light eaters can have sandwiches, ploughman's salads and omelettes, and there is also home-made soup and a selection of daily specials such as turkey fricassee, baked trout or braised oxtail. Patio and garden. **Family pub**

## Grantchester *(Food)* — *Red Lion*

High Street · *Cambridgeshire* · Map 5 C2
Cambridge (0223) 840121

*Brewery* Greene King
*Landlords* Mr & Mrs D. W. Gration

Poacher's pie £2.75 Chocolate mousse £1.10 (Last order 10pm)
Greene King IPA, Abbot Ale; Guinness; Harp; Kronenbourg; Taunton cider. *Real ale*

The cold buffet, with its tempting selection of quiches, pies and salads, is a popular lunchtime attraction at this well-run pub in a village immortalised by Rupert Brooke. There are plenty of hot choices, too, from robust French onion soup to basket meals, beef bordelaise, poacher's pie and grilled trout with almonds. Mousses and gâteaux to finish. Garden. **Family pub**

## Great Ayton *(B & B)* — *Royal Oak Hotel*

Middlesbrough, Cleveland · *North Yorkshire* Map 4 C2
Great Ayton (0642) 722361

*Brewery* Scottish & Newcastle
*Landlords* Mr & Mrs D. Monaghan

**BEDROOMS 5 Grade 2 £C**
Scottish & Newcastle Exhibition; Younger's IPA, Tartan; Guinness; Carlsberg Hof; Cavalier; cider.

Captain Cook attended school close to this welcoming village pub beside the village green. It provides a comfortable overnight stay in five spacious, well-kept bedrooms, all with TVs and tea-makers. One room has a private bathroom, while a public one serves the rest. Guests can relax in either of the two bars or in the residents' lounge. Good breakfasts. Accommodation closed December. **Family pub**

## Great Chishill *(Food)* — *Pheasant Inn*

Near Royston · *Hertfordshire* · Map 5 C2
Royston (0763) 838535

*Free House*
*Landlord* Denis Ryan
Beef casserole £1.95 Scampi provençale £4.45 (Last order 9.30pm. No bar food Sun lunch & Mon)
Younger's IPA, Scotch Bitter, Tartan; Greene King IPA; Tolly Cobbold Original; McEwans Export; Harp. *Real ale*

Formerly a jockey, landlord Denis Ryan has made this peaceful village pub a good bet for tasty, wholesome food. Home-made soup served in the cosy, antique-furnished bar is a welcome addition to sandwiches and salads, and hot dishes range from omelettes, fish and grills to beef casserole or scampi provençale. Steaks are an evening speciality. Closed Mon lunchtime.
**Family pub** (lunchtime)

## Great Oxendon *(Food)* — *George*

Near Market Harborough · *Leicestershire*
Map 5 B2
Market Harborough (0858) 65205

*Free House*
*Landlords* George & Dorothy Taylor
Fish chowder £1.50 Game pie £4.95 (Last order 10.30pm. No bar food Mon eve)
Hoskins Bitter; Samuel Smith's Old Brewery Bitter; Shipstone's Bitter; Stella Artois; cider. *Real ale.*

Wholesome country fare matches the cosy charm of this meticulously kept inn, where you can admire a fine collection of old pewter. Stockpot soup and fish chowder have a loyal following, and there are also salads, pâté, prawn-stuffed trout and delicious game pie served with fresh vegetables. Chocolate mousse and spicy apple pie are among the irresistible sweets. Garden.

## Great Ryburgh *(Food, B & B)* — *Boar Inn*

Near Fakenham · *Norfolk* · Map 5 D1
Great Ryburgh (032 878) 212
*Free House*
*Landlords* Mr & Mrs J. Corson & Mr & Mrs I. Lewis
**BEDROOMS 4 Grade 2 £B**
Lasagne £1.75 Madras beef curry £1.85 (Last order 9.45pm)
Tolly Cobbold Original, Bitter; Bass Springfield Bitter; Guinness; Hansa; Carling Black Label; Taunton cider. *Real ale*

Two ex-RAF men and their wives run this friendly village inn. The ladies do the cooking, producing excellent fare that ranges from flavoursome vegetable soup to shepherd's pie, ham salad and a splendid sherry trifle. Decor and furnishings are mainly traditional, both in the comfortable bar and in the modestly equipped bedrooms, which share a simple shower room. All have colour TVs. **Family pub**

## Great Shefford *(Food)* — *Swan*

Newbury Road · *Berkshire* · Map 6 A3
Great Shefford (048 839) 271

*Brewery* Courage
*Landlords* Mr & Mrs M. Lovett
Summer buffet £2.75 Home-made beefburger with salad & chips £1.95 (Last order 9.45pm. No bar food Sun & Mon eves)
Courage Directors Bitter, Best Bitter; Guinness; Kronenbourg; Hofmeister; Taunton cider. *Real ale*

The garden of this pink-washed pub beside a stream is a delightful place to enjoy your pick from the appetising summer buffet of cold meats, fish and colourful salads. In winter, the cosy bar serves satisfying hot snacks such as leek and potato soup, lamb chops in sherry and splendid home-made beefburgers. Book for the traditional Sunday lunch. **Family pub**

## Great Stainton *(Food)* — *Kings Arms*

*Co. Durham* · Map 4 C1
Sedgefield (0740) 30361

*Brewery* Whitbread
*Landlord* Gordon Mitchell

Cold meat salad £1.95 Kidneys in red wine £2.45 (Last order 10pm. No bar food Sun eve)
Whitbread Trophy, Castle Eden Ale; Heineken; Stella Artois; cider. *Real ale*

About 300 years old, this white-painted pub in a pretty village has cosy, traditional decor in its beamed bar, where a fire burns in winter. An extensive blackboard menu caters for most tastes with substantial dishes like seafood platter, ham in onion and mushroom sauce, lamb Reform or a tender, rich beef casserole. Sweets include trifle and coffee mousse. Garden.

## Great Waltham *(Food)* ★ *Windmill*

*Essex* · Map 5 C2
Chelmsford (0245) 360292

*Free House*
*Landlord* Mr Martin Ridgewell

Steak, kidney & mushroom pudding £3.75 Pheasant in red wine £5.50 (Last order 9.30pm. No bar food Sat lunch & all Sun)
Adnams Bitter; Carling Black Label. *Real ale*

Generous portions of tasty, well-prepared food brings hungry crowds to this comfortable roadside pub. Steak, kidney and mushroom pudding, and pheasant in red wine are typically satisfying choices, and you could also try the home-cured bloaters and spaghetti bolognese. There are sandwiches, too, and splendid puddings like steamed syrup sponge or blackberry and apple fool. **Family pub**

## Great Wolford *(Food, B & B)* *Fox & Hounds*

Near Shipston-on-Stour · *Warwickshire*
Map 5 A2
Barton-on-the-Heath (060 874) 220
*Free House*
*Landlords* Mr & Mrs C. Olcese
**BEDROOMS 4 Grade 1 £B**
Steak & kidney pie £2.35 Lasagne £2.50 (Last order 10pm)
Manns Bitter; Ben Truman; Webster's Yorkshire Bitter; Guinness; Foster's; Carlsberg; cider. *Real ale*

The genial Signor Olcese and his Scottish wife make a fine team at this pleasant old Cotswold-stone inn. His welcome is warm and sunny, her bar snacks simple and delicious, ranging from ploughman's and country broth to spaghetti bolognese, omelettes and a really good chicken curry. Overnight guests are accommodated in four neatly kept bedrooms with TVs and well-appointed modern bathrooms. Garden. **Family pub**

## Greatford *(Food)* *Hare & Hounds*

Main Street, Near Stamford · *Lincolnshire*
Map 5 B1
Greatford (077 836) 332

*Brewery* Manns
*Landlords* Mr & Mrs P. Wilkins
Turkey & ham pie £2.95 Apple pie 75p (Last order 9pm. No bar food Mon except Bank Hols)
Manns Bitter, Triple Crown; Webster's Yorkshire Bitter; Ben Truman; Guinness; Holsten; Carlsberg; cider.

The river Glen runs just across the road from this cosy, cottagy pub, where Mrs Wilkins produces a good choice of robust, homely fare. Steak and kidney pie, devilled gammon and a mighty mixed grill are meaty main dishes, and grilled lemon sole is a firm favourite with fish-lovers. To finish, perhaps trifle or a delicious apple and blackberry pie. Garden. Closed 2 weeks October.

## Greenhalgh *(Food)* *Blues*

Fleetwood Road, Near Kirkham · *Lancashire*
Map 3 B3
Weeton (039 136) 283

*Brewery* Thwaites
*Landlord* Mr Kevin Ratcliffe

Prawn salad platter £1.50 Seafood casserole £4.25 (Last order 10pm)
Thwaites Bitter, Best Mild; Guinness; Stein; cider. *Real ale*

Just north of junction 3 of the M55, this pub is worth seeking out for its enjoyable bar food. Start with pâté, deep-fried onion rings or a hearty broth, and go on to seafood casserole, lasagne or a good traditional steak and kidney pie. There are also nice sweets. In summer you can sit out on the terrace or in the garden with its attractive duck pond and children's playground equipment. **Family pub**

## Greta Bridge *(Food, B & B)* — *Morritt Arms Hotel*

Near Barnard Castle · *Co. Durham* · Map 4 C2
Teesdale (0833) 27232

*Free House*
*Landlords* Mr & Mrs S. R. Waldron
**BEDROOMS 26 Grade 1 £A**
Smoked mackerel £1.95 Fresh salmon salad £4.75 (Last order 10.30pm)
Theakston's Best Bitter; Newcastle Exhibition, Scotch Bitter; Harp; Carlsberg; cider. *Real ale*

Charles Dickens stayed at this roadside inn while writing *Nicholas Nickleby*, as visitors are reminded by murals in the welcoming, beamed bar. Tasty snacks include home-made soups, gamy venison pâté, sandwiches, cold meats and salads. Overnight guests have 26 comfortable bedrooms furnished in a variety of styles, most with their own bathrooms. There's also a small TV room. Garden. **Family pub**

## Grimsthorpe *(Food, B & B)* — *Black Horse Inn*

Near Bourne · *Lincolnshire* · Map 5 B1
Edenham (077 832) 247

*Free House*
*Landlords* Mr & Mrs Fisher

**BEDROOMS 4 Grade 1 £A**
Mrs Beeton's steak, kidney & mushroom pie £2.99 Bramley apple tart with cream £1.39 (No bar food eves or Sun)
Sam Smith's Sovereign

The delightful bar of this Georgian coaching inn has beams and a flagstone floor, and there's a residents' lounge with TV. Bedrooms are comfortable and cosy, with pretty floral decor, private bathrooms and extras such as hairdryers. Delicious lunchtime snacks have a distinctly English slant: Lincolnshire rarebit and potatoes, Yorkshire beef pasties, sausage and mash, treacle tart. Closed 1 week Christmas.
**Family pub**

## Grindleford *(Food, B & B)* — *Maynard Arms Hotel*

Main Road · *Derbyshire* · Map 4 C3
Hope Valley (0433) 30321

*Free House*
*Landlords* Bob & Thelma Graham

**BEDROOMS 13 Grade 1 £A**
Yorkshire meat pudding £2.25 Neptune salad £3.25 (Last order 9.30pm)
Stones Traditional Bitter, Keg Bitter; Carling Lager. *Real ale*

This fine Victorian hotel in the Peak District National Park retains attractive original features like wood panelling, stained-glass windows and a splendid oak staircase. Modernised bedrooms are very well appointed, with direct-dial phones, TVs and trouser presses, and all have private facilities. Satisfying bar snacks include ravioli, steak and kidney pie and filled Yorkshire puddings; there's also a lunchtime cold table (except Sunday). Patio.

## Groombridge *(B & B)* — *Crown Inn*

Near Tunbridge Wells · *Kent* · Map 6 C3
Groombridge (089 276) 361

*Free House*
*Landlords* Jeffrey & Barbara Chambers

**BEDROOMS 4 Grade 2 £C**
Harvey's Best Bitter; Courage Directors Bitter; Bass; Mitchells & Butlers Springfield Bitter; Guinness; Hofmeister; cider. *Real ale*

Full of nooks and crannies, the cosy beamed bars of this handsome 16th-century pub are perfect for an intimate chat and a well-kept pint. The attractive garden adjoining the village green is ideal for summer drinking. Pretty floral duvets have brightened the spotlessly clean bedrooms with their solid traditional furniture, and the public bathroom is in perfect order. Tasty breakfasts. **Family pub**

## Guisborough *(B & B)* — *Fox Inn*

10 Bow Street · *Cleveland* · Map 4 C2
Guisborough (0287) 32958

*Brewery* Scottish & Newcastle
*Landlords* Mr & Mrs Williamson

**BEDROOMS 7 Grade 1 £C** (No dogs)
Scottish & Newcastle Exhibition; Younger's Scotch Bitter; McEwan's 80/-, Guinness; Harp; Taunton cider.

This old pub continues to provide a welcoming haven for travellers, the mounting steps at the front recalling its days as a coaching inn. The seven bedrooms are comfortably furnished and all have colour TVs and tea-makers. They share two nicely kept public bathrooms. You can join the locals for a drink in the lively, beamed public bar or relax in the quieter cocktail bar. **Family pub**

## Guisborough *(B & B)* — *Moorcock Hotel*

West End Road · *Cleveland* · Map 4 C2
Guisborough (0287) 32342

*Brewery* Whitbread
*Landlord* Mr Alan Mitchell

**BEDROOMS 6 Grade 1 £C**
Whitbread Trophy; Guinness; Heineken; Stella Artois; cider.

Alan Mitchell offers a warm welcome and excellent accommodation at this modern purpose-built pub. There are two smart bars (one with pine panelling and plush seating), as well as a brightly furnished residents' lounge. Compact, well-maintained bedrooms have fitted furniture, TVs and up-to-date shower cabinets; there's a public bathroom too. Exemplary housekeeping throughout. Garden.

## Gunnislake *(B & B)* — *Cornish Inn*

The Square · *Cornwall* · Map 8 B4
Tavistock (0822) 832475

*Free House*
*Landlords* Messrs Lawrence & Chapple

**BEDROOMS 9 Grade 2 £C**
St Austell Tinner's Ale; Flower's Best Bitter; Younger's Tartan; Guinness; Carlsberg Hof. *Real ale*

A warm and friendly welcome awaits visitors to this white-painted pub in the centre of the village. Locals and tourists mingle in the convivial surroundings of the bar, and residents have a TV lounge with plenty of comfortable armchairs and settees. The homely, traditional style extends to the bright bedrooms, five of which have their own spotlessly maintained bathrooms. Patio.

## Hambleden *(B & B)* — *Stag & Huntsman Inn*

Near Henley-on-Thames, Oxfordshire
*Buckinghamshire* · Map 6 B3
Hambleden (049 166) 227

*Free House*
*Landlords* Mr & Mrs C. Hubbard

**BEDROOMS 3 Grade 2 £B**
Brakspear's Pale Ale; Wadworth's 6X; Chiltern Ale; Eldridge Pope Royal Oak; Guinness; Stella Artois; cider. *Real ale*

Overnight guests will find a warm welcome at this delightful little village pub. Comfortable bedrooms have neat modern furniture and an excellent breakfast will set you up for the day. The bar with its old beams and panelling has a loyal following of regulars and provides a cosy, friendly setting for a drink. Children not accommodated overnight. Garden. **Family pub**

# Let TWA be your guide to the USA.

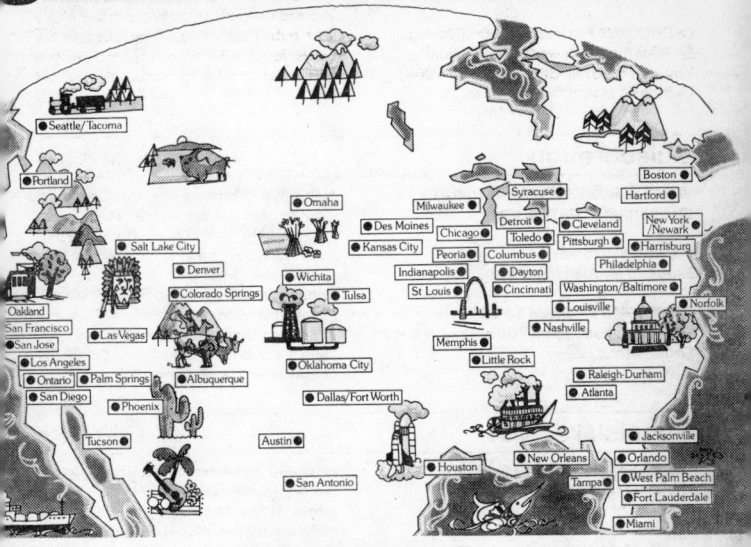


## TWA flies to over 60 US cities.

As someone who likes to follow a good guide, you probably get around a bit.

If you're going to America you can do that best with TWA.

TWA flies all over America. Not just to the great cities like New York, Boston, Los Angeles and Chicago, but some of the more picturesque—like New Orleans or Nashville. To the West, like Albuquerque and Phoenix. Smaller towns like Peoria. Sunny Florida. Spectacular California.

TWA flies to over 60 US cities. If you want a guide to get you around, then TWA's the one.

See your TWA Main Agent

You're going to like us TWA

## Handcross *(Food)* — *Royal Oak*

Horsham Road · *West Sussex* · Map 6 C4
Handcross (0444) 400703

*Brewery* Phoenix
*Landlords* Mr & Mrs E. H. R. Field

Guinness, steak & kidney pie £2.55
Cold seafood platter £5.85 (Last order 9.30 pm)
Tamplins Bitter; Watneys Stag Bitter; Webster's Yorkshire Bitter; Ben Truman; Guinness; Holsten. *Real ale*

Just off the A23, this trim little pub formed out of three adjoining cottages provides appetising snacks in its cosy bar. Wholesome pies including chicken and mushroom or steak and kidney are popular choices, and there are also tempting quiches served with salad, moussaka or perhaps beef crumble. Additional evening alternatives are provided by grills and a seafood platter. Patio.

## Harome *(Food)* — *Star Inn*

Near Helmsley · *North Yorkshire* · Map 4 C2
Helmsley (0439) 70397

*Free House*
*Landlord* Mr Tony Bowron

Star special sandwich £1.80 Mushroom soup 60p (No bar food eves)
Theakston's Best Bitter, Old Peculier; Cameron's Lion; Vaux Samson Ale; Carlsberg. *Real ale*

Carefully prepared soup, sandwiches and cheese make up the lunchtime bar menu at this delightful village pub with a thatched roof and masses of roses. The bar itself is full of country charm, while the sandwiches (white or brown bread) come with a score of fillings like egg and chives, tuna mayonnaise, home-cooked ham – even prawn curry. There's a pretty little rear garden. Closed Bank Holidays. **Family pub**

## Harpenden *(Food)* — *Silver Cup*

West Common, St Albans Road
*Hertfordshire* · Map 5 B2
Harpenden (058 27) 3095
*Brewery* Wells
*Landlord* Mr Roy Mills
Steak pie £1.95 Spaghetti bolognese £1.95 (No bar food eves or all Sun)
Wells Bitter, Bombardier, Noggin; Guinness; Kellerbräu; Red Stripe; cider. *Real ale*

This old whitewashed pub – its name a reminder of the horse races which used to take place on the nearby common – draws eager crowds with a tasty, wholesome selection of lunchtime snacks. Home-made soups and daily specials such as liver and bacon or chilli con carne are firm favourites, along with gammon steak and burgers. Freshly made sandwiches, pâté and various ploughman's are also in the running. Patio.

## Harrietsham — *Ringlestone Inn*

Tucked away in the Kentish countryside, this splendid old inn is a great place to enjoy a pint and soak up the antiquity. Uneven floors, exposed brickwork, blackened beams and gnarled woodwork characterise the three small rooms, whose furnishings include sturdy little oak tables, pews and fine old high-backed chairs. **Family pub**

Near Maidstone · *Kent* · Map 6 C3
Maidstone (0622) 859207
*Free House* *Landlord* Mr M. Millington-Buck
Boddingtons Bitter, Wadworth's 6X; Gibbs Mew Bishop's Tipple; Everards Tiger; Heineken; Carlsberg; cider. *Real ale*

## Harrogate *(B & B)* — *West Park Hotel*

West Park · *North Yorkshire* · Map 4 C2
Harrogate (0423) 524471

*Brewery* Tetley
*Landlord* Mr Charles Gillis

**BEDROOMS 18 Grade 1 £A** (No dogs)
Tetley's Bitter, Dark Mild; Guinness; Skol; Castlemaine; cider. *Real ale*

Major refurbishment has transformed this pleasant old inn, which stands in the heart of the city overlooking verdant West Park Stray. Well-proportioned bedrooms are bright, modern and comfortable, with TVs, tea-makers, trouser presses and fully tiled shower rooms. The relaxing main bar features an ornate plaster ceiling, while the cocktail bar is smartly up to date in pale grey and pink. **Family pub**

## Hartfield *(Food)* — *Anchor*

Church Street · *East Sussex* · Map 6 C3
Hartfield (089 277) 424

*Free House*
*Landlords* Ken & Janis Thompson

Seafood cassoulet £4.50 Lamb & beef kebabs £4.75 (Last order 10pm)
Fremlins Tusker; King & Barnes Sussex Bitter, Festive; Shepherd Neame Masterbrew; Guinness; Stella Artois; cider. *Real ale*

A verandah runs along the front of Ken and Janis Thompson's handsome pub, where a fine selection of delicious snacks is served in the bar. Simple sandwiches, ploughman's and burgers are supplemented by excellent lamb and beef kebabs, steaks and a range of seafood dishes which includes moules marinière, seafood cassoulet and goujons of sole. Garden. **Family pub**

## Hartwell *(Food)* — *Bugle Horn*

Aylesbury · *Buckinghamshire* · Map 5 B2
Aylesbury (0296) 748209

*Brewery* Benskins
*Landlords* Antony & Lady Rose Saint

Beef casserole £2.25 Stuffed baked potatoes £1.65 (Last order 10pm)
Benskins Bitter; Ind Coope Burton Ale; John Bull Bitter; Guinness; Oranjeboom; Skol; cider. *Real ale*

The lunchtime cold buffet is a popular feature at this whitewashed 17th-century pub set in a very attractive garden. Cooked meats, pâtés and quiches are displayed temptingly at one end of the bar, and there's also a large selection of freshly filled rolls and baps. Hot options include stuffed baked potatoes and a daily special, perhaps chicken curry or chunky beef casserole.

**Family pub**

## Haslemere *(Food)* — *Crown & Cushion*

Weyhill · *Surrey* · Map 6 B3
Haslemere (0428) 3112

*Brewery* Friary Meux
*Landlord* Benjamin Heath

Spinach & bacon bake £2.95 Fillet of lamb with rosemary & redcurrant £4.25 (Last order 10.30pm)
Friary Meux Bitter; Ind Coope Burton Ale; Guinness; Löwenbräu; Skol; cider. *Real ale*

Sandwiches, jacket potatoes, quiches and pâté are just a few of the choices on offer at this smart pub. Tasty hot dishes range from soup served with wholemeal bread to grills, rabbit in mustard sauce, vegetable curry, lamb with rosemary and spinach and bacon bake. If you're still hungry, there are some delicious home-made sweets, too. Garden.

## Hastingwood Common — *Rainbow & Dove*

Not far from the M11, but the surroundings are so peaceful and rural that the age of the motor car seems far removed from this friendly old pub. It's been dispensing hospitality since the 17th century, and the bars, with their low beams, sturdy wooden furniture and warming fires, are delightfully welcoming. There's a pretty garden, too.

Near Harlow · *Essex* · Map 6 C3
Harlow (0279) 415419
*Brewery* Ind Coope *Landlords* Joyce and Tony Bird
John Bull Bitter; Double Diamond; Guinness; Löwenbräu; Skol; cider.

## Hatherleigh *(Food, B & B)* — *George Hotel*

Near Okehampton · *Devon* · Map 8 B3
Okehampton (0837) 810454

*Free House*
*Landlords* Mr & Mrs M. E. F. Giles
**BEDROOMS 12 Grades 1 & 2 £C**
Prawn curry £4.25 Fruit pie £1.10 (Last order 9.30pm)
Courage Directors Bitter, Best; John Smith's Trophy; Simmonds Bitter; Guinness; Hofmeister; cider. *Real ale*

Originally a monk's retreat and later a coaching inn, this fine old thatched pub continues to provide excellent hospitality. The large beamed bar is the setting for a wide range of tasty fare, from light snacks – ploughman's, toasted sandwiches, delicious tomato soup – to hearty fry-ups, grills and curries. Spick-and-span bedrooms, most with private facilities, have sturdy traditional furnishings. Courtyard.

**Family pub**

## Hawk Green *(Food)* — *Crown Inn*

Marple, Near Stockport · *Greater Manchester*
Map 4 C3
061-427 2678

*Brewery* Robinson
*Landlord* Mr T. C. Lane

Mushrooms à la grecque £1.65 Pork Normandy £3.45 (Last order 9.45pm)
Robinson's Best Bitter, Mild; Guinness; Einhorn; Tennent's Lager. *Real ale*

A friendly, popular pub, whose spick-and-span bar is a comfortable setting for enjoying a wide variety of excellent fare. Follow French onion soup or deep-fried whitebait with a succulent steak, tandoori-style chicken or a daily special like delicious beef olives. Also salads and open sandwiches, seafood and tempting sweets. Food is served from noon to closing time on Sunday. Garden.

**Family pub** (lunchtime)

## Hawkhurst *(B & B)* — *Royal Oak Hotel*

Highgate · *Kent* · Map 6 C3
Hawkhurst (058 05) 2184

*Brewery* Courage
*Landlord* Mr David Jackson

**BEDROOMS 15 Grade 2 £B**
Courage Best Bitter, Director's Bitter; Guinness; Hofmeister; Kronenbourg; Taunton cider. *Real ale*

Old-fashioned charm and character abound in this handsome black and white hostelry in the middle of the village. Three homely bars are popular with both tourists and the local community, and there's a tranquil sitting room with comfortable armchairs and sofas. Spacious bedrooms are also traditional in style; one has its own bathroom, two others showers. Garden.

**Family pub**

## Hawkhurst *(Food, B & B)* — *Tudor Arms Hotel*

Rye Road · *Kent* · Map 6 C3
Hawkhurst (058 05) 2312

*Owner* Mr Basil Sanderson
*Landlord* Karen Bradbury

**BEDROOMS 13 Grade 1 £A**
Lasagne & salad £2.25 Cottage pie £1.80 (Last order 9pm)
Fremlins Bitter; Whitbread Best Bitter; Stella Artois; cider. *Real ale*

Bedrooms are very comfortably furnished at this handsome brick pub standing in pleasant grounds beside the A268. All have fitted carpets and trouser presses, and nine have TVs and well-fitted private bathrooms. The panelled bar offers an appetising range of snacks like home-made soup, quiche, cottage pie, lasagne and delicious blackberry and apple pie. **Family pub**

## Hawkshead *(Food, B & B)* — *Queen's Head*

*Cumbria* · Map 3 B2
Hawkshead (096 66) 271

*Brewery* Hartley
*Landlord* Mr Allan Whitehead

**BEDROOMS 8 Grade 2 £B** (No dogs)
Venison pâté £2.25 Beef & beer casserole £3.25 (Last order 9pm)
Hartley's Best Bitter, Mild; Guinness; Heineken; cider. *Real ale*

The panelled bar of this busy village pub provides a convivial setting for enjoying some very good snacks. Venison liver pâté and local smoked trout make tasty light meals, and more substantial offerings range from deep-fried scampi to beef and beer casserole. There are also lunchtime sandwiches. Simply furnished bedrooms are well maintained, and there's a plush TV room. No under-tens overnight. **Family pub**

## Haytor Vale *(Food, B & B)* — *Rock Inn*

Newton Abbot · *Devon* · Map 8 C4
Haytor (036 46) 305

*Free House*
*Landlord* Mr C. F. H. H. Graves
**BEDROOMS 9 Grades 1 & 2 £B**
Stuffed chicken £2.85 Salcombe smokie £1.35 (Last order 10pm)
Eldridge Pope Royal Oak, Dorset IPA, Dorchester Bitter; Guinness, Stella Artois; Faust Export; Taunton cider. *Real ale*

This friendly, welcoming inn stands in a tiny village below Dartmoor's tallest tors. Low beams and milk-churn tables give a rustic feel to the main bar, where snacks range from soup and sandwiches to pâtés, smoked mackerel and curries, with nice home-made sweets to finish. Airy, spacious bedrooms (all with TV) feature bright floral patterns and many home comforts. Five of them have en suite bathrooms. Patio and garden. **Family pub**

## Helford *(Food)* — *Shipwright's Arms*

Near Helston · *Cornwall* · Map 8 A4
Manaccan (032 623) 235

*Brewery* Devenish
*Landlords* Mr & Mrs Flynn
Ploughman's £1.50 Local crab salad £3.95 (Last order 9.15pm. No bar food Mon–Wed in winter)
Devenish Cornish Best Bitter, Mild; Whitbread Tankard; Guinness; Grünhalle; cider. *Real ale*

You can walk straight down to the sea from the terrace of this charming little thatched pub perched above the Helford estuary. Lunchtime fare consists mainly of ploughman's and a tempting range of salads featuring home-cooked ham, beef or seafood. On winter evenings there are warming dishes like steak and kidney soup or scallops Mornay to be enjoyed in the panelled bar. The covered patio is useful for children.

## Helston *(B & B)* — *Angel Hotel*

Coinage Hall Street · *Cornwall* · Map 8 A4
Helston (032 65) 2701

*Free House*
*Landlords* Mr & Mrs S. W. Hudson

**BEDROOMS 21 Grade 2 £B**
Devenish Cornish Bitter; Worthington Bitter; Whitbread Best Bitter; Flowers Bitter; Guinness; Heineken; Stella Artois. *Real ale*

This welcoming hotel in the town centre has a history stretching back over 500 years. A well complete with a little water-wheel is an unusual feature in the foyer-lounge, and there's a comfortable TV lounge-cum-writing room as well as two bars. Bedrooms of various sizes have pretty floral wallpaper and freestanding furniture. Accommodation closed 1 week Christmas. Terrace. **Family pub**

## Henfield *(Food)* — *White Hart*

High Street · *West Sussex* · Map 6 B4
Henfield (0273) 492006

*Brewery* Charrington
*Landlords* Mr John Dean & Mr A. Sephton
Braised lamb's liver £1.95 Carbonnade of beef £2.45
Bass; Charrington's Mild; Stones Bitter; Worthington Best Bitter; Guinness; Carling Black Label; Tennent's Extra; Taunton cider. *Real ale*

Distinctive glass lanterns cast a rosy glow in the traditionally furnished bar of this friendly, welcoming pub, where capable chef Christopher Boyle provides some delicious fare. Nourishing home-made soups are backed up by tasty main courses such as chicken Marengo, sole provençale and grills. There are salads and Danish open sandwiches too, and simple sweets include fruit pie and cheesecake. Only light snacks available Monday and Tuesday evenings.

## Henley-on-Thames *(Food)* — *Argy!!*

Market Place · *Oxfordshire* · Map 6 B3
Henley-on-Thames (0491) 573400

*Brewery* Morland
*Landlord* Mr R. K. Boswell
Beef stew with dumplings & vegetables £2.30 Chicken & mushroom pie with salad £2.20 (No bar food eves)
Morland's Best Bitter, Bitter, Mild; Guinness; Heineken; Stella Artois. *Real ale*

Tartan carpets and regimental prints lend a Scottish flavour to this cosy town-centre pub, but the emphasis is on traditional English fare when it comes to bar snacks. The well-laden hot and cold buffet offers dishes like stuffed shoulder of lamb or beef stew with dumplings, as well as tasty quiche lorraine and crisp, fresh salads. Don't miss the lovely treacle tart. Less choice Sunday lunch. Patio.

## Henley-on-Thames *(Food)* ★ — *Little Angel*

Remenham Hill · *Oxfordshire* · Map 6 B3
Henley-on-Thames (0491) 574165

*Brewery* Brakspear
*Landlord* Mr Paul Southwood

Open seafood sandwich £2.95 Cottage pie £3 (Last order 10pm)
Brakspear's Bitter, Old Ale; Guinness; Heineken; cider. *Real ale*

In the bustling beamed bars or out on the patio you can enjoy food of outstanding quality at this pretty 16th-century pub. Seafood is something of a speciality (hors d'oeuvre or open sandwich), and the steak and pheasant pie is absolutely bursting with goodness and flavour under its lovely light puff pastry lid. Other delights include subtly smooth pâté, French cheeses and heavenly sweets. Summer cold table.

## Henley-on-Thames *(Food, B & B)* — *Victoria*

Market Place · *Oxfordshire* · Map 6 B3
Henley (0491) 575628
*Brewery* Wethered
*Landlord* Mr Worsdell
**BEDROOMS 4 Grade 2 £C**
Steak & kidney pie & vegetables £1.95
Pork in cream & cider £3.75 (Last order 10.30pm)
Wethered's Bitter, SPA, Winter Royal; Whitbread Best Bitter, Mild; Heineken; cider. *Real ale*

There's a wide variety of tasty home-cooked fare to keep the customers happy at this cheerful pub behind the town hall. Beef and beer stew, casseroled chicken and pork in cream and cider are hearty main courses, with sandwiches and Cornish pasties among the lighter snacks. Nice sweets, too, and a Sunday lunchtime roast. Recently refurbished bedrooms share two public bathrooms. Patio. **Family pub**

## Henton *(Food, B & B)* — *Peacock*

Near Chinnor · *Oxfordshire* · Map 6 B3
Kingston Blount (0844) 53519

*Free House*
*Landlord* Mr H. S. Good
**BEDROOMS 3 Grade 1 £A** (No dogs)
Salmon trout £4.45 T-bone steak £5.85 (Last order 10pm)
Tetley's Bitter; Hall & Woodhouse Badger Best Bitter; Hook Norton Best Bitter; Adnams Bitter; Guinness; Carlsberg; cider. *Real ale*

An attractive thatched village pub, complete with ducks and peacocks in the garden. Very good snacks are served in the comfortable bar, including sandwiches and salads, salmon trout and barbecued lamb ribs. Roast beef can be enjoyed hot or cold, and chocolate fudge cake makes a fine finale. Three spotless bedrooms have smart freestanding furniture and excellent modern bathrooms. Accommodation closed 1 week February.

We neither seek nor accept hospitality, and we pay for all food, drinks and accommodation in full.

## Hereford *(Food)* — *Cock of Tupsley*

Ledbury Road, Tupsley · *Hereford & Worcester*
Map 7 D2
Hereford (0432) 274911

*Brewery* Wolverhampton & Dudley
*Landlords* Mr & Mrs P. & C. Hancox

Tupsley pie £1.90 Smoked salmon quiche £1.90 (No bar food eves or Sun)
Banks's Mild, Bitter; Guinness; Harp; Kronenbourg; cider.

Food is taken seriously at this friendly modern pub, and a large part of the bar is devoted to the enjoyment of tasty, home-prepared snacks. The appetising cold table features pâtés, quiches and salads, and there are also hot daily specials like liver and bacon. A delicious passion cake makes an excellent finish. Light snacks only on Saturday. Garden. **Family pub**

## Hetton *(Food)* — *Angel Inn*

Near Skipton · *North Yorkshire* · Map 4 C2
Cracoe (075 673) 263

*Free House*
*Landlords* Denis & Juliet Watkins

Salade niçoise £1.70 Braised oxtail & vegetables £2.50
Theakston's Bitter, XB; Taylors Landlord; Younger's Scotch Bitter; Webster's Light Mild; Guinness; Carlsberg. *Real ale*

A wide variety of tasty bar food is available at this trim roadside pub, a cheerful sight with its climbing plants and window boxes. In the beamed bars or out on the forecourt you can enjoy anything from flavoursome terrine and smoked fish mousse to lasagne verdi, grills or a generous bowl of salade niçoise. Also sandwiches, home-cooked meats and simple sweets.

## Hexworthy *(B & B)* — *Forest Inn*

Near Princetown · *Devon* · Map 8 B4
Poundsgate (036 43) 211

*Free House*
*Landlords* Mr A. Wise & Mr A. Oake

**BEDROOMS 15 Grade 2 £C**
Bass; Hancocks Bitter; Worthington Best Bitter; Guinness; Tennent's Extra; Pilsner; cider. *Real ale*

Set in a landscape of rugged, desolate beauty, this sturdy Dartmoor inn is a splendid base for tourists and also offers facilities for fishing and horse-riding. The bedrooms, all centrally heated, provide simple, practical comforts and nine have private bathrooms. There are two welcoming bars and a pleasant covered patio hung with climbing plants. Good breakfasts, both in choice and quality. **Family pub**

## High Halden *(Food, B & B)* — *Chequers Inn*

Near Ashford · *Kent* · Map 6 C3
High Halden (023 385) 218

*Brewery* Whitbread
*Landlords* John & Pauline Shaw

**BEDROOMS 3 Grade 2 £C**
Chicken curry £1.75 Chocolate brandy cake 85p (Last order 9pm)
Fremlin's Bitter, Mild; Guinness; Stella Artois; Heineken; cider. *Real ale*

A friendly and convivial atmosphere pervades this fine old roadside pub in the heart of the Kentish countryside. The saloon bar is a suitably homely setting for Pauline Shaw's simple, tasty snacks, which range from sandwiches and hearty soups to curries, grills and basket meals. Sweets like cheesecake and lemon mousse are a strong point. Three modest bedrooms share the family bathroom. Terrace and garden.

## High Offley *(Food)* — *Royal Oak*

Grubb Street · *Staffordshire* · Map 3 B4
Woodseaves (078 574) 579

*Free House*
*Landlords* Lynne & Shirley Hartley

Steak & kidney pudding £2 Fish pie £2 (Last order 10pm. No bar food Sat eve or Sun lunch)
Younger's Traditional, Tartan, Mild; Newcastle Bitter; McEwan's Lager. *Real ale*

A sympathetically modernised village pub run with pride by sisters Lynne and Shirley Hartley. The bar fare ranges from quick snacks like sandwiches and ploughman's platters to deliciously filling vegetable soup, cottage pie, smoked trout salad and a hearty helping of tasty veal fricassee. More limited menu in the evening. Closed Bank Holidays and last two weeks August. Garden.

## Highclere *(B & B)* — *Yew Tree Inn*

Andover Road, Near Newbury · *Berkshire*
Map 6 A3
Newbury (0635) 253360

*Free House*
*Landlords* Mr & Mrs A. M. Greenwood

**BEDROOMS 4 Grade 1 £B** (No dogs)
Wadworth's 6X; Bourne Valley Andover Ale, Henchard Bitter; Guinness; Kestrel; Beck's Bier; Taunton cider. *Real ale*

Everything is kept in apple-pie order at this comfortably refurbished 17th-century inn, a warm and friendly spot for an overnight stop. The bedrooms have very comfortable beds, ample wardrobe space and modern bath or shower rooms with big towels. The spacious open-plan bar boasts two splendid inglenook fireplaces. Patio. **Family pub**

## Hildenborough *(Food)* — *Gate Inn*

Rings Hill · *Kent* · Map 6 C3
Hildenborough (0732) 832103

*Brewery* Whitbread Fremlin
*Landlord* Mr G. R. M. Sankey

Lamb provençale £3 Beef carbonnade £3 (Last order 10pm. No bar food Sun)
Wethered's Bitter; Fremlins Bitter; Tusker Bitter; Guinness; cider. *Real ale*

Seafood is a great attraction at this welcoming inn, with lobster and crayfish at the top of the list. Our beautifully cooked skate with black butter was a really super treat, and there are also meat dishes among the lunchtime hot specials served in the bar. Available at both sessions are soup, salads, prime English cheeses and smashing home-made sweets. Garden. Bar closed Bank Holiday Mondays.

## Hindon *(Food, B & B)* — *Lamb at Hindon*

High Street, Near Salisbury · *Wiltshire*
Map 6 A3
Hindon (074 789) 225
*Free House*
*Landlord* Mr C. Nell
**BEDROOMS 16 Grades 1 & 2 £A**
Lunch dish of the day with vegetables £2.25
Fresh salmon salad £3.50 (Last order 10pm)
Wadworth's 6X; McEwan's Export; Usher's Triple Crown; Guinness; Carlsberg Hof; Kestrel; cider. *Real ale*

The lounge bar of this fine old pub offers a good choice of light snacks such as pâtés, pies, ploughman's and tempting salads featuring local ham or fresh salmon. Curry served with lots of little side dishes is a popular choice among more substantial dishes. Bedrooms are simply furnished – except for one with a four-poster – and six have their own well-kept bathrooms. There's also a small TV lounge. Garden.

## Hipperholme *(Food)* — *Hare & Hounds*

Denholme Gate Road, Near Halifax
*West Yorkshire* · Map 4 C3
Halifax (0422) 202661
*Owners* Viking Taverns
*Landlords* Mr & Mrs B. Anderson
Roast beef & Yorkshire pudding £1.90
Meat & potato pie £1.70 (Last order 10pm. No bar food Sat & eves except Tues & Thurs)
Webster's Yorkshire Light, Bitter; Guinness; Foster's; Holsten; Carlsberg; cider. *Real ale*

Simple, wholesome dishes are well prepared and attractively presented at this welcoming beamed pub. Home-made soup gets things off to a good start, and you could follow with a roast and trimmings, meat and potato pie, lasagne or a cold meat salad. Sweet lovers have plenty to choose from, with desserts like cheesecake and a delicious mandarin flan. Terrace.

## Holcombe *(Food, B & B)* — *Duke of Cumberland*

Near Bath · *Somerset* · Map 8 D3
Stratton-on-the-Fosse (0761) 232412
*Free House*
*Landlords* Mr & Mrs E. G. Pockson
Lasagne & salad £1.70 Tandoori chicken £2.65 (Last order 9.30pm. No bar food Sun lunch & all Mon)
**BEDROOMS 2 Grade 2 £C** (No dogs)
Wadworth's 6X, IPA; Farmer's Glory; Tisbury Local Bitter; Worthington 'E'; Carlsberg Export Hof. *Real ale*

Exotic delights like tandoori chicken, lamb korma and spicy Armenian lamb make for an enterprising menu at the Pocksons' friendly pub. Simpler tastes are catered for by pizzas, lasagne and salads, and you can always ask for a sandwich. Overnight guests have two neat, comfortable bedrooms sharing the family bathroom. Children not accommodated. Terrace. Closed Monday lunch.

## Holmbury St Mary *(Food)* — *Royal Oak*

Near Dorking · *Surrey* · Map 6 B3
Dorking (0306) 730120

*Brewery* Friary Meux
*Landlords* Jacques & Irene Lestrade
French steak sandwich £2.25 Pickwick pie £2.95 (Last order 10.30pm. No bar food Sun eve)
Friary Meux Bitter; Ind Coope Burton Ale, John Bull; Guinness; Skol; Löwenbräu; cider. *Real ale*

A Gallic touch to the food adds to the gastronomic charm of this pretty and thoroughly English village pub. French onion soup makes a satisfying start, and to follow you could have cannelloni, crab salad, a pork chop or perhaps a delicious steak sandwich served with locally made mustard. The restaurant trolley provides a tempting array of sweets. Garden.

**Family pub**

## Holme *(B & B)* — *Smithy Inn*

Via Milnthorpe · *Cumbria* · Map 3 B2
Burton (0524) 781302

*Brewery* Yates & Jackson
*Landlords* Mr & Mrs Barrett

**BEDROOMS 2 Grade 1 £C**
Yates & Jackson Bitter, Mild; Guinness; Heineken; Stella Artois. *Real ale*

The old blacksmith's shop has been cleverly incorporated into this attractively modernised coaching house in a peaceful village. A lot of original stonework survives in the comfortable bars, and there's a pleasant courtyard for drinks in summer. The two bedrooms are very neat and tidy, with washbasins and good-quality furniture; they share a well-equipped modern bathroom. Good breakfast.

## Holt *(Food, B & B)* — *Old Ham Tree*

Near Trowbridge · *Wiltshire* · Map 8 D3
North Trowbridge (0225) 782581

*Free House*
*Landlords* John & Carol Francis
**BEDROOMS 3 Grade 2 £C**
Cheese, leek & ham pie £1.90 Baked fresh mackerel £1.95 (Last order 10pm)
Marston's Pedigree; Eldridge Pope Royal Oak; Wadworth's 6X; Usher's Country Bitter, PA; Carlsberg; cider. *Real ale*

Almost opposite the green, this friendly, cream-painted pub serves a good selection of simple, appetising fare. Home-made soup, plaice on the bone and cottage pie are typical items on the blackboard menu, and apple and mincemeat crumble is a delicious way to round things off. Three neat little bedrooms with modern furniture share an up-to-date bathroom. Garden.

**Family pub**

## Holton — *Old Inn*

This pleasant little whitewashed pub not far from the A303 is a great place for enjoying a drink and chat with the locals. It's very much in the tradition of village pubs, with beams and rafters, flagstoned floors and a welcoming fire in the hearth. Polished wooden tables and comfortable banquettes complete the homely scene.

Near Wincanton · *Somerset* · Map 8 D3
Wincanton (0963) 32002
*Free House* *Landlords* Colin & Jenny Davey
Wadworth's 6X; Hall & Woodhouse Badger Best Bitter; Guinness; Carlsberg Hof; cider. *Real ale*

## Holywell *(Food)* — *Ye Olde Ferry Boat Inn*

Near St Ives, Huntingdon · *Cambridgeshire*
Map 5 C2
St Ives (0480) 63227

*Free House*
*Landlord* Mrs Joyce Edwards
Seafood pancake £2.45 Home-made sorbet & ice cream coupe £1.70 (Last order 10pm)
Greene King IPA, Abbot Ale; Adnams Bitter; Guinness; Carling Black Label; Tennent's Extra; Taunton cider. *Real ale*

With records dating back more than a thousand years, this characterful inn on the banks of the Ouse can claim to be the oldest continuously operating hostelry in the country. It's a popular place for bar meals, offering anything from sustaining vegetable soup and toasted snacks to substantial dishes like flavoursome savoury pancakes, Dover sole and sirloin steak. Sweets include subtly spiced apple pie. Garden. **Family pub**

## Holywell Green *(B & B)* — *Rock Hotel*

Near Halifax · *West Yorkshire* · Map 4 C3
Halifax (0422) 79721

*Free House*
*Landlord* Mr Robert Vinsen

**BEDROOMS 18 Grade 1 £B**
Younger's IPA, Scotch Bitter; Matthew Brown's John Peel, Lion Bitter; Slalom; Kronenbourg; Taunton cider. *Real ale*

Travellers on the M62 will find unusually comfortable pub accommodation at this modernised 17th-century inn close to junction 24. Smartly furnished bedrooms have fitted carpets, colour TVs, telephones, radios, tea-makers and even drinks trays. All have neat little shower rooms, and some enjoy pleasant country views. The split-level bar is a cosy place for a drink. **Family pub**

## Hope *(Food)* — *Poachers Arms*

Castleton Road · *Derbyshire* · Map 4 C3
Hope Valley (0433) 20380

*Free House*
*Landlord* Anton & Barbara Singleton

Game casserole £2.85 Crab claws £3.80 (Last order 10.30pm)
Webster's Dark Mild; Wilson's Bitter; Carlsberg; Foster's; cider. *Real ale*

Fresh local produce, including seasonal game, is used for the delicious bar snacks served at this charming little roadside hotel. A mug of vegetable soup makes a good warming starter, preceding garlic mussels, grilled gammon or steak and kidney pie. Try a hot roll filled with minced meat and cheese for a tasty quick snack. Patio. *For accommodation see Egon Ronay's Lucas Hotel & Restaurant Guide 1985.* **Family pub**

# 'SCOTCH – It's All A Question Of Taste'

Malt whiskies, as produced in individual distilleries all over Scotland, vary widely in taste and character. Just as wine differs between the variety of grapes, so no two single malt whiskies are exactly the same. Some are forceful and peaty, while others are lighter and gentler. In addition, they all have their own 'nose' or aroma.

What causes this variation is a complex matter involving the location of the distillery, the peat and water, the shape and size of the still, the operation of the still, the air and the climate.

These varied elements contribute to the fact that whiskies produced at, for example, the Lagavulin Distillery on Islay, the Cardhu Distillery in Speyside and the Talisker Distillery on the Isle of Skye all differ in style and character.

There are two distinct types of Scotch whisky – malt and grain. Malt whisky is distilled in a pot-still from malted barley, while the grain spirit is produced in a patent or continuous still from maize mashed with malted barley.

Malts tend to be more expensive than blended whiskies, and are traditionally divided into four geographical regions – Highland, Lowland, Islay and the two remaining distilleries in Campbeltown. Highland malt whiskies are distilled to the north of an imaginary line running from Dundee to Greenock, while the Lowland variety come from the south of Scotland.

Most brands of Scotch sold to the public are blends of malt and grain whiskies. Blending is the art of combining a number of single whiskies so that each makes its particular contribution, though none predominates. The blender's object is to achieve a distinctive whisky of the highest possible quality, consistent in flavour and bouquet from one year to another.

# MAPS

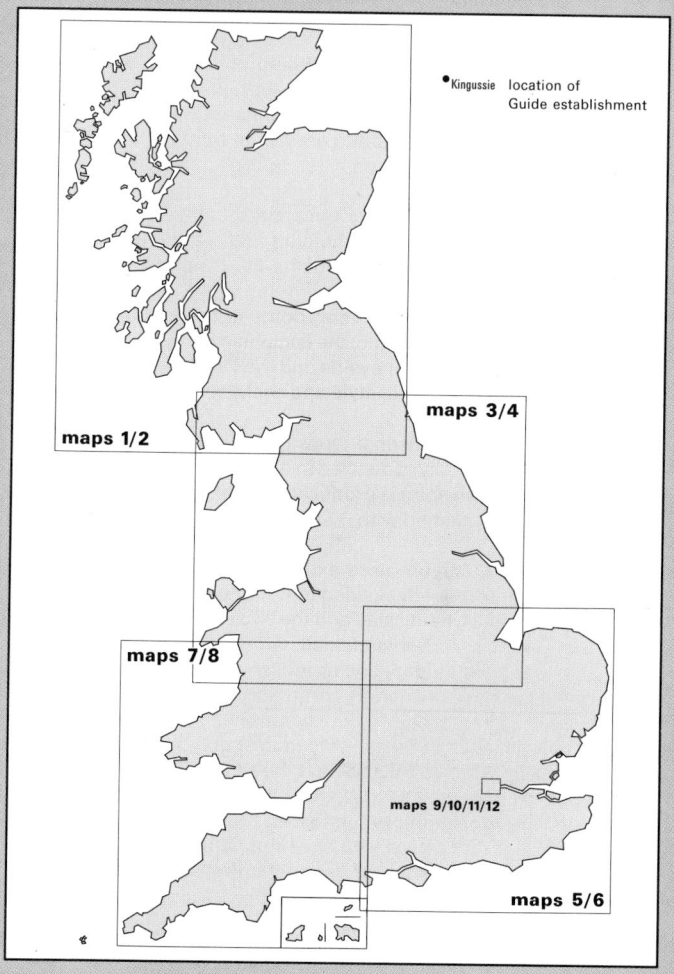
Kingussie location of Guide establishment
maps 1/2
maps 3/4
maps 7/8
maps 9/10/11/12
maps 5/6

CRAWFORD'S *Old Scotch Whisky* CRAWFORD'S

The taste is too good to forget

CRAWFORD'S *Old Scotch Whisky*

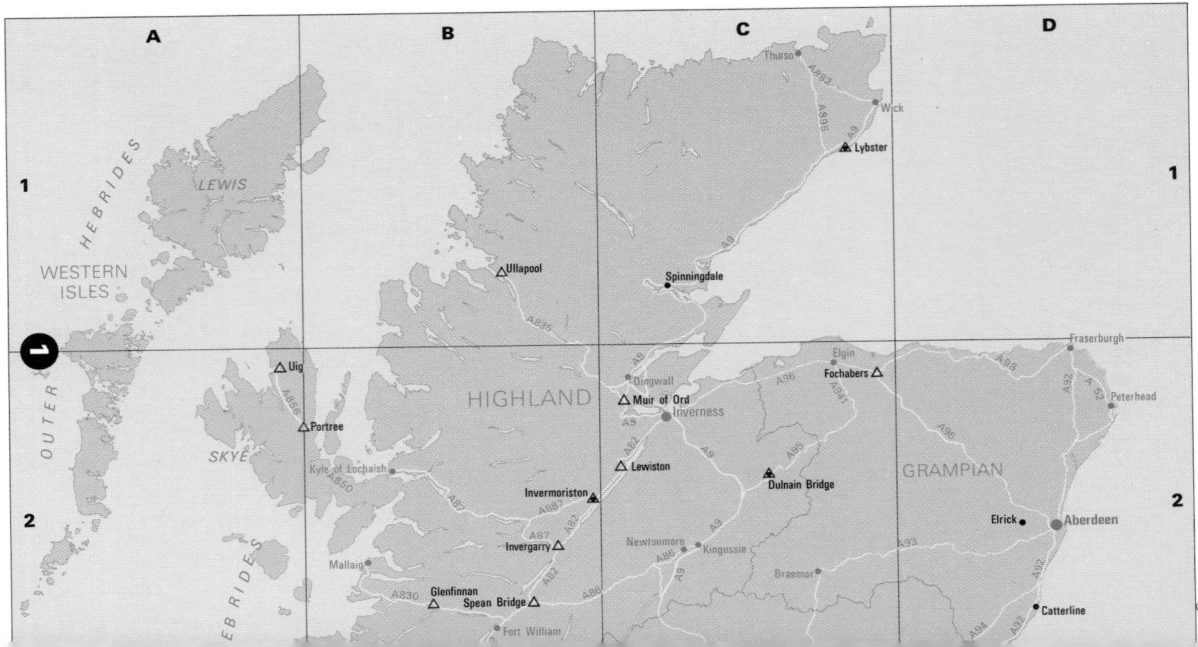

CRAWFORD'S *Old Scotch Whisky*

CRAWFORD'S *Old Scotch Whisky* CRAWFORD'S

The taste is too good to forget

A
B
1
2
3
4
DUMFRIES AND GALLOWAY
Dumfries
Canonbie
New Abbey
Castle Douglas
Metal Bridge
Rockcliffe
Carlisle
Talkin
Warwick-on-Eden
Faugh
Armathwaite
Melmerb
Cockermouth
Bassenthwaite Lake
Workington
Pooley Bridge
Keswick
Askham
Penrith
Whitehaven
Loweswater
CUMBRIA
Wasdale Head
Langdale
Elterwater
Calderbridge
Kirkby Step
Boot
Little Langdale
Troutbeck
Eskdale
Hawkshead
Bowland Bridge
Winster
Kendal
Andreas
ISLE OF MAN
Ramsey
Cartmel Fell
Lowick
Levens
Peel
Douglas
Sandside
Beetham
Holme
Barbo
Caster
Ho-
Ribb
Port St Mary
Barrow-in-Furness
Morecambe
Lancaster
Slaidburn
Forton
Fleetwood
Whitewell
Chipping
Blackpool
Greenhalgh
LANCAS
Preston
Mellor
Blackbur
Southport
Standish
Ainsw
Bolton
Wigan
MERSEYSIDE
MANCHES
Bootle
Burtonwood
Risley
Wallasey
LIVERPOOL
Warrington
Little Bollingto
ANGLESEY
Birkenhead
Widnes
Holyhead
Runcorn
Beaumaris
Colwyn Bay
Parkgate
Ellesmere Port
Plumley
Menai Bridge
Bangor
Conwy
Betws-yn-Rhos
Holywell
Ledsham
Wincham
Lov
Peo
Llanfyllin
Bodfari
Babell
Bridge Trafford
Sandiway
Llanrug
Caernarfon
Mold
Chester
Tarporley
CHESH
Ruthin
Betws-y-coed
CLWYD
Crewe
Wrexham
Nantwich
Newcastle-unt
Morfa Nefyn
Porthmadog
GWYNEDD
Llangollen
Whitchurch
Llanarmon Dyffryn Ceiriog
Oswestry
Penmaenpool
Dolgellau
POWYS
SHROPSHIRE
Shrewsbury
Telford
Machynlleth
© 1985 Egon Ronay's Guides
Crown Copyright Reserved

# head by its nose

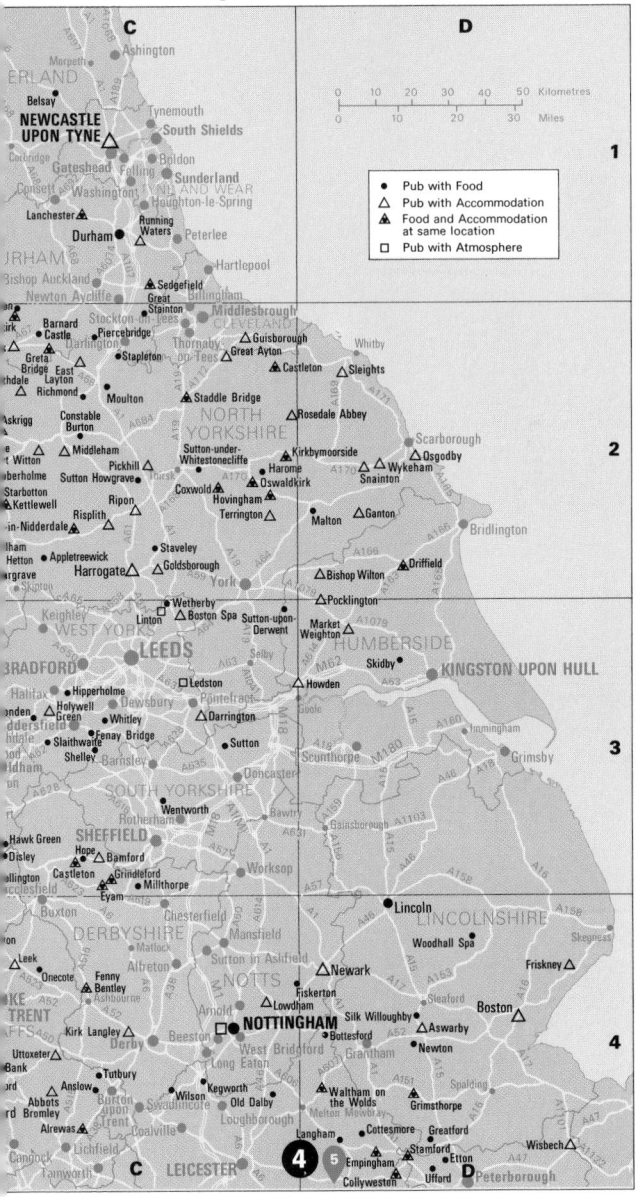


head by its nose

WHITE HORSE Ahead by its nose

Johnnie Walker®

Johnnie Walker®

The perfect Scotch at all even

Johnnie Walker® Johnn

A B C D

1 2 3 4 5 7

Leek Onecote Mansfield Sutton in Ashfield Alfreton Matlock Newark Woodhall Spa Skegness Frisknev

Fenny Bentley STAFFS DERBYSHIRE NOTTS LINCOLNSHIRE Fiskerton Lowdham Arnold Ashbourne Seaford

NOTTINGHAM Beeston Silk Willoughby Boston Wells-next-the-Sea Cromer

Kirk Langley Derby West Bridgford Bottesford Aswarby Hunworth Briston

Uttoxeter Long Eaton Newton Dersingham Bircham Blicking

Tutbury Anslow Kegworth Grantham Great Ryburgh Winterton-on-Sea

Stafford Abbots Bromley Wilson Old Dalby Waltham on the Wolds Spalding King's Lynn East Dereham

Alrewas Burton upon Trent Swadlincote Loughborough Melton Mowbray Grimsthorpe Cromer

Cannock Coalville Cottesmore Greatford Wisbech Norwich Great Yarmouth

Lichfield Langham Oakham Stamford Stow Bardolph Swaffham Bawburgh

Tamworth LEICESTERSHIRE Empingham Etton Downham Market NORFOLK

WOLVERHAMPTON Collyweston Ufford Peterborough March

Wednesbury Sutton Coldfield LEICESTER Wansford Nassington Whittlesey

West Bromwich Hinckley Lyddington Fotheringhay Bungay Lowestoft

Coleshill Bedworth Nuneaton Weldon Beccles

Stourbridge BIRMINGHAM Harborough Corby Great Oxendon Rothwell Thetford Scole Southwold

Solihull Kettering CAMBRIDGESHIRE Ely Diss Brome

COVENTRY Keyston Molesworth Mildenhall

Bromsgrove Rugby Huntingdon Needingworth

Dunchurch NORTHAMPTONSHIRE East Haddon Fen Drayton Holywell

WARWICKSHIRE Wellingborough Elsworth Horningsea Bury St Edmunds Framlingham

Redditch Leamington Spa Warwick Madingley Newmarket Easton

Sambourne Aston Cantlow Weedon Northampton St Neots Woodditton SUFFOLK

Wilmcote Wellesbourne Priors Hardwick Eltisley Kirtling Needham Market

Stratford-upon-Avon Grantchester Newton Cambridge Bromeswell

Bidford-on-Avon Blakesley Hartwell Bedford Linton Long Melford Chelsworth Woodbridge Orford

Evesham Mickleton Fowlmere Cavendish Clare Ipswich

Chipping Campden Shipston on Stour Shennington Stony Stratford Royston Duxford Little Walden Kersey Washbrook

Bourton-on-the-Hill Great Wolford Moreton-in-Marsh West Adderbury Westbury Ashwell Great Chishill Saffron Walden Boxford Upper Layham Levington

Toddington Winchcombe Broadwell Chipping Norton Buckingham Milton Keynes Newton Gestingthorpe Stoke-by-Nayland Pin Mill Felixstowe

Kineton Naunton Stow-on-the-Wold Upper Oddington Bledington Enstone Weston-on-the-Green Woburn Bletchley Willian Walkern Little Hadham Braintree Chappel Dedham Harwich

Winslow Marsh Gibbon Stewkley Dunstable Stevenage Puckeridge Colchester

Mentmore Luton Bishop's Stortford Coggeshall

Johnnie Walker®

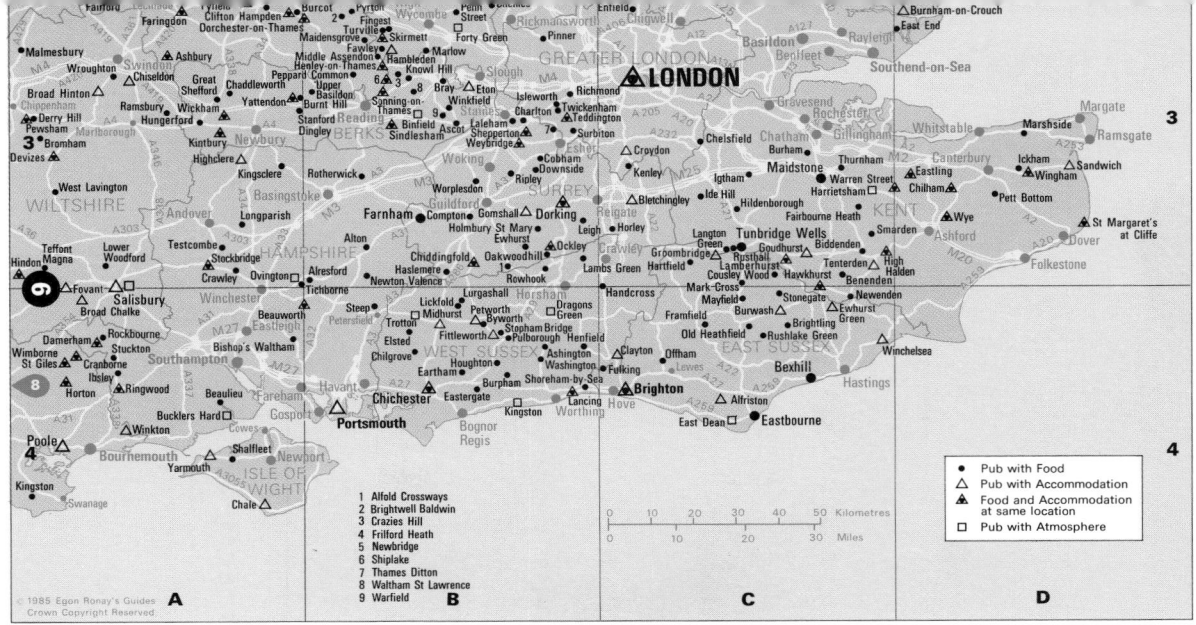


The perfect Scotch at all events

Johnnie Walker®

Johnnie Walker®

THE OLDEST NAME IN SCOTCH WHISKY

# Don't be vague, ask for HAIG

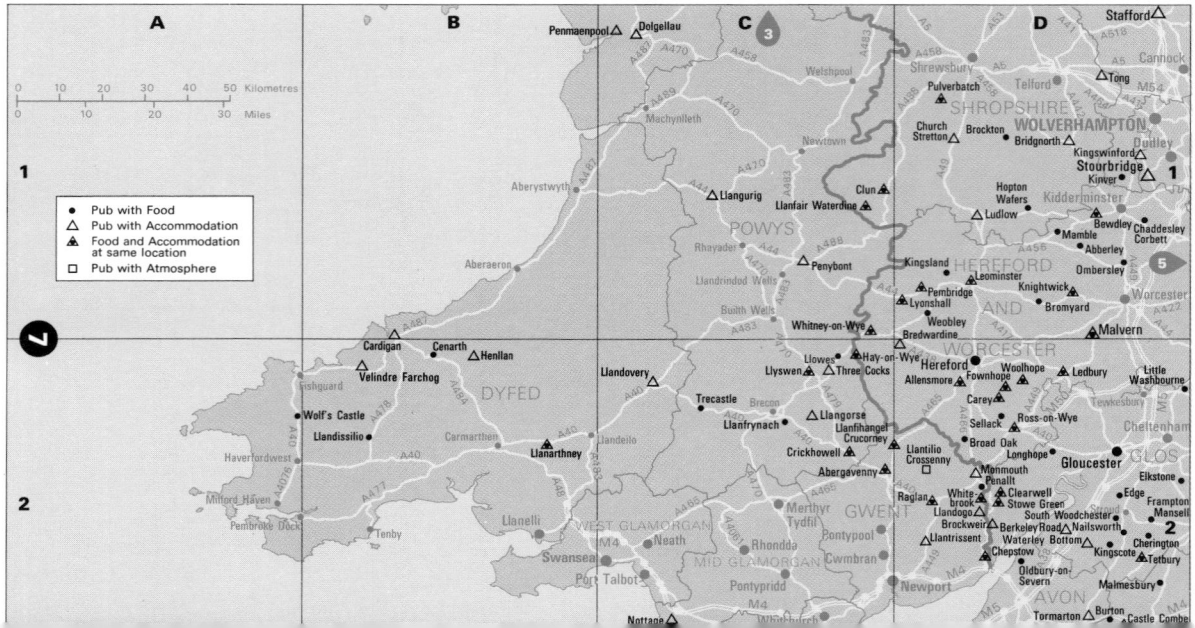


HAIG

Don't be vague, ask for HAIG

THE OLDEST NAME IN SCOTCH WHISKY

Don't be vague, ask for HAIG

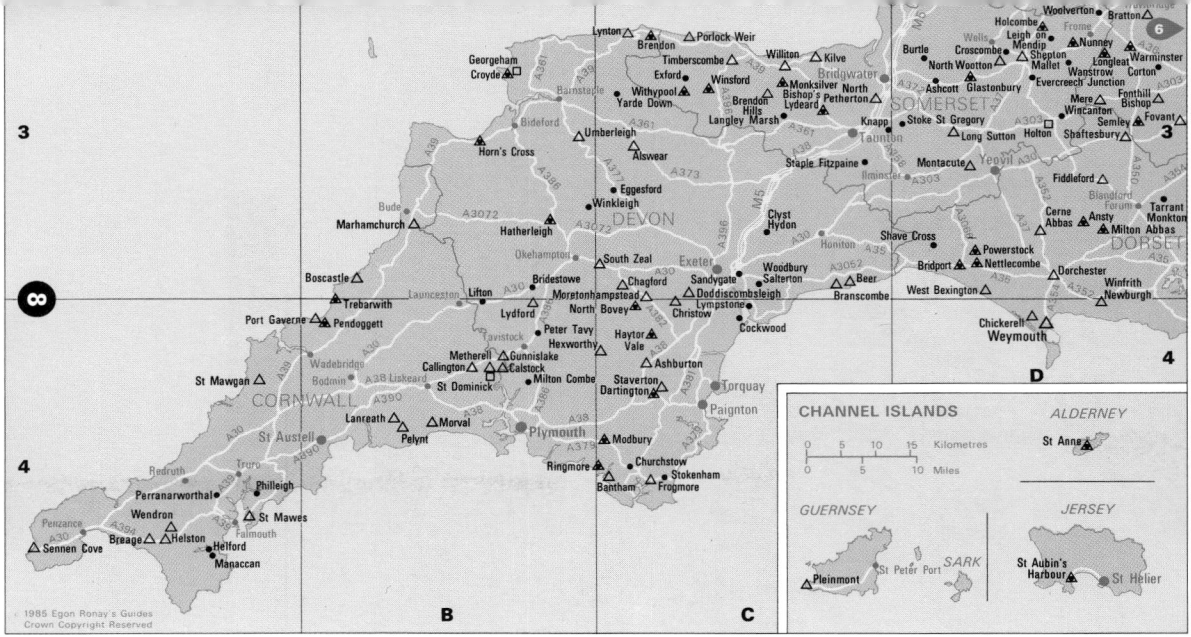


Don't be vague, ask for HAIG

# People go to great lengths to eat the best.

People like you, who use Egon Ronay guides, expect the best whenever they eat out.

Which is why you'll expect Uncle Ben's to be served with your favourite rice dish.

Because Uncle Ben's is the best rice in the world.

And whether you eat fluffy Long Grain, Natural Wholegrain or the more exotic Long Grain & Wild, the same high standards of quality apply.

So go to great lengths to eat the best rice. Uncle Ben's is well worth the effort.

**Uncle Ben's®**

**The Best Rice in the World.**

Uncle Ben's Rice, Dornay Foods, P.O. Box 15, Hansa Road, King's Lynn, Norfolk

HINE COGNAC

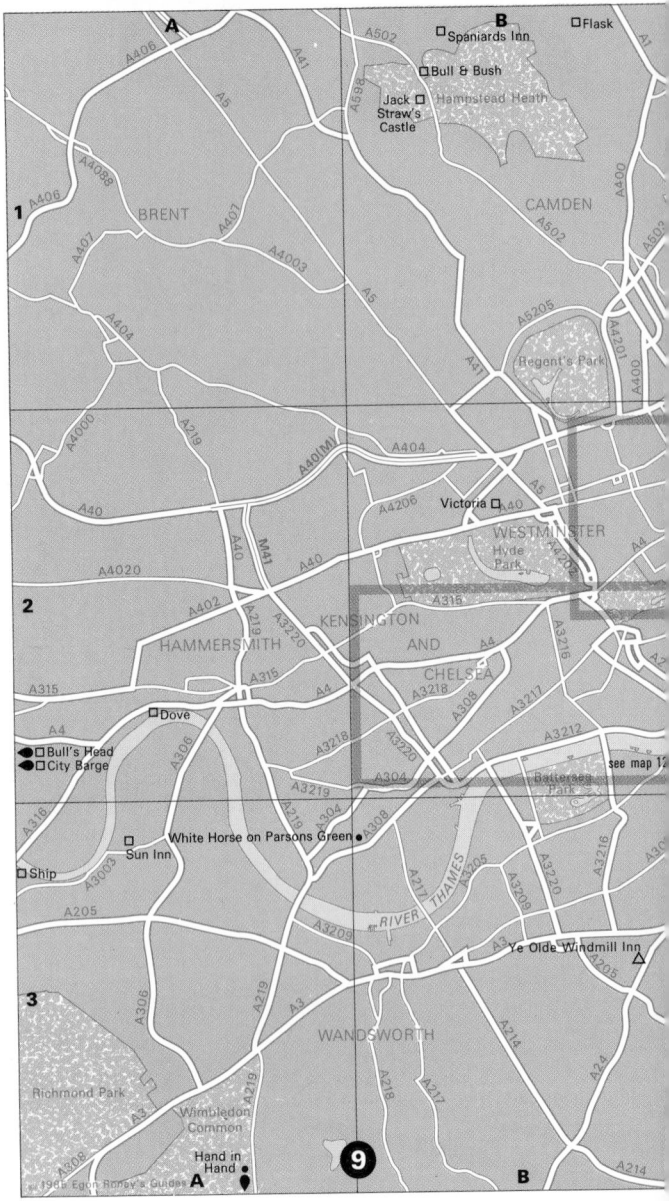


HINE COGNAC HINE COGNAC

Savour the moment

HINE COGNAC

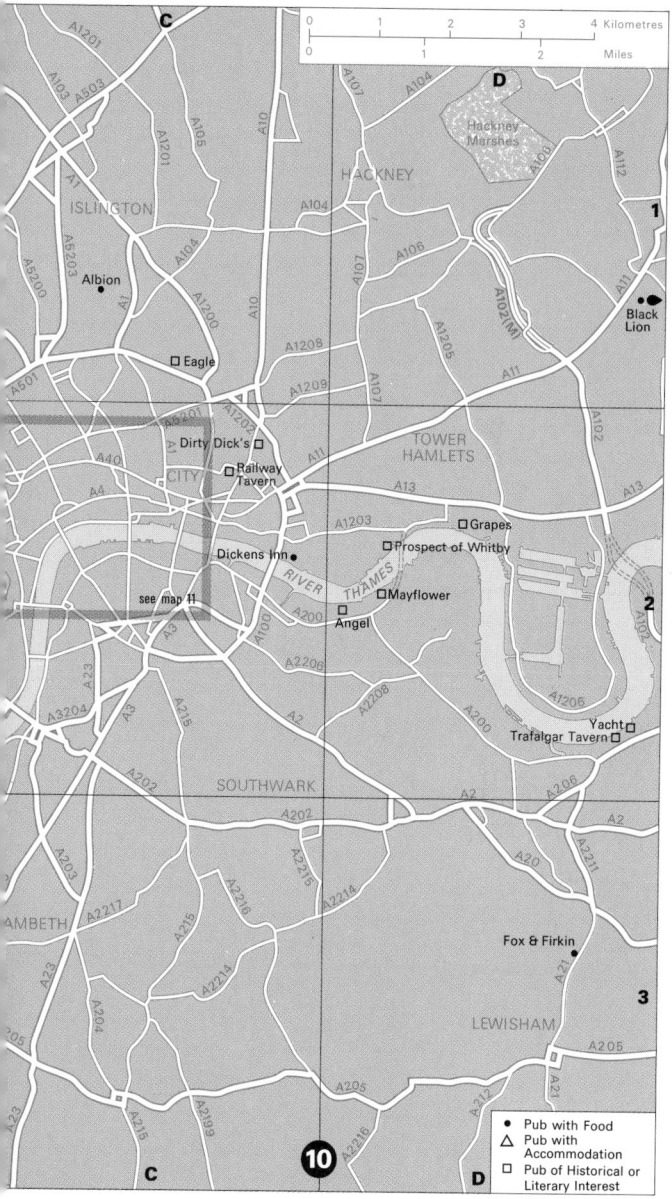


HINE COGNAC HINE COGNAC

Savour the moment

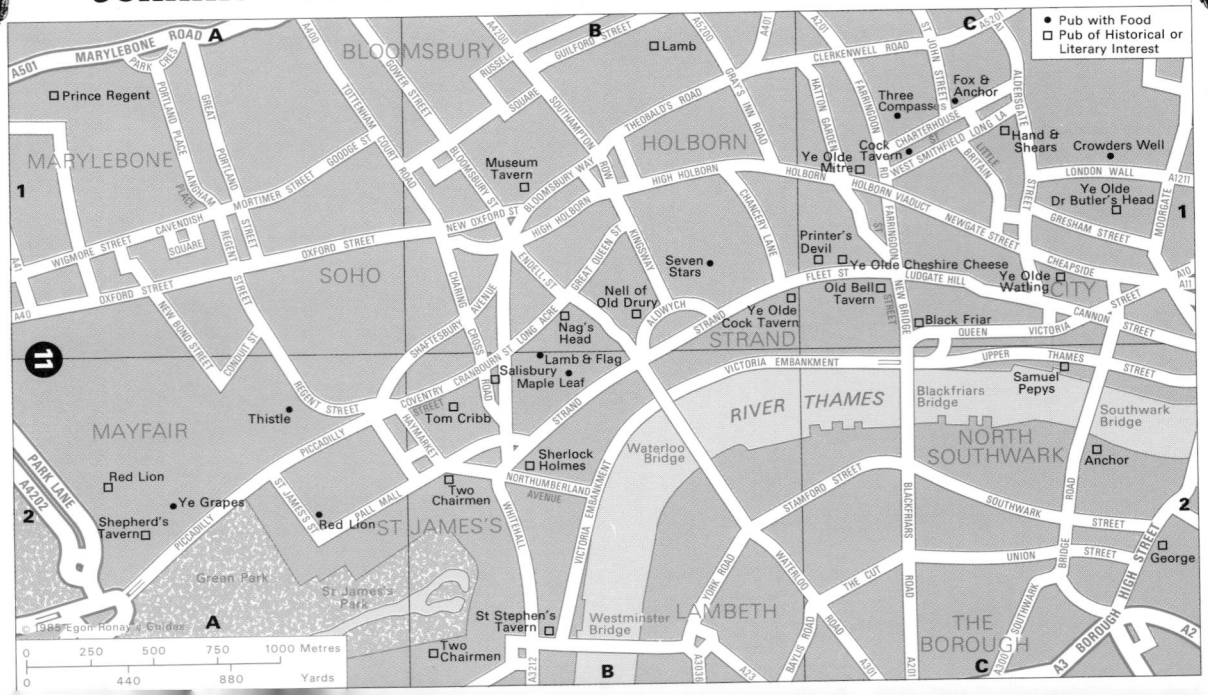


Other pleasures pale beside it

Johnnie Walker® BLACK LABEL

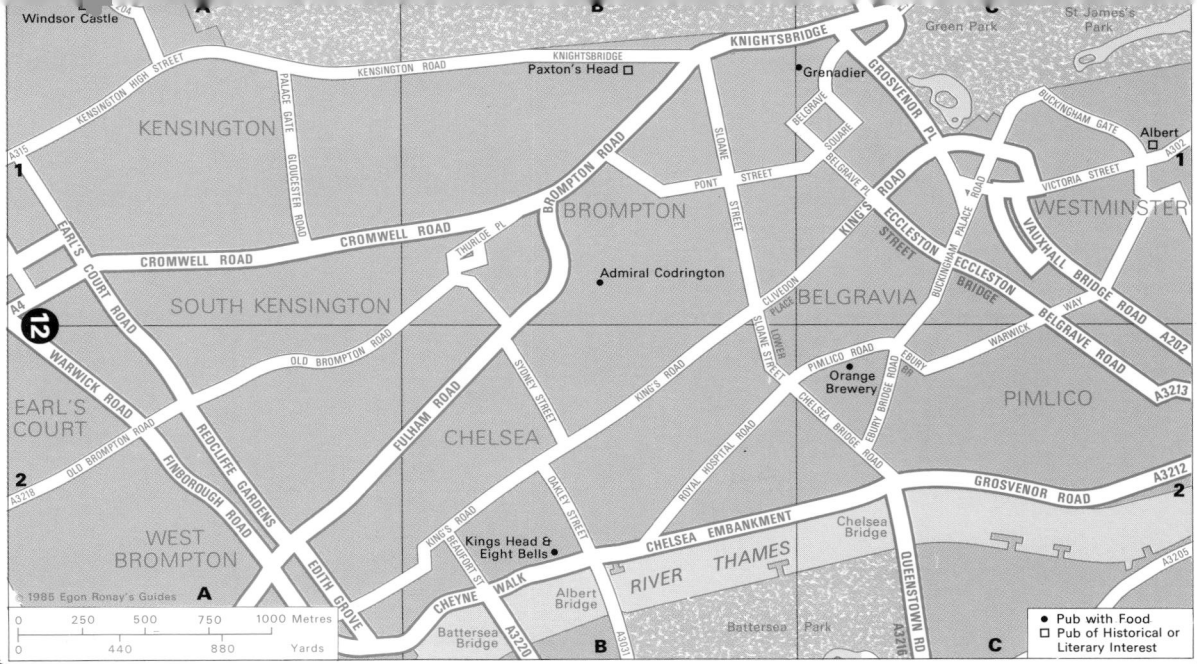




Johnnie Walker® BLACK LABEL Johnnie Walker® 12

OTHER PLEASURES PALE BESIDE IT

**Whether on business or vacation in Great Britain & Ireland, consult *Egon Ronay's Lucas Guide 1985* to Hotels, Restaurants & Inns**

It recommends the 2,500 best UK hotels and restaurants, spotlighting de luxe, country house and executive hotels as well as those with sporting and leisure facilities. Restaurants with above average food are starred. There is also an extensive economy section including hundreds of bargain weekend breaks and inexpensive evening meals in London.

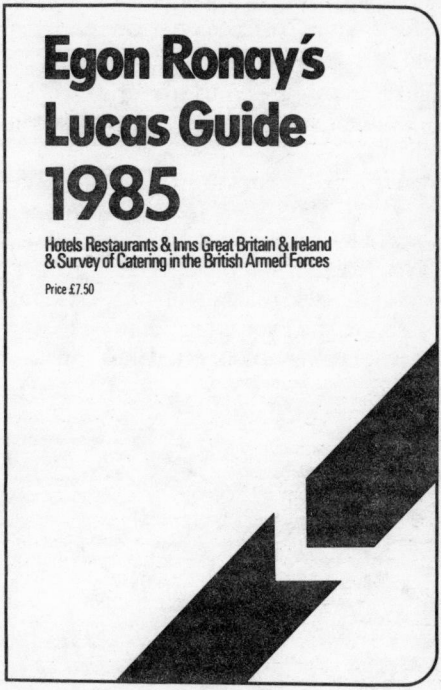


Contains 832 pages including 56 pages of maps

£7.50 from bookshops everywhere or £8.60 including postage and packing from:

Egon Ronay Organisation Ltd, Greencoat House,
Francis Street, London SW1P 1DH

*See colour pages and page 14 for news about Egon Ronay's other 1985 guides.*

# CHEERS FOR ENGLISH CHEESE

IF CHEESE and wine is a comparatively modern pairing – in this country at any rate – cheese and ale has represented the successful marrying of traditional food and drink for longer than anyone can remember.

Both are an integral part of our way of life, and the cheeses of England and Wales form a natural part of every good pub menu.

There are nine traditional English and Welsh cheeses, although new variations are constantly being developed, with additions of herbs, pickles and spices, as well as with the introduction of English soft blue cheeses.

Even today cheese making remains a natural, traditional process. Just as grape juice is fermented into wine and hops into beer, so whole milk is converted into cheese.

The English Cheese Quality Mark signifies that Mark cheese is of a uniformly high standard.

Implemented by established graders with years of experience in selecting cheese, the Mark is awarded only to those cheeses which meet the required standards of quality and consistency set by the English Country Cheese Council.

Cheese naturally complements every drink from local-brewed ciders to real ales. Wines in particular often help bring out the subtlest of flavours – Cheddar, for example, is delicious with a full claret or burgundy, while Lancashire is especially suited to a dry red wine.

Double Gloucester and Cheshire show up particularly well against a light claret or a tawny port, Derby with a ruby port. Stilton and Leicester will be appreciated when eaten with a red burgundy, tawny or vintage port, while the subtlety of Wensleydale and Caerphilly are enhanced by a hock, a fino sherry or a dry white wine.

Chances are you'll find English and Welsh cheese in your local, so enjoy some at lunch today, as a wholesome meal with a pint of cider, ale or milk or as a natural snack with a glass of red or white wine or port.

## RED LEICESTER

This russet red cheese is recognisable both by its colour and its clean, buttery flavour. Best when about three months old, it's at its peak when its cutting leaves a smear on the knife.

## LANCASHIRE

Lancashire is a creamy white cheese with a crumbly texture and mild, country fresh flavour. It makes mouthwatering melted toppings and sauces.

## CAERPHILLY

Caerphilly, the pride of Wales, is a young white cheese with a close, moist texture and fresh, mild taste. It's specially good with bread and celery.

## WENSLEYDALE

Mild flavoured and flaky, Wensleydale melts in your mouth, leaving a delicious honeyed after-taste. A marvellous way to end a meal, especially with fresh fruit.

## DERBY

Mild when young, Derby develops a distinct and unique tang as it matures. Sage Derby, flavoured with chopped sage leaves, is a Christmas favourite.

## CHEDDAR

Cheddar is the most popular cheese in Britain. Quality Selected Mild Cheddar is at least 8 weeks old, while Mature Cheddars are aged for at least 5 months.

Creamy yellow with a full bodied, nutty flavour, Cheddar is ideal for a hearty ploughman's lunch.

## CHESHIRE

Cheshire is the oldest English cheese. Red and White Cheshire have a mild, slightly salty flavour and a crumbly texture. Blue Cheshire is mellow and creamy.

## STILTON

This King of Cheese is well known for its cream-white colour, royal blue veins and rough, amber crust. The flavour is rich and creamy and blends beautifully with vintage Port.

## DOUBLE GLOUCESTER

Golden in colour, Double Gloucester is a smooth, sophisticated cheese with a unique mellow flavour. A marvellous companion to fresh fruit and salads.

**English Cheese. Only the best is up to the Mark.**

English Country Cheese Council, 5-7 John Princes Street, London W1M 0AP.

## Hopton Wafers *(Food)* — *Crown Inn*

Near Cleobury Mortimer · *Shropshire*
Map 7 D1
Cleobury Mortimer (0299) 270372

*Free House*
*Landlord* Mrs L. V. G. Harrison
Hot crab pâté £1.80 Filled pancakes & salad £2.10 (Last order 10pm)
Marston's Pedigree; Younger's Tartan; Guinness; Carlsberg; Stella Artois; Taunton cider. *Real ale*

You'll find a varied assortment of tasty dishes at this pleasant, creeper-clad pub. Hot saffron prawns and savoury stuffed pancakes are firm favourites, and you can also get things like steak, lasagne and salads. To finish there's a super selection of sweets – from meringue gâteau and syrup sponge to ice creams and sorbets. Children's menu too. Closed Monday except Bank Holidays. **Family pub**

## Horley *(Food)* — *Ye Olde Six Bells*

Church Road · *Surrey* · Map 6 C3
Horley (029 34) 2209

*Brewery* Vintage Inns
*Landlords* Geoffrey & Rish Noble
Home-cooked cold meats with salads from £3 Hot pot £4 (Last order 9.30pm. No bar food Sun lunch)
Charrington's IPA; Bass; Toby; Tennent's Extra; Carling Black Label; Guinness; Taunton cider. *Real ale*

The Nobles take great pride in running this fascinating old pub, whose history can be traced back more than a thousand years. Under an extraordinary beamed roof (mind your head) you'll find some very good bar snacks, from succulent cold meats and crisp salads to hot dishes such as cottage pie and evening specials like Somerset pork. Free hot herb bread at Sunday lunchtime. The large rear garden borders the river Mole.

## Horningsea *(Food)* — *Plough & Fleece*

High Street · *Cambridgeshire* · Map 5 C2
Cambridge (0223) 860795

*Brewery* Greene King
*Landlords* Mr & Mrs K. Grimes

Suffolk ham hot pot £2.40 Welsh fish pie £3.25 (Last order 9.30pm. No bar food Sun & Mon eves)
Greene King Abbot Ale, IPA, Mild; Guinness; Harp; Kronenbourg; cider. *Real ale*

Imaginative, tasty bar fare complements the charms of this pretty village pub. Mr and Mrs Grimes' tempting menu features dishes like hot garlic cockles, Suffolk ham hot pot and casseroled pigeon. There are salads, too, and some marvellous desserts like cherry cobbler and treacle tart. Sandwiches are an additional option at lunchtime. Ploughman's only for Sunday lunch. Garden.

## Horn's Cross *(Food, B & B)* — *Hoops Inn*

Near Bideford · *Devon* · Map 8 B3
Horn's Cross (023 75) 222

*Free House*
*Landlords* June & Jimmy Malcolm
**BEDROOMS 14 Grade 1 £B**
Cheesy hammy eggy £1.35 Home-made sweets 90p (Last order 10pm)
Whitbread Best Bitter, Flower's Best Bitter, IPA; Guinness; Heineken; Stella Artois; cider. *Real ale*

A steaming bowl of home-made soup in front of a log fire provides an inviting introduction to this cosy old thatched pub. Other simple bar snacks include the popular ham, egg and grilled cheese on toast and tempting puds, and June Malcolm also does a good breakfast. Delightful traditional bedrooms in the main building are surpassed by modern ones in the converted coach house, which boast TVs, drinks, fridges and luxurious bathrooms.

## Horton *(Food, B & B)* — *Horton Inn*

Cranborne, Near Wimbourne · *Dorset*
Map 6 A4
Witchampton (0258) 840252
*Free House*
*Landlords* Mr & Mrs P. J. Purtill
**BEDROOMS 5 Grade 1 £C** (No dogs)
Steak & kidney pie £3.25 Crevettes in garlic butter £2.95 (Last order 10pm)
Wadworth's 6X; Burton's Bitter; Poole's Bitter; Guinness; Löwenbräu; Oranjeboom; cider. *Real ale*

New owners have many plans for this handsome 18th-century inn standing outside the village on the B3078. The five immaculate bedrooms are spacious, airy and very comfortable, and two have large private bathrooms. Excellent snacks served in the bar include pâté en croûte, garlic prawns and flavour-packed steak and kidney pie, with home-made ice creams and splendidly rich chocolate mousse to finish. Garden.

## Horton in Ribblesdale *(B & B)* — *Crown Hotel*

Near Settle · *North Yorkshire* · Map 3 B2
Horton in Ribblesdale (072 96) 209

*Brewery* Matthew Brown
*Landlord* Mr Richard Hargreaves

**BEDROOMS 10 Grade 2 £C**
Matthew Brown's John Peel, Bitter, Mild; Guinness; Slalom; cider. *Real ale*

Grouse-shooting parties and hikers alike favour this old whitewashed inn standing right on the Pennine Way just off the A65. Comfortable bedrooms are warm and attractively decorated and share two neat bathrooms. Guests can relax in the homely TV lounges or in the welcoming beamed bars with French windows opening on to the beer garden. **Family pub**

## Houghton *(Food)* — *George & Dragon Inn*

Near Arundel · *West Sussex* · Map 6 B4
Bury (079 881) 559

*Free House*
*Landlord* Mr Tyler

Roast beef salad £3.75 Trout £4.25 (Last order 10pm)
Young's Special; Fuller's London Pride; King & Barnes Bitter; Guinness; Carlsberg; Holsten; cider. *Real ale*

Charles II is said to have stopped at this fine old flint inn while fleeing after the battle of Worcester. It's best, however, not to rush over the well-prepared bar snacks, which range from egg mayonnaise or pâté to devilled whitebait, cold meat salads, fresh trout and daily specials like king prawns or lamb cutlets. There are some tempting sweets, too, plus grills in the evening. Garden.

## Hovingham *(Food, B & B)* — *Worsley Arms Hotel*

*North Yorkshire* · Map 4 C2
Hovingham (065 382) 234

*Free House*
*Landlord* Mr B. Precious
**BEDROOMS 14 Grade 1 £A+**
Home-made quiche £1.65 Cold meats & salad £2 (No bar food eves)
Theakston's Best Bitter, Old Peculier; Younger's Tartan; Double Diamond; Guinness; Carlsberg; cider. *Real ale*

Good food and comfortable accommodation are to be found at this handsome Georgian stone inn. Lunchtime snacks in the bar include tasty soups and pâtés, plus salads, flans and fresh fish, with delicious sweets to finish. Overnight guests have 14 prettily decorated bedrooms, all with their own bathrooms, and can relax in the cosy lounge or TV room. Garden.
**Family pub**

## Howden *(B & B)* — *Bowmans Hotel*

Bridgegate · *Humberside* · Map 4 D3
Howden (0430) 30805

*Brewery* North Country Breweries
*Landlord* Mr Tomas Munoz

**BEDROOMS 13 Grade 1 £A**
North Country Old Traditional, Ridings Bitter, Mild; Guinness; Stella Artois; cider. *Real ale*

Horse brasses and old prints recall coaching inn days in the bars of this welcoming hostelry. It's a very good place for an overnight stop, being in the centre of town and just a short drive from the M62. Centrally heated bedrooms are neat and comfortable, with smart white fitted furniture, floral print duvets, TVs and telephones. All but two have compact tiled bathrooms. Patio.
**Family pub**

## Hubberholme *(Food, B & B)* — *George Inn*

Kirk Gill, Near Skipton · *North Yorkshire*
Map 4 C2
Kettlewell (075 676) 223

*Free House*
*Landlord* John Frederick
**BEDROOMS 4 Grade 2 £C**
Steak & kidney pudding £2.35 Chicken & ham pie £2.35 (Last order 9.30)
Younger's IPA, Scotch Bitter; Harp; Taunton cider. *Real ale*

A walk in the fells is just the thing to work up an appetite for the tasty, robust fare served at this welcoming village pub by the river. Thick soups, pies, casseroles and home-cooked ham are all featured on the menu, along with a splendid apple pie. Four prettily decorated bedrooms cater for overnight guests who can enjoy a hearty breakfast in the morning. Children under eight not accommodated. Patio. **Family pub**

## Hungerford *(Food)* — *Bear at Hungerford*

Charnham Street · *Berkshire* · Map 6 A3
Hungerford (0488) 82512

*Owners* Fine Inns
*Landlords* Mrs J. Dickson & Mr D. Evans

Spinach flan £1.85 Rare beef open sandwich £2.15 (Last order 9.30pm)
Arkell's BB, BBB; Morland's Pale Ale; Guinness; Carlsberg Hof; Arkell's 1843 Lager; cider. *Real ale*

An ancient and historic inn, where snacks are served in two characterful bars boasting splendid fishing trophies. Soup, spinach flan and devilled whitebait are popular for starters or light meals, while main courses include eggs and bacon, roast turkey salad and cooked-to-order steak and kidney pie. Also sandwiches at lunchtime. Patio. *For accommodation see Egon Ronay's Lucas Hotel & Restaurant Guide 1985.* **Family pub**

## Huntingdon *(Food, B & B)* — *George*

George Street · *Cambridgeshire* · Map 5 B2
Huntingdon (0480) 51947

*Free House*
*Landlord* R. L. Gardiner

**BEDROOMS 25 Grade 1 £A**
Ploughman's platter £1.60 Lasagne verdi £2.95 (Last order 9.30pm)
Greene King IPA, Abbot Ale; Younger's Tartan; Stones Bitter; Carlsberg. *Real ale*

A fine galleried courtyard is just one of the many charming period features of this old posting house. Tasty snacks served in the comfortable, popular bar include sandwiches, quiches, salads from the cold buffet and hot dishes like lasagne or braised liver (less choice evenings and Sunday lunch). Bedrooms are spacious and nicely furnished; and all have TVs and most have private bathrooms. **Family pub**

## Huntingdon *(Food)* ★ *Old Bridge Hotel*

1 High Street · *Cambridgeshire* · Map 5 B2
Huntingdon (0480) 52681

*Free House*
*Landlord* Mr R. Waters

Tortellini carbonara £3.25 Gruyère cheese fritters £2.65 (Last order 10.30pm)
Ruddle's County; Paine's St Neots Bitter; Tolly Cobbold Best Bitter; Adnams Southwold Bitter; Kestrel. *Real ale*

This smart, ivy-clad Georgian house by the Great Ouse offers high-quality bar snacks in comfortable, civilised surroundings. Gruyère fritters and richly flavoured chicken liver pâté are splendid starters, which you might follow with tortellini carbonara or delicious seafood pancakes. There's also a popular cold buffet and some lovely sweets. Garden. *For accommodation see Egon Ronay's Lucas Hotel & Restaurant Guide 1985.* **Family pub**

## Hunworth *(Food)* *Bell Inn*

The Green, Near Holt · *Norfolk* · Map 5 D1
Holt (026 371) 2300

*Free House*
*Landlords* Brian & Dolores Bunting
Gammon with salad & chips £3.20 Home-cooked ham £2.20 (Last order 8.30pm)
Adnams Bitter; Whitbread Mild; Sam Smith's Sovereign; Woodforde's Bitter; Guinness; Hansa; Löwenbräu; Taunton cider. *Real ale*

Bar snacks are simple and satisfying at this welcoming, 17th-century village pub. Soups, pâtés and ploughman's are supplemented by steaks and daily specials like spaghetti bolognese, game pie, home-cooked ham and delicious pork and vegetable hot pot. Barbecues are a popular feature in summer, and there are always salads and sandwiches, too. Garden.
**Family pub**

## Hyde Heath *(Food)* *Plough*

Near Amersham · *Buckinghamshire* · Map 6 B3
Chesham (0494) 783163

*Brewery* Benskins
*Landlord* Mrs S. Willcocks
Prawn & asparagus au gratin £2.25 Beef carbonnade £2 (Last order 10pm. No bar food Sun eve)
Benskins Bitter, Pale; Ind Coope John Bull Bitter; Guinness; Skol; Löwenbräu; cider. *Real ale*

Sandra Willcocks provides an imaginative, flavoursome range of bar snacks at this cosy little village pub. Hot garlic mushrooms, prawn and asparagus au gratin, paprika pork casserole and beef carbonnade are some of the tempting items on her menu, and there are also splendid salads like lettuce with walnuts and cucumber. Fish or sausage and chips caters for simpler tastes. Garden.

## Ibsley *(Food)* *Old Beams Inn*

Near Ringwood · *Hampshire* · Map 6 A4
Ringwood (042 54) 3387

*Free House*
*Landlords* Major family
Steak pie £3.50 Grilled steak from £5.70 (Last order 10.15pm)
Ringwood Best Bitter; Wadworth's 6X, Old Timer; Gibbs Mew Bishop's Tipple; Eldridge Pope Royal Oak; Guinness; Harp; cider. *Real ale*

A huge display of a score of eye-catching salads is a feature of the bar at this delightful old pub made up of two thatched cottages. There's also a wide choice of hot dishes such as vegetable soup, steak pie, braised oxtail and excellent roast lamb. If you're still hungry, finish with sherry trifle or a home-made fresh fruit pie. Garden.
**Family pub**

## Ickham *(Food)* — *Duke William*

The Street · *Kent* · Map 6 D3
Canterbury (0227) 721308

*Free House*
*Landlord* Mr A. R. McNeill
Braised rabbit & veg £2.95 Steaks from £4.50
(Last order 10pm)
Young's Bitter, Special; Fuller's London Pride; Shepherd Neame Masterbrew; Guinness; Tennent's Extra; Hurliman's Lager; cider. *Real ale*

Festooned with hops, the bar of this pretty high-street inn is a cosy place to enjoy a pint and a tasty snack from Mr McNeill's wide-ranging menu. Salt beef, poached haddock, braised rabbit, steak and quiche are all featured on the menu, along with simpler items like sandwiches, salads and soup. Nice sweets, too, such as blackberry and apple pie. Garden and patio.

**Family pub**

## Ide Hill *(Food)* — *Cock Inn*

Near Sevenoaks · *Kent* · Map 6 C3
Ide Hill (073 275) 310

*Brewery* Friary Meux
*Landlord* Mr Arnett

Plate of fresh prawns £2.50 Gammon, egg & chips £3
(Last order 8.30pm. No bar food Sun eve)
Friary Meux Bitter; Ind Coope Mild, Burton Ale; Guinness; Löwenbräu; cider. *Real ale*

Facing the village green, this 15th-century inn is popular with locals who like to gather round the inglenook fireplace in the beamed bar. Mr Arnett's wholesome snacks range from herb sausages and pâté and cheese to burgers served with crisp chips, cold meat and seafood salads and toasted sandwiches. Steak and kidney pie is a tasty winter special. Sandwiches only Sunday lunchtime. Terrace.

## Ightham *(Food)* — *George & Dragon*

The Street, Near Sevenoaks · *Kent* · Map 6 C3
Borough Green (0732) 882440

*Brewery* Whitbread
*Landlord* Mr T. K. Peters
Steak & kidney pie £2.50 Chicken curry £2.40
(Last order 10pm. No bar food Sun & Mon eves)
Whitbread Best Mild, Bitter; Wethered's Bitter; Guinness; Heineken; Stella Artois; cider. *Real ale*

Parts of this handsome pub date back to the 16th century, and it still has a splendid timbered façade. Inside you will find a welcoming atmosphere and appetising snacks such as delicious home-made soups, rich, tender steak and kidney pie, chicken curry and ham carved off the bone. For a lighter snack there's a wide choice of sandwiches. The large garden is an additional asset.

## Isleworth *(Food)* — *London Apprentice*

62 Church Street · *Middlesex* · Map 6 B3
01-560 6136

*Brewery* Watneys
*Landlord* A. Cain

Ploughman's £1.05 Beef salad £2.25
(Last order 9.30pm)
Watneys Stag Bitter, Special, Coombe Bitter; Ben Truman; Guinness; Foster's; cider. *Real ale*

Royal patrons at this famous 500-year-old pub are said to have included Henry VIII, Charles II and Lady Jane Grey. Nowadays, there's a cheerful welcome in the long bar, and next door is a fine display of cold meats and fresh salads. At lunchtime, there are also a few hot dishes such as steak and kidney pie (except Sunday). Patio.

**Family pub**

## Kegworth *(Food)* — *White House*

London Road, Near Derby · *Leicestershire*
Map 4 C4
Kegworth (050 97) 2245

*Brewery* Bass
*Landlord* John Batchelor
Cold mixed seafood £4.75 Nigerian peppered chicken £4.75 (Last order 10pm)
Bass; Worthington 'E'; Mitchells & Butlers Mild; Guinness; Carling Black Label; Taunton cider. *Real ale*

The patio of this cheerful pub on the outskirts of town overlooks the river Soar. Enjoyable food served in the bar includes a cold buffet featuring seafood, home-cooked joints and a variety of colourful salads. There are basket meals and grills, too, and a few hot specials such as the unusual Nigerian peppered chicken. Lunchtime specials like cottage pie provide further choice. **Family pub** (lunchtime)

## Kenley *(Food)* — *Wattenden Arms*

Old Lodge Lane · *Surrey* · Map 6 C3
01-660 8638

*Brewery* Charrington
*Landlords* Joan & Ron Coulston

Steak pie £2 Curried chicken Madras £2 (Last order 9pm)
Charrington's IPA; Bass; Mitchells & Butlers Mild; Stones Bitter; Guinness; Carling Black Label; Taunton cider. *Real ale*

Former airline steward Ron Coulston now looks after his customers on terra firma, and has built up a reputation for cheery hospitality and fine food. In the cosy panelled bar of his village pub you can choose from a tempting display of mouth-watering cold joints, fresh crab and smooth garlicky pâté, or go for one of the hot dishes like curry, steak and kidney pie or a mammoth plateful of ham, egg and chips. Sandwiches only on Sundays. Garden.

## Kersey — *Bell Inn*

Attractive flower baskets festoon the timbered facade of this fine old inn in a village once renowned for its cloth industry, now known for its main-street watersplash and picture postcard prettiness. Open fires keep winter at bay in the brass-bedecked bars, while in summer the large garden comes into its own.

The Street, Near Ipswich · *Suffolk* · Map 5 D2
Hadleigh (0473) 823229
*Free House* *Landlords* Mr & Mrs G. Slater
Adnams Bitter; Mauldon's Bitter; Greene King Abbot Ale; Guinness; Skol; Carlsberg Hof; cider. *Real ale*

## Keswick *(B & B)* — *Pheasant Inn*

Crossthwaite Road · *Cumbria* · Map 3 B2
Keswick (0596) 72219

*Brewery* Jennings
*Landlords* Mr & Mrs Wright

**BEDROOMS 3 Grade 2 £C**
Jennings Traditional, Bitter, Mild; Stones Bitter; Guinness; Ayinger Bräu; Taunton cider. *Real ale*

A popular spot with the locals, this homely little pub stands just off the A66 about a mile from the centre of town. Cartoons of hunting scenes lend interest to the panelled bar, and there's a patio for fair-weather sipping. The three modestly furnished bedrooms (two of them of a suitable size for families) share a modern bathroom.

## Kettlewell *(B & B)* — *Bluebell Hotel*

Near Skipton · *North Yorkshire* · Map 4 C2
Kettlewell (075 676) 230

*Free House*
*Landlord* Mr J. A. F. Croft

**BEDROOMS 8 Grade 2 £B**
Theakston's Best Bitter, Old Peculier; Tetley's Bitter, Mild; Guinness; Foster's; Carlsberg Hof; cider. *Real ale*

Popular with trout fishermen and walkers on the Yorkshire Dales, this whitewashed pub with a pleasant beer garden at the rear stands near the river Wharfe. The bar is a welcoming place for a hard-earned drink, and the TV lounge is well provided with deep armchairs. Comfortable bedrooms, furnished in a variety of styles, are warm and neatly kept. **Family pub**

## Kettlewell *(Food, B & B)* — *Racehorses Hotel*

Near Skipton · *North Yorkshire* · Map 4 C2
Kettlewell (075 676) 233

*Free House*
*Landlords* Mr & Mrs Rowbottom

**BEDROOMS 16 Grade 1 £B**
Steak pie £2.50 Lasagne £1.50 (Last order 9pm)
Younger's Scotch Bitter; Webster's Yorkshire Bitter; Tetleys Bitter; Taunton cider. *Real ale*

Enjoyable bar snacks and comfortable accommodation make this friendly old pub beside the river Wharfe a good base for exploring the Dales. Delicious local trout is a popular choice on the menu, which also offers soup, lasagne, cold meat salads and steak and kidney pie. Overnight guests have 16 bright, practical bedrooms, five with well-fitted private bathrooms. TV lounge. **Family pub**

We have raised our standards considerably since last year. The omission of some houses that appeared in last year's Guide is no reflection on their standing.

## Keyston *(Food)* — *Pheasant Inn*

Near Huntingdon · *Cambridgeshire* · Map 5 B2
Bythorn (080 14) 241

*Free House*
*Landlord* Mr Steve Klamer

Paris mushrooms £2.85 Swordfish in raspberries £4.25 (Last order 10.30pm)
Tolly Cobbold Bitter; Ruddle's County; Younger's Tartan; Stella Artois. *Real ale*

Once the village bakehouse, this smart thatched pub offers a combination of familiar favourites and more unusual items on its chalked-up snack menu. Start perhaps with soup, pâté or deep-fried squid and go on the flavoursome turkey and mushroom pie, sweet and sour chicken or maybe something really different like swordfish marinated with raspberries. Cold buffet in summer. Patio. **Family pub**

## Kilve *(B & B)* — *Hood Arms*

Near Bridgwater · *Somerset* · Map 8 C3
Holford (027 874) 210

*Free House*
*Landlords* Mr C. R. Rutt & Mr N. A. White

**BEDROOMS 6 Grade 1 £B**
Flowers Original, IPA; Whitbread Bitter, Trophy; Guinness; Heineken; Taunton cider. *Real ale*

Named after Admiral Hood, this smoothly run village pub provides very satisfactory accommodation. Neatly furnished bedrooms have pretty floral fabrics and are equipped with tea-makers; iced water and pot plants are thoughtful touches. Residents can watch TV in a charming little lounge or drink in either of the two convivial bars. There's also a skittle alley. No under-sevens overnight.

## Kineton *(B & B)* — *Halfway House*

Near Guiting Power, Cheltenham
*Gloucestershire* · Map 5 A2
Guiting Power (045 15) 344

*Brewery* Donnington
*Landlords* Mr & Mrs D. Marshall

**BEDROOMS 3 Grade 2 £C** (No dogs)
Donnington's Special, Best Bitter; Carlsberg; cider. *Real ale*

Hospitality comes naturally to the Marshalls, who run this popular village pub in the heart of rural Gloucestershire. Corn dollies and farm implements adorn the spacious bar, where you can relax with a drink or join the locals in a game of darts. Three simple, spotless bedrooms share a neat bathroom. No under-sevens overnight. Accommodation closed ten days Christmas. Garden. **Family pub** (lunchtime)

## Kingsclere *(Food)* — *Crown*

Near Newbury · *Berkshire* · Map 6 A3
Kingsclere (0635) 298956

*Brewery* Courage
*Landlords* Mr & Mrs G. Worrall

Trawlerman's pie £2.50 Treacle tart & cream £1 (Last order 9.45pm. No bar food Sun eve)
Courage Directors Bitter, Best Bitter, Mild; Hofmeister; Kronenbourg; Taunton cider. *Real ale*

The daily-changing blackboard menu at this welcoming old pub on the high street offers unusual delights like steak kebab, Thai chicken with brown rice or bratwurst, as well as lasagne, steak and kidney pie and quiche. There are also toasted sandwiches, plus a few more elaborate dishes in the evening. Less choice Sunday lunchtime. Children's room for family eating at lunchtime (weekends only in winter). Patio.

## Kingscote *(Food)* — *Hunter's Hall Inn*

Near Tetbury · *Gloucestershire* · Map 7 D2
Dursley (0453) 860393

*Free House*
*Landlords* Mr & Mrs David Barnett-Roberts
Seafood pancakes £2.50 Sauté of kidneys with watercress sauce £2.50 (Last order 9.45pm)
Bass; Fussell's Best Bitter; Guinness; Carling Black Label; Tennent's Extra; Taunton cider. *Real ale*

More than 500 years old, this welcoming inn on the A4135 has four cosy, panelled bars with cheerful log fires to ward off the cold. A tempting buffet features pâtés, meats and colourful salads, and there are also tasty hot dishes like seafood pancakes, chicken curry and cottage pie. Don't miss out on the deliciously rich chocolate mousse. Garden. **Family pub**

## Kingsland *(Food)* — *Angel Inn*

Near Leominster · *Hereford & Worcester*
Map 7 D1
Kingsland (056 881) 355

*Free House*
*Landlords* Mr & Mrs M. W. Thompson

Steak & kidney pie £2.50 Pheasant casserole £3.50 (Last order 9.45pm)
Marston's Pedigree, Best Bitter; Guinness; Carlsberg; cider. *Real ale*

Mr and Mrs Thompson's bar menu caters for all tastes at this fine old half-timbered inn. There are staple items such as pâté, salads, scampi in the basket and steak and kidney pie, as well as more unusual things like delicious cauliflower soup and an excellent pastry-topped venison and pheasant casserole. Toasted sandwiches, too. **Family pub**

## Kingston *(Food)* — *Scott Arms*

Near Corfe Castle · *Dorset* · Map 6 A4
Corfe Castle (0929) 480270

*Brewery* Devenish
*Landlord* Gerald Lomax
Steak & kidney pudding & vegetables £2.20 Dorset apple cake 65p (Last order 9.15pm. No bar food Sun eve)
John Devenish Bitter, Wessex Bitter, John Groves; Guinness; Taunton cider. *Real ale*

Pretty flower displays make the two cosy bars especially welcoming at this creeper-clad pub. Tasty light snacks include crab pâté, pizzas, ploughman's and a selection of home-cooked meats, while steak and kidney pudding caters for hearty appetites. Leave room for sweets such as Dorset apple cake or rich treacle tart. Garden. **Family pub**

## Kingston — *Juggs*

Nestling under the South Downs, this pretty, tile-hung pub dating from the 15th century is one of the most picturesque drinking places in the area. Its bars are full of character, with low ceilings, beams and a brass-hooded open fireplace. As well as the family room, there are two gardens and a children's play area. **Family pub**

Near Lewes · *West Sussex* · Map 6 B4
Brighton (0273) 472523
*Free House* *Landlord* Mr F. A. Browne
Harveys Best Bitter; King & Barnes Festive Bitter; Guinness; Tennent's Extra; Carling Black Label; Taunton cider. *Real ale*

## Kingswinford *(B & B)* — *Summerhill House Hotel*

Swindon Road · *West Midlands* · Map 7 D1
Kingswinford (0384) 295254

*Brewery* Allied
*Landlord* Mr R. H. Beatty

**BEDROOMS 10 Grade 2 £C** (No dogs)
Ansells Bitter, Mild, Castlemain XXXX; Harp; Skol; Löwenbräu. *Real ale*

Fine gardens and trees surround this extended Regency house, which stands on top of a hill to the west of the town centre. The spacious bar is in plush Edwardian style, while good-sized bedrooms have a more contemporary appeal, with practical freestanding furniture, tea-makers and telephones. Bathrooms (two private, three public) are well fitted and smartly maintained. There's a pleasant TV lounge. **Family pub**

## Kintbury *(Food, B & B)* — *Dundas Arms*

*Berkshire* · Map 6 A3
Kintbury (0488) 58263

*Free House*
*Landlords* David & Wendy Dalzell-Piper
**BEDROOMS 6 Grade 1 £A** (No dogs)
Smoked salmon pâté £1.60 Cornish pasty with chips & peas £1.70 (No bar food eves or Sun)
Morland's Bitter; Usher's Best Bitter; John Smith's Bitter; Guinness; Carlsberg Hof; Anchor Export; Taunton cider. *Real ale*

The patio of this large pub beside the canal is a pleasant place to enjoy a pint in summer. A fine display of china plates is a feature of the bar, which offers enjoyable snacks like smoked salmon pâté, ploughman's and tempting daily specials such as crab au gratin. Smartly furnished bedrooms, including one in a separate chalet, all have neat private bathrooms. Accommodation closed Christmas–New Year.

## Kinver *(Food)* — *Whittington Inn*

Near Stourbridge, West Midlands
*Staffordshire* · Map 7 D1
Kinver (038 483) 2496

*Owners* Messrs Hickman & Mucklow
*Landlord* Miss Julie Pike
Cold meat salad £2.75 Chilli £2 (Last order 10.15pm)
Courage Directors Bitter; Bass; Marston's Pedigree, Owd Rodger (winter only); Guinness; Stella Artois; cider. *Real ale*

Excellent snacks served in the upstairs wine bar-cum-bistro are a popular feature of this fine timber-framed pub which stands just outside the village on the A449. Julie Pike's menu ranges from delicious home-made soup, fresh-cut sandwiches and a tempting buffet of cold meats and salads to hot specials like cannelloni, chilli con carne and a hearty beef stew. Good English cheeses, too. Garden.

## Kirk Langley *(B & B)* — *Meynell Arms Hotel*

Ashbourne Road · *Derbyshire* · Map 4 C4
Kirk Langley (033 124) 515

*Brewery* Bass
*Landlords* Mr & Mrs J. R. Richards

**BEDROOMS 10 Grades 1 & 2 £B**
Bass; Worthington Bitter; Stones Bitter; Mitchells & Butlers Mild; Tennent's Lager. *Real ale*

Converted from a handsome Georgian farmhouse, this well-maintained three-storey hotel stands alongside the A52 between Derby and Ashbourne. Ten bedrooms – five with their own up-to-date bathrooms – provide comfortable overnight accommodation; all have central heating, TVs and thoughtful extras like information folders. The bars are simply furnished. Garden. **Family pub**

## Kirkby Stephen *(Food, B & B)* ★ — *King's Arms Hotel*

*Cumbria* · Map 3 B2
Kirkby Stephen (0930) 71378

*Brewery* Whitbread
*Landlords* Mr K. Simpson & Mrs J. Reed

**BEDROOMS 9 Grade 2 £B**
Toasted steak sandwich £2.10 Curry £1.75 (Last order 8.45pm)
Castle Eden Ale; Whitbread Trophy; Heineken; cider. *Real ale*

The bar food is of very high quality at this attractive old town-centre posting inn. Succulent home-baked ham is delicious in sandwiches and salads or with eggs scrambled or fried, and other choices include soup, curries, beautifully cooked steaks and mouthwatering sweets. Smaller evening choice (served in the restaurant). Colourful, well-furnished bedrooms offer plenty of modern comfort, and there's a pleasant lounge with TV. Garden.

## Kirkbymoorside *(Food, B & B)* — *George & Dragon*

Market Place · *North Yorkshire* · Map 4 C2
Kirkbymoorside (0751) 31637
*Free House*
*Landlords* Mr & Mrs Curtis & Mr & Mrs Austin
**BEDROOMS 23 Grade 1 £A** (No dogs)
Steak & kidney pie £2.25 Roast beef & Yorkshire pudding £2.25 (No bar food eves or Sun)
Theakston's Best Bitter; Younger's Scotch Bitter; Guinness; Carlsberg; Taunton cider. *Real ale*

Lunchtime crowds appreciate the tasty home-made fare served in the beamed bar of this welcoming old coaching inn. Soup, steak and kidney pie and roast beef are among the hot dishes, and there are also salads, sandwiches and a delicious sherry trifle. Neat modern bedrooms in converted granaries across the courtyard provide comfortable accommodation. No children under five overnight.

## Kirtling *(Food, B & B)* — *Queen's Head*

Near Newmarket · *Cambridgeshire* · Map 5 C2
Newmarket (0638) 730253

*Brewery* Tolly Cobbold
*Landlord* Ann Bailey

**BEDROOMS 3 Grade 2 £C**
Fidget pie £2.50 Chocolate rum log £1.20 (Last order 9.30pm. No bar food Thurs eve)
Tolly Cobbold Original, Ordinary, Best Bitter, Mild; Guinness; Hansa; cider. *Real ale*

Built during the reign of Elizabeth I, this attractive inn is run with energy and charm by horse-loving Ann Bailey. Snacks served in the cosy bars range from ploughman's platters and spicy crab pâté to omelettes, fried plaice and flavour-packed savoury pies. Overnight guests climb a winding staircase to reach the simply fitted bedrooms, which share a spotless bathroom. Garden.

## Knapp *(Food)* — *Rising Sun*

North Curry, Near Taunton · *Somerset*
Map 8 C3
Taunton (0823) 490436
*Free House*
*Landlords* Derek & Gena Geneen
Grilled lamb steak £3.95 Baked cheesecake 90p (Last order 10pm. No bar food Mon lunch except Bank Holidays)
Flower's Original, IPA; Carne's Falmouth Bitter; Whitbread Trophy; Guinness; Heineken. *Real ale*

Antiques add to the rustic charm of this splendid former cider house, down a narrow country lane off the beaten track but well worth the search for its very enjoyable bar snacks. A blackboard announces the day's choice, which ranges from sandwiches and ploughman's to super smoked mackerel pâté, cauliflower cheese and beef Stroganoff. Leave room for the delicious speciality cheesecake baked to a German recipe. Garden. **Family pub**

## Knightwick *(Food, B & B)* — *Talbot Hotel*

Near Worcester · *Hereford & Worcester*
Map 7 D1
Knightwick (0886) 21235
*Free House*
*Landlords* Mr D. Hales & Mrs J. Clift
**BEDROOMS 10 Grade 1 £C**
Chicken & prawn pie £2.75 Venison pie £2.75 (Last order 10pm)
Whitbread IPA; Wethered's Bitter; Banks's Bitter; Bass; Guinness; Heineken; cider. *Real ale*

Regular supplies of market-fresh fish and meat make for excellent eating at this popular riverside pub. Trout with bacon, prawns and garlic bread, lamb curry and venison pie are typical treats on a nicely varied menu, and syrupy steamed pudding is a good, old-fashioned sweet. Well-carpeted bedrooms have practical modern furnishings and most have their own up-to-date bathrooms. Garden. **Family pub**

## Knowl Hill *(Food)* — *Bird in Hand*

Near Maidenhead · *Berkshire* · Map 6 B3
Littlewick Green (062 882) 2781

*Free House*
*Landlords* Jack & Moira Shone

Chicken in garlic & honey £3.50 Steak & kidney pudding £3.50 (Last order 10.15pm)
Brakspear's Pale Ale, Old Ale; Young's Special; Courage Directors Bitter; Guinness; Carlsberg Hof; cider. *Real ale*

Mrs Shone's well-laden lunchtime cold table is a popular attraction at this old red-brick pub beside the A4. Fresh salmon, roast beef, gammon, turkey and sausages compete for attention amidst a host of imaginative salads. For something hot there's always soup served with lovely home-baked bread, as well as a daily special like steak and kidney pudding or chicken casserole. Less choice in the evening.

## Knutsford *(Food, B & B)* — *Angel Hotel*

King Street · *Cheshire* · Map 3 B3
Knutsford (0565) 52627

*Brewery* Greenall Whitley
*Landlords* Mr & Mrs A. Nardi

**BEDROOMS 12 Grade 2 £B** (No dogs)
Beef stew £1.80 Plaice, chips & peas £1.90 (No bar food eves)
Greenall Whitley Bitter, Best Mild; Guinness; Grünhalle.

The bar of this old coaching inn is very cosy with its beams and various little snugs, and it provides an enjoyable range of lunchtime snacks, from soup, salads and vol au vents to fish and chips, roast chicken and beef stewed in ale. Bright, well-kept bedrooms are comfortably furnished and all have TVs and shower cubicles. **Family pub**

## Lacock *(Food, B & B)* — *Red Lion*

Near Chippenham · *Wiltshire* · Map 7 D2
Lacock (024 973) 456

*Brewery* Wadworth
*Landlord* Mr J. Levis
**BEDROOMS 3 Grades 1 & 2 £B**
Fresh Cornish shrimps & garlic mayonnaise £1.75 Lacock beef pie £3.20 (Last order 9pm. No bar food Sun eve)
Wadworth's 6X, IPA, Farmers Glory, Northgate Bitter; Guinness; Heineken. *Real ale*

Home cooking is a strong point at this fine old coaching inn, where a large courtyard is a popular summer alternative to the cosy, rustic bars. Start with the day's soup and proceed to delicious baked sole, special sausages or beef pie, finishing with lovely home-made ice cream. Three spacious bedrooms with traditional furnishings include one with its own modern bathroom.

## Laleham *(Food)* — *Three Horseshoes*

Shepperton Road · *Surrey* · Map 6 B3
Staines (0784) 52617

*Brewery* Watneys
*Landlords* Roland & Frances Thanisch
Egg & prawn sandwich 95p Roast pork salad £3.20 (Last order 9.45pm. No bar food Sun & Bank Holidays)
Watneys Stag Bitter, London Bitter; Webster's Yorkshire Bitter; Ruddle's County; Guinness; Carlsberg. *Real ale*

A huge variety of sandwiches caters for all tastes at this charming little roadside pub; generous, interesting fillings might be Camembert and onion or prawn and asparagus. As an alternative, there are also fresh, colourful salads to go with fish, cold meats and the unusual fidget pie, plus several pâtés including the tasty duck and brandy. Homely sweets to finish. Garden.

## Lamberhurst *(Food, B & B)* — *Chequers Inn*

The Broadway · *Kent* · Map 6 C3
Lamberhurst (0892) 890260

*Brewery* Whitbread
*Landlord* Mr K. C. Smith
**BEDROOMS 4 Grade 2 £C**
Home-made soup from 60p Veal escalope à la crème £5.30 (Last order 9.30pm)
Fremlins Bitter; Whitbread Best Bitter, Mild; Guinness; Heineken; Stella Artois; cider. *Real ale*

Standing in the heart of the village by the little river Teise, this friendly old coaching inn provides good food and comfortable accommodation. Snacks served in the beamed bars include soup and sandwiches, lasagne and cauliflower cheese, with more substantial evening choices such as garlicky chicken Kiev. Cheerful, good-sized bedrooms (three with TV) have solid furniture and private bathrooms. Garden.

## Lamberhurst *(B & B)* — *George & Dragon Inn*

High Street · *Kent* · Map 6 C3
Lamberhurst (0892) 890277

*Free House*
*Landlords* Reg & Pat Godward

**BEDROOMS 8 Grade 1 £C**
Harvey's Bitter; Charrington's IPA; Toby Bitter; Carling Black Label; Tennent's; Taunton cider. *Real ale*

The landlord's welcome is warm and friendly at this whitewashed roadside inn with flower boxes at the front and a neat garden running down to the river Teise at the back. Bright, cheerful bedrooms – some quite small, others almost palatial – have modern furniture and tea-makers. Breakfast is a positive feast! The convivial bar is a popular local meeting place.

## Lambs Green *(Food)* — *Lamb Inn*

Near Rusper · *West Sussex* · Map 6 B3
Rusper (029 384) 336

*Free House*
*Landlords* John & Kathy Thompson
Salmon trout £4.50 Half pheasant £4.25 (Last order 10pm)
Badger Best Bitter; Courage Directors Bitter; Young's Bitter; Sussex County Ale; Guinness; Tennent's Extra; Holsten; Taunton cider. *Real ale*

Landlord John Thompson is a welcoming host at this village pub, and his wife Kathy helps to keep customers happy with excellent, nourishing bar snacks. Try her rich meat and vegetable soup or a helping of home-made meat pie with especially delicious gravy. You can also get fresh fish, game in season and curry. If you're not too hungry, go for a ploughman's or a toasted sandwich. Patio.

## Lanchester *(Food, B & B)* — *Kings Head*

Station Road · *Co. Durham* · Map 4 C1
Lanchester (0207) 520054

*Brewery* Scottish & Newcastle
*Landlord* Mr H. Bainbridge

**BEDROOMS 5 Grade 2 £C**
Roast of the day £1.95 Steak & kidney pie £1.65 (No bar food eves & all Sun)
Scottish & Newcastle Exhibition; McEwan's Scotch; Harp; Taunton cider.

A short lunchtime menu of enjoyable cooked dishes is a popular feature of this stone pub at a crossroads. Besides the daily roast, you might find liver and bacon, steak and kidney pie or grilled lamb cutlets. There are also salads, sandwiches and sweets like blackberry sponge. Bedrooms have neat modern furniture, TVs and tea-makers. Accommodation closed 21 December–1 Jan.

## Lancing *(Food, B & B)* — *Sussex Pad*

Old Shoreham Road · *West Sussex* · Map 6 B4
Shoreham-by-Sea (079 17) 4647

*Free House*
*Landlord* Mr Wally Pack
**BEDROOMS 6 Grade 1 £A**
Double-decker sandwich £1.35 Local crab salad £4.75 (Last order 10pm. No bar food Sat eve)
Tetley's Bitter; Ind Coope John Bull; Guinness; Skol; Löwenbräu; cider.

Just opposite Shoreham airport, this modernised pub offers good accommodation and tasty bar fare. Spacious bedrooms with practical fitted units have TVs, telephones, tea-makers and smart modern bathrooms. Head for the plush Edwardian Bar to find freshly cut sandwiches, a splendid steak and kidney pie, plus a lunchtime buffet featuring salads, cold meats and delicious local crab. **Family pub**

## Langdale *(Food)* — *Pillar Hotel, Hobson's Pub*

Near Ambleside · *Cumbria* · Map 3 B2
Langdale (096 67) 302

*Free House*
*Landlord* Mr Jim Craig

Beef in Guinness casserole £3.25 Baked lemon sole £3.25 (Last order 9.30pm)
Hartleys Best Bitter, Mild; Tetley's Bitter; Skol; cider. *Real ale*

Check directions when heading for this rustically styled modern pub, a self-contained element in an impressive hotel-cum-country club complex. Bar snacks are quite a feature and include sandwiches, salads, Barnsley chops and the popular Cumberland sausage. The spacious terrace is a pleasant summer alternative to the stone-floored bar. *For accommodation see Egon Ronay's Lucas Hotel & Restaurant Guide 1985.*

## Langham *(Food)* — *Noel Arms*

Near Oakham · *Leicestershire* · Map 5 B1
Oakham (0572) 2931

*Free House*
*Landlord* Alan Eacott

Steak & kidney pie £2.30 Roast meat salad £4.20 (Last order 10pm)
Ruddle's County, Rutland Bitter; Whitbread Trophy; Guinness; Stella Artois; Taunton cider. *Real ale*

A selection from the eye-catching cold buffet is your best bet in the nicely furnished bar of this fine old converted farmhouse. Ham, turkey and sirloin, roasted on the premises, are carved to order and accompanied by a serve-yourself selection of freshly prepared salads. Ploughman's is a popular choice for a quick snack. Patio. **Family pub**

## Langley Marsh *(Food)* ★ — *Three Horseshoes*

Near Wiveliscombe · *Somerset* · Map 8 C3
Wiveliscombe (0984) 23763

*Free House*
*Landlords* Mr & Mrs J. Marsden

Trout pâté £1.40 Pineapple & lentil curry £1.30 (Last order 10.30pm)
Golden Hill Exmoor Ale; Cotleigh Tawny Bitter; Hall & Woodhouse Badger Best Bitter; Palmer's IPA, Tally Ho; cider. *Real ale*

Jill Marsden's adventurous cooking is the crowning glory of this charming village pub, and she is always coming up with new ideas to tempt the customers. Super soups and traditional specialities such as roast beef salad and stargazey pasty are first class, and there's always a vegetarian dish like our subtle vegetable curry accompanied by hot granary bread and butter. You can finish on a high note with sublime souffléed orange. Less choice Thurs eve.

## Langton Green *(Food)* — *Greyhound*

Near Tunbridge Wells · *Kent* · Map 6 C3
Langton (089 286) 2028

*Brewery* Courage
*Landlords* Mr & Mrs Keith Parker

Ham, leek & mushroom pie £1.50 Bacon & onion roll £1.50 (Last order 10pm)
Courage Best Bitter, Directors Bitter, JC, Dark Mild; Guinness; Kronenbourg; cider. *Real ale*

On the edge of the village green, this attractive red-brick and timbered pub is a popular place for bar snacks. Wholesome home-cooked dishes like ham, leek and mushroom pie or bacon and onion roll are great favourites, perhaps followed by some excellent apple and mince pie. Sandwiches, ploughman's and salads make lighter bites. A traditional roast is an extra feature for Sunday lunch.

## Lanreath *(B & B)* — *Punch Bowl Inn*

Near Looe · *Cornwall* · Map 8 B4
Lanreath (0503) 20218

*Free House*
*Landlords* Mr & Mrs T. C. Mansfield

**BEDROOMS 18 Grade 1 £B**
Bass; Tinner's Ale; Worthing Best Bitter, Dark; Guinness; Carling Black Label; cider. *Real ale*

First licensed in 1620, this fine old hostelry has been at various times a court house, coaching inn and smugglers' distribution house. The beamed bars, agleam with copper and brass ornaments, are cosy, welcoming spots, and there's a lounge with a pool table. Bedrooms vary from traditionally furnished (two have four-posters) to more modern extension rooms with smart fitted units. Most have TVs. Garden.
**Family pub**

## Leafield *(Food)* — *Old George Inn*

Near Witney · *Oxfordshire* · Map 5 A2
Asthall Leigh (099 387) 288

*Free House*
*Landlords* Bob & Valerie Taylor

10oz sirloin steak £4.95 Ploughman's lunch £1 (Last order 10.30pm)
Wadworth's 6X; Hook Norton Best Bitter; Glenny's Witney Bitter; Guinness; Tennent's; Carling Black Label; Taunton cider. *Real ale*

People come from a wide area to tuck into the tasty, tender steaks that are the speciality of this well-kept inn. Valerie Taylor's menus offer plenty of other choice, too, from quick lunchtime snacks like sandwiches and ploughman's platters to basket meals, baked trout and lightly cooked veal escalope. Tables are well spaced in the comfortable bar. Garden.

## Ledbury *(B & B)* — *Feathers Hotel*

High Street · *Hereford & Worcester* · Map 7 D2
Ledbury (0531) 2600

*Brewery* Mitchells & Butlers
*Landlord* Mr Michael Hester

**BEDROOMS 11 Grade 1 £A+**
Mitchells & Butlers Brew XI, Springfield Best Bitter; Bass; Guinness; Carling Black Label; cider. *Real ale*

The interior of this handsome half-timbered building at the centre of town is suitably rich in heavy oak beams and fine old furniture. The large, old-fashioned bedrooms provide modern conveniences like TVs, radio-alarms and tea-makers and all have well-fitted private bathrooms. The public bar is a convivial place for a drink; you can also relax in the spacious foyer-lounge with its cheerful winter fire.
**Family pub**

## Ledbury *(Food, B & B)* — *Verzons Country Hotel*

Trumpet · *Hereford & Worcester* · Map 7 D2
Trumpet (053 183) 381
*Free House*
*Landlords* Phillip & Mary Stanley
**BEDROOMS 6 Grade 1 £B**
Deep-fried potato skins with garlic mayonnaise 65p Pork chop in cider & cheese sauce £2.25 (Last order 10pm)
Marston's Pedigree; Ind Coope Burton Bitter; Guinness; Stella Artois: Marston's Pilsner; cider. *Real ale*

A quiet rural setting alongside the A438 is enjoyed by this splendid Georgian house, where the welcoming Bistro Bar serves a good selection of tasty fare. Deep-fried potato skins with garlic mayonnaise make a scrumptious snack, and other choices include quiches, savoury pies and navarin of lamb. Bedrooms (all with TV) are divided between compact singles and comfortable doubles with modern bath or shower rooms. Garden.

## Ledbury *(B & B)* — *Ye Olde Talbot Hotel*

New Street · *Hereford & Worcester* · Map 7 D2
Ledbury (0531) 2963

*Brewery* Ansells
*Landlords* Mr & Mrs E. Harrison

**BEDROOMS 6 Grade 2 £C** (No dogs)
Gibbs Mew Bitter; Tetley's Bitter; Ansells Bitter; Guinness; Löwenbräu; Skol; cider. *Real ale*

The panelled dining room of this lovely half-timbered pub was once the scene of a bloody Civil War struggle, and evidence of the fray can still be seen. It's more peaceful now, although a mischievous poltergeist apparently makes his presence felt from time to time! You can relax in one of the beamed bars or watch TV in the cosy little upstairs lounge, and you'll rest easy in the neat, sturdily furnished bedrooms (two with bathrooms). **Family pub**

## Ledsham *(Food)* — *Tudor Rose*

Two Mills, South Wirral · *Cheshire* · Map 5 B2
051-339 2399

*Brewery* Higsons
*Landlord* Mr F. Fairclough

Chicken Kiev £2 Grilled trout £2
(Last order 9.45pm)
Higsons Best Bitter, Mild; Bass; Guinness; Carling Black Label; cider. *Real ale*

Copper and brassware, plates and jugs adorn the bar of this smart modern pub at the junction of the A540 and A550. Lunch-time and evening bar snacks provide plenty of choice, with hot dishes like soup, grills, home-made pie and tasty omelettes. You can also get cold meat salads, filled baps and some fine English cheeses. Garden.

## Ledston — *White Horse*

Graham Bedford is the affable landlord at this busy village pub, modernised but still retaining much of its original appeal. Stuffed birds and animals, horse brasses and harnesses are decorative features in the long bar, with beams, copper-topped tables and cheerful fires all contributing to the warm, welcoming atmosphere. **Family pub**

Main Street, Near Castleford · *West Yorkshire* · Map 4 C3
Castleford (0977) 553069
*Brewery* Whitbread *Landlord* Mr Graham Bedford
Whitbread Castle Eden Ale, Trophy, BYB; Guinness; Stella Artois; Heineken; cider. *Real ale*

## Leek *(B & B)* — *Three Horseshoes Inn*

Blackshaw Moor · *Staffordshire* · Map 4 C4
Blackshaw (053 834) 296

*Free House*
*Landlords* Bill & Jill Kirk

**BEDROOMS 7 Grade 1 £C**
McEwan's Scotch, 80/-, 70/-, Export, Lager; Guinness; Kestrel; Taunton cider. *Real ale*

Dating back some 300 years, this well-kept former farmhouse enjoys a superb setting north of Leek on the A53. The views are lovely from the cottage-style bedrooms, which feature pine furniture and colour TVs. Six have shower cabinets, and there are two carpeted bathrooms. The public bar is cheerful and lively, the beamed lounge bar more intimate. Accommodation closed 1 week Christmas. Garden.

**Family pub**

## Leigh *(Food)* — *Plough Inn*

Church Road, Near Reigate · *Surrey* · Map 6 B3
Dawes Green (030 678) 348

*Brewery* King & Barnes
*Landlords* Mr J. Browning & Mr M. Morrell

Steak & kidney pie with vegetables £1.95
Pâté £1.40 (Last order 9pm. No bar food Sun)
King & Barnes Festive, Sussex Bitter, Old Ale (winter only); Guinness; Carling Black Label; Heineken; cider. *Real ale*

The oldest part of this well-kept village pub is the low ceilinged lounge bar with original 16th-century beams. Generous portions of tasty, home-prepared dishes are served in this characterful setting, including pâté and ploughman's, jumbo sausages and scampi. The day's special could be chicken pie or chilli con carne, and the lunchtime sandwiches are replaced in the evening by simple grills. Garden.

## Leigh *(Food)* — *Seven Stars*

Bunce Common Road, Near Reigate · *Surrey*
Map 6 B3
Dawes Green (030 678) 254

*Brewery* Ind Coope
*Landlord* Mr Tom Doyle
Moussaka £2.25 Home-cooked ham & salad £2.75 (Last order 10pm)
Friary Meux Bitter; Ind Coope Burton Ale, Double Diamond; Guinness; Löwenbräu; cider. *Real ale*

A warm welcome from landlord Tom Doyle and enjoyable bar fare keep the customers flocking to this charming old country pub. You can sit by the fire and enjoy winter specials like savoury pies and curries, while in summer there are appetising salads to go with quiche and home-cooked joints. Ploughman's, mixed grills and fry-ups are available all year, along with sweets like delicious apple pie. Garden.

## Leigh on Mendip *(Food)* — *Bell Inn*

Near Bath · *Somerset* · Map 8 D3
Mells (0373) 812316
*Free House*
*Landlords* Dick Erith & Ian Holdsworth
Seafood Thermidor £4.50 Fried chicken breast stuffed with prawns & crab £5.20
(Last order 9.30pm)
Wadworth's 6X; Devenish Bitter; Worthington Best Bitter; Carling Black Label; Youngers; Guinness; Löwenbräu; Taunton cider. *Real ale*

This whitewashed 17th-century inn in a quiet village provides some excellent bar fare. The regular menu features interesting dishes like duck and port pâté, pizza and curries – served complete with poppadums and chutney – and there are also tempting blackboard specials such as pepper chicken, seafood Thermidor and Norfolk venison. Garden. Closed Monday lunchtime except Bank Holidays. **Family pub**

## Leominster *(Food, B & B)* — *Royal Oak Hotel*

South Street · *Hereford & Worcester* · Map 7 D1
Leominster (0568) 2610

*Free House*
*Landlord* Mr John Pallant
**BEDROOMS 16 Grade 1 £B**
Beef sandwiches £1.50 Mushroom omelette £3.45 (Last order 9pm)
Wood's Parish Bitter; Hook Norton Best Bitter; Younger's Dark Mild; Guinness; Carlsberg Hof; cider. *Real ale*

Sandwiches generously filled with rare roast beef are one of the favourite snacks at this welcoming Georgian inn with two comfortable bars. There's also home-made soup and pâté, omelettes, steaks and tasty lunchtime specials such as chicken espagnole. Overnight accommodation is in 16 well-maintained bedrooms, all equipped with TVs, tea-makers and spacious modern bathrooms. There's a smart lounge, and staff are helpful. Patio **Family pub**

## Levens *(Food)* — *Hare & Hounds Inn*

Near Kendal · *Cumbria* · Map 3 B2
Sedgwick (0448) 60408

*Brewery* Vaux
*Landlords* Myra & Jim Stephenson
Cumberland sausage with chips £2.05 Ploughman's £1.30 (Last order 9pm. No bar food Mon eve)
Vaux Sunderland Bitter, Mild, Samson; Guinness; Tuborg; Taunton cider. *Real ale*

A turning off the A590 leads to this friendly village pub with its relaxing lounge bar where you can enjoy Myra Stephenson's splendid home-cooked fare. Start with soup or pâté, and go on to Cumberland sausage, scampi or chicken served with a baked potato, chips or salad. Home-cooked ham and beef make delicious toppings for open sandwiches, and there are steaks in the evening. Patio.
**Family pub** (lunchtime)

## Levington *(Food)* — *Ship*

Gun Hill, Ipswich · *Suffolk* · Map 5 D2
Nacton (047 388) 573

*Brewery* Tollemache & Cobbold
*Landlords* Mr & Mrs L. Wenham

Mariner's tart £2.50 Bread pudding & cream 70p (No bar food eves)
Tolly Cobbold Bitter, Original; Guinness; Hansa. *Real ale*

The location, atmosphere and cooking are all delightful at this 14th-century smuggler's inn overlooking the Orwell estuary. Nautical knick-knacks deck the cosy beamed bar, and a tame parrot aids a piratical touch. Lunchtime snacks include home-smoked ham, hearty savoury pies, ploughman's and quiches; crab is a summer favourite, and there are some lovely old-fashioned puddings. Ploughman's and prawns only on Sunday. Terrace.

## Ley Hill *(Food)* — *Swan Inn*

Chesham · *Buckinghamshire* · Map 6 B3
Chesham (0494) 783025

*Brewery* Benskins
*Landlords* Mr & Mrs Brian Williams

Cottage pie £1.50 Fruit crumble 85p (Last order 9pm. No bar food Sun eve)
Benskins Bitter; Ind Coope Burton Ale; John Bull Bitter; Guinness; Skol; Löwenbräu; cider. *Real ale*

This cosy, intimate and inviting inn opposite the village green was originally a hunting lodge and dates back to the 16th century. It's a fine place for snacks – country vegetable soup with granary bread, smoked mackerel and trout, cider-baked gammon, daily specials like tuna bake or chilli con carne. Puddings feature seasonal fruits. Soup and ploughman's only Sunday lunchtime. Garden.

## Lickfold *(Food)* — *Lickfold Inn*

Near Petworth · *West Sussex* · Map 6 B4
Lodsworth (079 85) 285

*Free House*
*Landlord* Mr C. Tyler
Lasagne £2.50 Steak & kidney pie with vegetables £2.95 (Last order 10pm)
Fuller's London Pride, ESB; Hall & Woodhouse Badger Best Bitter, Tanglefoot; Marston's Pedigree; Eldridge Pope Royal Oak; Guinness; cider. *Real ale*

This 500-year-old pub with a handsome timber-framed façade serves enjoyable fare in its comfortable, beamed bars. The wide choice ranges from salads and sandwiches to grills, pies, omelettes and fresh fish. Lasagne, moussaka and spare ribs are other options, with more elaborate specialities like chicken cordon bleu in the evening. Leave room for sweets such as the delicious rum crunch. **Family pub**

## Lifton *(Food)* — *Arundell Arms*

*Devon* · Map 8 B3
Lifton (0566) 84666

*Free House*
*Landlord* Anne Voss-Bark

Cold buffet £4 Arundell Arms pâté with French bread £1.85 (No bar food eves)
Usher's Country Bitter; Carlsberg. *Real ale*

Anne Voss-Bark's attractive creeper-clad hotel is a super place for a lunchtime bar snack. The cold buffet, with succulent cooked meats, crisp, light quiches and colourful fresh salads, is the chief attraction, supported by creamy vegetable soup and the occasional hot dish. Sweets include treacle tart and a nice light lemon soufflé. **Family pub**

## Lincoln *(Food)* — *Wig & Mitre*

29 Steep Hill · *Lincolnshire* · Map 4 D4
Lincoln (0522) 35190

*Brewery* Samuel Smith
*Landlord* Mr Michael Hope

Waldorf salad £1.50 Chicken cordon bleu £4.25 (Last order 10.30pm)
Samuel Smith's Old Brewery Bitter; Pils; Alpine. *Real ale*

A wide range of imaginative fare is served all day in this charming pub-cum-wine bar, where breakfast starts the day at 8 o'clock. Then come sandwiches, pâtés and tempting blackboard specials like delicious spinach and mushroom soup, ham and sweetcorn cheesecake and rich, beery harvest casserole, as well as plenty of vegetarian specialities. Superb puddings include a marvellous banana Pavlova. Garden. **Family pub**

## Linton *(Food)* — *Crown*

11 High Street · *Cambridgeshire* · Map 5 C2
Cambridge (0223) 891759

*Free House*
*Landlords* Luis & Doreen Sanz
Deep-fried stuffed mushrooms £3.35 Fresh grilled salmon £3.95 (Last order 9.30pm. No bar food Sun eve)
Adnam's Bitter; Greene King IPA; Younger's Tartan; Guinness; Carlsberg. *Real ale*

Fresh seafood is a feature of the varied menu at this whitewashed village pub. Delicious and unusual soups like carrot and curry are served with lovely granary bread, and other favourites include deep-fried mushrooms stuffed with cream cheese, liver pâté, quiche lorraine and cannelloni. Cold meat salads, too. Garden.

## Linton — *Windmill Inn*

Standing at the heart of a pleasant little village, this 200-year-old converted farmhouse retains a great deal of rustic charm and character. Winter fires warm the two bars, whose stone walls are hung with a variety of highly polished brassware. A popular, convivial place with delightful staff and good beer. **Family pub**

Near Wetherby · *West Yorkshire* · Map 4 C3
Wetherby (0937) 62938
*Brewery* Younger's *Landlord* Mrs J. Oxley
Younger's No. 3 Ale, Scotch Bitter; McEwan's Lager. *Real ale*

## Little Bollington *(Food)* — *Ye Olde No. 3*

Lymm Road, Near Altrincham · *Greater Manchester* · Map 3 B3
Lymm (092 575) 6115

*Brewery* John Smith
*Landlords* Bill & Thelma Bentley
Steak & kidney pie, chips & vegetables £1.30
Omelette with chips or salad £1.30
(Last order 10pm. No bar food Sun eve)
John Smith's Bitter, Mild; Guinness; Hofmeister; cider.

Once the third posting house on the Liverpool to London coach route, this friendliest of pubs is kept in absolutely sparkling condition by delightful Bill and Thelma Bentley. Satisfying bar snacks are simple: sandwiches and salads or such hot dishes as omelettes, fish and a superb steak and kidney pie. Roast for Sunday lunch. Less choice evenings. Garden.

## Little Hadham *(Food)* — *Nag's Head*

The Ford, Near Ware · *Hertfordshire*
Map 5 C2
Albury (027 974) 555
*Brewery* Rayment
*Landlord* Mr M. Robinson
Prawns Thermidor £2.95 Veal steak with rice £4.20 (Last order 9pm. No bar food Sun eve)
Rayment's Bitter; Greene King Abbot Ale; Guinness; Kronenbourg; cider. *Real ale*

Local ladies provide the superb cakes and sweets which are the undoubted winners at this friendly, 16th-century village pub. We finished our meal with a sublime Austrian coffee cake that was simply out of this world. The rest of the menu is full of variety, and you can get anything from salads and freshly cut sandwiches to liver and bacon, prawns Thermidor, steaks and nicely cooked veal. There are tables outside on the patio.

## Little Langdale *(B & B)* — *Three Shires Inn*

Near Ambleside · *Cumbria* · Map 3 B2
Langdale (096 67) 215

*Free House*
*Landlords* Neil & Sheila Stephenson

**BEDROOMS 8 Grade 1 £B** (No dogs)
Wilsons Bitter, Mild; Guinness; Carlsberg; Foster's; cider

The beer garden beside the beck running through the garden is the perfect place to appreciate the idyllic setting of this immaculate pub. It's also pleasant inside, whether in the walkers' bar or the slate-walled cocktail bar. Bedrooms are first-rate with modern furniture, pretty fabrics and dainty prints – not to mention the glorious views from the windows. Bathrooms are spotlessly clean.

## Little Walden *(Food)* ★ *Crown Inn*

Saffron Walden · *Essex* · Map 5 C2
Saffron Walden (0799) 27175

*Free House*
*Landlord* Mr Chris Oliver

Apple pie with cream 95p Local trout £4.50 (Last order 9.30. No bar food Sun)
Ruddle's County, Bitter; Courage Bitter, Directors; Ben Truman; Kronenbourg; Taunton cider. *Real ale*

An enticing selection of superb seafood is the jewel in the crown of this lovely old village pub, where all the bar snacks are freshly prepared with great skill and care. Crab, Dover sole and stuffed rainbow trout are among the fishy favourites, and samphire makes an unusual and delicious starter. Also sandwiches, hearty winter pies and an exquisitely spiced apple pie. Garden.

## Little Washbourne *(Food)* *Hobnails Inn*

Near Tewkesbury · *Gloucestershire*
Map 7 D2
Alderton (024 262) 237

*Brewery* Whitbread
*Landlord* Mr S. Farbrother
Gammon & pineapple bap £1 Steak & mushroom bap £1.50 (Last order 10.30pm)
Whitbread West Country Pale Ale; Flowers Original, Best Bitter; Guinness; Heineken; Stella Artois; cider. *Real ale*

Speciality baps and gorgeous sweets bring customers from far and wide to this small roadside pub. The choice of fillings for delicious fresh, farmhouse-style baps ranges from gammon and pineapple to liver and onions or steak, egg and mushrooms. Mouthwatering gâteaux, flans and ice creams make a splendid finish to the meal. Patio. **Family pub**

## Liverpool *Philharmonic Dining Rooms*

Built in 1898 by Walter Thomas, the Philharmonic is a marvellous example of late-Victorian extravagance. Rich rosewood panelling, polished mahogany and glittering chandeliers combine in a dazzling symphony of style, and even the fittings in the gents are made of pink marble! Definitely one of the sights of Liverpool. **Family pub**

36 Hope Street · *Merseyside* · Map 3 B3
(051) 709 1163
*Brewery* Tetley Walker *Landlord* Mr Stroud
Tetley's Bitter, Mild; Guinness; Skol; cider. *Real ale*

## Llanfair Waterdine *(Food, B & B)* *Red Lion*

Near Knighton, Powys · *Shropshire* · Map 7 C1
Knighton (0547) 528214

*Free House*
*Landlords* Mr & Mrs S. J. Rhodes

**BEDROOMS 3 Grade 2 £B** (No dogs)
Cheese & bacon flan £1.50 Lemon gâteau 75p (Last order 10pm)
Ansells Pale Ale, Dark Mild; John Smith's Bitter; Wrexham Lager; cider. *Real ale*

Once frequented by drovers, this appealing stone-built pub stands on the banks of the river Teme (watch for the sign on the B4355). Sturdily furnished bedrooms in traditional style are quite comfortable. In the two homely bars you'll find simple snacks like smooth pâté, as well as quiches and pizzas. No children under 15 overnight; sometimes closed at lunchtime in winter. Garden.

## Long Hanborough *(Food)* — *Bell*

Near Oxford · *Oxfordshire* · Map 5 A2
Freeland (0993) 881324

*Brewery* Morrell's
*Landlord* Mr Graham Laer

Chicken & turkey pie 95p Beef & venison casserole in port 95p (No bar food eves)
Morrell's Varsity; Guinness; Harp; Kronenbourg; cider. *Real ale*

Good food at old-fashioned prices is the trademark of this traditional, welcoming village pub, where the lunchtime snacks – prepared by a gifted local lady – consist of simple, homely dishes like a bowl of Berkshire broth, hot pot luck and an Oxfordshire pâté. Dressed crab with mayonnaise sandwiches and ploughman's too, and a hot treacle pudding not to be missed. Less choice weekends. Patio.

## Long Melford *(Food, B & B)* — *Crown Inn Hotel*

Near Sudbury · *Suffolk* · Map 5 C2
Sudbury (0787) 77666

*Free House*
*Landlords* Mr & Mrs B. Sell

**BEDROOMS 14 Grades 1 & 2 £B**
Pâté & toast £1.20 Steak & kidney pie £2.15 (Last order 9pm)
Adnams Bitter; Mauldon's Bitter; Greene King IPA; Carlsberg Hof. *Real ale*

Cheerful awnings and window boxes adorn the front of this old village inn, and the interior retains its beams and antique furniture. Simple snacks in the bar include tasty herb pâté, pies, scampi and chips and nice sweets like treacle tart. Bedrooms in the main building are traditional in style, those in the annexe neat and modern, with TVs, tea-makers and small private bathrooms. Garden. **Family pub**

## Long Sutton *(B & B)* — *Devonshire Arms*

Near Langport · *Somerset* · Map 8 D3
Long Sutton (045 824) 271

*Free House*
*Landlords* John & Maureen Hodder

**BEDROOMS 4 Grade 2 £B** (No dogs)
Wadworth's 6X; Hancock's HB; Toby; Worthington Best Bitter; Guinness; Carling Black Label; Taunton cider. *Real ale*

Good standards of maintenance and housekeeping prevail at this ivy-clad 18th-century inn, built by the Duke of Devonshire as a private shooting lodge. Spacious bedrooms have sturdy traditional furniture, tea-makers and colour TVs and share two well-equipped bathrooms. There's a smart lounge area and a delightful, immaculately kept walled garden. **Family pub**

## Longframlington *(Food, B & B)* — *Granby Inn*

*Northumberland* · Map 2 D4
Longframlington (066 570) 228

*Brewery* Bass
*Landlord* Mr G. Hall

**BEDROOMS 6 Grade 1 £B** (No dogs)
Steak & kidney pie £2.65 Fresh cod & chips £2.55 (Last order 9.30pm)
Piper Best Scotch Bitter; Stones Bitter; Guinness; Carling Black Label; Taunton cider.

The Halls extend a friendly welcome at this roadside coaching inn, where visitors flock to enjoy reliably prepared bar snacks like smooth chicken liver pâté, sandwiches, salads, grills and the ever-popular steak and kidney pie (lunch only). Attractive bedrooms (including three compact chalet rooms) with colour TVs and tea-makers provide first-rate comfort. No undertens overnight. No accommodation 23 December–2 January. Patio.

## Longhope *(Food)* — *Nags Head*

Ross Road · *Gloucestershire* · Map 7 D2
Gloucester (0452) 830284

*Free House*
*Landlord* Roger & Roslyn Salter

Steak & kidney pie £1.50 Moussaka £1.50 (Last order 10pm)
Brain's SA; Smiles Best Bitter; Wadworth's Northgate Bitter; Tetley's Bitter; Carlsberg Hof; cider. *Real ale*

This welcoming pub on the A40 is a spruce little black and white building with tables on its tiny front lawn. In Oscar's Wine Bar (there's another bar as well) you can enjoy straightforward, home-prepared fare like spaghetti bolognese, chilli con carne and trout with almonds. Simple starters, ice creams to finish. For Sunday lunchtime, only a traditional roast is served.

**Family pub**

## Longleat *(Food, B & B)* — *Bath Arms*

Near Warminster · *Wiltshire* · Map 8 D3
Maiden Bradley (098 53) 308

*Free House*
*Landlords* Beryl & Joseph Lovatt
**BEDROOMS 7 Grade 1 £B**
Turkey & mushroom pie £2.95 Brixham pot pie £2.95 (Last order 10pm)
Eldridge Pope Dorchester Bitter; Bass; Wadworth's 6X; Guinness; Holsten; Carlsberg; cider. *Real ale*

Right in the middle of the Longleat Estate, this well-managed hostelry is the place for good food and excellent accommodation. Fresh fish and seasonal game are highlights of the enterprising bar menu, which also offers quiches and casseroles, curries and a cold buffet in summer. Attractively furnished bedrooms (six with private bathrooms) have tea-makers and TVs. There are three splendidly rustic bars and a cosy residents' lounge. **Family pub**

## Longparish *(Food)* — *Plough Inn*

Near Andover · *Hampshire* · Map 6 A3
Longparish (026 472) 358

*Brewery* Whitbread
*Landlord* Mr Trevor Colgate
Home-made pâté & toast £1.40 Venison sausages, tomato & egg £2.95 (Last order 10.30pm. No bar food Mon eve)
Whitbread Poacher Bitter, Best Bitter, Strong Country Bitter; Devenish Wessex Best Bitter; Guinness; cider. *Real ale*

Very much food-orientated, this popular, brick and tile pub and its pretty garden stand about a mile from the A303 in a picturesque little village. Among the dried hops in the thatched bar you can kick off with a superb chicken liver pâté and go on to a grill, venison sausages or a tasty daily special like squab pie. Also toasted snacks, ploughman's and nice home-made puds.

## Lowdham *(B & B)* — *Springfield Inn*

Old Epperstone Road · *Nottinghamshire*
Map 5 B1
Nottingham (0602) 663387

*Free House*
*Landlords* Gordon & Mavis Ferriman
**BEDROOMS 11 Grade 1 £B**
Mansfield Bitter, Mild; Mitchells & Butlers Springfield Bitter; Marston's Pedigree; Home Brewery Bitter; Guinness; Foster's; cider. *Real ale*

You're staying with an aircraft enthusiast at this gabled inn, converted and extended from a private house. The extensive lawned grounds are in fact a licensed helipad and parachute drop zone, and some of the propellers decorating the walls of the spacious bars come from planes owned by welcoming landlord Gordon Ferriman. Bedrooms furnished in simple contemporary style have tea-makers, colour TVs and either showers or bathrooms.

## Lower Peover *(Food)* — *Bells of Peover*

Near Knutsford · *Cheshire* · Map 3 B4
Lower Peover (056 581) 2269

*Brewery* Greenall Whitley
*Landlord* Mr J. R. Fisher

Beef sandwich 70p Prawn sandwich £1.40
(Last order 10pm)
Greenall Whitley Local Bitter, Mild; Guinness; Grünhalle; cider. *Real ale*

Keep your eyes peeled for the narrow cobbled lane that leads from the B5081 to this captivating whitewashed inn. The tiny snug bar features a fascinating collection of Toby jugs, and in the comfortable lounge bar there are some fine antiques, including a splendid Welsh dresser. Bar snacks consist of freshly cut sandwiches with generous fillings of beef, prawns, turkey or cheese. Patio.

## Lower Woodford *(Food)* — *Wheatsheaf*

Near Salisbury · *Wiltshire* · Map 6 A3
Middle Woodford (072 273) 203

*Brewery* Hall & Woodhouse
*Landlord* Mr Peter Charlton
Smoked mackerel pâté with toast £1.40
Steak & kidney pie with vegetables £2.25
(Last order 10pm)
Hall & Woodhouse Badger Best Bitter, Tanglefoot; Guinness; Brock; Stella Artois; Taunton cider. *Real ale*

Relax in the garden or enjoy the darts and other games inside this charming village pub. A bridge over a fish pond makes a novel entrance to the dining area, where you can tuck into freshly prepared soup or tasty pâté with toast, followed perhaps by steak, chicken Kiev or rainbow trout. Home-made fruit pie makes an excellent finish. Special children's menus – even cold milk on draught! **Family pub**

## Loweswater *(Food, B & B)* — *Kirkstile Inn*

Near Cockermouth · *Cumbria* · Map 3 B2
Lorton (090 085) 219

*Free House*
*Landlord* Mr Joe Habens
**BEDROOMS 10 Grade 1 £C**
Ham, egg & chips £3.50 Pasties 90p (Last order 9pm)
Jennings Best Bitter; Younger's Scotch Bitter, Tartan; Guinness; Ayingerbräu; cider. *Real ale*

Stunning views of lakes and fells are a feature of this friendly old inn next to the village church. The characterful beamed bars are the setting for some enjoyable and satisfying snacks, from nice meaty pasties to baked potatoes, omelettes and sirloin steak. Comfortable bedrooms – most with modern private bathrooms – have good carpets and practical fitted furniture. Breakfasts are excellent. **Family pub**

## Lowick *(Food, B & B)* — *Farmers Arms*

Near Ulverston · *Cumbria* · Map 3 B2
Greenodd (022 986) 376

*Brewery* Scottish & Newcastle
*Landlords* Philip & Dorothy Broadley
**BEDROOMS 13 Grade 2 £B**
Steak & kidney pie £2 Stilton & walnut pâté £1.50 (Last order 10pm)
Younger's Scotch Bitter, No. 3; McEwan's 80/-, Export; Guinness; Harp; Taunton cider. *Real ale*

Tasty bar snacks can be enjoyed in the flagstoned bars or out on the patio of this agreeable old inn, once a farmhouse that brewed its own beer. Chicken liver pâté, steak and kidney pie and haddock with chips are typical fare, and at lunchtime there are also sandwiches. Bedrooms are furnished in simple, traditional style and there's a comfortable TV room.
**Family pub** (lunchtime)

## Ludlow *(B & B)* — *Angel Hotel*

Broad Street · *Shropshire* · Map 7 D1
Ludlow (0584) 2581

*Free House*
*Landlords* Colin & Joan Espley

**BEDROOMS 16 Grades 1 & 2 £B** (No dogs)
Flowers Bitter; Whitbread Bitter; Stella Artois; Heineken; cider. *Real ale*

Back in 1802, this fine half-timbered coaching inn played host to Lord Nelson on a trip to the Forest of Dean to inspect oak trees felled for the building of the fleet. Today's visitors sleep soundly in the unassuming, traditionally furnished bedrooms (the four large ones with neat modern bathrooms are the most appealing). There's also a comfortable, relaxing bar and a large first-floor TV lounge with deep armchairs and settees.

## Lurgashall *(Food)* — *Noah's Ark*

The Green, Near Petworth · *West Sussex*
Map 6 B4
Northchapel (042 878) 346
*Brewery* Friary Meux
*Landlord* Mr Ted Swannell
Moussaka £2.10 Fish pie £2.25 (Last order 10pm. No bar food Sun)
Friary Meux Bitter; Ind Coope Burton Ale, Mild, John Bull; Löwenbräu; Guinness; cider. *Real ale*

Standing on the edge of a delightful village, this old beamed pub is full of charm There's a daily blackboard menu of enjoyable snacks ranging from rich game soup to tasty moussaka, chilli con carne or gammon and chips. You can also have salad with crab, prawns, beef, turkey or tongue, as well as a wide variety of plain and toasted sandwiches. Nice sweets like apple pie or sherry trifle. Garden.

**Family pub**

## Lyddington *(B & B)* — *Marquess of Exeter*

Main Street, Near Uppingham · *Leicestershire*
Map 5 B1
Uppingham (0572) 822477

*Free House*
*Landlord* Mr B. W. B. Cousins

**BEDROOMS 15 Grade 1 £A** (No dogs)
Ruddle's Bitter, County; Bateman's Bitter; Adnams Southwold Bitter; Greene King Bitter; Guinness; Stella Artois; cider. *Real ale*

On the main village street, this handsome 16th-century pub is full of period charm, with flagstone floors and low-beamed ceilings. Hunting prints and horse-racing photographs abound, and the splendidly comfortable bedrooms in a quiet annexe are named after local hunts. All have excellent carpeted bathrooms and are very well equipped, with double glazing, colour TVs and direct-dial telephones. No under-fives overnight. Patio.

## Lydford *(B & B)* — *Castle Inn*

Near Okehampton · *Devon* · Map 8 B4
Lydford (082 282) 242

*Free House*
*Landlords* Mr & Mrs S. B. Reed

**BEDROOMS 7 Grade 2 £C**
Bass; St Austell Tinner's Ale; Ben Truman; Guinness; Carlsberg; cider. *Real ale*

This charming old village pub enjoys a delightful setting next to the ancient castle and just a short walk from the dramatic Lydford Gorge. The low-beamed bars are full of old-world appeal, with open fires, oil lamps, Victorian pictures and a fine collection of old plates. Comfortably furnished bedrooms, all with washbasins, share two well-equipped bathrooms. No under-tens overnight. Garden.

**Family pub**

## Lympstone *(Food)* — *Globe Inn*

Near Exmouth · *Devon* · Map 8 C4
Exmouth (0395) 263166

*Brewery* Heavitree
*Landlords* Mr & Mrs Smith

Mixed seafood salad £3.95 Fresh salmon sandwich £1 (Last order 10.15pm)
Flowers Original; Bass; Whitbread Best Bitter; Worthington 'E'; Guinness; Taunton cider. *Real ale*

Fishing nets on the walls and a tempting display of incomparably fresh seafood set the tone in this popular harbourside pub. Superb fresh salmon, lobster, succulent king prawns and excellent dressed crab are used for salads and sandwiches, while meat-lovers can tuck into cold joints, pies and pasties. There are also hot dishes in winter, and gorgeous sweets like fruity apple tart and butterscotch crunch come topped with rich clotted cream.

## Lynton *(B & B)* — *Crown Hotel*

Sinai Hill · *Devon* · Map 8 C3
Lynton (059 85) 2253

*Free House*
*Landlords* Alan & Thelma Westgarth

**BEDROOMS 16 Grade 1 £A**
Bass; Whitbread Best Bitter, Trophy; Flowers IPA; Carling Black Label; Foster's; cider. *Real ale*

Housekeeping and maintenance are both first-class at this 200-year-old former coaching inn, whose lofty situation affords lovely views of both sea and countryside. First-class bedrooms are comfortable and well equipped, with sturdy traditional furnishings, TVs, radio-alarms, tea-makers and carpeted bathrooms. Five boast fully draped four-posters, and there are three family suites. Residents' lounge. Accommodation closed January. **Family pub**

## Lyonshall *(Food, B & B)* — *Royal George Inn*

Near Kington · *Hereford & Worcester* · Map 7 D1
Lyonshall (054 48) 210

*Brewery* Whitbread
*Landlord* Mr John Allen

**BEDROOMS 3 Grade ?. £C** (No dogs)
Lamb goulash £3.75 L priot curry £2.75 (Last order 10pm)
Flower's Original, IPA; Guinness; Heineken; Stella Artois; cider. *Real ale*

Landlord John Allen bids visitors a warm welcome to this pleasant old whitewashed inn, where good food and homely accommodation are the order of the day. The bar snacks are tasty and satisfying, from vegetable soup and king-size sausages to gammon steak and really splendid moussaka. Three neatly kept bedrooms with TVs and tea-makers share a modern shower room. Garden.

## Madingley *(Food)* — *Three Horseshoes*

Cambridge · *Cambridgeshire* · Map 5 C2
Madingley (0954) 210221

*Brewery* Tollemache & Cobbold
*Landlord* Mr Iain Twinn

Turkey & mushroom pie £3.75 Chocolate mousse £1.25 (Last order 10pm)
Tolly Cobbold Original, Bitter; Hansa Lager; Taunton cider.

Food is a major attraction at this splendidly run thatched pub, where a blackboard lists the day's offerings in the smart beamed bar. Salad cocktails served in large glass bowls are a very popular feature, and hot items include tasty soups, savoury pies and grilled steaks. Avocado and fresh mint cheesecake is one of several deliciously different sweets. Garden. **Family pub**

## Maidensgrove *(Food)* ★ *Five Horseshoes*

Near Henley · *Oxfordshire* · Map 6 B3
Nettlebed (0491) 641282

*Brewery* Brakspear
*Landlords* Colin & Hazel Funnell
Beef fillet in green peppercorn sauce £3.90 Chicken Kiev £3.90 (Last order 10pm. No bar food Sun eve in winter)
Brakspear's Ordinary Bitter, Special Bitter; Guinness; Heineken; cider. *Real ale*

As the name suggests, your luck is really in when you visit this cosy red-built pub, where Colin Funnell is the genial host, his wife Hazel the talented chef. Her repertoire ranges from soups and pâtés to chicken Kiev, nutty pork casserole and tender slices of beef in a creamy green peppercorn sauce. Ploughman's and jacket potatoes for quick snacks, home-made ice cream to finish. Garden.

## Malham *(B & B)* *Buck Inn*

Near Skipton · *North Yorkshire* · Map 4 C2
Airton (072 93) 317

*Free House*
*Landlord* Ruth Robinson

**BEDROOMS 10 Grade 2 £B**
Theakston's Bitter, XB, Old Peculier; Younger's Bitter; Guinness; Kestrel; Harp; Taunton cider. *Real ale*

Popular with walkers and motorists alike, this sturdy old stone-built inn enjoys a setting of great beauty among the lovely Yorkshire Dales. The two bars are both characterful and convivial, and residents have a cosy little TV room. There are some fine old furnishings in the bedrooms, four of which are family size. Two rooms have good showers. **Family pub**

## Malmesbury *(Food)* *Suffolk Arms*

Tetbury Hill · *Wiltshire* · Map 7 D2
Malmesbury (066 62) 2771

*Free House*
*Landlords* Mr & Mrs C. Johnson
Steak, kidney & mushroom pie with vegetables £2.50 Cottage pie with vegetables £1.70 (Last order 9.45pm. No bar food Sun eve)
Wadworth's 6X, IPA; Archer's Village Bitter; Ben Truman; Guinness; Carlsberg Pilsner. *Real ale*

The rustic lounge bar of this handsome ivy-clad inn on the Tetbury road is a popular spot for a drink and a simple, tasty bar snack. The choice includes soup, pâté, sandwiches, local sausages with jacket potatoes, plus a few daily specials like steak and kidney pie, venison pie or seafood pancakes. Mousses and flans are typical delicious sweets. **Family pub**

## Malton *(Food)* *Green Man Hotel*

Market Street · *North Yorkshire* · Map 4 D2
Malton (0653) 2662

*Free House*
*Landlord* Mrs J. Tate-Smith

Hot carvery & vegetables £3.05 Steak & kidney pie £2.15 (Last order 10pm)
Tetley's Bitter; Younger's Scotch Bitter; Cameron's Lion Bitter; Guinness; Skol; Carlsberg Hof; cider. *Real ale*

Several generations of Tate-Smiths have run this agreeable white-shuttered pub near the market square. Bar snacks are a popular feature, and the lunchtime cold buffet with appetising quiches and cooked joints is much in demand. There's also plenty of hot choice, from Yorkshire pudding with onion gravy to a daily roast. Pleasant sweets, too. Grills, sandwiches and things like lasagne in the evening. **Family pub**

# Bring out the Branston. Bring out the best.

**Branston,*** the original sweet pickle, has been Britain's vourite since it was first produced over 60 years ago – and still made with the same care and in the same traditional ıanner. There are those who try to imitate it – but there is ılly one **Branston** Pickle.

So ask for it by name when you next have a pub lunch.

**You and Crosse & Blackwell make tastier meals.**

CROSSE & BLACKWELL REGD

**ranston** is a registered trade mark.

# JUST A BITE

## Egon Ronay's Lucas Guide

**for Gourmets on a Family Budget**

**— 1985 —**

for the best British light meals and snacks in some 1,000 cafés, tearooms, wine bars, wholefood and vegetarian restaurants, fish and chip shops, pizzerias and hamburger places, coffee shops and many other modest eating places serving high-quality food:

including **EATING ON & OFF MOTORWAYS**

With many new recommendations replacing the old ones after reappraisal.

£3.95 from bookshops everywhere or £4.50 to include postage and packing (limited to addresses in the United Kingdom) from:

Egon Ronay Organisation Ltd,
Greencoat House, Francis Street
LONDON SW1P 1DH

*See colour pages and page 14 for news about another Egon Ronay 1985 Guide.*

BEJAM BM 603 MICROWAVE COOKER

# DISCOVER THE 4 MINUTE MEAL.

Discover the speed and efficiency of today's microwaves at Bejam.

Discover how perfectly a microwave complements your freezer.

Bejam have one of the best selections anywhere.

And some of the best prices.

With all the specialist help and advice you need to make the right choice.

DISCOVER

**Bejam**

**THE WORLD OF FROZEN FOOD**

Enjoy a bottle and ...
Make friends with the wines of France.

## Malvern *(Food)* — *Foley Arms Hotel*

Worcester Road · *Hereford & Worcester*
Map 7 D1
Malvern (068 45) 3397

*Free House*
*Landlords* Mr N. Ivanzo

Foley special £1.95 Self-service buffet £2.40
(Last order 8.30pm. No bar food Sun)
Bass; Marston's Pedigree; Guinness; Carlsberg; Tennent's Extra. *Real ale*

Excellent snacks are served in the bar of this handsome coaching inn, which enjoys splendid views of the Severn Valley. The Foley special – a steak sandwich served with salad or chips – is a great favourite, and other choices include soup, casseroles and local salmon. The self-service buffet is popular at lunchtime. Terrace. *For accommodation see Egon Ronay's Lucas Hotel & Restaurant Guide 1985.* **Family pub**

## Malvern *(Food, B & B)* — *Mount Pleasant Hotel*

Bellevue Terrace · *Hereford & Worcester*
Map 7 D1
Malvern (068 45) 61837
*Free House*
*Landlord* Mr & Mrs R. J. Downing
**BEDROOMS 8 Grade 1 £A** (No dogs)
Rabbit & gooseberry pie £3.20 Vegetable macaroni & cheese £1.65 (Last order 9pm)
Marston Pedigree; Albion Bitter; Burton Bitter; Hook Norton Bitter; Guinness; Stella Artois; cider. *Real ale*

Wholesome, well-prepared bar snacks are appreciated by locals and tourists alike at this friendly hotel overlooking the priory. The choice is wide, from flavoursome chicken liver pâté to scampi, beef curry and a spirited chocolate and rum mousse. Antiques abound in the bar, lounges and very comfortable bedrooms, which have TVs and well-appointed bathrooms. No children under 10 overnight. Closed 1 week Christmas. Patio.

**Prices given are as at the time of our research and are comparative indications rather than firm quotes.**

## Mamble *(Food)* — *Sun & Slipper*

Near Kidderminster · *Hereford & Worcester*
Map 7 D1
Bewdley (0299) 22307

*Free House*
*Landlord* Mr P. Fort
Stuffed mushrooms £1.40 Whole plaice £2.35
(Last order 10pm)
Banks's Bitter; Mitchells & Butlers Bitter; Holdens; Wadworth's Old Original; Guinness; Tuborg; cider. *Real ale*

French landlord Philippe Fort offers a tempting choice of well-prepared bar fare at his tall, white-painted Victorian pub. Everything is home-made, from deliciously rich beef and vegetable soup and well-seasoned meat pâté to sausages, stuffed aubergines and a particularly good lasagne. Other choices range from filled rolls to trout, sirloin steak and chilli con carne. Garden. **Family pub**

## Manaccan *(Food)* — *New Inn*

Near Helston · *Cornwall* · Map 8 A4
Manaccan (032 623) 323

*Free House*
*Landlord* Mr Patrick Cullinan

Steak & kidney pie £3.50 Fresh local salmon £5.50 (Last order 9.30pm. No bar food Tues eve)
Devenish Cornish Bitter, John Devenish Bitter; Guinness; Grünhalle. *Real ale*

Set in one of the loveliest parts of Cornwall, this fine old country pub serves excellent food in civilised, convivial surroundings. Everything is home-cooked, from soup with a real taste of the stock pot to fish quenelles, first-rate steak and kidney pie and lamb cutlets in a mint and orange sauce. Sandwiches and salads for lighter snacks, and a terrific treacle tart to finish. Garden. **Family pub**

## Manchester *(Food)* — *Sinclairs*

Shambles Square · *Greater Manchester*
Map 3 B3
061-834 0430

*Brewery* Samuel Smith
*Landlords* Peter & Jean Wild

Seafood platter £2 Beef & oyster pie £2.50 (No bar food eves)
Sam Smith's Old Brewery Bitter, 4X Mild; Ayinger Bräu; cider. *Real ale*

Oysters are a popular feature of the lunch-time snacks at this fine old half-timbered inn, served either fresh on the half shell or gently cooked in the excellent beef and oyster pie. There's also a tempting display of other seafood, cold meats and salads, along with a regularly changing selection of hot specials. Upstairs is a soup and sandwich bar. Sandwiches are the only snacks available on Sundays. Patio.

## Marhamchurch *(B & B)* — *Bullers Arms*

Near Bude · *Cornwall* · Map 8 B3
Widemouth Bay (028 885) 277

*Free House*
*Landlords* Mr & Mrs Kneebone

**BEDROOMS 7 Grade 1 £C**
St Austell Tinner's Ale, Hick's Special Draught; Whitbread Best Bitter; Worthington Best Bitter; Guinness; Carlsberg; cider. *Real ale*

Bill Kneebone offers very comfortable accommodation for tourists and travellers in this peacefully situated village pub. Spacious bedrooms, which are furnished in simple modern style, have TVs and spotlessly clean bathrooms. Five suites have kitchen/dining/lounge areas. Most drinkers choose to relax in the popular beamed Hunter's Bar; the other bar is smaller and more intimate. Garden. **Family pub**

## Mark Cross *(Food)* — *Mark Cross Inn*

*East Sussex* · Map 6 C3
Rotherfield (089 285) 2423

*Brewery* Whitbread
*Landlord* Mr Martin Roberts

Plate of prawns £1.20 Beef & mushroom casserole £1.90 (Last order 10pm)
Fremlins Bitter, Tusker; Whitbread Best Bitter; Guinness; Stella Artois; Heineken; cider. *Real ale*

Meals are served from the smart tiled counter of the comfortable bar at this large pub with a garden. You can choose from eight sorts of ploughman's and there's also an ample selection of cold meat and seafood salads. Hot dishes include rich, satisfying farmhouse soup, beef and mushroom casserole, tasty turkey pie – even a vegetarian dish of the day. **Family pub**

## Market Drayton *(B & B)* — *Corbet Arms Hotel*

High Street · *Shropshire* · Map 3 B4
Market Drayton (0630) 2037

*Free House*
*Landlords* Mr & Mrs John Beckett

**BEDROOMS 10 Grade 1 £B**
Mitchells & Butlers Springfield Bitter, Mild; Stones Bitter; Guinness; Carling Black Label; Tennent's Pilsner; Taunton cider. *Real ale*

Much of Market Drayton's social life is centred on this creeper-clad coaching inn, whose attractions include a splendid bowling green. Open-plan bars offer abundant space for exercising elbows, and there's a restful residents' lounge. Bedrooms, too, are large and comfortable, with practical modern furnishings, colour TVs and well-appointed bathrooms. Bachelors speak warmly of the amorous lady ghost that haunts room 7. Good breakfasts. **Family pub**

## Market Weighton *(B & B)* — *Londesborough Arms*

High Street · *Humberside* · Map 4 D3
Market Weighton (0696) 72219

*Brewery* North Country Breweries
*Landlords* Mr & Mrs Cuckston

**BEDROOMS 14 Grade 1 £B**
North Country Riding Bitter, Old Tradition, Mild; Hopfenperle; Stella Artois. *Real ale*

Located in the town centre, this handsome Georgian hotel has a classical red-brick facade and a white-painted portico. There are two comfortable bars, one of them named after a celebrated 18th-century giant, William Bradley (you can still see his chair). Potted plants add a homely touch to the spacious bedrooms, which have modern built-in units, colur TVs and neat, compact bathrooms. **Family pub**

## Marlow *(Food)* — *Hare & Hounds*

Henley Road · *Buckinghamshire* · Map 6 B3
Marlow (062 84) 3343

*Brewery* Whitbread
*Landlords* Mr & Mrs Gladman

Seafood crumble £1.85 Beef & duck pie £1.95
(No bar food eves or Sun lunch)
Wethered's Bitter, SPA; Guinness; Stella Artois; Heineken; cider. *Real ale*

This delightful creeper-clad pub is as pretty as a picture, and inside there are two cosy beamed bars where you can enjoy a delicious snack in convivial surroundings. The menu is full of interesting and tempting fare, ranging from creamy chilled summer soup and a 'breakfast' sandwich to terrine with apricot relish, moussaka and chicken curry. You can also get a straightforward ploughman's.

## Marsh Gibbon *(Food)* — *Greyhound Inn*

Near Bicester · *Oxfordshire* · Map 5 B2
Stratton Audley (086 97) 365

*Free House*
*Landlords* Sylvia & Henry Phillips

Venison pie £2.25 Steak & kidney pie £2
(Last order 9pm. No bar food Sat eve)
Phillips Heritage, Allric's Old Ale; Newcastle Bitter; Kestrel; cider. *Real ale*

Marvellous atmosphere and real ale brewed on the premises are just two of the many good things about this fine, spotlessly kept pub. Excellent bar food is another, including home-roasted meats, beautifully baked pies, full-flavoured pâtés and splendid seasonal game. Fresh herbs feature in many dishes, and you can finish your meal with some prime English cheeses. Closed Monday lunchtime. Patio. **Family pub**

## Marshside *(Food)* — *Gate Inn*

Near Canterbury · *Kent* · Map 6 D3
Chislet (022 786) 498

*Brewery* Shepherd Neame
*Landlord* Christopher John Smith

Gateburger in wholemeal bread 75p Black pudding ploughman's £1.10 (Last order 10.15pm. No bar food Sun lunch)
Shepherd Neame Best Bitter, Masterbrew, Mild, Stock Ale; Taunton cider. *Real ale*

Nothing could be simpler or more delightful than this super village pub with its enthusiastic landlord, lovely rose garden, fine locally brewed beer and no-nonsense food. In the beamed bar you can tuck into an excellent home-made hamburger (served in a bap or delicious wholemeal bread) or choose a hearty sandwich of bacon, sausage, cheese or black pudding. And in winter you can enjoy a bowl of soup before the roaring fire. **Family pub**

## Mayfield *(Food)* — *Rose & Crown*

Fletching Street · *East Sussex* · Map 6 C4
Mayfield (0435) 872200

*Free House*
*Landlords* Richard & Claudette Leet
Seafood pancake £1.55 Chicken curry mayonnaise £1.65 (Last order 9.45pm. No bar food Mon eve & all Sun)
Everards Old Original, Tiger; Adnams Best Bitter; Guinness; Tennent's Extra; cider. *Real ale*

Low beamed ceilings, log fires and sturdy old furniture create an atmosphere of mellow charm at this long, white-painted pub that was once a brewhouse. A blackboard announces the day's bar snacks, which range from soup to sirloin steak by way of savoury cheese slice, whitebait and smoked chicken with orange. There are salads in summer, when you can enjoy them outside in the garden.

## Mellor *(B & B)* — *Millstone Hotel*

Church Lane, Near Blackburn · *Lancashire*
Map 3 B3
**Mellor (0254 81) 3333**

*Brewery* Shire Inns
*Landlord* Mr A. Simmons

**BEDROOMS 16 Grade 1 £A+**
Thwaites Bitter, Mild; Guinness; Stein Lager. *Real ale*

Just a short drive from junction 31 of the M6, this pleasantly modernised hotel is popular with both businessmen and holiday-makers. Light oak is much in evidence in the open-plan lounge and bar and the dining room, where splendid breakfasts are served. Compact, well-furnished bedrooms are equipped with tea-makers, trouser presses and direct-dial telephones. Patio. **Family pub**

## Melmerby *(Food)* — *Shepherds Inn*

Near Penrith · *Cumbria* · Map 3 B1
Langwathby (076 881) 217

*Brewery* Marston
*Landlords* Martin & Christine Baucutt

Fillet of pork Thai style £3.20 Cumberland sausage hot pot £2.70 (Last order 9.45pm)
Marston's Pedigree; Ind Coope Burton Bitter; Mercian Mild; Marston's Pilsner; cider. *Real ale*

Home-prepared bar meals attract a loyal following at this pleasant village inn, where Martin Baucutt also keeps a good selection of real ales. Standard fare like ploughman's, scampi and steak are supplemented by specialities such as baked rainbow trout and flavoursome pork and mushrooms Thai style. Delicious sweets, too, including apricot and almond gâteau. A roast joint is the main Sunday lunchtime offering. Patio.

## Mentmore *(Food)* — *Stag Inn*

Near Leighton Buzzard, Bedfordshire
*Buckinghamshire* · Map 5 B2
Cheddington (0296) 668 423

*Brewery* Wells
*Landlords* Michel & Helen Rigal
Steak pie £2.25 Scampi with chips £2.50 (Last order 10pm. No bar food Sun lunch or Sat eve)
Wells Bitter, Noggin; Guinness; Red Stripe; Kellerbräu; cider. *Real ale*

Whether it's a sandwich or a generous helping of roast lamb, you can be sure that your chosen dish will be carefully prepared from good fresh ingredients at this friendly hilltop pub. The French onion soup is the real McCoy – dark, rich and full of flavour – and there's also quiche, cold meats, salads and simple sweets. Garden.

## Mere *(B & B)* — *Old Ship Hotel*

Castle Street · *Wiltshire* · Map 8 D3
Mere (0747) 860258

*Brewery* Hall & Woodhouse
*Landlord* Mr Philip Johnson

**BEDROOMS 24 Grades 1 & 2 £A**
Hall & Woodhouse Badger Best Bitter, Malthouse; Worthington Dark; Guinness; Brock; Stella Artois; Taunton cider. *Real ale*

Period charm and up-to-date comfort combine happily at this sturdy 17th-century coaching inn. The oak-panelled hotel bar is cosy and intimate, and the lounge bar, with its stone walls and splendid open fireplace, has a pleasantly rustic character. Bedrooms in the main building are also traditional in style, while annexe rooms with private bathrooms are smartly modern; all have tea-makers and TVs. Enjoyable breakfasts. **Family pub**

## Metal Bridge *(B & B)* — *Metal Bridge Inn*

Near Gretna · *Cumbria* · Map 3 B1
Rockcliffe (022 874) 206

*Brewery* Younger
*Landlord* Mr D. O'Brien

**BEDROOMS 5 Grade 1 £C**
Younger's IPA, Tartan, Scotch Bitter; McEwan's Export, Lager; Kestrel. *Real ale*

Motorists travelling between England and Scotland can pull in at this white-painted pub just off the A74 for a pleasant overnight stay. Spacious, spotlessly clean bedrooms with smart fitted units, TVs and tea-makers are double-glazed to keep out the winds and the traffic noise. Public bathrooms are functional. Visitors can enjoy a drink in the bar decorated with fishing prints or enjoy the views of the river Esk from the patio or the attractive conservatory. **Family pub**

## Metherell *(B & B)* — *Carpenters Arms*

Near Callington · *Cornwall* · Map 8 B4
St Dominick (0579) 50242

*Free House*
*Landlords* Douglas & Jill Brace

**BEDROOMS 3 Grade 2 £C**
Bass; Flower's Original; Guinness; Tennent's Pilsner; Heineken; cider. *Real ale*

The 15th and 20th centuries come together at this delightful old inn, which is tucked away just south of the A390 Gunnislake–Liskeard road. Flagstone floors, rough-hewn walls and black beams create a splendid old-world atmosphere in the bars, while the three bedrooms have a simple modern appeal. Neat and tidy, they have tea-makers and share a spacious shower room. Terrace. **Family pub**

## Mickleton *(Food)* — *Butchers Arms*

Near Chipping Camden · *Gloucestershire*
Map 5 A2
Mickleton (038 677) 285

*Brewery* Whitbread
*Landlords* Alan & Judy Strong
Ploughman's £1.65 Cotswold chicken casserole £2.70 (Last order 9.45pm. No bar food Sun eve)
Flowers IPA, Original Bitter, Best Bitter; Heineken; Stella Artois; cider. *Real ale*

Alan and Judy Strong take good care of this cosy little pub with its collection of antique weapons and military prints. Relax in the bar and enjoy some hearty, wholesome dishes like tasty chicken casserole in cider, beef pie or ragout of venison. Light eaters have a choice of sandwiches, salads and ploughman's, and you can finish with homely apple pie and whipped cream. Patio.

## Middle Assendon *(Food)* — *Rainbow Inn*

Near Henley-on-Thames · *Oxfordshire*
Map 6 B3
Henley-on-Thames (0491) 574879

*Brewery* Brakspear
*Landlords* Nick & Mary Carter

Herby beef casserole £2.60 Spicy lamb hot pot £2.30
Brakspear's Bitter, Special, Mild, Old Ale (winter only); Guinness; Heineken. *Real ale*

There's a thriving darts team at this friendly country pub, where Nick Carter is the jovial landlord and his wife Mary the capable chef. She hits the target every time with her simple, satisfying and flavoursome bar food, from salads and sandwiches to quiches, curries, hot pots and roasts – and her excellent fruit pies provide a splendid finish. Sandwiches only in the evening & restricted choice Sunday lunch. Garden.

## Middleham *(B & B)* — *Black Swan Hotel*

Market Place · *North Yorkshire* · Map 4 C2
Wensleydale (0969) 22221

*Free House*
*Landlords* Mr & Mrs K. B. Burton

**BEDROOMS 3 Grade 2 £C**
Theakston's Best Bitter, Old Peculier; John Smith's Best Bitter, Magnet; Carlsberg; Guinness; Taunton cider. *Real ale*

This delightful old inn makes an ideal base from which to explore the beauty of the Yorkshire Dales. You can while away the hours in the beamed bar while enjoying a pint and listening to the local tales. There's also a beer garden. Very pretty, tastefully decorated bedrooms are furnished in modest style and equipped with TVs and washbasins; one room at the top of the pub has its own spacious bathroom. Superb breakfasts. **Family pub**

## Midhurst *(B & B)* — *Angel Hotel*

North Street · *West Sussex* · Map 6 B4
Midhurst (073 081) 2421

*Brewery* Gale
*Landlord* Mr N. Gibson

**BEDROOMS 18 Grade 2 £B**
Gale's HSB, BBB; Guinness; Carlsberg. *Real ale*

The Pilgrim Fathers reputedly stayed at this handsome old inn, and today's visitors will find a wealth of period charm, with ships' timbers and fine panelling much in evidence. Bedrooms, all with TVs and tea-makers, are a mixture of old and modern, and there are two bars and a large, comfortable residents' lounge – once the local court room. Pretty rose garden. **Family pub**

## Mildenhall *(B & B)* — *Bell Hotel*

High Street · *Suffolk* · Map 5 C2
Mildenhall (0638) 712134

*Free House*
*Landlords* Carolyn & John Child

**BEDROOMS 18 Grades 1 & 2 £A**
Younger's IPA; Newcastle Bitter; McEwan's IPA; Adnams Bitter; Guinness; Carlsberg; Taunton cider. *Real ale*

There's a warm, friendly feel about this fine old inn opposite the church. A beamed foyer-lounge greets visitors, and the large bar area, warmed by open fires, is well filled with comfortable armchairs. Spotlessly maintained bedrooms have good modern furnishings, tea-makers and colour televisions; most of them have bath or shower rooms with plentiful supplies of towels. Patio. **Family pub**

## Millthorpe *(Food)* — *Royal Oak*

Holmsfield, Near Sheffield · *Derbyshire*
Map 4 C3
Sheffield (0742) 890870

*Free House*
*Landlords* Mr & Mrs Wills
Lasagne £1.50 Brie ploughman's £1.80 (Last order 9pm. No bar food Thurs–Sun eves)
Ward's Sheffield Bitter; Darley's Thorne Bitter; Guinness; Carlsberg; Norseman; Taunton cider. *Real ale*

The locals who crowd the main panelled bar of this attractive stone-built pub will testify to the excellence of the ploughman's lunches – great wedges of English cheese with a generous salad garnish. Equally tasty are the sandwiches – perhaps fresh crab – fluffy omelettes and winter-warmers like cottage or fisherman's pie. Apple and raisin pie is popular too. Sandwiches only Sunday lunch. Steak and baked potatoes provide further evening choice.

## Milton Abbas *(Food, B & B)* — *Hambro Arms*

Near Blandford Forum · *Dorset* · Map 8 D3
Milton Abbas (0258) 880233

*Brewery* Devenish
*Landlords* John & Judy Dance
**BEDROOMS 2 Grade 1 £C**
Venison in red wine sauce £3.75 Goulash & wild rice £2.65 (Last order 9.30pm)
Devenish Wessex Best Bitter, Ordinary Bitter, John Groves Bitter; Guinness; Heineken; Grünhalle; cider. *Real ale*

A friendly atmosphere prevails in this rustic thatched pub, where Judy Dance delights customers with her varied choice of delicious food. In summer the main attraction is a hot and cold lunchtime buffet, while at other times you can have classic stews, hot pots and pies, as well as things like creamy mushroom soup, haddock and cheese pancakes and curries. Comfortable bedrooms have pretty fabrics, tea-makers and shower cubicles. **Family pub**

## Milton Combe *(Food)* — *Who'd Have Thought It*

Yelverton · *Devon* · Map 8 B4
Yelverton (0822) 853313

*Free House*
*Landlords* Gary Rager & Keith Yeo

Beef pasty 90p Roast beef salad £2.60 (Last order 9.45pm)
Usher's Best Bitter; Wadworth's 6X; Golden Hill Exmoor Ale; Palmer's IPA; Guinness; Heineken; cider. *Real ale*

Nestling at the bottom of a valley in the heart of Dartmoor, this 16th-century village pub is a friendly place to enjoy some homely food in pleasant surroundings. As well as monster ploughman's and salad platters, you can feast on nourishing vegetable soup or – if you're lucky – one of the famous home-made pasties. There are also daily hot dishes like tasty cottage pie or chicken and bacon pie. Less choice Sunday lunch. Garden.

## Minster Lovell *(Food, B & B)* — *Old Swan Hotel*

Near Witney · *Oxfordshire* · Map 5 A2
Minster Lovell (0993) 75614

*Brewery* Halls
*Landlords* Mr & Mrs Tim Turner

**BEDROOMS 10 Grade 1 £A+** (No dogs)
Cotswold ploughman's £1.60 Chicken pie £2 (No bar food eves or Sun)
Halls Harvest Bitter; Ind Coope Burton Ale; Löwenbräu. *Real ale*

Take the Old Minster turning off the B4070 Witney to Burford road to find this marvellous 600-year old inn. Warmed by log fires in the flagstone-floored bar you can enjoy tasty lunchtime snacks ranging from sandwiches and pâté to salads and specials like chicken and mushroom pie. Comfortable, well-equipped bedrooms have TVs and excellent private bathrooms. No children overnight. **Family pub**

## Modbury *(Food, B & B)* — *Exeter Inn*

Church Street · *Devon* · Map 8 C4
Modbury (0548) 830239
*Brewery* Usher
*Landlord* Mr James Mogg
**BEDROOMS 2 Grade 1 £C** (No dogs)
Scallops & bacon in mushroom & cream sauce £2.95 Spanish chicken £5.50 (Last order 9.45pm)
Usher's Best Bitter, Founder's Ale, Triple Crown; Ben Truman; Guinness; Holsten Export; Carlsberg; cider. *Real ale*

Present-day travellers are well cared for at this fine old coaching inn. Friendly, hard-working landlord James Mogg offers an excellent choice of imaginative food in the large beamed bar – from stuffed baked mushrooms to steak and Guinness casserole or succulent scallop and prawn kebabs. There are two comfortable bedrooms, the one boasting a four-poster and huge bathroom with gold-plated fittings being quite luxurious. **Family pub**

## Molesworth *(Food, B & B)* — *Cross Keys*

Huntingdon · *Cambridgeshire* · Map 5 B2
Bythorn (080 14) 283

*Free House*
*Landlord* Mrs Frances Bettsworth
**BEDROOMS 4 Grade 2 £C**
Moussaka £2.25 Rhubarb crumble 75p (Last order 10.45pm)
Adnams Bitter; Stones Bitter; Younger's Tartan; McEwan's Export; Guinness; Carlsberg; cider. *Real ale*

Good breakfasts are a bonus of a stay at this friendly, unpretentious pub, which offers simple overnight accommodation. The cosy bar is the setting for a local version of skittles and for some homely cooking. Pride of place on a menu of sandwiches, grills and salads goes to a real old-fashioned steak and kidney pie served with wholesome vegetables. Save room for some rhubarb crumble or a wedge of lemon meringue pie. **Family pub**

## Monksilver *(Food, B & B)* — *Notley Arms*

Near Taunton · *Somerset* · Map 8 C3
Stogumber (098 46) 217

*Brewery* Usher
*Landlords* Mike & Jill Robinson
**BEDROOMS 3 Grade 2 £C**
Hot roast beef in French bread £1.95 Beef casserole £3.45 (Last order 9.30pm)
Usher's Best Bitter, Triple Crown; Country Bitter; Guinness; Carlsberg; Taunton cider. *Real ale*

A barbecue in the lovely garden is a summertime attraction of this welcoming pub: Jill Robinson supplies diners with meat and jacket potatoes, after which it's DIY. Her lunchtime cold buffet is equally tempting, and other treats include onion soup, hot dishes like our steak and kidney pie, floaters (French bread with grilled topping) and delicious sweets. Neat little bedrooms are traditionally furnished and beautifully kept. No under-sevens overnight.

## Montacute *(Food, B & B)* — *Kings Arms Inn*

Bishopston · *Somerset* · Map 8 D3
Martock (0935) 822513

*Free House*
*Landlords* Mr & Mrs T. D. Hague
**BEDROOMS 10 Grade 1 £A** (No dogs)
Pâté & salad £2.50 Curry & rice £2.30 (Last order 10pm. No bar food Sun eve)
Bass, Toby, Worthington Best Bitter; Ben Truman; Guinness; Carlsberg; Taunton cider. *Real ale*

The Hagues extend a cordial welcome to guests at their plushly converted 16th-century inn, which offers excellent accommodation. Attractively decorated bedrooms have good fitted units. TVs, tea-makers and carpeted modern bathrooms. In the comfortable lounge bar the main attraction at lunchtime is a cold buffet, while at suppertime you can get things like tasty soup, mildly spiced curry and pizza with salad. Super sweets. **Family pub**

## Moreton-in-Marsh *(B & B)* — *Redesdale Arms Hotel*

High Street · *Gloucestershire* · Map 5 A2
Moreton-in-Marsh (0608) 50308

*Free House*
*Landlord* Mr G. R. Jewell

**BEDROOMS 14 Grades 1 & 2 £A**
Bass; Worthington Best Bitter; Guinness; Tennent's Extra; Carling Black Label; Taunton cider. *Real ale*

This is an attractive 18th-century inn of mellow sandstone. The cottagy, panelled bar is a pleasant place for a drink, and there's a patio for nice weather. Comfortable, well-maintained bedrooms (including some in the annexe) have good-quality furniture and carpeting, colour TVs and trouser presses; bathrooms are modern and fully tiled. Friendly staff add to the pleasure of a stay here. **Family pub**

## Moretonhampstead *(B & B)* — *White Hart Hotel*

The Square · *Devon* · Map 8 C3
Moretonhampstead (0647) 40406

*Free House*
*Landlord* Mr Peter Morgan

**BEDROOMS 16 Grades 1 & 2 £B**
Bass; Ansells Bitter; Tetley's Bitter; Whitbread Trophy; Guinness; Skol; Carlsberg Export; cider. *Real ale*

Once a posting house on the Plymouth–London mail route, this pleasant, well-kept Georgian inn retains much period charm. The beamed public bar is a cosy, friendly meeting place, and there's a relaxing lounge bar. Centrally heated bedrooms (all with TVs, tea-makers and extras like hair-dryers) vary in size and style; most have good modern bathrooms. No under-tens overnight. Patio. **Family pub**

## Morval *(B & B)* — *Snooty Fox Hotel*

Near Looe · *Cornwall* · Map 8 B4
Widegates (050 34) 233

*Free House*
*Landlord* Mr D. S. Mutton

**BEDROOMS 10 Grade 1 £A**
Flower's Original; Whitbread Best Bitter; McEwan's Export; Guinness; Stella Artois; Heineken; cider. *Real ale*

Views of the lovely Cornish countryside are a feature of this pleasant hotel, a popular base for tourists. Bedrooms are of a uniformly high standard, with good fitted carpets, modern furnishings, tea-makers and TVs. All have spotless, well-appointed bathrooms. Public rooms have plenty to offer: comfort in the spacious lounge bar, conviviality in the games room, peace and quiet in the cosy reading room. Garden.

## Moulton *(Food)* ★ *Black Bull Inn*

Near Richmond · *North Yorkshire* · Map 4 C2
Barton (032 577) 289

*Free House*
*Landlords* Mr & Mrs Pagendam

Welsh rarebit £1.50 Cottage cheese, prawns & salad £2.50 (No bar food eves or Sun)
Theakston's Best Bitter, Old Peculier; Black Bull Bitter; Carlsberg. *Real ale*

At lunchtime visitors from far and wide are drawn to this simple roadside pub by the excellent snacks served in the charming bar. You might tuck into tasty French onion soup, a first-rate rough terrine finely flavoured with herbs or a sandwich with a mouthwatering filling like smoked salmon. A few luscious sweets – the huge brandy snaps bursting with cream are famous – and superb cheeses, including local Swaledale. Closed 1 week Christmas.

## Murcott *(Food)* *Nut Tree Inn*

Near Islip · *Oxfordshire* · Map 5 B2
Charlton-on-Otmoor (086 733) 253

*Free House*
*Landlords* Gordon & Diane Evans
Fish with potatoes & salad £3.50 Rump steak with chips & salad £6.50 (Last order 9pm. No bar food Sun)
Wadworth's 6X; Ind Coope Burton Ale; Hall's Harvest Bitter; Guinness; Skol; Löwenbräu; cider. *Real ale*

Gordon Evans runs a particularly friendly ship at this delightful old thatched inn, circulating among his customers in the cosy beamed bar. His wife Diane, who looks after culinary matters, produces a good range of tasty bar snacks – from cold meats, salads and sandwiches to basket meals, local trout and game and a first-rate beef curry. To finish, nice home-made sweets and a varied cheeseboard. Garden.

## Nailsworth *(Food)* *Tipputs Inn*

Bath Road · *Gloucestershire* · Map 7 D2
Nailsworth (045 383) 2466

*Free House*
*Landlords* Mr & Mrs S. Whitebread

Roast gammon £3.75 Beef curry £2.75 (Last order 10.15pm)
Hook Norton Best Bitter; Robinson's Best Bitter; Ruddles County; Newcastle Bitter; Guinness; Carlsberg; Taunton cider. *Real ale*

This attractive stone pub south of town has a plush, nicely furnished bar as well as both patio and garden for alfresco snacks. The bar menu is varied: ploughman's with your choice from six cheeses, smooth chicken liver pâté, open baps, hot snacks such as Tipputs Brunch (2 jumbo sausages, fried egg and chips, served with salad) or substantial dishes like curry, chicken pie, baked trout and roast gammon. **Family pub**

## Nantwich *(Food, B & B)* *Lamb*

Hospital Street · *Cheshire* · Map 3 B4
Nantwich (0270) 625286

*Brewery* Greenall Whitley
*Landlords* Mr & Mrs R. Jones

**BEDROOMS 16 Grades 1 & 2 £B**
Ravioli pinocchio £1.95 Chicken casserole £1.95 (Last order 10pm)
Greenall Whitley Bitter, Mild; Guinness; Grünhalle Lager; cider. *Real ale*

Bar snacks served at this comfortable old coaching inn range from plain and toasted sandwiches to full-flavoured chicken liver pâté, shepherd's pie and ravioli with a peppy sauce made with fresh tomatoes. There are also puddings at lunchtime; only sandwiches on Sunday. Spacious bedrooms have mostly sturdy freestanding furniture; eight have private facilities. Courtyard.

## Nassington *(Food)* — *Black Horse Inn*

Near Peterborough, Cambridgeshire
*Northamptonshire* · Map 5 B1
Stamford (0780) 782324
*Free House*
*Landlord* Mr Tom Guy
Seafood pancake £3.35 Stir-fried chicken with shrimps & mushrooms £5.65
(Last order 10.15pm)
Greene King IPA; John Smith's Bitter; Guinness; Harp; Kronenbourg; Taunton cider. *Real ale*

Hungry travellers need make only a short diversion from the Great North Road to enjoy the excellent bar fare served at this attractive old stone pub. The regular menu offers anything from pâté and pasta to game pie and pepper steak, while a blackboard proclaims fresh fish dishes and other specials like our beautifully tasty beef in beer. Super sweets, too. Summer cold table. Garden. **Family pub**

## Naunton *(Food, B & B)* — *Black Horse*

Near Cheltenham · *Gloucestershire*
Map 5 A2
Guiting Power (045 15) 378

*Brewery* Donnington
*Landlords* Adrian & Jennie Bowen-Jones
**BEDROOMS 3 Grade 2 £C** (No dogs)
Mixed meat ploughman's £1.50 Pork in cider with chips £2.50 (Last order 9.30pm)
Donnington's SBA, BB; Carlsberg; cider. *Real ale*

Adrian and Jennie Bowen-Jones – he behind the bar, she in the kitchen – take excellent care of visitors to their friendly village pub. In the lounge bar you can enjoy anything from a light snack such as egg mayonnaise or rarebit to filling lasagne or a juicy sirloin steak, and you should always leave room for the super chocolate roulade. For overnight guests (no children) there are three homely bedrooms sharing a simple modern bathroom. Patio.

## Needham Market *(Food, B & B)* — *Limes Hotel*

High Street · *Suffolk* · Map 5 D2
Needham Market (0449) 720305

*Free House*
*Landlords* Terry & Stephanie Watts
**BEDROOMS 11 Grade 1 £A+**
Steak pie & vegetables £2.50 Spare ribs with sweet & sour sauce £2 (Last order 10pm)
Adnams Bitter; Tolly Cobbold Bitter; Younger's Tartan; Guinness; Kestrel; Skol; Taunton cider. *Real ale*

Spacious, well-equipped bedrooms (tea-makers, TVs, telephones, spotless modern bathrooms) provide first-rate comfort at this pleasant Georgian-fronted inn. Carefully prepared snacks on offer in the smartly rustic Bugs Bar include sandwiches, ploughman's and chicken liver pâté. There are also tasty daily hot dishes such as braised liver and onions and cottage pie, and a cold buffet brings further weekday lunchtime choice. **Family pub**

## Needingworth *(B & B)* — *Pike & Eel*

Overcote Lane · *Cambridgeshire* · Map 5 C2
St Ives (0480) 63336

*Free House*
*Landlord* J. M. Stafferton

**BEDROOMS 9 Grade 2 £B** (No dogs)
Greene King IPA, Abbot Ale; Adnams Bitter; Bass; Guinness; Carling Black Label; Harp; Kronenbourg; Taunton cider. *Real ale*

River-borne visitors can tie up at private moorings outside this attractive old inn on the Ouse. It's very popular with anglers as well as boaters, and mounted fish form part of the decor in the comfortable lounge bar. Centrally heated bedrooms with practical modern furniture and colour TVs provide excellent overnight accommodation, and there's a cosy lounge and writing room. Garden. **Family pub**

## Nettlecombe *(Food, B & B)* — *Marquis of Lorne*

Near Bridport · *Dorset* · Map 8 D3
Powerstock (030 885) 236

*Brewery* Palmer
*Landlords* Bob & Philippa Bone

**BEDROOMS 8 Grade 2 £B** (No dogs)
Steak & kidney pie £2.25 Chocolate mousse 95p (Last order 10pm)
Palmer's IPA, Bridport Bitter; Guinness; Shilthorn. *Real ale*

Ramblers and holiday-makers are drawn to this friendly, stone-built pub. The menu in the snug bar offers something for all tastes, from sandwiches and salads (home-cooked ham, juicy prawns) to basket meals and delicious daily specials like rabbit, chicken and corn pie or whole lobster salad. Lovely puds, too. Simple, cheerful accommodation includes four family rooms. There's a residents' TV lounge, as well as a children's playground in the garden. **Family pub**

## Newark *(B & B)* — *Robin Hood Hotel*

Lombard Street · *Nottinghamshire* · Map 4 D4
Newark (0636) 703858

*Owners* Anchor Hotels Ltd
*Landlord* Diana Wildbur

**BEDROOMS 20 Grade 1 £A+**
John Courage Bitter; John Smith's Best Bitter, Lager; Guinness.

Within striking distance of Sherwood Forest and nearby industrial centres, this 17th-century coaching inn is a popular base for tourists and business people. Spacious, simply furnished bedrooms have fitted units, tea-makers and colour TVs, plus adequate private bathrooms. Downstairs there are two bars – the plush Sheriff's, which is medieval in style, and the Friar Tuck, where children are welcome.
**Family pub**

## Newbridge *(Food)* — *Maybush*

Near Witney · *Oxfordshire* · Map 6 A3
Standlake (086 731) 624

*Brewery* Morland
*Landlords* Mr & Mrs J. Phillips
Seafood Thermidor £1.35 Toasted beef & horseradish sandwich 80p (Last order 10pm. No bar food Mon eve Oct–Feb)
Morland's Best Bitter, Bitter, Mild; Whitbread Tankard; Guinness; Heineken; cider. *Real ale*

A terrace and garden overlooking the Thames are great summer attractions at this well-kept pub. There or in the low-ceilinged bar you can enjoy Mrs Phillips' dependable home cooking. Favourite daily specials like spaghetti bolognese or curry (lunchtime only) are backed up by omelettes, toasted sandwiches and scampi, and her tempting sweets include the popular apple turnover and banana split.

## Newcastle upon Tyne *(B & B)* — *Corner House*

Heaton Road, Heaton · *Tyne & Wear*
Map 4 C1
Newcastle upon Tyne (0632) 659602

*Brewery* Scottish & Newcastle
*Landlords* Roland & Brenda Barnes

**BEDROOMS 7 Grade 1 £C** (No dogs)
McEwans 80/-; Younger's Scotch Bitter; Scottish & Newcastle Exhibition, Newcastle Bitter; Guinness; Taunton cider. *Real ale*

Situated by a busy roundabout on the eastern outskirts of the city, this cheerful pub provides good accommodation for the traveller. Quiet bedrooms (all at the rear of the building) have well-designed fitted furniture, tea-makers and colour TVs. The two public bathrooms are large and nicely maintained. Downstairs, visitors will find three spacious bars: a panelled snug bar, a modernised lounge bar and a public bar with games. Garden.

## Newenden *(Food)* — *White Hart*

*Kent* · Map 6 C4
Northiam (079 74) 2166

*Brewery* Courage
*Landlord* Mr A. E. Faulkner

Shepherd's pie £1.50 Fishcakes & chips £1.25 (Last order 10pm)
Courage Best Bitter, Directors Bitter; Guinness; Harp; Taunton cider. *Real ale*

Mrs Faulkner's excellent bar snacks draw the crowds to this rustic weatherboarded pub close by the Rother River. At lunchtime the attraction is superb crab pâté, shepherd's pie, fishcakes and sweets such as blackberry and apple pie, while in the evening there are more adventurous dishes like delicious poached salmon with light, lemony hollandaise, Rye scallops and hefty, good-quality steaks. Sandwiches and salads too. Garden. **Family pub**

## Newton *(Food)* — *Queen's Head*

Near Cambridge · *Cambridgeshire* · Map 5 C2
Cambridge (0223) 870436

*Free House*
*Landlord* D. M. V. Short

Soup 75p Sandwiches from 60p (Last order 10.30pm)
Adnams Bitter, Old Ale (winter only); Guinness; Tuborg Gold; cider. *Real ale*

Run by the Short family for over 20 years, this ancient village pub oozes old-world charm. A huge inglenook fireplace warms the saloon bar, and fine old furniture is a feature throughout. The snack menu couldn't be simpler – mugs of nourishing soup, baked potatoes (lunchtime only) and super wholemeal bread with generous fillings of cheese, smoked salmon and excellent cooked meats. **Family pub**

## Newton *(Food)* — *Red Lion Inn*

Near Sleaford · *Lincolnshire* · Map 4 D4
Folkingham (052 97) 256
*Free House*
*Landlords* Mr & Mrs J. W. Power
Lincolnshire stuffed chine & salads £4
Coffee gâteau 80p (Last order 10pm. No bar food Sun eve & all Mon, except Bank Holidays)
Bateman's Bitter; Manns Triple Crown; Whitbread Tankard; Guinness; Heineken; Stella Artois; cider. *Real ale*

Arrive early, as the fame of the marvellous cold buffet brings the crowds flocking to the bar of this friendly stone-built pub near the A52. Sugar-baked gammon, rare roast beef, turkey, pâté and the outstanding herb-stuffed chine of pork are served with a selection of crisp, super-fresh salads. There are also sandwiches, winter soups and a delectable lemon meringue pie. Patio.
**Family pub**

## Newton *(B & B)* — *Saracen's Head*

Near Sudbury · *Suffolk* · Map 5 C2
Sudbury (0787) 79036

*Brewery* Tollemache & Cobbold
*Landlords* Mr & Mrs J. Eglin

**BEDROOMS 3 Grade 2 £C** (No dogs)
Tolly Cobbold Original, Bitter; Guinness; Hansa. *Real ale*

The cordial Eglins put out the welcome mat at their roadside public house. The bars with their old oak beams and winter fires are cosy and inviting, the public bar being a popular local meeting place. Cheerfully decorated bedrooms, all with tea-makers, radios and plenty of wardrobe space, share a well-maintained bathroom. Accommodation closed 1 week Christmas. Garden. **Family pub**

## Newton-in-Bowland *(Food, B & B)* — *Parkers Arms Hotel*

Near Clitheroe · *Lancashire* · Map 3 B3
Slaidburn (020 06) 236

*Brewery* Whitbread
*Landlord* Mr H. Rhodes

**BEDROOMS 3 Grade 2 £C** (No dogs)
Steak & kidney pie £1.95 Salmon salad £3 (Last order 10.30pm)
Whitbread Trophy, Best Mild; Guinness; Heineken.

In the heart of the beautiful Hodder Valley, this former deer-keepers cottage offers peaceful accommodation in its simple, well-kept bedrooms. Residents also have a cosy lounge with colour TV. Bar snacks are nicely varied, with fresh fish dishes like our lovely salmon salad a regular and popular feature. Home-made soup, pâtés, pies and sandwiches round off the choice. Accommodation closed 2 weeks Christmas. **Family pub**

## Newton Valence *(Food)* — *Horse & Groom*

Near Alton · *Hampshire* · Map 6 B3
Tisted (042 058) 220

*Brewery* Watneys
*Landlord* Mr A. Gill
Prawns on toast with tomato sauce & cheese £1.95 Grilled gammon steak £3 (Last order 9pm)
Watneys Stag Bitter; Usher's Best Bitter; Webster's Yorkshire Bitter; Gale's HSB; Guinness; Holsten; cider. *Real ale*

Visitors to this imposing roadside pub are assured of a friendly welcome from Mr Gill, as well as some really tasty bar food. For a quick snack there are sandwiches and tempting savouries like prawns with tomato sauce and cheese. And if you're looking for something more substantial, the menu offers cold meats with help-yourself salads, various grills and a daily special like ham risotto or cottage pie. The glazed patio is useful for children.

## North Bovey *(Food, B & B)* — *Ring of Bells*

Near Moretonhampstead · *Devon* · Map 8 C4
Moretonhampstead (0647) 40375

*Free House*
*Landlords* George & Cora Batcock

**BEDROOMS 6 Grades 1 & 2 £A** (No dogs)
Devonshire hot pot £1.65 Sirloin steak £6.50 (Last order 9.30pm. No bar food Sun lunch)
Wadworth's 6X; Flowers Traditional; Whitbread Trophy; Heineken; cider. *Real ale*

This sturdy old thatched inn lies at the heart of one of Devon's prettiest villages. George and Cora Batcock are delightful hosts and the bar fare is tasty and well prepared: ploughman's, baked potatoes and cottage pie for lunch, anything from local trout to roast pheasant in the evening. Charming bedrooms (two with four-posters) have their own neat bathrooms. Accommodation closed January. Garden. **Family pub**

## North Cerney *(Food, B & B)* — *Bathurst Arms*

Near Cirencester · *Gloucestershire* · Map 6 A3
North Cerney (028 583) 281

*Free House*
*Landlords* Mrs V. N. Judd & Mr C. R. Kite
**BEDROOMS 4 Grade 1 £B** (No dogs)
Steak & kidney pie £1.95 Ploughman's £1.40 (Last order 10pm)
Flowers Original Bitter; Archer's Best Bitter; McEwan's Export; Heineken; Stella Artois; cider. *Real ale*

Attractive, well-furnished bedrooms with splendid modern bathrooms provide excellent overnight accommodation at this converted farmhouse with a pretty riverside garden. There are three bars, including the beamed lounge bar with its own dining area and table service. Snacks range from salads and ploughman's to lasagne, steaks and daily specials like our lovely fresh grilled sole. **Family pub** (lunchtime)

## North Petherton *(B & B)* — *Walnut Tree Inn*

Fore Street, Near Bridgwater · *Somerset*
Map 8 C3
North Petherton (0278) 662255

*Free House*
*Landlords* Mr & Mrs Goulden

**BEDROOMS 11 Grade 1 £A**
Wadworth's 6X Bitter; Whitbread Trophy; Exmoor Ale; Younger's Tartan Bitter. *Real ale*

There's a comfortable, homely feel about this spotlessly maintained coaching inn, which stands in the middle of the village opposite a 13th-century church. Bedrooms (some in a motel-style block at the rear) are prettily decorated and sturdily furnished; all have tea-makers, TVs and carpeted bathrooms with colourful modern suites. The bars are warm and welcoming, too.
**Family pub**

## North Wootton *(B & B)* — *Crossways Inn*

Near Shepton Mallet · *Somerset* · Map 8 D3
Pilton (074 989) 237

*Free House*
*Landlords* John & Cynthia Kirkham

**BEDROOMS 7 Grade 2 £C** (No dogs)
Wadworths 6X; Bass; Usher's Triple Crown; John Smith's Yorkshire Bitter; Tetley's Bitter; Guinness; Hofmeister; cider. *Real ale*

The rural setting makes for a peaceful stay at this rambling inn. The traditionally furnished bedrooms offer simple comforts, and two have their own compact shower rooms. Stone walls and sturdy oak furniture give a rustic feel to the spacious bar, and there's a cosy residents' lounge with TV. Plans include more bedrooms and improvements to the little patio. No children under two overnight. **Family pub**

## Nottingham *(Food)* — *Lord Nelson Inn*

11 Thurgarton Street, Sneinton
*Nottinghamshire* · Map 4 C4
Nottingham (0602) 54801

*Brewery* Hardys & Hansons
*Landlord* Mr Chris Smith

Home-made steak & potato pie £2 Roast beef salad £2.50 (No bar food eves or Sun)
Hardy's and Hansons Bitter; Guinness; Heineken; cider. *Real ale*

Two converted farmhouses make up this cosy pub on the outskirts of the city. There are four little beamed bars, in one of which you will find a tempting lunchtime display of cold meats, pies and wedges of English cheese to go with fresh, crisp salads. Chris Smith also offers jacket potatoes and hot daily specials like cottage pie. Finish with gâteau or delicious apple pie. Sandwiches only for Saturday lunch. Terrace.

## Nottingham — *Ye Olde Trip To Jerusalem Inn*

A public house since 1189 (reputedly the oldest in the land), this unique inn has a 16th-century facade that hides a maze of cellars, rooms and passages carved out of the rock on which Nottingham Castle stands. Each room has its own appeal: note especially the snug, with its ancient weapons and extraordinary cavernous ceiling.

Brewhouse Yard, Castle Road · *Nottinghamshire* · Map 4 C4
Nottingham (0602) 473171
*Free House* *Landlords* Mr & Mrs E. Marshall
Samuel Smith's Old Brewery Bitter; Marston's Pedigree; Everards Old Original; Heineken; Taunton cider. *Real ale*

## Nunney *(Food, B & B)* — *George Inn*

11 Church Street · *Somerset* · Map 8 D3
Nunney (037 384) 458

*Free House*
*Landlord* Mr J. Lewis
**BEDROOMS 12 Grade 1 £B**
Somerset beef & Guinness casserole £2.75 Apple charlotte £1 (Last order 10pm)
Bass; Butcombe Bitter; Double Diamond; Younger's Tartan; Guinness; Carling Black Label; Löwenbräu; Taunton cider. *Real ale*

Food and accommodation are both excellent at this charming 14th-century inn in the shadow of the castle. Home-made soups and sandwiches make tasty light snacks, or you could opt for something more substantial like mushroom and turkey pie, beef curry, rabbit casserole – even seasonal game. Comfortable bedrooms decorated in a pretty, cottagy style include six new ones; some have TVs and private bathrooms. There's a residents' lounge. **Family pub**

## Oakwoodhill *(Food)* — *Punchbowl Inn*

Near Ockley · *Surrey* · Map 6 B3
Oakwood Hill (030 679) 249

*Free House*
*Landlords* Rob & Shirley Chambers
Curried chicken £2.75 Steak & kidney pudding £3.50 (Last order 10pm)
King & Barnes Sussex Bitter; Hall & Woodhouse Badger Bitter; Young's Special Bitter; Charrington IPA; Guinness; Taunton cider. *Real ale*

In this ancient country cottage dating back 600 years, locals and visitors now gather to sample excellent local brews and some really tasty food. You can help yourself to a bowl of soup or tuck into something like a sandwich, sausage with French bread or superb home-cooked ham, eggs and chips. There's also a daily special such as a pie, a casserole or a dish of pasta. And to round things off try one of the nice puddings.
**Family pub**

## Ockley *(Food, B & B)* — *King's Arms*

Stane Street · *Surrey* · Map 6 B3
Dorking (0306) 711224

*Free House*
*Landlords* Mrs Mary Kates Doyle & family
**BEDROOMS 3 Grade 1 £B**
Prawn curry £2.30 Chicken & ham pie with chips £1.95 (Last order 9.45pm)
King & Barnes Sussex Bitter; Fuller's ESB; Hall & Woodhouse Badger Bitter; Guinness; Carlsberg; Foster's; cider. *Real ale*

Mary Kates Doyle is admirably assisted by her daughters and grandchildren in this immaculate, tile-hung pub, and you couldn't wish for a more friendly welcome. The bar food is good and wholesome, with a choice ranging from salads, sandwiches and ploughman's to smooth chicken liver pâté and tasty steak and kidney pie. For overnight visitors there are three traditionally furnished bedrooms which share an attractive little bathroom. Garden. **Family pub**

## Offham *(Food)* — *Blacksmith's Arms*

Near Lewes · *East Sussex* · Map 6 C4
Lewes (079 16) 2971

*Free House*
*Landlords* Peter & Ann Blackburn
Beef salad £3.95 Pie of the day with chips or salad £2.50 (Last order 9.30pm)
Young's Special Bitter; Harvey's Best Bitter; King & Barnes Sussex Bitter; Guinness; Tennent's Extra, Pilsner; Tuborg; cider. *Real ale*

An eye-catching cold buffet is a central feature of this welcoming roadside pub, where Peter and Ann Blackburn offer a good selection of tasty bar snacks. The menu ranges from omelettes and a choice of sandwiches (our roast beef was lovely and rare) to specials like full-flavoured turkey Stroganoff and a generous seafood platter. French apple flan makes a super sweet. Closed Monday. **Family pub**

## Old Dalby *(Food)* — *Crown Inn*

Near Melton Mowbray · *Leicestershire* · Map 5 B1
Melton Mowbray (0664) 823134

*Free House*
*Landlords* Lynne Bryan & Salvatore Inguanta
Seafood pancake £2.95 Chicken medley £3.95 (Last order 10.15pm. No bar food Sun & Mon eves)
Marston's Pedigree, Owd Rodger, Merrie Monk, Burton Bitter; Ruddles County; Adnams Bitter. *Real ale*

Full of character and atmosphere, with friendly regulars and cheerful staff, this 200-year-old inn is tucked modestly away so ask directions. Delicious food is served in the cosy bars, from flavoursome cream of mushroom soup and crab-filled baked avocado to lamb kebabs, seafood pancakes and our excellent chicken with tomato sauce in a pastry case, served with crisp fresh vegetables. Garden.

**Family pub**

## Old Heathfield *(Food)* — *Star Inn*

Church Street · *East Sussex* · Map 6 C4
Heathfield (043 52) 3570

*Brewery* Watneys
*Landlord* Mr Ron Gilbert
Home-made pâté & toast £1.45 Turkey & ham pie £2.50 (Last order 9.45pm. No bar food Sun & Mon eves)
Tamplins Bitter; Webster's Yorkshire Bitter; Gale's HSB; Guinness; Foster's; Carlsberg; cider. *Real ale*

Generous helpings of good, honest fare keep the customers smiling at this most convivial and reliable of pubs, run in admirable fashion by Ron Gilbert and his family. A varied menu of familiar favourites includes richly flavoured pâté, savoury pies and omelettes, and the delicious bubble and squeak is always in demand. Simple sweets to finish. There are two cosy bars and a lovely garden. **Family pub**

## Oldbury-on-Severn *(Food)* — *Anchor Inn*

Near Bristol · *Avon* · Map 7 D2
Thornbury (0454) 413331
*Free House*
*Landlord* Mr Michael J. Dowdeswell
Steak, kidney & mushroom pie £1.45 Langoustines in garlic butter £2.50 (Last order 9.30pm)
Theakston's Best Bitter, Old Peculier; Marston's Pedigree; Robinson's Best Bitter; Butcombe Best Bitter; Guinness; Taunton cider. *Real ale*

Food plays an important part in this attractive converted mill house. Expansive host Michael Dowdeswell offers an appetising cold selection that includes fresh Severn salmon, rare beef and smoked spare ribs to enjoy with tasty salads. Or you might tuck into one of the daily-changing hot dishes such as liver and bacon casserole, followed by an Oldbury tart that's packed with gooseberries steeped in brown sugar. Garden.

## Ombersley *(Food)* — *Kings Arms*

*Hereford & Worcester* · Map 7 D1
Worcester (0905) 620315

*Brewery* Mitchells & Butlers
*Landlords* Chris & Judy Blundell
Moussaka & salad £2.95 Steak & kidney pie with chips & peas £2.95 (Last order 9pm. No bar food Sun)
Bass; Mitchells & Butlers Brew XI, Springfield Bitter, Mild; Guinness; Carling Black Label; Taunton cider. *Real ale*

Stuffed birds, brass kitchen utensils and other bric-à-brac add to the charm of this lovingly kept 15th-century pub. Snacks cater for even the heartiest appetite: there's steak or a pork chop, rich home-made steak and kidney pie, salad or a ploughman's, and daily specials might include treats like smoked salmon and asparagus quiche, with gooseberry fool to finish. There are also well-filled cobs at lunchtime. Patio.

**Family pub**

## Onecote *(Food)* — *Jervis Arms*

Near Leek · *Staffordshire* · Map 4 C4
Onecote (053 88) 206
*Free House*
*Landlords* Mr & Mrs D. Smith
Home-cooked ham £1.75 12oz. sirloin steak £4 (Last order 10pm. No bar food Mon lunch except Bank Hols, also Tues–Fri lunch in winter)
Ruddle's County; Marston's Pedigree; McEwan's P70; Younger's Scotch, IPA; Guinness; Carlsberg; Taunton cider; Kestrel. *Real ale*

The river Hamps flows past this agreeable old inn, whose cosy beamed bars are a very busy, convivial setting in which to enjoy Mrs Smith's popular snacks. The choice is excellent, and whether you want a simple ploughman's, a super ham salad or a flavoursome shepherd's pie, you'll find good quality matched by good value. To finish, try the home-made chocolate gâteau. Garden. **Family pub**

## Orford *(Food, B & B)* — *King's Head Inn*

Front Street, Near Woodbridge · *Suffolk*
Map 5 D2
Orford (039 45) 271

*Brewery* Adnams
*Landlords* Mrs P. Shaw & Mr A. Shaw
**BEDROOMS 5 Grade 2 £B** (No dogs)
Home-made pâté with salad £1.85 Hot cockle salad with cottage loaf £1.85 (No bar food eves)
Adnams Bitter; Skol. *Real ale*

Local seafood features prominently on the menu of this charming pub, parts of which date back to the 13th-century. You can also get home-made pâté, delicious hickory-smoked ham and a range of freshly cut sandwiches. Bedrooms are comfortable and homely and a splendid breakfast awaits guests in the morning. Accommodation closed 5–28 Jan.

## Osgodby *(B & B)* — *Barn*

Near Scarborough · *North Yorkshire* · Map 4 D2
Scarborough (0723) 583536

*Brewery* Younger
*Landlords* Paul & Karen Waugh

**BEDROOMS 7 Grade 2 £C** (No dogs)
Younger's No. 3 Ale; Scotch Bitter; Newcastle Bitter; Kestrel; Harp. *Real ale*

Standing about a mile from the sea on the site of an ancient manor house, this welcoming pub is a pleasant place for an overnight stay. Centrally heated bedrooms in an adjoining house vary in size; all have identical modern fittings, tea-makers and televisions. They share a simple bathroom and shower room. There are two bars, one with games machines and a pool table.
**Family pub** (summer)

## Oswaldkirk *(Food, B & B)* — *Malt Shovel Inn*

Near Helmsley · *North Yorkshire* · Map 4 C2
Ampleforth (043 93) 461
*Brewery* Samuel Smith
*Landlords* Ian & Carol Pickering
**BEDROOMS 3 Grade 2 £C** (No dogs)
Sweetcorn & crab pancake £1.70 Shovel bun with chicken curry filling £2.65 (Last order 9.30pm. No bar food Mon eve except Bank Holidays)
Samuel Smith's Old Brewery Bitter; Alpine. *Real ale*

An interesting menu really gets the taste buds tingling at this fine old 17th-century manor house. Spinach roulade or tuna mousse with diced cucumber makes a lovely light snack, while more substantial offerings include cold meat salads, lamb cutlets, game pie and the unique Shovel buns – little cottage loaves filled with delicious curried chicken. Three homely bedrooms share a well-maintained bathroom. Garden. **Family pub**

## Ovington — *Bush Inn*

A lovely tree-lined lane leads from the A31 to this delightful rose-covered pub, whose garden runs down to the peaceful river Itchen, famous for its trout fishing. The setting is enchanting, and the bars, with their nooks and crannies and gleaming copperware, are cosy and convivial. The oldest part is 17th century, the rest 19th century.

**Family pub**

Near Alresford · *Hampshire* · Map 6 A3
Alresford (096 273) 2764
*Free House* *Landlords* Mr & Mrs G. M. Draper
Strong's Country Bitter; Flower's Original; Wadworth's 6X; Wethered's Spa Bitter; Guinness; Stella Artois; cider. *Real ale*

## Oxford *(Food)* — *Perch*

Binsey · *Oxfordshire* · Map 6 A3
Oxford (0865) 240386

*Brewery* Halls
*Landlords* Andy & Julie Little

Lasagne £1.85 Apple crumble 40p (Last order 9.30pm. No bar food Sun & Mon eves)
Halls Harvest Bitter, Mild; Ind Coope Burton Ale, Double Diamond; Guinness; Skol; Löwenbräu; cider. *Real ale*

Check directions when setting out for this attractive old thatched pub linked by a path to the river Thames. The menu in the roomy flagstoned bar sticks mainly to standard pub fare such as soup, ploughman's platters, lasagne and a good meaty steak and kidney pie with plenty of rich gravy. To finish, there's a nice crunchy apple crumble. Garden.

## Oxford *(Food, B & B)* — *Turf Tavern*

5 Bath Place, Holywell Street · *Oxon* · Map 6 A3
Oxford (0865) 243235
*Owner* Mr Wally Ellse
*Landlord* Keith Roberts
**BEDROOMS 9 Grade 2 £B**
Beef, wine & mushroom pie £2.95
Lasagne £2.35 (Last order 10pm)
Hook Norton Best Bitter, Old Hookey; Theakston's Old Peculier (winter only); Webster's Yorkshire Bitter; Guinness; Harp; cider. *Real ale*

Tucked away in the shadow of New College tower, this historic inn is very much an Oxford institution. Immensely popular even out of term, it offers a fine selection of bar snacks, both hot and cold: tasty flans and pies, fresh, crunchy salads, shepherd's pie, beef casserole, old-fashioned puddings. Cosy bedrooms in adjacent cottages share two neat little bathrooms. TV lounge. Two beer gardens. **Family pub**

## Parkgate *(Food, B & B)* — *Ship Hotel*

The Parade Wirral · *Cheshire* · Map 3 B3
051 336 3931

*Owners* Anchor Hotels
*Landlord* Mr Michel Kaiser

**BEDROOMS 26 Grade 1 £A+** (No dogs)
Quiche lorraine £1.90 Parkgate platter £2.20 (No bar food eves or Sun)
John Smith's Bitter, Mild; Guinness; Harp; Kronenbourg; Taunton cider.

Savoury pies remain firm favourites among the super lunchtime snacks served in this stone-built inn overlooking the Dee estuary. There are also excellent sandwiches and salads and a roast or fish dish as the daily special. Comfortably furnished bedrooms are splendidly appointed, with tea-makers, direct-dial telephones and neat carpeted bathrooms. High standard of maintenance, and excellent breakfasts.

**Family pub**

## Pelynt *(B & B)* — *Jubilee Inn*

Near Looe · *Cornwall* · Map 8 B4
Lanreath (0503) 20312

*Free House*
*Landlord* Mr F. E. Williams

**BEDROOMS 10 Grades 1 & 2 £B**
Whitbread Best Bitter; Flower's Original; Poachers Bitter; Guinness; Stella Artois; Heineken; cider. *Real ale*

A cosy, welcoming atmosphere pervades this pleasant pink-washed inn, which started life as a farmhouse in the 14th century. Its present name dates from 1887 (the 50th year of Queen Victoria's reign), and there's a display of commemorative china in the beamed main bar. Spacious bedrooms, six with private bathrooms, range from traditional to more modern, and there's a snug lounge. Garden.

## Pembridge *(Food, B & B)* — *New Inn*

Market Square · *Hereford & Worcester*
Map 7 D1
Pembridge (054 47) 427

*Brewery* Whitbread
*Landlord* Jane Melvin
**BEDROOMS 7 Grade 2 £C**
Lasagne £1.95 Pork & apricot pie £1.95 (Last order 9.45pm)
Flower's IPA; Whitbread Dark Mild, Light Mild; Stella Artois; Heineken; cider. *Real ale*

The food is good and tasty at this ancient black and white inn, where log fires create a warm, cosy atmosphere in the bars. Ploughman's and baked potatoes are popular quick snacks, while for a full menu you could follow kipper pâté with chicken casserole, beefsteak pie or sugar-baked gammon, with a nice pudding to follow. Modest bedrooms share a bathroom and separate shower. Patio. **Family pub**

## Pendoggett *(Food, B & B)* — *Cornish Arms*

St Kew · *Cornwall* · Map 8 B4
Port Isaac (020 888) 263

*Free House*
*Landlords* Nigel Pickstone & Alan Wainwright

**BEDROOMS 7 Grade 1 £B**
Salmon pie £1.60 Roast beef salad £1.75 (Last order 10pm)
Bass; Flowers Original Bitter; Guinness; Carlsberg Hof; cider. *Real ale*

The welcome is warm and the atmosphere convivial at this fine old Cornish inn, where the lunchtime centre of attraction is a splendid buffet of cold meats and salads. Other options include soup, quiches and a terrific treacle tart. Less evening choice; sandwiches only at Sunday lunchtime. Smartly furnished bedrooms (four with private bathrooms) provide excellent accommodation. No under-14s overnight. Garden.

## Penn Street *(Food)* — *Hit or Miss*

Near Amersham · *Buckinghamshire*
Map 6 B3
High Wycombe (0494) 713109

*Free House*
*Landlord* Mr Mel James
Chicken provençale with rice £1.90
Tongue sandwich 90p (Last order 10pm)
Wethered's SPA; Younger's Tartan; McEwan's Export; John Smith's Bitter; Guinness; Heineken; cider. *Real ale*

There's nothing hit or miss about the bar food in this attractive, wistaria-clad pub with its own cricket pitch and team. You might open your innings with potted shrimps or a salami salad, and follow on with sausage and chips, a ploughman's or the day's special, such as chicken fricassee, beef bourguignon or quiche lorraine. To finish there are gâteaux, cheesecakes and ices, plus sweets like bread and butter pudding. Garden.

## Peppard Common *(Food)*

### *Red Lion*

Near Henley · *Oxfordshire* · Map 6 B3
Rotherfield Greys (049 17) 329

*Brewery* Brakspear
*Landlords* Ian & Pauline Wadhams

Jacket potato with Swiss steak £1.70 Cannelloni £1.95 (Last order 10pm)
Brakspear's Bitter, Special, Mild; Guinness; Heineken; cider. *Real ale*

This little white pub on the edge of the common serves a good selection of tasty lunchtime and evening snacks in pleasant, friendly surroundings. Jacket potatoes, filled with anything from cheese and butter to steak and vegetables, are popular house specials, and other choices include sandwiches, pâté and pot meals – cannelloni, seafood au gratin, sweet and sour pork. Garden. **Family pub**

## Perranarworthal *(Food)*

### *Norway Inn*

Near Truro · *Cornwall* · Map 8 A4
Truro (0872) 862081

*Brewery* Devenish
*Landlord* Mr W. C. Herbert

Steak & kidney pie £3.25 3-course set dinner £6 (Last order 10pm)
Devenish Cornish Best Bitter; Mild; Whitbread Tankard; Guinness; Grünhalle; Taunton cider. *Real ale*

Mahogany panelling, little booths and soft lighting make the bar of this popular roadside inn pleasantly intimate. Go to the room next door for a well-laden lunchtime buffet featuring succulent cold meats, fresh seafood and salads. There's also a barbecue on Saturday and Sunday nights, while weekday evenings and Sunday lunch bring a splendid roast. **Family pub**

We have raised our standards considerably since last year. The omission of some houses that appeared in last year's Guide is no reflection on their standing.

## Pett Bottom *(Food)*

### *Duck Inn*

Bridge, Near Canterbury · *Kent* · Map 6 D3
Canterbury (0227) 830354

*Free House*
*Landlords* Mr & Mrs L. C. Boothright

Fish pâté £1.35 Steak & kidney pie £2.95 (Last order 9.45pm)
Shepherd Neame Bitter; Marston's Pedigree; Gibbs Salisbury; Fuller's London Pride; Canterbury Ale; cider. *Real ale*

A well-balanced selection of robust snacks is available at this friendly old country pub, where a large garden is a popular summer alternative to the cosy bars. Steak and kidney pie, garlicky fish pâté and fiery chilli are served with lovely hot rye bread, and there's a choice of salads, ploughman's and jacket potatoes. Nice sweets like treacle tart from the restaurant menu. Closed Monday.

## Petworth *(B & B)* — *Angel*

Angel Street · *West Sussex* · Map 6 B4
Petworth (0798) 42153

*Free House*
*Landlords* Mr & Mrs Pope

**BEDROOMS 4 Grade 2 £B**
Flowers Bitter; Whitbread Best Bitter; John Smith's Bitter; Courage Best Bitter; Guinness; Heineken; cider. *Real ale*

Sloping beamed ceilings and low doorways give a quaint character to the bedrooms in this welcoming town-centre inn. Each is furnished in a mixture of styles, and there are some pretty fabrics to add a splash of colour. Two carpeted public bathrooms have modern suites. On cold winter days you can snuggle round the log fire that burns in one part of the attractive old bar. Garden. **Family pub**

## Pewsham *(Food, B & B)* — *Lysley Arms*

Near Chippenham · *Wiltshire* · Map 6 A3
Chippenham (0249) 652864

*Free House*
*Landlord* Mr Peter Reeves
Steak & kidney pie £2.50 Baked crab £1.50 (Last order 10pm)
**BEDROOMS 4 Grade 2 £C**
Bass; Worthington 'E'; Mitchells & Butlers Brew XI; Guinness; Tennent's Extra; Taunton cider. *Real ale*

A distinctive white building on the A4 between Chippenham and Calne. Bar meals are a popular feature, and a cold table displays cooked meats and salads. There are also sandwiches, ploughman's and hot dishes ranging from baked crab and omelettes to basket meals, grills and specials like mussels and tasty braised oxtail. Nicely furnished bedrooms have neat modern bath/shower rooms. Garden. **Family pub**

## Philleigh *(Food)* — *Roseland Inn*

Truro · *Cornwall* · Map 8 A4
Portscatho (087 258) 254

*Brewery* Devenish
*Landlords* Margaret & Desmond Sinnott
Seafood mornay £1.90 Savoury pancake £1.50 (Last order 9pm. No bar food eves except July & August)
John Devenish Bitter; Cornish Best Bitter; Whitbread Tankard; Guinness; Heineken; Grünhalle; Taunton cider. *Real ale*

Country lanes wind their way to this charming 17th-century inn, whose decor reflects the area's strong links with farming and the sea. Seafood is a popular choice among the wholesome bar snacks, which also include sandwiches, Cornish pasties and splendid ploughman's platters. Summer pudding makes a delicious sunshine sweet, while winter brings stockpot soup and home-made game pie. Patio. **Family pub**

## Pickhill *(B & B)* — *Nags Head*

Near Thirsk · *North Yorkshire* · Map 4 C2
Thirsk (0845) 567391

*Free House*
*Landlords* Messrs E. & R. Boynton

**BEDROOMS 8 Grade 2 £B**
Theakston's Best Bitter, XB, Old Peculier; Younger's Scotch Bitter; Tetley's Best Bitter; Guinness; Carlsberg Export; cider. *Real ale*

Not far from the A1, the Nags Head is a pleasant brick building with bedrooms in a modern annexe. The eight spick-and-span rooms have attractive pine furniture, radio-alarms, tea-makers and very good bath or shower rooms. All are equipped with colour TVs. Features of the lounge and public bars are respectively a copper-hooded fireplace and an impressive collection of neckties. Garden. **Family pub**

## Piercebridge *(Food)* — *George*

Near Darlington · *Co. Durham* · Map 4 C2
Piercebridge (032 574) 576

*Brewery* Vaux
*Landlord* Mr Ray Wade

Panackletie £2.40 Raspberry surprise £1 (No bar food eves)
Vaux Samson; Lorimer's Scotch Bitter; Guinness; Norseman; cider.

Nestling on the banks of the river Tees just off the A67, this traditional coaching inn offers a simple choice of lunchtime bar food. You might start with a crock of home-made soup or smoked salmon pâté and go on to a hamburger, steak and kidney pie or deep-fried local cod; and to finish there are simple sweets like banana split or chocolate nut sundae. Eat in the cosy bar or outside in the garden. **Family pub**

## Pin Mill *(Food)* — *Butt & Oyster*

Chelmondiston · *Suffolk* · Map 5 D2
Ipswich (0473) 84224

*Brewery* Tollemache & Cobbold
*Landlords* Dick & Brenda Mainwaring

Pork en croûte £2.50 Smoked salmon £1.60 (Last order 10pm)
Tolly Cobbold Bitter, Original, Mild; Guinness; Hansa Lager; Taunton cider. *Real ale*

Little has changed down the years at this splendid old inn, whose main bar, with its well-worn wooden floor and yellowing walls, is a room of great character. Seafarers and landlubbers alike appreciate the tasty bar snacks, which range from sandwiches and ploughman's to garlic prawns, savoury mince pie and pork en croûte with apricot sauce. Less choice Sunday lunch. The setting right on the river Orwell is especially noteworthy. **Family pub**

## Pinner *(Food)* — *Queens Head*

High Street · *Middlesex* · Map 6 B3

*Brewery* Benskins
*Landlord* Mr Passey

Steak & kidney pie £2.50 Prawn sandwich 85p (No bar food Sun lunch)
Benskins Bitter; Ind Coope Burton Ale; Guinness; Skol; Löwenbräu; cider. *Real ale*

Right in the middle of Pinner High Street, this attractive black and white inn of timber construction has a sign dated 1705. The comfortable bar, with its beams and dark-wood panelling, is a warm, mellow setting for enjoying a simple range of lunchtime snacks, including salads, cottage pie and a very tasty meat and vegetable pasty. Only sandwiches in the evening and sausages Saturday lunchtime. Garden.

## Plumley *(Food)* — *Smoker Inn*

Near Knutsford · *Cheshire* · Map 3 B3
Lower Peover (056 581) 2338

*Brewery* Robinson
*Landlord* Mr Jorge Masso

Steak & kidney pie £2 Moussaka £1.75 (Last order 9.45pm)
Robinson's Best Bitter, Best Mild, Lager; Guinness. *Real ale*

A warm welcome and splendid bar snacks are a winning combination at Jorge Masso's appealing thatched inn alongside the A556. The lunchtime menu offers a wide choice, from sandwiches and salads to Cumberland sausage, cottage pie and turkey fricassee, and from the chef's native India comes samosas and kofta curry. There are no puddings. Less evening choice; only sandwiches Saturday evening and Sunday lunch. Garden.

## Plymouth *(Food)* — *Unity*

Eastlake Street · *Devon* · Map 8 B4
Plymouth (0752) 262622

*Brewery* Halls
*Landlords* Antony & Theresa Irish

Seafood pie £1.40 Stilton sandwich £1.20 (No bar food eves except Sun)
Ind Coope Burton Ale; Tetley's Bitter; Harvest Bitter; Löwenbräu; Skol. *Real ale*

There's a distinctly Edwardian atmosphere about this popular city-centre pub, with its padded leather seating and mahogany-framed mirrors. At lunchtime, crowds pack in for well-filled French sticks, sandwiches bursting with juicy roast beef, pork or prawns and assorted meat salads with vinaigrette or home-made mayonnaise. Creamy tuna flan and mixed seafood pie are other typical choices. No sweets. Closed Sunday lunch.

## Pocklington *(B & B)* — *Feathers Hotel*

Market Place · *Humberside* · Map 4 D3
Pocklington (075 92) 3155

*Brewery* Younger
*Landlord* Mr K. F. Suttle

**BEDROOMS 12 Grade 1 £A** (No dogs)
Younger's Scotch Bitter, No. 3; Guinness; Kestrel; Cavalier; Taunton cider. *Real ale*

This handsome pebbledash inn really buzzes with life on market days, when drinkers crowd into the cheerful main bar to chat and warm themselves by the open fires; there's also a cosy smaller bar. Excellent bedrooms in the main building are solidly furnished in traditional style (the bridal suite has a tester bed); rooms across the car park are in chalet style. All have colour TVs, tea-makers and spotlessly clean bathrooms. Garden. **Family pub**

**We neither seek nor accept hospitality, and we pay for all food, drinks and accommodation in full.**

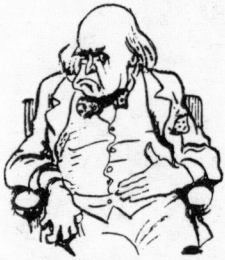

## Poole *(B & B)* — *Inn in the Park*

26 Pinewood Road, Branksome Park · *Dorset*
Map 6 A4
Bournemouth (0202) 761318

*Free House*
*Landlords* Paula & Alan Potter

**BEDROOMS 5 Grade 1 £C**
Wadworth Farmer's Glory, 6X; Poole Dolphin Bitter; Guinness; Löwenbräu; Carlsberg; Taunton cider. *Real ale*

Half a mile from Branksome Chine and the sea, this comfortable inn has been converted from a handsome Victorian house. A log fire keeps winter at bay in the roomy bar, and there's a patio for fair-weather drinking. Overnight accommodation consists of five spacious bedrooms with smart modern furniture, tea-makers and colour TVs; two have private bathrooms. **Family pub**

## Pooley Bridge *(B & B)* — *Crown Hotel*

Near Penrith · *Cumbria* · Map 3 B1
Pooley Bridge (085 36) 217

*Brewery* Whitbread
*Landlords* Mr & Mrs J. W. Huddart

**BEDROOMS 5 Grade 2 £C** (No dogs)
Whitbread Trophy, Mild; Guinness; Heineken; Stella Artois.

The river Eamont flows through the large garden of this trim, white-painted hotel, which the Huddart family has looked after for over three decades. There are two bright, spacious bars and a homely residents' lounge with TV. Roomy, well-carpeted bedrooms are furnished either in traditional or more contemporary style, and they share a single modern bathroom.

## Porlock Weir *(B & B)* — *Anchor Hotel & Ship Inn*

*Somerset* · Map 8 C3
Porlock (0643) 862753

*Free House*
*Landlords* D. H. Wade, P. D. Sechiari, H. F. Jeune

**BEDROOMS 24 Grade 1 £A**
Usher's Best Bitter, Triple Crown Bitter; Bass; Ben Truman; Guinness; Fosters; Taunton cider. *Real ale*

The 19th-century Anchor Hotel and 16th-century Ship Inn are harbourside neighbours, whose picturesque settings afford fine views across the Bristol Channel to the Welsh coast. Homely beamed bedrooms, most with private bath, have darkwood furniture, TVs and tea-makers. Best public rooms are the relaxing bar and lounge in the hotel. Patio. Accommodation closed 2 weeks January. **Family pub**

## Port Gaverne *(B & B)* — *Port Gaverne Hotel*

Near Port Isaac · *Cornwall* · Map 8 A4
Port Isaac (020 888) 244

*Free House*
*Landlords* Mr & Mrs F. P. Ross

**BEDROOMS 17 Grade 1 £A**
St Austell HSD; Whitbread Bitter; Flower's Best Bitter; Guinness; Heineken; Stella Artois; cider. *Real ale*

Half a mile from Port Isaac on the unspoilt North Cornish coast, this fine old inn combines a delightful location with high standards of service and accommodation. Stylishly modern bedrooms, many with patios, are well stocked with reading matter and all have excellent private facilities. There's an absorbing collection of local photographs and paintings in the bars. Closed 12 Jan–23 Feb. **Family pub**

## Portsmouth *(B & B)* — *Sally Port Hotel*

High Street, Old Portsmouth · *Hampshire*
Map 6 B4
Portsmouth (0705) 821860

*Free House*
*Landlord* Mr K. Moore

**BEDROOMS 12 Grades 1 & 2 £B** (No dogs)
Whitbread Strong Country Bitter; Usher's Best Bitter; Bass; Gale's HSB; Guinness; Stella Artois; Foster's Taunton cider. *Real ale*

A splendid Georgian spiral staircase, supported by the mast of an 18th-century frigate, is a striking feature of this historic inn named after the gate in the defence wall through which officers sallied forth to their ships. Characterful bedrooms with sloping floors and a wealth of oak timbers have pretty furnishings, tea-makers and TVs. Most have shower cubicles. No children overnight. Accommodation closed two weeks Christmas.

## Potten End *(Food)* — *Red Lion*

The Green, Berkhamsted · *Hertfordshire*
Map 6 B3
Berkhamsted (044 27) 4318

*Brewery* Benskins
*Landlords* Mr & Mrs E. Gleeson
Filled potatoes £1.20 Quiches £1 (Last order 10pm. No bar food Sun)
Benskins Best Bitter, Pale Ale; Ind Coope Burton Ale; John Bull Bitter; Guinness; Löwenbräu; cider. *Real ale*

Standing on the green of an attractive village, this popular, brick-built pub serves a good range of straightforward bar snacks at lunchtime. Baked potatoes filled with anything from cheese and ham to chilli con carne are long-standing favourites, along with sandwiches, sausages, burgers and rich, tasty cottage pie. Quiches and salads, too. Sandwiches and hot dishes in the evenings. Garden.

## Powerstock *(Food, B & B)* — *Three Horseshoes*

Bridport · *Dorset* · Map 8 D3
Powerstock (030 885) 328

*Brewery* Palmer
*Landlords* Pat & Diana Ferguson

**BEDROOMS 4 Grade 2 £C**
Seafood soup with crusty bread £1.10 Pint of prawns with garlic dip £2.50 (Last order 10pm)
Palmer's Best Bitter, IPA; Guinness; Shilthorn; cider. *Real ale*

This stone-built pub with fine views from its garden has the flavour of a real local. Fresh seafood is something of a speciality here, and in the welcoming bar you can tuck into pan-fried plaice or a shellfish platter, as well as summer salads, ploughman's and warming dishes like beef curry, with apple pie for afters. Bright bedrooms with traditional furnishings and tea-makers are pleasant for an overnight stop.

## Priors Hardwick *(Food)* — *Butchers Arms*

Near Southam · *Warwickshire* · Map 5 A2
Byfield (0327) 60504

*Free House*
*Landlords* Pires family

Beefburger £1.50 Goujonnades of plaice £1.95 (No bar food eves or weekends)
Mitchells & Butlers Brew XI, Springfield Bitter; Carling Black Label; Tennent's Extra.

The owners are Portuguese, but the decor, atmosphere and cooking are distinctly English at this pleasant village inn. Low oak beams, log fires and gleaming brassware give a delightfully rustic appeal to the bar, where you can order anything from the restaurant menu – a satisfying bowl of soup or perhaps grilled sardines, succulent giant prawns, even roast partridge. Sweets include a fine crème brûlée. **Family pub**

## Puckeridge *(Food)* — *White Hart*

High Street, Near Ware · *Hertfordshire*
Map 5 C2
Ware (0920) 821309

*Brewery* McMullen
*Landlord* Colin & Rita Boom

Crab & prawn mayonnaise £4.95 Baked plaice stuffed with prawns £3.95 (Last order 9.45pm)
McMullen's Country Bitter, AK Mild; Guinness; Hartsman. *Real ale*

Fresh seafood is the major gastronomic attraction in this black and white pub. You can sit round the huge open fireplace in the plush lounge bar and enjoy anything from smoked salmon pâté and rollmop herring stuffed with firm, tasty prawns to dressed crab and lobster. Meat-lovers are tempted by steak, cold ham and turkey and mushroom pie, while simple sweets like trifle satisfy those with a sweet tooth. Garden.
**Family pub**

## Pulborough *(Food)* — *Waters Edge*

Station Road · *West Sussex* · Map 6 B4
Pulborough (079 82) 2451

*Brewery* Friary Meux
*Landlord* John Salmon
Wholemeal quiche £1.95 Individual steak & kidney pie cooked in Guinness £3.25 (Last order 10.30pm)
Friary Meux Bitter; Ind Coope Burton Ale, John Bull; Guinness; Skol; Löwenbräu; cider. *Real ale*

Food takes high priority at this agreeable and popular pub, whose long bar has picture windows overlooking the river Arun. The carvery and salad bar offer an excellent choice of hot and cold dishes, and you'll also find soups, pâté, sandwiches (lunchtime only) and daily specials like macaroni cheese or tasty pork casserole. Nice sweets, too. Less choice weekends and Monday. Garden.

## Pulverbatch *(Food, B & B)* — *White Horse*

Near Shrewsbury · *Shropshire* · Map 7 D1
Dorrington (074 373) 247

*Brewery* Whitbread
*Landlords* Margaret & Hamish MacGregor
**BEDROOMS 3 Grade 1 £C**
Smoked trout pâté £1.25 Salmon goujons £2.10 (Last order 10pm)
Flower's Original, Flower's Best Bitter; Whitbread Best Bitter; Guinness; Stella Artois, cider. *Real ale*

This thriving old timbered inn, set in rolling countryside south of Shrewsbury, is very much geared to the service of food. Everything on the long bar menu is fresh and flavoursome, from smoked trout pâté or eggs à la russe to generous toasted sandwiches, burgers and curries. Neat little bedrooms, which share a well-kept bathroom, have smart white unit furniture and floral duvets. **Family pub**

## Pye Corner *(Food)* — *Plume of Feathers*

Gilston, Near Harlow, Essex · *Hertfordshire*
Map 5 C2
Harlow (0279) 24154
*Brewery* Courage
*Landlord* Mr G. R. Ellis
Mushroom omelette £1.85 Roast beef salad £2.95 (Last order 10pm. No bar food Sun eve)
Courage Best Bitter, Directors Bitter; John Smiths Yorkshire Bitter; Guinness; Hofmeister; Kronenbourg; Taunton cider. *Real ale*

Sandwiches are served in splendid variety at this characterful black and white pub: choose them plain, club or toasted, or try one of the popular baps packed with anything from peanut butter to prawn and coleslaw. There's also pâté, salads and omelettes, plus specials like stuffed plaice or steak and kidney pie. Only sandwiches Sunday lunchtime. Patio and garden.

## Pyrton *(Food)* — *Plough Inn*

Near Watlington · *Oxfordshire* · Map 6 B3
Watlington (049 161) 2003

*Free House*
*Landlords* Jackie & Jeremy Hunt

King prawns in garlic butter with salad £4.25 Beef romana with jacket potato & peas £3.25 (Last order 10pm)
Adnams Bitter; Hall & Woodhouse Badger Bitter; Brakspears Bitter; Guinness. *Real ale*

The very model of a traditional country pub, with thatched roof, low beams, a roaring fire and charming hosts in Jackie and Jeremy Hunt. Good, simple home cooking is another attraction, with bar snacks ranging from sandwiches and ploughman's (lunchtime only) to filled jacket potatoes, pies, roast pheasant and flavoursome casseroles. You'll also find tasty soups, pâtés and terrines and some smashing sweets. Garden. **Family pub**

## Ramsbury *(Food)* — *Bell at Ramsbury*

The Square · *Wiltshire* · Map 6 A3
Marlborough (0672) 20230

*Free House*
*Landlord* Mr Michael Benjamin

Marengo pie £1.95 Shellfish & fruit platter £3.95 (Last order 9.30pm. No bar food Sat eve)
Wadworth's IPA, 6X; Younger's Tartan; Guinness; Carlsberg Hof; cider. *Real ale*

There's plenty of interest on the menu of this cheerful pebbledash pub with canopies at its windows. Besides home-made soups and pâtés, you might find tempting salmon and dill pie, an eye-catching shellfish platter or spicy Calcutta lamb. There are also colourful fresh salads and a selection of lovely sweets. Garden. **Family pub**

## Richmond *(Food)* — *Orange Tree*

45 Kew Road · *Surrey* · Map 6 B3
01-940 0944

*Brewery* Young
*Landlord* Mr D. J. Murphy

Steak & kidney pie £2.80 Duck in orange sauce £3.80 (Last order 10pm. No bar food Sun eve)
Young's Bitter, Special Bitter; Guinness; John Young's London Lager; cider. *Real ale*

The mood is lively and friendly at this solid Victorian pub, where the main centre of eating activity is the smart Cellar Bar with its quarry-tiled floor, red-brick walls and plush seating. The eye-catching cold buffet offers a good choice of cooked meats and salads, while blackboard-listed hot specials might include stuffed peppers, steaks and duck in orange sauce. Patio.

## Richmond *(Food)* — *Castle Tavern*

Market Place · *North Yorkshire* · Map 4 C2
Richmond (0748) 3187

*Brewery* Vaux
*Landlords* Mr & Mrs M. Carter

Castle terrine £1.50 Swaledale pie £2 (No bar food eves & all Mon)
Vaux Sunderland Bitter, Samson; Guinness; Tuborg. *Real ale*

Cooking has a definite Yorkshire slant at this welcoming pub, where snacks are served in the lounge bar at lunchtime. Dishes like pheasant or pigeon casserole, fisherman's pie or rabbit stew with Yorkshire pudding are tasty and satisfying, and there are some nice traditional sweets, too, such as curd tart or apple pie made with a layer of Wensleydale cheese.
**Family pub**

## Ringmore *(Food, B & B)* — *Journey's End Inn*

Near Kingsbridge · *Devon* · Map 8 B4
Bigbury-on-Sea (054 881) 205
*Free House*
*Landlords* Mr & Mrs R. T. Hollins
**BEDROOMS 4 Grades 1 & 2 £B** (No dogs)
Sausages & mash with onion sauce £1.95 Open ham sandwich topped with fried egg £1.50 (Last order 10pm)
Badger's Best Bitter; Bate's Bitter; Golden Hill Exmoor Ale; Wadworth's 6X; Guinness; Harp; Hofmeister; cider. *Real ale*

Winding country lanes lead to this enchanting little inn, where the panelled lounge bar is especially cosy. Wholesome bar snacks might include home-made celery soup with crusty bread, succulent steak and delicious blackberry and apple pie. Neat modern bedrooms have TVs, tea-makers and radio-alarms. There is a games room with video games. No under-tens overnight. Garden.
**Family pub**

## Ringwood *(Food, B & B)* — *Original White Hart*

Market Place · *Hampshire* · Map 6 A4
Ringwood (042 54) 2702
*Brewery* Eldridge Pope
*Landlord* Mr T. G. Eales
**BEDROOMS 8 Grade 2 £B**
Steak & kidney pie £2.95 Home-cooked ham salad £2.95 (Last order 10pm. No bar food Sun eve)
Eldridge Pope Dorchester Bitter, IPA, Royal Oak, 1880; Guinness; Faust; Taunton cider. *Real ale*

Food plays a major role at this fine old inn, whose attractive bars contain a wealth of period detail. Well-prepared snacks are exemplified by soup, home-baked ham and the popular steak and kidney pie with plenty of tender meat and rich, tasty gravy. There are also sandwiches and a good apple pie. Bedrooms are simple and traditional, spacious and spotlessly clean. Patio. **Family pub**

## Ripley *(Food)* — *Anchor*

High Street · *Surrey* · Map 6 B3
Guildford (0483) 224120

*Brewery* Friary Meux
*Landlord* Mrs Christine Beale

Steak & kidney pie £1.40 Beef curry £1.80 (No bar food eves)
Friary Meux Bitter; Ind Coope Burton Ale; Guinness; Skol; Löwenbräu; cider. *Real ale*

This handsome red-brick building is over 700 years old and its low-ceilinged lounge bar is filled with knick-knacks, brass ornaments and pretty porcelain. Best of the bar snacks are the tasty home-baked savoury pies – the steak and kidney is always in demand – and daily specials like beef curry. Filled rolls and ploughman's platters for lighter bites. Patio.

## Ripon *(B & B)* — *Unicorn Hotel*

Market Place · *North Yorkshire* · Map 4 C2
Ripon (0765) 2202

*Free House*
*Landlords* Mr & Mrs D. T. Small

**BEDROOMS 27 Grade 1 £A+**
Theakstons Bitter; Smith's Bitter; Guinness; Carlsberg Hof; Hofmeister; Taunton cider. *Real ale*

Hospitality has long been a feature of this handsome old posting house, which occupies a prominent position on the historic market square. The beamed public bar has a cheerful, rustic charm, and there's a smart cocktail bar and comfortable residents' lounge. Lofty, simply furnished bedrooms offer plenty of space, with TVs, teamakers and functional bath or shower rooms.

## Ripponden *(Food)* — *Old Bridge Inn*

Priest Lane · *West Yorkshire* · Map 4 C3
Halifax (0422) 822595

*Free House*
*Landlord* Mr Ian Hargreaves Beaumont
Fisherman's pie £2.50 Goujons of sole £2.25 (Last order 10pm. No bar food Sat eve & Sun lunch)
Younger's Scotch Bitter; Webster's Pennine Bitter; Tetley's Mild; Taylor's Golden Best; Guinness; Carlsberg Hof; cider. *Real ale*

The nearby river Ryburn adds to the charm of this ancient whitewashed inn with its quaint, cottagy beamed bars. At lunchtime the help-yourself cold buffet of home-made quiches, tender roast beef, spicy Virginia ham and crisp salads is deservedly popular, while in the evening there are sandwiches (plain or toasted), along with tasty hot dishes such as savoury pancakes and chilli con carne with garlic bread.

## Risley *(Food)*

Near Warrington · *Cheshire* · Map 3 B3
Padgate (0925) 812022

*Brewery* Greenall Whitley
*Landlords* Tony & Maureen Edwards

Danish open sandwich from 55p Steak & kidney pie with chips & vegetables £1.85 (Last order 10pm. No bar food Sun & Mon eves)
Greenall Whitley's Original Bitter, Local Bitter, Mild; Grünhalle. *Real ale*

## *Noggi*

Maureen Edwards takes care of the cookir at this pleasant roadside pub, where blac boards proclaim an interesting selection tasty, well-prepared dishes. Open sane wiches, steaks and fresh haddock ar regular favourites, while daily-changin specials could include casseroles, currie and savoury pies. Sunday lunchtime bring a traditional roast plus several other dishe Home-made fruit pies and trifles to finis Terrace. **Family pub** (weekend lunchtime

## Risplith *(B & B)*

Pateley Bridge Road, Near Ripon
*North Yorkshire* · Map 4 C2
Sawley (076 586) 214

*Free House*
*Landlords* Mr & Mrs Byron Brader

**BEDROOMS 3 Grade 2 £C** (No dogs)
Theakston's Best Bitter; Younger's Scotch Bitter; John Smith's Bitter, Mild; Hofmeister; Taunton cider. *Real ale*

## *Black-a-Moor Inn*

This solid stone-built pub stands beside th B6265 about five miles west of Ripon. It's cheerful, popular place, where the Brader are the friendliest of hosts. You can enjoy chat with the locals in the spacious bar c play pool in a separate room. Bedrooms ar unpretentious with washbasins and simpl furnishings. No children overnight. Close Monday lunchtime.

## Rochester *(B & B)*

Near Otterburn · *Northumberland* · Map 2 D4
Otterburn (0830) 20668

*Free House*
*Landlords* Alan & Connie Robertson

**BEDROOMS 11 Grade 2 £C** (No dogs)
Drybrough Heavy; Stones Bitter; McEwan's Scotch Bitter; Carling Black Label; cider.

## *Redesdale Arms*

The Scottish border is only a dozen mile from this greystone hostelry, which ha been welcoming travellers for the last 60 years. Friendly farmers congregate in th public bar, leaving visitors to enjoy the fir in the beamed lounge bar or do a bit c viewing in the TV lounge. Spotless bed rooms have all the traditional comfort (two have four-posters), and the three old fashioned bathrooms are well maintained All rooms have TVs. Garden.

## Rockbourne *(Food)* ★

Near Fordingbridge · *Hampshire* · Map 6 A4
Rockbourne (072 53) 236

*Brewery* Whitbread
*Landlords* Mr & Mrs P. A. Read

Steak & kidney pie £3.95 Fresh seafood from £4 (Last order 9.30pm)
Whitbread Pompey Royal, Strong Country Bitter, Best Bitter; Guinness; Heineken; Stella Artois; cider. *Real ale*

## *Rose & Thistle*

Tended by the Reads with loving care, this delightful thatched pub is a classic village hostelry offering wonderful bar food. Pride of place must go to the superb local sea-food – lobster, beautifully sweet giant crab and a daily special like mussels, sole o bass. And it doesn't stop there, as othe delights include pea and ham soup, home-cooked Wiltshire ham and a delectable apple pie flavoured with cloves. Garden.

## Rockcliffe *(Food)* — *Crown & Thistle*

lear Carlisle · *Cumbria* · Map 3 B1
ockcliffe (022 874) 378

*rewery* Scottish & Newcastle
*andlords* Kevin & Joane Dempsey
oast ham & salad £1.95 Creamy apple
âteau 75p (Last order 9pm. No bar food
un eve)
Younger's Scotch Bitter, Dark Ale,
raditional IPA; McEwan's Export; Guinness;
larp; Taunton cider. *Real ale*

Bar snacks are a popular feature at this pleasant old pub on the outskirts of the village. Among a wide range of offerings look for the succulent ham and tender, pink beef, both prepared on the premises. Sweets are home-made, too: try the lovely light creamy apple gâteau. Service is cheerful. Only soup and sandwiches are available on Mondays. Patio.

## Romaldkirk *(Food, B & B)* — *Rose & Crown*

eesdale · *Co. Durham* · Map 4 C2
eesdale (0833) 50213

*ree House*
*andlords* Mr & Mrs D. Jackson
**EDROOMS 15 Grade 1 £A**
asagne £2.35 Local Cotherstone cheese &
iscuits £1.25 (Last order 10pm)
Theakston's Best Bitter; Tetley's Bitter;
'ameron's Bitter; Carlsberg; Hansa; Taunton
ider. *Real ale*

There's a genuine warmth and friendliness about this fine old coaching house, whose bars provide a characterful setting for some enjoyable home cooking. Garlic mushrooms, robustly flavoured pâté, lemon sole and lasagne are typical items on the varied menu, and the cold buffet is a popular summertime feature. Very comfortable bedrooms range from traditional in the main building to smartly modern in the courtyard block. **Family pub**

## Rosedale Abbey *(B & B)* — *Blacksmiths Arms*

lartoft End · *North Yorkshire* · Map 4 D2
astingham (075 15) 331

*ree House*
*andlords* Mr & Mrs Barrie

**EDROOMS 12 Grade 1 £B**
Younger's Scotch Bitter; John Smith's
itter; Newcastle Exhibition; Guinness;
lofmeister; McEwan's Lager; Taunton cider.
*eal ale*

Built in the 16th century with stone taken from Rosedale Abbey, this handsome farmhouse is now a comfortable and welcoming hotel. Its lovely, quiet position is a major asset, and the cottagy bars and homely residents' lounge with TV are inviting and relaxing. Bedrooms have simple modern furniture and tea-makers; the seven in the wing offer private facilities. Patio. **Family pub**

## Rosedale Abbey *(B & B)* — *White Horse Farm Hotel*

lear Pickering · *North Yorkshire* · Map 4 D2
astingham (075 15) 239

*ree House*
*andlords* Mr & Mrs Wilcock

**EDROOMS 15 Grade 1 £A**
Tetley's Bitter, Mild; Cameron's Lion
itter; Skol; cider. *Real ale*

Set high up in the heart of the Yorkshire moors, this sturdy stone pub is a popular base for tourists. A cheerful fire wards off winter in the welcoming bar with its fine old church pew seating, and the well-appointed bedrooms are neat, bright and modern. All have colour TVs and tea-makers, plus compact bath or shower rooms. Garden. **Family pub**

## Ross-on-Wye *(Food, B & B)*

### *Rosswyn Hote*

High Street · *Hereford & Worcester* · Map 7 D2
Ross-on-Wye (0989) 62733
*Free House*
*Landlord* R. Livesey
**BEDROOMS 10 Grade 2 £B**
Rabbit, mushroom & ham pie £1.40 Ratatouille & cheese £1.20 (Last order 10pm. No bar food Sun)
Wadworth's 6X; Sam Smith's Old Brewery Bitter; Bass; Whitbread Trophy; Mitchells & Butlers Springfield Bitter; Carling Black Label; Harp; cider. *Real ale*

A fine Elizabethan fireplace and handsom antiques set the characterful tone for th friendly 15th-century hostelry. The snac menu changes daily, offering simple, enjoy able fare like chicken liver pâté, sandwiche salads and savoury pies. Sweets includ chocolate brandy cake and luscious home made ice cream. Bedrooms (three with fou posters) offer good comfort, and five hav private bathrooms. Garden. **Family pu**

## Rotherwick *(Food)*

### *Coach & Horse*

The Street, Near Hook · *Hampshire* · Map 6 B3
Hook (025 672) 2542

*Free House*
*Landlord* Mrs T. A. Williams

Steak & kidney pie £2.30 Home-made soup 65p (Last order 10.30pm)
Hall & Woodhouse Badger Bitter, Tanglefoot; Ringwood Old Thumper; Guinness; Taunton cider. *Real ale*

The hungry and the thirsty are really we provided for at this convivial village pub which offers a good choice of bar food and u to a dozen real ales. Ploughman's, pâtés, pie and pasties typify the simple delicious far which customers can enjoy in the cheerfu bars or separate eating area. Sweets include deliciously crisp, rich Danish chocolate gâteau Roasts only on Sunday. Garden. **Family pu**

## Rowhook *(Food)*

### *Chequers Inn*

Near Horsham · *West Sussex* · Map 6 B3
Slinfold (0403) 790480

*Brewery* Whitbread
*Landlord* Mr P. A. Barrs

Steak & mushroom pie £2.25 Fillet steak £5.75 (Last order 10pm. No bar food Sun eve)
Flowers Bitter; Whitbread Pompey Royal, Strong Country Bitter; Guinness; Stella Artois; Heineken; cider. *Real ale*

Mrs Barrs' cooking is a major attraction a this charming old whitewashed inn dee in rural Sussex. Lunchtime brings ligh snacks, quiches, steak and mushroom pie and the popular home-cooked ham, while the evening menu extends to th restaurant-style dishes like chicke béchamel or Scotch fillet steak. Dessert include sorbets, chocolate fudge cake and traditional English trifle. Garden.

## Running Waters *(B & B)*

### *Three Horse Shoes*

Sherburn House, Near Durham · *Co. Durham*
Map 4 C1
Durham (0385) 720286

*Brewery* Vaux
*Landlords* Derek & Leslie Crehan

**BEDROOMS 3 Grade 1 £C**
Vaux Samson; Lorimer's Scotch; Guinness; Tuborg. *Real ale*

There's no mistaking the warmth of th welcome at Derek Crehan's well maintained inn perched high up alongside the A181 between Durham and Hartlepool It's a comfortable spot for an overnigh stop, all the pleasant bedrooms having tea makers, TVs, washbasins and showe cabinets. Leslie Crehan's freshly cooke breakfasts are a further attraction. There are two bars, the public one being very popular with locals. Garden.

## Rushlake Green *(Food)* — *Horse & Groom*

Near Heathfield · *East Sussex* · Map 6 C4
Rushlake Green (0435) 830320

*Brewery* Board's of Lewes
*Landlords* Anton & Elaine Levy

Sussex smokies £1.60 Steak & oyster pie £3.50 (Last order 9.30. No bar food Sun & Mon eves)
Board's Traditional Sussex Bitter; Guinness; Carlsberg Hof; Hürlimann; cider. *Real ale*

Winding country lanes lead to this friendly pub, where low ceilings and oak beams provide a pleasant, cosy ambience for sampling the tasty bar snacks. Start perhaps with soup or an enjoyably different cream cheese pâté, and follow up with lasagne or lovely grilled lemon sole. There are also substantial salads, a good selection of puds and some well-kept cheeses. Garden. **Family pub**

## Rusthall *(Food)* — *Red Lion*

Near Tunbridge Wells · *Kent* · Map 6 C3
Tunbridge Wells (0892) 20086

*Brewery* Whitbread
*Landlords* Mr & Mrs B. Cooter

Smoked salmon pâté with toast £1.30 Kidneys in red wine £1.10 (Last order 11pm)
Whitbread Bitter; Fremlins Bitter, Tusker; Guinness; Stella Artois; Heineken; cider. *Real ale*

Mrs Cooter's lunchtime bar snacks are a popular feature at this handsome old pub, parts of which date from the 15th century. Chicken liver pâté, soup and salads are familiar favourites, with more unusual options being offered by paprika roast chicken and savoury meatballs served in a curry sauce. Cheese and sandwiches only in the evenings and on Sunday. There are two pleasant bars and a beer garden.

## Saffron Walden *(Food)* — *Eight Bells*

Bridge Street · *Essex* · Map 5 C2
Saffron Walden (0799) 22790

*Brewery* Benskins
*Landlord* Mr R. Moore

Fresh wing of skate £3.75 Coffee meringue £1 (Last order 9.30pm)
Benskins Bitter; Ind Coope Burton Ale, John Bull; Guinness; Skol; Oranjeboom; cider. *Real ale*

Spot the eight brass bells on the sign of this fine old hostelry, whose inviting beamed bar offers a varied menu of imaginative, well-prepared snacks. Start perhaps with pâté or home-made soup and go on to lasagne, super grilled swordfish or prawn-stuffed chicken breast with a saffron-flavoured sauce. There's even a children's menu, and at lunchtime sandwiches (except weekends) and a cold buffet widen the choice. **Family pub**

## Saffron Walden *(Food)* ★ — *Saffron Hotel*

10 High Street · *Essex* · Map 5 C2
Saffron Walden (0799) 22676
*Free House*
*Landlords* Craddock family
French onion soup 85p Steak, kidney & Guinness pie with vegetables £2.85 (Last order 9.30pm. No bar food Sun)
Greene King IPA; John Smith's Bitter; Ruddles County; Younger's Tartan; Guinness; Carlsberg; Kronenbourg; Taunton cider. *Real ale*

Quality and variety are outstanding features of the bar snacks served in this friendly Georgian hostelry. French onion soup and chicken liver pâté are splendid preludes to main courses that range from omelettes and seafood to steak, kidney and Guinness pie. Also pasta and pizzas, as well as salads, sandwiches and super sweets. Patio. *For accommodation see Egon Ronay's Lucas Hotel & Restaurant Guide 1985.* **Family pub**

## St Dominick — *Who'd Have Thought It Inn*

Perched high on a hill with distant views of the Tamar Valley and Plymouth, this sturdy stone house has been an inn since 1849. It's a great favourite with locals and tourists, and there's a choice of three bars, all featuring handsome old furnishings, brassware and china. The amazing name has absolutely no relevance to anything!

Near Saltash · *Cornwall* · Map 8 B4
Liskeard (0579) 50214
*Free House* *Landlord* Mr D. Potter
Bass; Courage Directors Bitter; Worthington Best Bitter; Ben Truman; Guinness; Carling Black Label. *Real ale*

## St Margaret's at Cliffe *(Food, B & B)* — *Cliffe Tavern*

High Street · *Kent* · Map 6 D3
Dover (0304) 852749

*Free House*
*Landlords* Westby family
**BEDROOMS 12 Grade 1 £B**
Cliffe Tavern fruits de mer £4.40 Chicken pie £1.55 (Last order 10pm)
Shepherd Neame Masterbrew; Courage Directors Bitter; Fremlins Bitter; Guinness; Carlsberg; Taunton cider. *Real ale*

The Westby family run this attractive clapboard pub with great warmth and attention to detail. In the cheerful, old-fashioned bar you can tuck into tasty snacks like rich smoked haddock chowder, excellent crab sandwiches and huge seafood platters, as well as good-looking salads and grills. Accommodation is a strong point, too, neat bedrooms with TVs and excellent bathrooms being superbly furnished. Garden.

## St Mawes *(B & B)* — *Rising Sun Inn*

*Cornwall* · Map 8 A4
St Mawes (0326) 270233

*Brewery* St Austell
*Landlord* Mrs Campbell Marshall

**BEDROOMS 16 Grade 1 £A**
St Austell Best Bitter, Extra; Guinness; Carlsberg Pilsner, Hof; cider. *Real ale*

Mrs Campbell Marshall ensures a warm welcome and high standards of comfort at this charming hotel overlooking the harbour. There are two cosy little bars, a sunny terrace for summer drinking and a peaceful lounge. Bedrooms are tastefully furnished and bathrooms are immaculately kept. Four rooms in a separate cottage have splendid sea views. Good breakfasts. Accommodation closed Christmas–14 January. **Family pub**

## St Mawgan *(B & B)* — *Falcon Inn*

Near Newquay · *Cornwall* · Map 8 A4
St Mawgan (063 74) 860225

*Free House*
*Landlords* Mr & Mrs P. Joyce

**BEDROOMS 4 Grade 2 £C**
St Austell Best Bitter, Tinners Ale; McEwan's Bitter, Worthington Bitter; Bass; Guinness; cider. *Real ale*

A huge magnolia tree, a wishing well and a well-equipped children's room are all to be found in the garden of this 16th-century country inn, where the Joyces are the friendly hosts. The popular bar is large and convivial, and there's a peaceful residents' lounge with TV. Homely, spick-and-span bedrooms share a pink-tiled public bathroom. No children overnight July and August. Accommodation closed Christmas week. **Family pub**

## St Neots *(Food)* — *Chequers Inn*

St Marys Street · *Cambridgeshire* · Map 5 B2
Huntingdon (0480) 72116

*Free House*
*Landlords* David & Ann Taylor

Smoked mackerel mousse £1.50 Spiced minced beef kebab £2.95 (Last order 10pm)
Paine's St Neots, XXX; Stones Bitter; Younger's Tartan; Carling Black Label; Carlsberg. *Real ale*

The appetising smell of the stockpot wafts from the kitchen of this delightful 17th-century pub, where the Taylors are the most engaging of hosts. There's an excellent choice of delicious bar food, from warming soups and smoked fish pâté to pasta, stuffed peppers and steak pie. Also sandwiches, sweets from the trolley and a summer lunchtime cold buffet. Patio.
**Family pub**

## St Neots *(B & B)* — *Stephenson's Rocket*

Cross Hall Road · *Cambridgeshire* · Map 5 B2
Huntingdon (0480) 72773

*Free House*
*Landlords* Mr & Mrs B. Stephenson

**BEDROOMS 9 Grade 1 £A** (No dogs)
Adnams Bitter; Paines St Neots Bitter; Ben Truman; Charles Wells Redstripe Lager. *Real ale*

About a mile from St Neots at the junction of the A1 and A45, this family-run pub offers excellent motel-style accommodation. Nine bedrooms in a modern red-brick annexe have practical fitted furniture, colour TVs and up-to-date telephones, plus well-appointed tiled bathrooms. In the main building (once a farmhouse) there's a comfortable bar with plush banquette seating. Patio. **Family pub**

## Salisbury — *Haunch of Venison*

Right in the city centre overlooking the ancient Poultry Cross, this fine old half-timbered pub has a history going back to 1320. The little bar, with its solid pewter counter, abounds in warmth and character. Another tiny room, known as the House of Lords, was reputedly once used as a discreet tippling place by local church dignitaries. **Family pub**

1 Minster Street · *Wiltshire* · Map 6 A4
Salisbury (0722) 22024
*Brewery* Courage *Landlords* Mr & Mrs Leroy
Courage Directors Bitter, Best Bitter; Guinness; Hofmeister. *Real ale*

## Salisbury *(B & B)* — *High Post Hotel*

High Post · *Wiltshire* · Map 6 A4
Middle Woodford (072 273) 293

*Free House*
*Landlords* Messrs Reader & Simpson

**BEDROOMS 15 Grade 1 £B**
Wadworth's 6X; Hall's Harvest Bitter; Ind Coope Burton Ale; Courage Director's Bitter; John Bull Bitter; cider. *Real ale*

Built in 1936 as an airport control tower, this pleasant tiled pub alongside the A345 offers plenty of space and comfort for todays land-based travellers. The bedrooms, restfully decorated in creams and light browns, have smart modern furniture, tea-makers and radio-alarms. Most also are equipped with TVs and private facilities. There are three roomy bars and quiet residents' lounge. Garden. **Family pub**

## Salisbury *(B & B)* — *King's Arms*

9 St John Street · *Wiltshire* · Map 6 A4
Salisbury (0722) 27629

*Owners* Wessex Hosts
*Landlords* Mr & Mrs Tim Wright

**BEDROOMS 16 Grade 2 £B**
Usher's Best Bitter, Pale Ale, Triple Crown; John Smith's Yorkshire Bitter; Carlsberg; cider. *Real ale*

Period charm oozes from every nook and cranny of this fine old half-timbered inn near the cathedral. The residents' lounge, with its dark oak panelling, Tudor fireplace, maps and tapestries, is particularly delightful, and there are two little beamed bars. Bedrooms, too, are appealingly old-fashioned; one boasts a splendid William and Mary four-poster. All have tea-makers. Patio. **Family pub**

## Sambourne *(Food)* — *Green Dragon*

Near Redditch · *Warwickshire* · Map 5 A2
Astwood Bank (052 789) 2465

*Brewery* Bass
*Landlords* Mr & Mrs Joseph Kimber
Lemon sole £4 Home-cured gammon £2.75 (Last order 10pm. No bar food Mon eve & all Sun)
Bass; Mitchells & Butlers Springfield Bitter, Brew XI; Guinness; Carling Black Label; Taunton cider. *Real ale*

Overlooking the village green, this white-washed pub makes a cheerful sight in summer with its window boxes and hanging baskets. Snacks served in the cosy beamed bars range from soup and sandwiches to omelettes, steak and kidney pie, home-cured gammon, fresh fish and curries. There's a good selection of English cheeses, and nice sweets include fruit pies and trifle. Patio. **Family pub**

## Sandiway *(Food)* — *Blue Cap*

520 Chester Road, Near Northwich · *Cheshire*
Map 3 B4
Sandiway (0606) 883006

*Owners* Lanchester Taverns
*Landlords* Mike & Joan Beaman
Steak pie £2.25 Lasagne £2.25 (Last order 9.30pm. No bar food Sun–Tues eves)
Wilson's Great Northern Bitter, Special Mild; Guinness; Carlsberg; Holsten; Foster's; cider. *Real ale*

Friendly service brings warmth to the plain bar and lightwood panelled lounges of this large pub. Homely food includes soups, sandwiches and simple hot dishes, grilled fish, steaks and omelettes. There is also a selection of cold meats with help-yourself salads. Finish with trifle or apple pie. Sandwiches only in the evening. Patio. **Family pub**

## Sandon Bank *(Food)* — *Seven Stars Inn*

Near Stafford · *Staffordshire* · Map 4 C4
Sandon (088 97) 316

*Brewery* Burtonwood
*Landlords* Gill & Ron Roestenburg

Chicken chasseur £3 Apple pie 85p (Last order 10pm)
Burtonwood Bitter, Dark Mild, Top Hat; Guinness; Tuborg Gold, Pils; cider. *Real ale*

Ron Roestenburg is the dedicated landlord and chef at this friendly pub, which stands on a hilltop alongside the B5066. Regular favourites among the tasty bar snacks include rainbow trout and beef curry, with additional choice provided by popular daily specials like chicken à la grecque or pork in cider. Sandwiches, ploughman's and salads available at lunchtime (except Sunday). Nice sweets. Garden. **Family pub**

## Sandside *(B & B)* — *Ship Inn*

Near Milnthorpe · *Cumbria* · Map 3 B2
Milnthorpe (044 82) 3113

*Brewery* William Younger's Inns
*Landlord* Mr John Nancarrow

**BEDROOMS 5 Grade 2 £C** (No dogs)
Younger's Scotch Bitter, Dark Mild; Kestrel; Taunton cider. *Real ale*

Standing right on the Kent estuary, this well-patronised inn affords fine views of the sea and the distant Cumbrian hills. The smartly refurbished bar is roomy and comfortable, and in good weather you can sit outside and watch the tide rushing in. Cheerful, traditionally furnished bedrooms share a single modern bathroom. Children not accommodated overnight. **Family pub**

## Sandwich *(B & B)* — *Fleur-de-Lis*

Delf Street · *Kent* · Map 6 D3
Sandwich (0304) 611131

*Brewery* Whitbread
*Landlord* Mr R. J. Tillings

**BEDROOMS 8 Grades 1 & 2 £C**
Wethered's Bitter, Fremlins Bitter, Tusker; Guinness; Heineken; Stella Artois; cider. *Real ale*

The landlord's love of the sea is reflected in the nautical knick-knacks that adorn one of the bars in this cheerful red-brick pub. There are three bars in all, including one with a pool table and video game machines. Comfortable bedrooms in the main building have a pleasantly traditional appeal, while annexe rooms with shower cabinets are more modern. All have TV.

## Sandygate *(Food)* — *Blue Ball Inn*

Near Exeter · *Devon* · Map 8 C3
Topsham (039 287) 3401

*Brewery* Whitbread
*Landlords* Mr & Mrs Courtenay

Beef steak & oyster pie £3.95 Chicken Marengo £3.50 (Last order 10pm)
Flowers Best Bitter; Whitbread Best Bitter; Bass; Heineken; cider. *Real ale*

Scallops with ratatouille, butter-roasted chicken with courgettes and garlicky tomato sauce, sweet and sour lamb on rice – such enterprising daily specials, many with a Middle Eastern accent, draw the crowds to this modest thatched pub situated down a narrow lane near junction 30 of the M5. Fiery chilli con carne with crusty bread remains popular, and you can also get ploughman's, sandwiches and salads. Ice cream to finish. **Family pub**

## Saunderton *(Food, B & B)* — *Rose & Crown Inn*

Wycombe Road · *Buckinghamshire* · Map 6 B3
Princes Risborough (084 44) 5299

*Free House*
*Landlords* R. M. & J. G. Watson
**BEDROOMS 15 Grade 1 £A+** (No dogs)
Steak & Guinness pie £2.25 Home-made soup 95p (Last order 10pm)
Morrell's Varsity Bitter; Morland's Bitter; Wethered's Bitter; Whitbread Best Bitter; Guinness; Heineken; cider. *Real ale*

Five attractive new bedrooms have been added to this roadside inn on the A4041; all rooms are comfortably furnished, with colour TVs and radio-alarms. The bow-fronted bar features a tempting display of cold meats and salads, and there are also hot dishes like home-made soup, chicken in the basket and Welsh rarebit. Fresh local seafood is particularly well represented in summer. No under-eights overnight. Accommodation closed 25 Dec–1 Jan. Garden.

## Scole *(Food, B & B)*

### *Scole Inn*

Near Diss · *Norfolk* · Map 5 D2
Scole (037 978) 481

*Free House*
*Landlord* Mr Bob Nylk
**BEDROOMS 20 Grade 1 £A**
Duck & lamb casserole £2.40 Lymeswold ploughman's £1.10 (Last order 10pm)
Adnam's Bitter; Stones Bitter; McEwan's Export; Guinness; Tennents's Extra; Carling Black Label; Taunton cider. *Real ale*

This impressive roadside inn, which has been dispensing hospitality since 1655, offers a warm welcome. In the cheerful bars you can enjoy simple, well-prepared snacks like soup, sandwiches and salads, plus hot dishes such as tasty liver and onions or roast lamb. Bedrooms (all with baskets of fruit and colour TV) range from traditional ones in the main building to especially well-equipped modern rooms in the converted stable block. **Family pub**

## Seahouses *(B & B)*

### *Olde Ship Hotel*

*Northumberland* · Map 2 D4
Seahouses (0665) 720200

*Free House*
*Landlords* Alan & Jean Glen

**BEDROOMS 9 Grade 2 £B** (No dogs)
Scottish & Newcastle Exhibition, Newcastle Bitter; McEwan's Best Scotch, 80/-; Guinness; Cavalier; cider.

The lounge and bars of this quaint little inn above the picturesque harbour are veritable museums of naval bric-à-brac. The pub is popular with the locals, and fishermen radio in their drinks orders while still out at sea! Shipshape bedrooms, most with modern tiled bath or shower rooms, have traditional furniture, colour TVs and teamakers. Breakfast is appropriately hearty. Accommodation closed mid-Oct to Easter. **Family pub**

## Sedgefield *(Food)*

### *Nag's Head Inn*

8 West End · *Co. Durham* · Map 4 C1
Sedgefield (0740) 20234

*Brewery* Charrington
*Landlords* Mr & Mrs I. Campbell

Sirloin steak £4.50 Tacos with rice & salad £2.95 (Last order 10pm)
Bass; Stones Bitter; Guinness; Carling Black Label; Taunton cider. *Real ale*

The enterprising Campbells offer plenty of attractions in this 300-year-old white-painted pub. There's an interesting choice of bar snacks including American hamburgers and some Mexican specialities like spicy tacos and deep-fried ice cream, as well as pub favourites such as piping-hot French onion soup, grills and lasagne. A sandwich bar provides extra variety at lunchtime, and the pub also has an extensive cocktail list. **Family pub**

## Sedgefield *(B & B)*

### *New Dun Cow*

43 Front Street · *Co. Durham* · Map 4 C1
Sedgefield (0740) 20894

*Owners* Ramside Estates
*Landlord* Mr Geoff Raynor

**BEDROOMS 6 Grade 1 £C**
Scottish & Newcastle Exhibition, Newcastle Bitter; Younger's Tartan; McEwan's Best Scotch; Guinness; Harp; Taunton cider.

Motorists travelling along the A1 will find this welcoming white-painted pub convenient for an overnight stop. You can unwind with a drink in the intimate cocktail bar or the comfortable Victorian-style public bar. After that you can retire to one of the spotlessly clean bedrooms, which are attractively furnished in traditional style and equipped with radios, TVs and telephones. Tasty breakfasts. Terrace.

## Seighford *(Food)* — *Hollybush*

Near Stafford · *Staffordshire* · Map 4 C4
Seighford (078 575) 280

*Brewery* Ansell
*Landlord* Mr & Mrs J. Fowden

Lasagne £2.45 Lemon syllabub 95p (Last order 10pm)
Ansell's Bitter, Mild; Tetley's Traditional Bitter; Guinness; Skol; Löwenbräu; cider. *Real ale*

This fine 17th-century pub is a characterful venue for a quiet drink and tasty snack. Richly flavoured mushroom soup, garlic prawns and hot Brie in breadcrumbs make excellent starters or light meals, while more substantial items include chicken Kiev, chilli and a good meaty steak and kidney pie. Leave room for a sweet – perhaps cider-baked apple or exquisite lemon syllabub. Garden. **Family pub**

## Sellack *(Food)* — *Loughpool Inn*

Near Ross-on-Wye · *Hereford & Worcester*
Map 7 D2
Harewood End (098 987) 236
*Free House*
*Landlord* Mr P. Whitford
Pork with peach sauce £3.75 Beef Stroganoff £4.95 (Last order 10pm)
Bass; Mitchells & Butlers Springfield Bitter; Wadworth's 6X; Worthington Best Bitter; Guinness; Carling Black Label; Harp; cider. *Real ale*

One look at the blackboard menus will tell you that this is a pub where they take their food seriously! In the friendly surroundings of the beamed bar you might start your meal with whitebait, deep-fried Brie or stuffed mushrooms with tasty garlic mayonnaise. Main courses could include moussaka, trout with prawns and garlic fried chicken, and the cold buffet is a popular summer feature. Garden. **Family pub**

## Semley *(Food, B & B)* — *Benett Arms*

Near Shaftesbury · *Wiltshire* · Map 8 D3
East Knoyle (074 783) 221

*Brewery* Gibbs Mew
*Landlord* Mr Joe Duthie

**BEDROOMS 6 Grade 1 £B**
Steak & kidney pie £2.50 Chocolate mousse £1.20 (Last order 9.45pm)
Gibbs Premium Bitter; Guinness; Tuborg Gold; cider. *Real ale*

The lively Joe Duthie has established a loyal following of regulars at this white-washed village pub. A good selection of tasty bar snacks ranges from salads, home-made soup and pâté to satisfying casseroles, game pie and garlic mushrooms. Dishes from the restaurant menu add further choice. Attractive bedrooms, including some in a modern annexe, have colour TVs and tea-makers. **Family pub**

## Sennen Cove *(B & B)* — *Old Success Inn*

Land's End · *Cornwall* · Map 8 A4
Sennen (073 687) 232

*Free House*
*Landlords* John & Anne Cutler

**BEDROOMS 18 Grade 2 £C** (No dogs)
St Austell Tinner's Ale, Best Bitter; Carne's Falmouth Bitter; John Smith's Yorkshire Bitter; Guinness; Carlsberg; cider. *Real ale*

Overnight guests wake to the sound of the surf at this delightful old inn, which stands right above a sandy cove near Land's End. The simply furnished bedrooms – eight with their own bathrooms – are bright and cheerful, and many enjoy lovely views out to sea. There are two bars (one a popular spot with local fishermen) and a comfortable first-floor residents' lounge with TV. Patio. **Family pub**

## Shaftesbury *(B & B)* — *Mitre Inn & Sunridge Hotel*

23 High Street · *Dorset* · Map 8 D3
Shaftesbury (0747) 2488

*Brewery* Eldridge Pope
*Landlord* Mr W. M. Davis-Sellick

**BEDROOMS 18 Grades 1 & 2 £C**
Eldridge Pope Royal Oak, IPA; Guinness; Faust Pilsner, Export; Taunton cider. *Real ale*

The Mitre is a fine, traditional stone-built inn with cosy, homely bars and nice views over Blackmoor Vale. It also has eight comfortable bedrooms, while ten more modern ones with private bath and showers are in the nearby Sunridge Hotel, which also boasts a health and leisure centre. All rooms have colour TVs. **Family pub**

## Shalfleet *(Food)* — *New Inn*

Yarmouth Road · *Isle of Wight* · Map 6 A4
Calbourne (098 378) 314

*Brewery* Whitbread
*Landlords* Nigel & Brenda Simpson

Steak pie £1 Pint of prawns £1.40 (Last order 10.30pm)
Whitbreads Best, Pompey Royal, Strong Country; Flower's Original; Guinness; Stella Artois; cider. *Real ale*

A pint of prawns, served in the shell with garlic mayonnaise or shellfish sauce, is typical of the simple yet delicious bar snacks served at this popular and characterful old inn. Local crab and lobster, rainbow trout and conger eel are among the many other fishy favourites, while meat-eaters can tuck into steak pies, country sausages and home-cooked joints. Garden.

## Shave Cross *(Food)* — *Shave Cross Inn*

Marshwood Vale, Near Bridport · *Dorset*
Map 8 D3
Broadwindsor (0308) 68358
*Free House*
*Landlords* Mr & Mrs W. B. Slade
Shave Cross sausages £1.30 Ploughman's lunch 95p (Last order 9.30pm)
Hall & Woodhouse Badger Best Bitter; Devenish Wessex Best Bitter; Eldridge Pope Royal Oak; Bass; Guinness; Carlsberg; Carling Black Label; cider. *Real ale*

The medieval charm of this delightful thatched pub is preserved in flagstone floors, beamed ceilings and a fine inglenook fireplace. It also has a lovely rose garden with a wishing well. Bar snacks include ploughman's platters, herby Dorset pâté and excellent locally made sausages, with summer treats like fresh crab and lobster salads. Difficult to find, so ask directions. Closed Monday (except Bank Holidays). **Family pub**

## Shelley *(Food)* — *Three Acres Inn*

Roydhouse · *West Yorkshire* · Map 4 C3
Huddersfield (0484) 602606

*Free House*
*Landlord* Mr D. Truelove
Creamed mushrooms in port £1.25 Ham & asparagus pancake £2.75 (Last order 9.30pm. No bar food Sun eve)
Tetley's Bitter, Mild; Stones Bitter; Theakston's Best Bitter; Guinness; Carlsberg; cider. *Real ale*

The Trueloves (father and son) know how to welcome visitors to this stone-built pub on the moors. In the roomy bar you can tuck into generous platefuls of home-made steak, kidney and mushroom pie, a traditional roast or perhaps fresh crab salad. Sandwiches are available, too, and tasty starters like egg and prawn mayonnaise, with homely crumbles to finish. Closed lunchtime Monday and Saturday.
**Family pub**

## Shenington *(Food)* — *Bell*

*Oxfordshire* · Map 5 A2
Edge Hill (029 587) 274
*Free House*
*Landlords* Mr & Mrs Keith Brewer
Pheasant & venison casserole £4.75 Crispy Somerset lamb in cider £3.25 (Last order 10.30pm. No bar food Sun eve, also Sun lunch Nov–April)
Hook Norton Best Bitter; Wadworth's 6X; Bass Special; Worthington 'E'; Guinness; Harp. *Real ale*

You must book if you want to sample Vanessa Brewer's excellent and enterprising cooking in the pleasant bar of this lovely old pub. Start with rich, creamy spinach soup or fish pâté, and go on to delicious light asparagus quiche or something more substantial – perhaps liver and bacon hot pot, fiery pork vindaloo or crispy Somerset lamb in cider; there's also game in winter. Finish with fruity peach and almond tart or apple charlotte with cream. **Family pub**

## Shepperton *(B & B)* — *Anchor Hotel*

Church Square · *Middlesex* · Map 6 B3
Walton-on-Thames (0932) 221618

*Free House*
*Landlord* Peter Wilson

**BEDROOMS 24 Grade 1 £A**
Ruddle's County; Eldridge Pope Royal Oak, 1880 Ale; Webster's Yorkshire Bitter; Guinness; Foster's; Holsten Export; cider. *Real ale*

Richly carved oak panelling creates a solidly traditional atmosphere in the bars of this handsome white-painted hotel, which stands in a quiet square close to the river Thames. Double-glazed bedrooms, uniformly decorated in a bright, fairly modern style, have smart fitted units, TVs, tea-makers and neat, compact bathrooms. There's a pleasant terrace for alfresco summer sipping. **Family pub**

## Shepperton *(Food)* — *King's Head*

Church Square · *Middlesex* · Map 6 B3
Walton-on-Thames (0932) 221910

*Brewery* Courage
*Landlord* David Longhurst

Shepperton pie £1.45 Treacle tart 85p (Last order 10.10pm. No bar food Sun)
Courage Directors Bitter, Best Bitter; John Smith's Bitter; Guinness; Hofmeister; Kronenbourg; Taunton cider. *Real ale*

Here's a fine old pub, close by the Thames, sporting two 'characters': JC, the bull-terrier, and Maria, the long-serving Spanish lady whose versatile bar snacks are definite crowd-pullers of a lunchtime and evening. Her delicious versions of Welsh rarebit, cottage pie and hot treacle tart are distinguished by original touches; you might also choose soup (in winter), quiche, home-cooked ham or just a sandwich. Patio.

## Shepperton *(Food)* — *Thames Court*

Towpath · *Middlesex* · Map 6 B3
Walton-on-Thames (0932) 221957

*Free House*
*Landlord* Mr L. J. Negus
Prawn sandwich £1.15 Stuffed leg of lamb with potatoes & vegetables £2.20 (Last order 9.30pm)
Bass; Charrington's IPA; Stones Bitter; Tennent's Extra; Guinness; Carling Black Label; Taunton cider. *Real ale*

An attractive brick building in an idyllic location overlooking the Thames by Shepperton weir. At lunchtime in the finely panelled bar, you can enjoy hearty chicken soup and take your pick from a selection of salads to accompany cold meats and raised pies. There are also sandwiches, pâtés, good-looking cheeses and hot specials (October–April only) like veal provençale. For a finish with a flourish, try the fresh strawberry flan. **Family pub**

## Shepton Mallet *(B & B)* — *Kings Arms*

Leg Square · *Somerset* · Map 8 D3
Shepton Mallet (0749) 3781

*Brewery* Hall
*Landlords* Mr & Mrs Peter Swan

**BEDROOMS 3 Grade 2 £C**
Wadworth's 6X; Hall's Harvest Bitter; Ind Coope Burton Ale; Guinness; Löwenbräu; Skol; cider. *Real ale*

Visitors to this really appealing 17th-century stone pub can expect a right royal welcome from friendly hosts Mr and Mrs Swan. There are three charming rustic bars (one with a collection of marvellous old photographs), as well as a peaceful residents' lounge. Pretty bedrooms have traditional furniture and floral fabrics, plus tea-makers; the modern public bathroom is spotlessly clean. **Family pub**

## Shiplake *(Food, B & B)* — *Baskerville Arms*

Nr Henley-on-Thames · *Oxfordshire* · Map 6 B3
Wargrave (073 522) 3332
*Brewery* Whitbread
Landlords Harry & Pat Caffrey
**BEDROOMS 3 Grade 2 £A** (No dogs)
Chilli con carne £2.50 Steak & kidney pie £1.20 (Last order 9.30pm. No bar food Sun & Mon eves)
Wethered's Bitter, SPA; Flower's Original; Whitbread Best Bitter; Guinness; Heineken; Stella Artois; cider. *Real ale*

In the roomy bar of this sturdy, red-brick pub you can get anything from a sandwich to a three-course meal. Blackboard menus spell out the day's offerings, which could include quiche, home-cooked ham, excellent chilli con carne and deliciously light and tangy lemon syllabub. The three comfortable bedrooms all have TVs and share a well-fitted modern bathroom. Very good breakfasts. Garden. **Family pub**

## Shipston on Stour *(Food, B & B)* ★ — *White Bear*

High Street · *Warwickshire* · Map 5 A2
Shipston on Stour (0608) 61558
*Brewery* Bass
*Landlords* Mr & Mrs Hugh Roberts
**BEDROOMS 9 Grade 1 £C**
Steak & kidney pie £2.95 Fresh salmon quiche £3.75 (Last order 9.30pm. No bar food Sun eve)
Bass; Mitchells & Butlers Mild, Brew XI; Worthington 'E'; Guinness; Carling Black Label; Taunton cider. *Real ale*

The Robertses are the perfect hosts at this handsome pub, which is justly renowned for its marvellous bar food. Blackboards announce the day's specials, such as deliciously herby vegetable soup, grilled sardines, Lancashire hot pot and pork casserole. There are also lots of salads, sandwiches and glorious puddings. Filled baguettes only for Sunday lunch. Super bedrooms (most with private bathrooms) are traditionally furnished. **Family pub**

## Shipton-under-Wychwood *(Food, B & B)* — *Lamb Inn*

High Street · *Oxfordshire* · Map 5 A2
Shipton-under-Wychwood (0993) 830465
*Free House*
*Landlords* Hugh & Lynne Wainwright
**BEDROOMS 5 Grade 2 £B** (No dogs)
George's Cotswold pie £3.25 Trout & sauté potatoes £2.95 (Last order 9.30pm. No bar food Sun lunch)
Hook Norton Best Bitter; Wadworth's 6X; Guinness (winter only); Löwenbräu; Grünhalle; Taunton cider (summer only). *Real ale*

The atmosphere is warm and welcoming, the bar food excellent at the Wainwrights' characterful Cotswold inn. Meat pies and savoury pancakes are popular choices, along with soup, summer salads, flavoursome pâtés and specials such as roast lamb. Up a steep staircase are five well-kept bedrooms with sturdy old furniture and tea-makers; four have private facilities. Good breakfasts. No children overnight. Terrace.

## Shipton-under-Wychwood *(Food, B & B)* *Shaven Crown Hotel*

High Street · *Oxfordshire* · Map 5 A2
Shipton-under-Wychwood (0993) 830330

*Free House*
*Landlords* Brookes family
**BEDROOMS 9 Grade 1 £A** (No dogs)
Steak, kidney & mushroom pie with vegetables £2.95 Mushroom & walnut pancake with salad £2.15 (Last order 9.30pm)
Flowers Best Bitter, Original; Heineken; Tuborg Gold, cider. *Real ale*

Rich in architectural history, this beautifully kept place – once a monk's hospice – is built around an attractive courtyard garden. Charming bedrooms with sturdy old furnishings provide comfortable overnight accommodation, while tasty bar snacks satisfy the inner man. The menu offers standard items like soup, lasagne and chilli con carne along with the popular grilled potato skins with bacon and cheese and an irresistible banana cake.

## Shoreham-by-Sea *(Food)* *Red Lion*

Old Shoreham Road · *West Sussex* · Map 6 B4
Shoreham (079 17) 3171

*Brewery* Phoenix
*Landlord* Norman Stevens
Prawns creole £2.50 Chilli con carne £1.75 (Last order 9.45pm. No bar food Mon eve & all Sun)
Gale's HSB; Usher's Best Bitter; Tamplins Bitter; Samuel Websters Yorkshire Bitter; Guinness; Holsten; cider. *Real ale*

There are lovely views of the South Downs from this low white-painted pub, whose fascinating history goes back to Saxon times. The new tenants take great pride in their bar food, and everything is good and fresh, from ploughman's with delicious home-boiled ham and warm cottage rolls to lasagne, quiche lorraine and kebabs. To finish, try the excellent spiced apple flan. Garden.

## Silk Willoughby *(Food)* *Horseshoes*

London Road, Sleaford · *Lincolnshire*
Map 5 B1
Sleaford (0529) 303153

*Brewery* John Smith
*Landlords* Mr & Mrs Cuñago

Seafood pancake £2.75 Charlotte russe 95p (Last order 10pm. No bar food Sun eve)
John Smith's Bitter, Mild, Lager; Guinness; Hofmeister.

Careful modernisation has enhanced the appeal of this 19th-century red-brick pub, which stands in a charmingly named village on the A15. The blackboard menu changes daily to present a good variety of tasty bar fare, from soup and pâté to halibut, lasagne and a really scrumptious steak and kidney pie. Nice sweets, too, including a moreish charlotte russe. Garden. **Family pub**

## Sindlesham *(Food, B & B)* *Walter Arms*

Bearwood Road · *Berkshire* · Map 6 B3
Wokingham (0734) 780260

*Brewery* Courage
*Landlords* Mr & Mrs W. M. Cox
**BEDROOMS 4 Grade 2 £B** (No dogs)
Country pie & vegetables £2 Hungarian pancakes £1.75 (Last order 10pm)
Courage Directors Bitter, Best Bitter, John Courage; Guinness; Kronenbourg; Hofmeister. *Real ale*

The three cosy, interconnecting bars of this imposing Victorian pub are busy at mealtimes, when Mrs Cox's tasty bar snacks attract a crowd. Her soups are flavoursome, and there's plenty of substantial fare like beef in burgundy, curry, moussaka and good home-made fruit pies. Well-cared-for bedrooms, traditionally furnished and all with colour TV, provide comfortable accommodation. No children overnight; bedrooms closed 23 Dec–1 Jan.

## Skidby *(Food)* — *Half Moon Inn*

16 Main Street · *Humberside* · Map 4 D3
Hull (0482) 843403

*Brewery* John Smith
*Landlord* Peter Madeley

Yorkshire pudding sandwich with beef £2.70
Steak & kidney pie with chips & mushy peas £2.10 (Last order 10pm)
John Smith's Bitter, Chestnut Mild; Guinness; Hofmeister; Harp.

Huge man-sized Yorkshire puddings, served with rich onion gravy, minced beef and asparagus, chilli con carne or even roast beef, are the claim to fame of this jolly white-painted pub just off the A164. At lunchtime you can also tuck into home-made soup, hot salt beef sandwiches or steak and kidney pie, and round things off with gâteau or apple pie. There's a more limited choice in the evening. Patio for fine-weather drinking. **Family pub**

## Skirmett *(Food, B & B)* — *King's Arms*

Near Henley-on-Thames, Oxfordshire
*Buckinghamshire* · Map 6 B3
Turville Heath (049 163) 247
*Free House*
*Landlords* Mr & Mrs R. Grahamslaw
**BEDROOMS 4 Grade 2 £B**
Beefburger with salad £1.20 Sirloin steak with potatoes £5.45 (Last order 10pm)
Ruddle's Bitter; Wethered's SPA, Bitter; Guinness; Stella Artois; Heineken; cider.
*Real ale*

Charming hosts Mr and Mrs Grahamslaw really make guests feel welcome at this friendly village pub. There's afternoon tea on arrival, and the cosy bedrooms offer thoughtful touches such as bottled spring water, books and tissues, plus ample storage space. Two have TVs and shower rooms. Downstairs, you'll find two pleasant bars where enjoyable bar snacks include soups, pasta, Cumberland sausages and home-made ice cream. **Family pub**

We have raised our standards considerably since last year. The omission of some houses that appeared in last year's Guide is no reflection on their standing.

## Slaidburn *(B & B)* — *Hark to Bounty Inn*

Near Clitheroe · *Lancashire* · Map 3 B2
Slaidburn (020 06) 246

*Free House*
*Landlords* Mr & Mrs P. Turner

**BEDROOMS 8 Grade 1 £A**
Thwaites Bitter, Mild; Theakston's Old Peculier; Guinness; Stein; Carlsberg; cider.
*Real ale*

The Turner family are maintaining admirable standards of friendly hospitality in this 13th-century stone pub. Locals gather for a pint and a chat in the spacious beamed bar, and there's a relaxing TV lounge for residents. Prettily decorated, simply furnished bedrooms (including an especially nice one in the attic) have radios and tea-makers; all but one also boast fully tiled modern bathrooms. Garden. **Family pub**

## Slaithwaite *(Food)* — *White House*

Huddersfield · *West Yorkshire* · Map 4 C3
Huddersfield (0484) 842245

*Free House*
*Landlord* Mrs Gillian Sykes
Fried mussels with garlic mayonnaise £1.75
Prawn cocktail platter £2.50 (Last order 10pm)
Tetley's Mild; Younger's IPA, Scotch Bitter, Chieftain; Guinness; McEwan's Lager. *Real ale*

Ask for directions to this charming country inn set above the village on the B6107 Marsden to Meltham road. Once there you'll be welcomed by Mrs Sykes and her loyal helpers and can look forward to a delicious snack in the beamed bar. As well as plain and toasted sandwiches and soup, you can get home-made burgers, a really tasty cottage pie made in the traditional style, flans, pizzas and specialities such as fried mussels with garlic mayonnaise.

## Sleights *(B & B)* — *Salmon Leap*

Near Whitby · *North Yorkshire* · Map 4 D2
Whitby (0947) 810233

*Brewery* Cameron
*Landlords* Mr & Mrs B. Gibson

**BEDROOMS 10 Grade 2 £C**
Cameron's Best Bitter, Strongarm; Lion; Guinness; Hansa; cider. *Real ale*

Perched high above the Esk valley, this sturdy stone inn provides comfortable accommodation in warm, friendly surroundings. Bedrooms in the modern extension are neat and compact, with well-designed fitted furniture, while those in the main building are more old-fashioned in style and roomy enough for families. Three bars offer plenty of elbow room for the thirsty and there's a very pretty garden.
**Family pub**

## Smarden *(Food, B & B)* — *Bell*

Bell Lane · *Kent* · Map 6 C3
Smarden (023 377) 283
*Free House*
*Landlord* Mr Ian Turner
**BEDROOMS 4 Grade 1 £C** (No dogs)
Clam fries £1.50 Gammon steak £2.95 (Last order 10pm)
Theakston's Old Peculier, Best Bitter; Shepherd Neame Masterbrew; Fuller's London Pride; Murphy's Stout; cider. *Real ale*

In the busy bar of this quintessential weatherboarded Kentish pub you can sample Ian Turner's fine real ales and delicious food: in addition to superb lasagne and the very popular rump steak, you can also get salads, pizzas and sandwiches, plus some nice old-fashioned puds. An exterior spiral staircase leads to the comfortable, tastefully furnished bedrooms, all with TV. Continental breakfast only. No accommodation Christmas week. **Family pub**

## Smarden *(Food)* — *Chequers Inn*

*Kent* · Map 6 C3
Smarden (023 377) 217

*Brewery* Courage
*Landlords* Mr & Mrs Frank Stevens

Chilli con carne £1.95 Steak & kidney pie £2.95 (Last order 10pm)
Courage Directors Bitter, Best Bitter, Dark Mild; Guinness; Hofmeister; Kronenbourg; Taunton cider. *Real ale*

Landlord Frank Stevens does most of the cooking in this friendly weatherboarded village pub, and he makes a very good job of it. We enjoyed subtly flavoured cream of vegetable soup with superb French bread (the real thing, specially imported), robust pork pâté and delicious weiner schnitzel; other tasty offerings include steaks, chilli con carne and home-made pies. Simple sweets. Garden.

## Snainton *(B & B)* — *Coachman Inn*

Near Scarborough · *North Yorkshire* · Map 4 D2
Scarborough (0723) 85231

*Brewery* Cameron
*Landlords* Mr & Mrs G. C. Senior

**BEDROOMS 12 Grade 1 £A**
Cameron's Best Bitter, Strongarm; Hansa; cider.

Set back from the A170 in pleasant gardens and paddocks, this rambling Georgian coaching house is a good base for exploring the North Yorkshire moors. The lounge is comfortable and homely, with fresh flowers and plenty of magazines, and there are two bars. Spacious bedrooms, most with their own bath/shower rooms, are furnished mainly in bright modern style. Garden. **Family pub**

## Sonning-on-Thames *(Food, B & B)* — *Bull Inn*

Near Reading · *Berkshire* · Map 6 B3
Reading (0734) 693901

*Brewery* Wethered
*Landlord* Mr D. T. Cotton

**BEDROOMS 5 Grade 2 £A+** (No dogs)
Selection of cold meats & salads from £3 Cheese & biscuits 70p (Last order 10pm)
Wethered's Bitter, SPA, Winter Royal; Heineken; cider. *Real ale*

As pretty as a picture, with wistaria hugging its walls, this centuries-old village pub is an excellent place for a lunchtime snack. A bar display offers cold meats and simple salads, and in winter there's soup, toasted sandwiches (the only evening choice) and a hot special. Simply furnished bedrooms (all with TV) share a single public bathroom. No children overnight. Accommodation closed 1 week Christmas. Patio.

## South Leigh *(Food)* — *Mason Arms*

Near Witney · *Oxfordshire* · Map 6 A3
Witney (0993) 2485

*Free House*
*Landlords* The Theobald family
Locally cured salt beef, chips & veg £3.50
Savoury fish pancake £1.95 (Last order 10pm. No bar food Sun eve)
Glenny's Witney Bitter; Younger's Scotch Ale; Newcastle Bitter; Guinness; Beck's. *Real ale*

Locally cured salt beef is a speciality at this attractive old thatched pub in a tiny village. Enjoy it with chips and peas, in salads or sandwiches, or with vegetables in a good warming broth. Other treats include home-cooked gammon, savoury pancakes and richly flavoured steak and kidney pie. To finish, there are some nice puddings made by ladies in the village. Closed Monday. Garden. **Family pub**

## South Woodchester *(Food)* — *Ram Inn*

Near Stroud · *Gloucestershire* · Map 7 D2
Amberley (045 387) 3329

*Free House*
*Landlord* Mr David Hicks
Whole prawns & garlic dip £1.95 Lamb & apricot pie £2.05 (Last order 10pm)
Archer's Village Bitter; Holden's Black Country Bitter; Hook Norton Old Hookey; Cirencester Bitter; Boddington's Bitter; Guinness. *Real ale*

This attractive little pub in a Cotswold village wins friends with a fine selection of real ales and some excellent home cooking. Mrs Hicks prepares tasty, satisfying dishes like succulent roast beef or lamb and apricot pie, along with pizza and savoury pancakes. There are some tempting cold choices, too, such as juicy whole prawns with a garlic dip. Nice views from the terrace.

## South Zeal *(B & B)* — *Oxenham Arms*

Near Okehampton · *Devon* · Map 8 C3
Sticklepath (083 784) 244

*Free House*
*Landlords* Mr & Mrs J. H. Henry

**BEDROOMS 8 Grades 1 & 2 £B**
Everards Tiger Bitter; Flower's Best Bitter; Guinness; Stella Artois; Kronenbourg; cider (summer only). *Real ale*

Believed to have been built by lay monks in the 12th century, this characterful pub stands in a peaceful village near the A30. Crackling fires warm the beamed public rooms, which include a cosy bar and a restful lounge with antiques and inviting armchairs. There are antiques, too, in many of the bedrooms, plus modern features like colour TVs and tea-makers. Six have private facilities. Garden. **Family pub**

## Southwold *(B & B)* — *Crown Hotel*

High Street · *Suffolk* · Map 5 D2
Southwold (0502) 722275

*Brewery* Sole Bay Hotels Ltd
*Landlord* Mrs H. Carpenter

**BEDROOMS 21 Grades 1 & 2 £A**
Adnam's Bitter; Skol; Stella Artois. *Real ale*

Comfortable overnight accommodation is provided at this pleasantly run Georgian coaching inn. Rooms at the top boast nice old beams and sloping ceilings, while others have a more modern feel. All are neat, well carpeted and equipped with radio-alarms and colour TVs, and most have their own smart bath or shower room. There's a spacious traditional lounge and two bars. Patio. **Family pub**

## Staddle Bridge *(Food, B & B)* ★ — *McCoy's at the Tontine*

Near Northallerton · *North Yorkshire*
Map 4 C2
East Harlsey (060 982) 207

*Free House*
*Landlords* McCoy Brothers
**BEDROOMS 6 Grade 1 £A+**
Seafood crêpe £2.85 Steak with red wine sauce £6.95 (Last order 10.30pm)
Cameron's Strongarm; Hansa; Guinness. *Real ale*

Snacks of outstanding quality are served in the informal cellar bar of the McCoy brothers' imposing stone house on the A19. Skill and flair shine through in every dish, from superb soups and succulent steaks to home-made pasta, seafood pancakes and fabulous fruit pies. Large, warm and very comfortable bedrooms are traditionally furnished with great charm. Superb breakfasts. **Family pub**

## Stafford *(B & B)* — *Swan Hotel*

Greengate Street · *Staffordshire* · Map 4 C4
Stafford (0785) 58142

*Owners* Berni Hotels
*Landlord* Mr J. Fiddler

**BEDROOMS 31 Grade 1 £A+** (No dogs)
Ansells Bitter, SDB, Mild; Double Diamond; Guinness; Skol; Löwenbräu. *Real ale*

High standards of housekeeping are maintained at this rambling old town-centre hotel, whose white façade includes attractive bow windows. Bedrooms are comfortable and well equipped, with smart fitted furniture, colour TVs, radio/alarms and tea-makers. One room features a four-poster, and all have compact bath or shower rooms. There are two traditionally furnished bars. Accommodation closed 2 weeks Christmas. Garden. **Family pub**

## Stamford *(B & B)* — *Bull & Swan Inn*

St Martin's · *Lincolnshire* · Map 5 B1
Stamford (0780) 63558

*Brewery* Melbourns
*Landlords* William & Rosa Morgado
**BEDROOMS 6 Grade 2 £B**
Lasagne £2 Mixed grill £2.90
(Last order 10.30pm)
Sam Smith's Old Brewery Bitter, Mild, Sovereign; Guinness; Diat Pils; Ayinger Bräu; cider. *Real ale*

A long tradition of hospitality is being continued at this attractive old coaching inn by the Morgadoes. Hungry visitors will find some tasty, homely bar fare, including chicken liver pâté, hearty ploughman's and steak sandwiches, as well as hot dishes like lasagne or perhaps trout provençale, with a selection of sweets to finish. Prettily decorated bedrooms, all with washbasins and colour TVs, share two public bathrooms. **Family pub**

## Stamford *(B & B)* — *Crown Hotel*

All Saints Place · *Lincolnshire* · Map 5 B1
Stamford (0780) 63136

*Free House*
*Landlords* Mr & Mrs R. D. McGahon

**BEDROOMS 18 Grade 2 £B**
Ruddle's County; Whitbread Trophy; Ansells Bitter; Guinness; Heineken; Skol; Stella Artois. *Real ale*

Robert and Eve McGahon extend a warm welcome at their fine old stone-built hotel, which stands near the town centre in the shadow of All Saints Church. Comfortable overnight accommodation is provided in 18 good-sized bedrooms, attractively decorated, solidly furnished and all boasting TVs and tea-makers. Ten have their own bathrooms. The bar is unpretentiously modern in style, and there's a simple lounge. **Family pub**

## Stamford *(Food)* ★ *George of Stamford*

St Martins · *Lincolnshire* · Map 5 B1
Stamford (0780) 55171

*Free House*
*Landlord* Mr Jolyon Gough

Antipasto £3.95 Braised oxtail £3.95 (Last order 11pm)
Ruddle's Bitter, County; Sam Smith's Old Brewery Bitter; Kestrel.

The comfortable bars, leafy garden lounge and cobbled courtyard are equally delightful settings for enjoying the truly super snacks served at this famous old coaching inn. An extensive cold buffet is available each lunchtime (summer evenings as well), and hot choices include soup, lasagne, delicious seafood pancakes and steak sandwiches. Lovely sweets, too. *For accommodation see Egon Ronay's Lucas Hotel & Restaurant Guide 1985.* **Family pub**

## Standish *(Food)* — *Foresters Arms*

Shevington Moor, Near Wigan · *Greater Manchester* · Map 3 B3
Standish (0257) 421337

*Brewery* Greenall Whitley
*Landlords* Ronnie & Jean Baxendale

Chicken & mushroom pie £1.20 Apple pie & cream 45p (Last order 10pm)
Greenall Whitley Bitter, Mild; Guinness; Grünhalle Lager; cider. *Real ale*

Good simple bar fare is available seven days a week at the Baxendales' friendly little pub, which stands behind a motel near junction 27 of the M6. Bumper beef or ham sandwiches make excellent quick snacks, and other choices range from tasty pizzas and savoury pies to scampi, roast chicken and T-bone steaks. To finish, home-made apple pie or cheesecake, and good fresh coffee. Garden.

## Stanford Dingley *(Food)* ★ *Old Boot Inn*

Near Bradfield · *Berkshire* · Map 6 B3
Bradfield (0734) 744292

*Free House*
*Landlords* John & Eliane Pratt

Roast beef & salad £3.50 Moules marinière £3.85 (Last order 9pm)
North Country Breweries Riding Bitter; Arkell's BBB; Fuller's London Pride; Ruddle's County; Guinness; Stella Artois. *Real ale*

Eliane Pratt's fine cooking makes it well worth seeking out this delightful 18th-century pub in deepest Berkshire. Garlic mushrooms with bacon on toast makes a tasty, satisfying snack, and other popular dishes include lasagne, moules marinière and rare roast beef with salad (hot roast Sunday lunchtime). Leave room for a delicious sweet like profiteroles or apple flan. The large terrace and attractive garden add to the pleasure in summer.

## Stanton Harcourt *(Food, B & B)* ★ *Harcourt Arms*

Near Eynsham · *Oxfordshire* · Map 6 A3
Oxford (0865) 882192

*Brewery* Morrell's
*Landlord* Mr George Dailey

**BEDROOMS 16 Grade 1 £B** (No dogs)
Grilled king prawns £2.50 Moules marinière £2.50 (Last order 9.30pm)
Morrell's Best Bitter, Varsity Bitter (winter); Guinness; Harp; cider. *Real ale*

Grilled king prawns with garlic mayonnaise are among the many delights that have put George Dailey's fine Cotswold pub firmly on the gastronomic map. Besides the renowned seafood, you'll find winter soups and pies and an excellent cold table in summer. Some lovely puddings too. Well-equipped bedrooms in charming stone cottages provide excellent comfort; most have TVs and private bathrooms. Patio and garden. **Family pub**

## Staple Fitzpaine *(Food)* ★ *Greyhound inn*

Near Taunton · *Somerset* · Map 8 C3
Hatch Beauchamp (0823) 480227
*Free House*
*Landlords* Martin Tarr & Paul Toogood
Celery & apple soup 85p Chicken & vegetable kebabs £2.95 (Last order 10pm. No bar food Sun eve)
Golden Hill Exmoor Ale; Eldridge Pope Royal Oak, Dorchester Bitter; Devenish Wessex Bitter; Guinness; Faust; Taunton cider. *Real ale*

Winding lanes lead from the A358 to this charming, creeper-clad pub, where the air is tranquil, the welcome warm and the cooking exceptional. The bar menu is full of lovely things, from sweetly succulent prawns with garlic mayonnaise to delicious seafood, pasta, imaginative vegetarian dishes and daily specials like lamb curry. Luscious puddings include a splendid treacle tart served with clotted cream. **Family pub**

## Stapleton *(Food)* ★ *Bridge Inn*

Near Darlington · *Co. Durham* · Map 4 C2
Darlington (0325) 50106

*Brewery* Vaux
*Landlords* Nicholas & Catherine Young
Salmon with hollandaise sauce £5.75 Lamb's kidneys with mushrooms & Madeira sauce £3.75 (Last order 10pm. No bar food Sun & Mon eves)
Vaux Samson; Guinness; Norseman; Taunton cider. *Real ale*

Skill, flair and enthusiasm shine through Nick Young's cooking at this unpretentious pub three miles from Darlington. Our celery soup was a delicious way to start a meal, and the lamb's kidneys with mushroom and Madeira sauce made a marvellous main course. Fresh fish is a great favourite, and toasted sandwiches are excellent quick snacks. Don't leave before trying one of Cathy Young's super sweets. Garden. **Family pub**

## Starbotton — *Fox & Hounds*

Rebuilt in 1834 after a fearsome flood inundated the village, this delightful little pub is a haven of warmth and hospitality – even the exterior looks friendly! A splendid open fireplace surrounded by burnished brassware dominates the tiny bar, which has a flagstoned floor and rough stone walls hung with paintings by local artists.

**Family pub**

Near Kettlewell, Upper Wharfedale · *North Yorkshire* · Map 4 C2
Kettlewell (075 676) 269
*Free House* *Landlord* Mrs B. Hartley
Theakston's Old Peculier, Best Bitter, Mild; Younger's Scotch Bitter; Carlsberg; cider. *Real ale*

## Staveley *(Food)* — *Royal Oak*

Near Knaresborough · *North Yorkshire*
Map 4 C2
Copgrove (090 14) 267

*Brewery* Younger
*Landlords* Peter & Elizabeth Gallagher

Game pie £2.50 Seafood open tart with vegetables £2.20 (No bar food eves)
Younger's Scotch Bitter, IPA; Guinness; McEwan's Lager. *Real ale*

The ebullient Gallaghers run this attractive little village pub. Hunting prints line the walls of the comfortable lounge bar, and there's an informal public bar where lunch-time snacks are served. Robust country fare includes soups, tasty quiches and well-filled French-bread sandwiches; best of all is the superb game pie, packed with good things and served with beautifully cooked vegetables. Garden. **Family pub**

## Staverton *(B & B)* — *Sea Trout Inn*

Near Totnes · *Devon* · Map 8 C4
Staverton (080 426) 274

*Free House*
*Landlord* Mr Bill McNeill

**BEDROOMS 6 Grade 2 £B**
John Smiths Yorkshire Bitter, Lager; Double Diamond; Simonds; Bates; Guinness; Hofmeister; cider. *Real ale*

Displays of stuffed fish and a large collection of salmon and sea trout flies give the cosy lounge bar of this peaceful village pub a distinctly piscatorial atmosphere. But for those who don't have angling aspirations there's also a little TV lounge. Prettily decorated bedrooms have modern furniture and are provided with tea-makers; bathrooms are spotlessly clean and well maintained. Patio. **Family pub**

## Steep *(Food)* — *Harrow Inn*

Near Petersfield · *Hampshire* · Map 6 B4
Petersfield (0730) 62685

*Brewery* Whitbread
*Landlord* E. C. McCutcheon

Ham salad £3.75 Stuffed Marrow £2.30 (Last order 9.30pm)
Whitbread Strong Country Bitter, Best Mild; Flowers Original; Guinness; Heineken; Stella Artois; cider. *Real ale*

Mr and Mrs McCutcheon maintain this pub in the nicest traditional style, with few concessions to the 20th century. In the charming atmosphere of the rustic public bar or the cottagy smoke room you can enjoy simple, hearty fare like ploughman's with home-cooked ham or rare roast beef, along with nourishing soup and daily hot dishes such as lasagne or really delicious stuffed marrow. There's a neat courtyard for fine-weather drinking.

## Stewkley *(Food)* — *Swan*

Near Leighton Buzzard, Bedfordshire
*Buckinghamshire* · Map 5 B2
Stewkley (052 524) 285
*Brewery* Courage
*Landlords* Colin & Carole Anderson
Chicken liver pâté & toast £1.30 Steak & kidney pudding with vegetables £2.20 (Last order 9.30pm. No bar food Sun)
Courage Directors Bitter, Best Bitter, JC; Guinness; Kronenbourg; Hofmeister; Taunton cider. *Real ale*

Colin and Carole Anderson generate a really friendly atmosphere in this cosy beamed pub, and Carole delights customers with her interesting choice of fare. As well as favourites like ploughman's and fried scampi, there are lunchtime specials such a superb meaty broth or bacon and onion dumpling. Sweets include a delicious sherry trifle. Grills, a pint of prawns or perhaps fish pie in the evening. Garden. Booking advisable. **Family pub**

## Stockbridge *(Food, B & B)* — *Vine Inn*

High Street · *Hampshire* · Map 6 A3
Andover (0264) 810652
*Brewery* Whitbread
*Landlord* Mr L. A. Wilkins
**BEDROOMS 4 Grade 2 £C**
Steak & kidney pie £2.35 Haddock bake £3.25 (Last order 9.30pm. No bar food Sat & Sun eves)
Flowers Original; Whitbread Strong Country Bitter, Best Bitter; Hampshire Bitter; Guinness; cider. *Real ale*

Mr Wilkins' daughter is queen of the kitchen in this homely little pub, and you can feast regally on her tasty bar snacks. There's plenty of choice ranging from crab mousse and filled jacket potatoes (try the cheesy smoked haddock) to sandwiches, salads and stuffed peppers, with excellent creamy trifle to finish. Four traditionally furnished bedrooms (all with colour TV) are kept in good order, and you'll start the day with a superb breakfast. **Family pub**

## Stockbridge *(Food, B & B)* — *White Hart Inn*

High Street · *Hampshire* · Map 6 A3
Andover (0264) 810475
*Free House*
*Landlord* Peter Curtis
**BEDROOMS 11 Grades 1 & 2 £C** (No dogs)
Steak & kidney & vegetables £2.25 Fisherman's lunch £1.75 (Last order 10.15pm)

Wadworth's 6X; Bass; Hancock's HB; Gale's HSB; Guinness; Carling Black Label; Taunton cider. *Real ale*

This inn is now a pleasant mixture of old and new. Bedrooms range from prettily decorated, beamed rooms in the main building to compact modern ones with up-to-date private bathrooms in converted stables; all have TV. In the two rustic bars you can tuck into flavoursome soups, home-made pâté, sandwiches and substantial dishes like curry or nourishing lamb casserole. Sweets, too, such as fruit pie. Three-course Sunday lunch. Terrace.

## Stoke-by-Nayland *(Food)* — *Crown*

Near Colchester, Essex
*Suffolk* · Map 5 D2
Nayland (0206) 262346

*Free House*
*Landlords* Keith & Tony Symonds
Cod & prawn lasagne £2.50 Steak & kidney pie £2.40 (Last order 10pm)
Tolly Cobbold Bitter, Original; McEwan's Export; Guinness; Carlsberg Hof; cider. *Real ale*

Inside, beams and lots of space, outside, a lovely garden with views over the rolling Suffolk countryside. Inside or out, you'll enjoy your meal at this large white-painted pub, whose extensive bar menu includes delicious soups, home-cooked ham, seafood lasagne and even fresh lobster. Steaks and basket meals are also popular, and sandwiches and salads are made to order. Plenty of sweets, too. **Family pub**

## Stoke St Gregory *(Food)* — *Rose & Crown*

Woodhill, Near Taunton · *Somerset* · Map 8 D3
North Curry (0823) 490296
*Free House*
*Landlords* Mr & Mrs Browning

Soup with granary bread 75p Scrumpy chicken £2.75 (Last order 10pm)
Golden Hill Exmoor Ale; Eldridge Pope Royal Oak, Dorchester Bitter, 1880; Bass Toby Bitter; Guinness; Faust; Taunton cider. *Real ale*

Twisting country lanes lead to this friendly old inn, whose interesting features include an illuminated well that's 60 feet deep. The menu, chalked up in the cosy bar, offers simple, well-prepared dishes served in generous portions. The choice ranges from soup and omelettes to cold meat salads, grilled gammon and succulent scrumpy chicken. There's excellent home-baked granary bread and some tempting sweets. Patio. **Family pub**

## Stokenham *(Food)* — *Tradesman's Arms*

Near Kingsbridge · *Devon* · Map 8 C4
Kingsbridge (0548) 580313

*Free House*
*Landlord* Allan Matthew

Avocado cream pâté £1.20 Honey roast, Madeira-flavoured gammon £2.95 (Last order 10pm)
Usher's Best Bitter; Carling Black Label; Worthington 'E'; cider. *Real ale*

An enormous range of malt whiskies and delicious bar food are among the attractions of this charming village inn. Avocado cream pâté or French onion soup is an excellent starter, and you could follow with Madeira-flavoured gammon or fresh fish from Plymouth. The Sunday lunchtime curry is a popular feature. Pub closed Mon–Thurs eves Dec–March. Patio and garden. **Family pub**

## Stonegate *(Food)* — *Bridge Inn*

Near Wadhurst · *East Sussex* · Map 6 C4
Burwash (0435) 883243

*Free House*
*Landlord* Mr John Blake

Mushroom pot £1.95 Savoury sausage pie £2.75 (Last order 10pm)
Young's Ordinary, Special Bitter; Friary Meux Bitter; John Bull Bitter; Guinness; Skol; Löwenbräu; cider. *Real ale*

John Blake and his young team provide a warm welcome at this friendly inn standing in extensive grounds. Snacks served in the cosy beamed bar are good and varied: well-filled sandwiches, garlicky mushroom pot, savoury pancakes, daily specials like excellent grilled plaice. Chilli con carne and curry cater well for spicier palates, and there's a barbecue on Friday evenings in summer. Garden.

## Stony Stratford *(B & B)* — *Bull Hotel*

64 High Street · *Buckinghamshire* · Map 5 B2
Milton Keynes (0908) 567104

*Brewery* Aylesbury
*Landlords* Mr & Mrs H. W. Willis

**BEDROOMS 12 Grade 2 £B** (No dogs)
ABC Bitter; Everards Tiger; Bass; Morell's Bitter; Burton Bitter; Guinness; Taunton cider. *Real ale*

Travellers staying at this friendly hotel in coaching days would swop tales with guests at the neighbouring Cock Hotel, allegedly giving rise to the cock and bull story. The tales are different now, but the welcome's just as warm, and the Vaults Bar is a favourite rendezvous for lovers of real ale. Comfortable, well-kept bedrooms have handsome pine furniture and TVs. No under-fives overnight.

## Stony Stratford *(B & B)* — *Cock Hotel*

72 High Street · *Buckinghamshire* · Map 5 B2
Milton Keynes (0908) 562109

*Free House*
*Landlords* Mr & Mrs D. P. Hoskins

**BEDROOMS 19 Grade 2 £A**
Hook Norton Best Bitter; Adnams Best Bitter; Wadworths 6X; Carlsberg Hof. *Real ale*

Four attractively furnished modern bedrooms with smart tiled bathrooms have recently been added to the accommodation at this agreeable old coaching inn, near neighbour of the Bull and existing on this site for five and a half centuries. Other rooms are comfortably old-fashioned; all have televisions. The public bar leads to a lovely garden with pretty shrubs and flower boxes. **Family pub**

## Stopham Bridge *(Food)* — *White Hart*

Near Pulborough · *West Sussex* · Map 6 B4
Pulborough (079 82) 3321

*Brewery* Whitbread
*Landlords* William & Elizabeth Bryce
Back bacon & mushroom sandwich £1.10
Daily special with fresh vegetables £1.75
(Last order 10pm)
Whitbread Best Bitter, Best Mild, Strong Country Bitter; Flowers Bitter; Guinness; Heineken; Stella Artois. *Real ale*

William and Elizabeth Bryce tempt customers to this attractive old pub on the river Arun with a simple menu of wholesome bar snacks. As well as sandwiches, filled jacket potatoes and nourishing dishes like cannelloni and grilled jumbo sausages, there is a daily special such as tasty cod pie topped with parsley-speckled pastry and served with nicely cooked vegetables. Garden. **Family pub**

## Stourbridge *(B & B)* — *Talbot Hotel*

High Street · *West Midlands* · Map 7 D1
Stourbridge (0384) 394350

*Brewery* Wolverhampton & Dudley
*Landlord* Mr Mark Chatterton

**BEDROOMS 23 Grades 1 & 2 £B**
Bank's Bitter, Mild; Guinness; Harp; Kronenbourg; cider. *Real ale*

This 500-year-old coaching inn in the town centre offers a warm welcome and good accommodation. Five bars provide plenty of choice for the thirsty, and in fine weather the covered courtyard comes into its own. Most bedrooms are furnished in a neat modern style, though antiques feature in two of them; all rooms have TVs and tea-makers, seven their own bathrooms.
**Family pub**

## Stow Bardolph *(Food)* ★ — *Hare Arms*

Near Downham Market · *Norfolk* · Map 5 C1
Downham Market (0366) 382229

*Brewery* Greene King
*Landlords* Mr & Mrs D. P. McManus

Steak & mushroom pie £1.95 Stilton & bacon soup 80p (No bar food Sun & eves)
Greene King Abbot Ale, IPA, Mild; Kronenbourg; Guinness; Harp; Taunton cider. *Real ale*

The lunchtime bar snacks are simple, wholesome and absolutely delicious at this homely gabled inn, run in the most friendly fashion by the McManuses. Generously filled sandwiches, ploughman's and salads are excellent cold fare, and the blackboard proclaims the day's soup – our turkey and vegetable was packed full of good things – and hot specials like lamb curry or super steak and mushroom pie. Lovely sweets, too. Garden. **Family pub**

## Stow-on-the-Wold *(B & B)* — *Royalist Hotel*

Digbeth Street · *Gloucestershire* · Map 5 A2
Cotswold (0451) 30670

*Free House*
*Landlords* Mr & Mrs E. J. Hardman

**BEDROOMS 13 Grades 1 & 2 £A** (No dogs)
Wadworth's 6X; Worthington Best Bitter; Flower's Original; Whitbread Trophy; Heineken; Carlsberg Export; cider. *Real ale*

Behind the 17th-century façade of this cosy hostelry are a thousand years of history. Open log fires warm the bars and lounge, and the bedrooms (most with private facilities) are centrally heated. Some rooms are splendidly old-fashioned in character, while the four in the annexe are functionally modern; all have tea-makers and TVs. No under-fives overnight. Garden. **Family pub**

## Stowe Green *(Food, B & B)* — *Travellers Rest Inn*

St Briavels, Near Coleford · *Gloucestershire*
Map 7 D2
Dean (0594) 530424
*Free House*
*Landlord* Mr C. Choremi
**BEDROOMS 3 Grade 2 £C** (No dogs)
Moussaka £3.30 Seafood salad £2.80 (Last order 10.30pm)
Bass; Toby Bitter; Stones Bitter; Worthington Best Bitter; Carling Black Label; Tennent's Extra; cider. *Real ale*

Lasagne, moussaka and spicy sausages are regular favourites at this secluded pub situated between St Briavels and Coleford, and there are savoury pies, the occasional fresh Wye salmon if you're lucky and a weekend carvery. Also sandwiches and salads, plus soups in winter. Three simple, well-kept bedrooms share a nice bathroom and separate shower. Pub closed Wednesday, accommodation closed 1 week Christmas. Garden. **Family pub**

## Stratford-upon-Avon *(Food)* — *Slug & Lettuce*

38 Guild Street · *Warwickshire* · Map 5 A2
Stratford-upon-Avon (0789) 299700

*Free House*
*Landlord* Mr Mark Coles

Mushrooms baked with bacon & garlic £2.25
Ragout of beef £3.25 (Last order 10pm)
Wadworth's 6X, IPA; Arkell's Best Bitter; Simpkiss Bitter; Guinness; Tuborg; Taunton cider. *Real ale*

Don't let the name put you off – the food is excellent at this pleasant, well-run pub. A blackboard menu in the panelled bar offers tempting dishes ranging from creamy soups and hot bacon sandwiches to barbecued pork casserole and our super baked chicken breast with avocado and cream cheese. Delicious sweets include chocolate mousse and a lovely sticky treacle tart. Terrace. **Family pub**

## Stuckton *(Food)* ★ — *Three Lions Inn*

Stuckton Road, near Fordingbridge
*Hampshire* · Map 6 A4
Fordingbridge (0425) 52489

*Brewery* Eldridge Pope
*Landlord* Karl Wadsack
Soufflé beignet Aida £1.85 Avocado seafood jambalaya £2.90 (Last order 9.15pm. No bar food Sun eve, Tues lunch & all Mon)
Eldridge Pope Royal Oak, Dorset IPA Dorchester Bitter; Faust. *Real ale*

It's best to book a table at this cosy pub to sample Karl Wadsack's brilliantly eclectic cooking. He borrows and blends ideas from all parts of the globe, creating wonderful dishes like rich game soup, herby Cumberland sausage with pungent sauerkraut and gingery pork fillet, to name but a few. Sweets too are out of this world. A la carte evening menu. Closed Feb, 1 wk Easter, last wk July, 1st wk Aug, 1 wk Sept–Oct & 1 wk Christmas.

## Studham *(Food)* — *Bell Inn*

Dunstable Road · *Bedfordshire* · Map 5 B2
Whipsnade (0582) 872460

*Brewery* Benskins
*Landlords* Ann & Ronald Harris

King-size sausages & chips £1.65 Steak & kidney pie £2.50 (Last order 9.45pm)
Benskins Bitter; Ind Coope Burton Ale, John Bull Bitter, Double Diamond; Guinness; Löwenbräu. *Real ale*

This friendly pub of traditional mien fits in well with its peaceful village setting. A straightforward bar menu featuring dishes like pâté, scampi or chicken in the basket is enlivened by an unusually varied selection of sausages – garlic, onion, apple, Cumberland – as well as flavoursome quiche and fresh, crisp salads. There are plenty of tables in the garden for fine weather eating and drinking.

## Surbiton *(Food)* — *Oak*

Maple Road · *Surrey* · Map 6 C3
01-399 1662

*Brewery* Charringtons
*Landlord* Mr Andy Christie

Coronation turkey £2.75 Apricot & lamb pie £2.20 (No bar food eves or Sun)
Charrington IPA; Bass; Guinness; Carling Black Label; Tennent's Extra; Taunton cider. *Real ale*

An attractive corner pub with one bar for drinking and another, a few steps down, with an eye-catching display of hot and cold dishes. Almost everything is made on the premises, and we very much enjoyed mildly curried coronation turkey and a pork hot pot with good lean meat and nicely browned potato topping. Soups and sweets in winter. Garden.

## Sutton *(Food)* — *Anne Arms*

Suttonfield Road, Near Doncaster
*South Yorkshire* · Map 4 C3
Doncaster (0302) 700500

*Brewery* John Smiths
*Landlords* Mr & Mrs J. R. Simm

Rabbit pie £1.50 Roast pork £1.50 (Last order 10.15pm. No bar food Sun)
John Smith's Bitter, Lager; Guinness; Hofmeister. *Real ale*

Mrs Simm's flavoursome rabbit pie is typical of the robust fare that brings the locals flocking to this ivy-clad village pub. The daily roast is another great favourite, and there are sandwiches, ploughman's and salads for smaller appetites. Sweets include traditional winter treats like treacle tart and jam roly-poly The beamed bar is warm and cosy, and there's a pleasant garden complete with gnome colony.

**Family pub**

## Sutton Howgrave *(Food)* — *White Dog Inn*

Near Ripon · *North Yorkshire* · Map 4 C2
Melmerby (076 584) 404

*Free House*
*Landlords* Pat & Basil Bagnall

Venison casserole £3.10 Chilli con carne £1.95 (No bar food eves)
Webster's Pennine Bitter; Carlsberg Hof.

In a sleepy village just off the B6267, this cottagy little pub is a charming setting for some very good lunchtime bar snacks. French onion soup is a great favourite, and other choices include prawn and ham salads, sirloin steak and a really hearty venison casserole. Sandwiches, too, and some tempting sweets. Closed Sun eve, Mon and 1st 2 weeks February. Garden.

## Sutton-u-Whitestonecliffe *(Food)* *Whitestonecliffe Hotel*

Near Thirsk · *North Yorkshire* · Map 4 C2
Thirsk (0845) 597271

*Free House*
*Landlords* Mr & Mrs A. Bartle
Pork fillet in cream & cider sauce £2.35
Gammon with egg & pineapple £2.35 (Last order 10pm)
Webster's Yorkshire Bitter; Younger's Scotch Bitter; Pennine Bitter; Guinness; Foster's; Carlsberg Export; cider. *Real ale*

The Bartles' appealing white-painted pub is building up an enthusiastic local following with its excellent bar snacks. Soups are nourishing and flavoursome, home-cooked ham makes lovely sandwiches and salads, and there are always interesting specials like fresh halibut, roast pheasant or fillet of pork in a creamy cider sauce. The sweets are just as tempting: try the sherry trifle or golden-topped blackberry and apple pie. Closed Monday lunch.

## Sutton-upon-Derwent *(Food)* *St Vincent Arms*

Near York, North Yorkshire · *Humberside*
Map 4 C3
Elvington (090 485) 349
*Free House*
*Landlords* Mr & Mrs R. F. Tyson
Steak, kidney & mushroom pie with vegetables £3.10 Prawn & sweetcorn quiche with salad & chips £1.75 (Last order 10pm)
Cameron's Best Bitter; Theakston's Best Bitter, Old Peculier; Younger's Scotch Bitter, IPA, Mild; Guinness; Carlsberg Hof. *Real ale*

Hospitality flows freely at Dick and Jean Tyson's handsome old timbered pub, whose cosy panelled bars offer an enterprising menu of well-prepared snacks. The super steak, kidney and mushroom pie is a perennial favourite, while other popular choices range from soup, salads and sandwiches to flavoursome liver and bacon pâté, American-style hamburgers and sirloin steaks. Less choice Sunday lunch. Garden. **Family pub**

## Talkin *(Food, B & B)* *Hare & Hounds Inn*

Near Brampton · *Cumbria* · Map 3 B1
Brampton (069 77) 3456

*Free House*
*Landlords* Les & Joan Stewart

**BEDROOMS 5 Grade 1 £C** (No dogs)
Steak £4.45 Gammon £2.45 (Last order 9pm)
Theakston's Best Bitter, Old Peculier, XB; Younger's Tartan; Drybrough Heavy; Guinness; Carlsberg; cider. *Real ale*

Homely and hospitable, this 200-year-old black and white inn stands in the centre of a quiet Cumbrian village. Bar snacks are a popular attraction, ranging from rolls and burgers to filled jacket potatoes, fish dishes and succulent steaks. Comfortable bedrooms, including two in the cottage annexe, are attractively furnished, and modern bathrooms are well equipped. Garden. **Family pub**

## Tarporley *(B & B)* *Swan Hotel*

50 High Street · *Cheshire* · Map 3 B4
Tarporley (082 93) 2411

*Brewery* Greenall Whitley
*Landlords* June & Bernard McQueen

**BEDROOMS 9 Grade 2 £B** (No dogs)
Greenall Whitley Bitter, Mild; Guinness; Grünhalle. *Real ale*

The facade is early Georgian, but some of the buildings at the back of the McQueens' imposing inn date from Tudor times. The Old Kitchen Bar, with its open fire, flagstone floor and burnished copperware, is a favourite local gathering place, and there's also the cosy Den Bar. Cheerfully decorated bedrooms, all with central heating, fitted carpets, TVs and tea-makers, are kept in apple-pie order.

## Tarrant Monkton *(Food)* — *Langton Arms*

Near Blandford Forum · *Dorset* · Map 8 D3
Tarrant Hinton (025 889) 225

*Free House*
*Landlords* Chris & Diane Goodinge

Steak & kidney pudding £2 Pancakes filled with jam 80p (Last order 10.15pm)
Bass, Toby; Worthington 'E', Best Bitter; Guinness; Carling Black Label; Taunton cider. *Real ale*

The prospect of cocktails, skittles and excellent food lures visitors to this out-of-the-way thatched pub. Start with a bowl of home-made soup (perhaps lentil and onion or mulligatawny), salmon mousse or a hot steak sandwich, and go on to chicken and vegetable curry, steak and kidney pudding or egg and mushroom mornay. There are also grills in the evening. Creamy gooseberry fool and orange sorbet are typical sweets. Garden.

## Teddington *(Food, B & B)* — *Clarence Hotel*

Park Road · *Middlesex* · Map 6 B3
01-977 8025

*Free House*
*Landlords* Mr R. J. Currall & Mrs R. A. Currall
**BEDROOMS 15 Grade 2 £B**
Steak & kidney pie £2 Turkey fillet with mushroom sauce £2 (Last order 10.30pm)
Wadworth's 6X; Ben Truman; Marston's Pedigree; Boddington's Bitter; Yorkshire Bitter; Guinness; Foster's; cider. *Real ale*

A cheerful, welcoming place, where the cooking is homely and portions are designed for hearty appetites. Tasty hot choices include succulent lamb chops, roast chicken and mixed grills, served with fresh vegetables, with perhaps apple and blackcurrant pie to finish. There are sandwiches, ploughman's and salads too. Traditional Sunday lunch. Bright bedrooms with tea-makers offer simple modern furnishings. **Family pub** (lunchtime)

## Teffont Magna *(Food)* — *Black Horse Inn*

Near Salisbury · *Wiltshire* · Map 6 A3
Teffont (072 276) 251

*Brewery* Ushers
*Landlords* Colin & Jacqui Carter

Pork Marengo £3 Steamed pudding 90p (Last order 10pm)
Bass; Usher's Founder's Ale, Best Bitter, Triple Crown; Watneys Mild; Ben Truman; Guinness; cider. *Real ale*

Rustic charm abounds in this friendly old village inn, where Colin Carter looks after the bars while his wife Jacqui attends to culinary matters. Succulent Wiltshire ham is one of her most popular offerings, with lasagne, pan-fried trout and steak and kidney pie high on the list of favourites. Sandwiches too. Desserts include fruit pies and delicious home-made ice cream. Patio and garden. **Family pub**

## Tenterden *(B & B)* — *White Lion Hotel*

High Street · *Kent* · Map 6 C3
Tenterden (058 06) 2921

*Free House*
*Landlord* Mr Gordon Wylde

**BEDROOMS 12 Grades 1 & 2 £A**
Whitbread Fremlins Bitter; Shepherd Neame Invicta; Guinness; Hurliman; cider. *Real ale*

Right in the heart of town, this handsome old coaching inn provides overnight accommodation of a high standard, including four characterful rooms with four-posters. All rooms have colour TVs and tea-makers and all except the simpler singles at the rear have their own well-appointed bath or shower room. There's a mellow beamed bar and a quiet upstairs residents' lounge. **Family pub**

## Terrington *(B & B)* — *Bay Horse Inn*

Near York · *North Yorkshire* · Map 4 C2
Coneysthorpe (065 384) 255

*Free House*
*Landlord* Grace Hoggard

**BEDROOMS 3 Grade 2 £C**
John Smith's Bitter; Younger's Scotch Bitter; Tetley Bitter; Guinness; Hofmeister; Carlsberg Hof; cider.

Hospitality comes naturally to Grace Hoggard, who takes good care of visitors to her lovely little country inn some 16 miles from York. A well-stoked fire keeps winter customers warm in the rustic front bar, while double glazing keeps the chill from the spotlessly kept modern bedrooms. These all have TVs and tea-makers and share a single neat bathroom. Terrific breakfasts. Garden. Closed Monday lunchtime except Bank Holidays. **Family pub**

## Testcombe *(Food)* — *Mayfly*

Near Stockbridge · *Hampshire* · Map 6 A3
Chilbolton (026 474) 283

*Brewery* Whitbread
*Landlord* Mrs Tuckett
Quiches £1.75 Chicken tandoori £2.45 (Last order 9.30pm. No bar food Sun & Mon eves)
Whitbread Strong Country Bitter, Pompey Royal, Best Bitter; Guinness; Stella Artois; Taunton cider. *Real ale*

The garden overlooking the river Test draws plenty of summer visitors to this charming red-brick pub, and tasty bar food is an additional attraction. Mrs Tuckett's imaginative menu offers delicious soups, quiches and cold meats to go with salads such as tomatoes with fennel dressing, and there are a few hot dishes like game pie or chicken tandoori. Nice traditional sweets, too, plus good cheeses.

## Tetbury *(Food, B & B)* ★ — *Gentle Gardener*

Long Street · *Gloucestershire* · Map 7 D2
Tetbury (0666) 52884

*Free House*
*Landlords* Mr & Mrs W. Knock
**BEDROOMS 5 Grade 2 £C**
Vegetable pie £1.65 Lemon Cotswold 80p (No bar food eves)
Usher's Founders Ale; Archer's Best Bitter; Cirencester Bitter; Ben Truman Bitter; Guinness; Carlsberg; cider. *Real ale*

A handsome old coaching inn, where super lunchtime snacks can be enjoyed in the comfortable bar or out in the courtyard. Filled rolls and ploughman's platters are popular quick bites, or you could start with flavour-packed celeriac soup and go on to duck pancake with cheese and apple or splendid spinach roulade. Five simple, spotless bedrooms share a large bathroom. Garden. **Family pub**

## Thames Ditton *(Food)* — *Crown Inn*

Summer Road · *Surrey* · Map 6 B3
01-398 2376
*Brewery* Watneys
*Landlords* John, Marion & Bob Wilder
Cheese salad £2.25 Beef & horseradish casserole & vegetables £2.35 (Last order 9.45pm)
Watneys Stag Bitter; Webster's Yorkshire Bitter; Hammerton's Porter; Coombes Bitter; Ruddles County; Guinness; Foster's; Carlsberg; cider. *Real ale*

Visitors to this convivial pub can look forward to a warm welcome and some splendid home cooking. The Wilders make their own pickles and chutneys to go with ploughman's and curries. Their menu also features soup (perhaps chicken and leek), mammoth portions of chunky steak and kidney pie served with heaps of fresh vegetables, plus burgers, salads, grills and sandwiches (plain or toasted). And to finish there are super fruit pies.

## Thetford *(B & B)* — *Historical Thomas Paine Hotel*

White Hart Street · *Norfolk* · Map 5 C2
Thetford (0842) 5631

*Free House*
*Landlords* Mr & Mrs T. Muir

**BEDROOMS 14 Grade 1 £A**
Adnams Original; Tolly Cobbold Original; Stones Bitter; Toby Bitter; Guinness; Carlsberg Hof; Tennent's Extra; Taunton cider. *Real ale*

An awning-covered walkway leads from the car park to the entrance of this attractive white-painted hotel, reputedly the birthplace of the political pamphleteer Thomas Paine in 1737. The spacious Franklin Bar is a pleasant spot for relaxing, and there's a cosy little residents' lounge. Comfortable bedrooms, most with private facilities, have smart modern furnishings, colour TVs, radios and tea-makers. Terrace.

**Family pub**

## Thurnham *(Food)* — *Black Horse*

Pilgrims Way · *Kent* · Map 6 C3
Maidstone (0622) 37185

*Brewery* Whitbread
*Landlords* Mr & Mrs Les Broughton

Madras lamb curry £2.50 Smoked turkey open sandwich £1 (Last order 9pm)
Whitbread Best Bitter; Fremlins Bitter; Tusker; Guinness; Heineken; Stella Artois; cider. *Real ale*

Once a hostelry on the old pilgrim's route to Canterbury, this popular pub attracts today's travellers with a selection of simple, well-prepared bar food. Crisp salads and tastily topped open sandwiches for quick snacks, with sausage, egg and chips, lasagne and a good spicy Madras lamb curry among the more substantial hot dishes. Soup in winter, sandwiches only at weekends. There's a pleasant beer garden.

## Tichborne *(Food)* — *Tichborne Arms*

Near Alresford · *Hampshire* · Map 6 B4
Alresford (096 273) 3760

*Free House*
*Landlord* Mrs J. M. Salter
Smoked mackerel pâté £1.15 Spare ribs with barbecue sauce £2.25 (Last order 10pm)
Courage Best Bitter, Directors Bitter; Wadworth's 6X; Marston's Pedigree; Guinness; cider. *Real ale*

Standing in a pretty Hampshire village surrounded by meadows and farmland, this attractive thatched pub is a most agreeable spot to pause for a snack. Everything is carefully prepared by Mrs Salter: salads, sandwiches, jacket potatoes with a choice of eight fillings, superb smoked mackerel pâté, along with popular daily specials like spare ribs or chicken curry. Nice sweets, too. Garden.

## Timberscombe *(B & B)* — *Lion Inn*

Near Dunster · *Somerset* · Map 8 C3
Timberscombe (064 384) 243

*Free House*
*Landlords* Mr & Mrs G. P. Christie

**BEDROOMS 5 Grade 2 £C** (No dogs)
Usher's Triple Crown, Best Bitter, Country; Younger's Scotch Bitter; McEwan's Export; Carlsberg; Taunton cider. *Real ale*

This charming whitewashed village pub stands in picturesque hunting country on the edge of Exmoor National Park. The main bar is a cosy, convivial spot, and next to it is a games room where children are welcome. Neatly kept bedrooms have practical modern furnishings and pretty floral duvets, and they share an up-to-date bathroom with shower. Terrace.

## Timperley *(Food)* — *Hare & Hounds*

1 Wood Lane, Near Altrincham · *Cheshire*
Map 3 B3
061-980 5299

*Brewery* Marston, Thompson & Evershed
*Landlords* Mr & Mrs J. B. W. Cunningham

Navarin of lamb £2 Poached fresh salmon £2 (Last order 10.30pm. No bar food Sun)
Marston's Pedigree, Mild, Burton Bitter; Guinness; Heineken; cider. *Real ale*

The French chef's magnificent cold table draws the lunchtime crowds to this eye-catching pub. Help yourself to cooked meats and fish, quiches and delicious salads like courgette and cauliflower or avocado and grapefruit, or go for one of the hot specials such as pork chops in cider. Do leave room for a sweet (we noted a light crème caramel) or a choice of fine cheeses. Sandwiches only evenings. Barbecues are a popular feature. **Family pub**

## Toddington *(Food)* — *Pheasant*

Near Cheltenham · *Gloucestershire* · Map 5 A2
Toddington (024 269) 271

*Brewery* Hall
*Landlord* Mr David Strathern
Game pie £2.50 Aloo gosht curry £2.50 (Last order 9pm. No bar food Tues eve in winter)
Hall's Harvest Bitter; Ind Coope Burton Ale; Tetley's Bitter; Ruddles County; Wadworth's 6X; Guinness; Löwenbräu; cider. *Real ale*

Only prime fresh ingredients go into the simple bar snacks that are a feature of this well-run pub. David Strathern uses high-quality beef for his excellent burgers, he grows his own vegetables, he makes his own soups and he grinds the spices that go into daily specials like his very popular curries. And the light, airy puff-pastry on the apple pie? Home-made of course! **Family pub**

## Tong *(B & B)* — *Bell Inn*

Newport Road, Near Shifnal · *Shropshire*
Map 7 D1
Weston-under-Lizard (095 276) 210

*Brewery* Wolverhampton & Dudley
*Landlords* Mr & Mrs Silvester

**BEDROOMS 3 Grade 1 £C**
Banks's Best Bitter, Best Mild; Kronenbourg; Harp; cider. *Real ale*

Francis and Valerie Silvester keep this red-brick roadside pub in perfect condition, both inside and out. Drinkers enjoy the homely atmosphere in the beamed bar, while overnight visitors can slumber soundly in the simple, traditionally furnished bedrooms and look forward to a hearty breakfast. Children under seven not accommodated overnight. Large, well-tended garden. Rooms closed 1 week Christmas.

## Toot Hill *(Food)* — *Green Man*

Near Ongar · *Essex* · Map 6 C3
North Weald (037 882) 2255

*Brewery* Watneys
*Landlord* Mr John Roads
Mexican chicken with vegetables £3.95 Lamb cutlets with vegetables £3.95 (Last order 10.15pm)
Webster's Yorkshire Bitter; Wilsons Great Northern Bitter; Ben Truman; Coombes Bitter; Guinness; Carlsberg; cider. *Real ale*

John Roads certainly has green fingers: both his front patio and the garden at the back are delightful places to sample his selection of champagnes, and the flower-bedecked bar is a charming setting in which to enjoy a well-prepared snack. Soups are made with home-grown vegetables, and main courses range from appetising ham salad to lamb cutlets, moussaka or beef Stroganoff. Salads and basket meals, too, and a roast lunch on Sunday.

## Tormarton *(B & B)* — *Compass Inn*

Near Badminton · *Avon* · Map 7 D2
Badminton (045 421) 242

*Free House*
*Landlords* Monyard family

**BEDROOMS 11 Grades 1 & 2 £B**
Bass; Wadworth's 6X, Old Timer (winter only); Archer's Village Bitter; Younger's Tartan; Carlsberg Hof. *Real ale*

Motorists leaving the M4 at junction 18 can set a course for this efficiently run inn, which offers good, comfortable accommodation. The best bedrooms are the spacious ones in the modern wing, which have spotless up-to-date bathrooms; six rooms in the main building are more compact. All have radios, TVs and tea-makers. There are four traditional Cotswold-stone bars, plus a glass-roofed orangery. Garden.
**Family pub** (lunchtime)

## Towersey *(Food)* — *Three Horseshoes*

Chinnor Road, Near Thame · *Oxfordshire*
Map 6 B3
Thame (084 421) 2322

*Brewery* Aylesbury
*Landlords* Mr & Mrs Smith

King prawn salad £4.30 Tandoori chicken £4.30
(Last order 9.30pm)
ABC Bitter; Everards Tiger; Ind Coope Pale Mild; Guinness; Skol; Carlsberg; cider. *Real ale*

The range and quality of the bar snacks are both admirable at this simple village inn. An eye-catching cold buffet is a popular feature in summer, and hot choices include evergreens like pâté, shepherd's pie and beef curry, plus more unusual items such as haddock cooked with coriander in a garlicky parsley sauce. Also vegetarian dishes and some nice sweets. Garden. **Family pub**

## Trebarwith *(Food, B & B)* — *Mill House Inn*

Near Tintagel · *Cornwall* · Map 8 B4
Camelford (0840) 770200

*Free House*
*Landlords* Mr & Mrs H. D. Thomas
**BEDROOMS 9 Grade 1 £A**
Chicken curry £2.50 Beef Stroganoff £2.50
(Last order 10pm)
Flower's Original, IPA; Younger's Tartan; Guinness; Heineken; Stella Artois; cider. *Real ale*

The Thomases are friendly, welcoming hosts at this cosy, slate-built inn situated off the B3263. Tasty snacks are served in the bars, from soup and sandwiches to pizza, chicken curry and home-made puddings. Overnight accommodation (no children under ten) comprises nine attractively decorated bedrooms, all with TVs and private facilities. There's a charming residents' lounge with antique furniture. Garden. **Family pub**

## Trotton — *Keepers Arms*

Hanging baskets and flower tubs make a nice splash of colour outside this welcoming roadside pub, which started life about 150 years ago when a blacksmith decided to open an ale house for his customers. There are fine views over the downs, and the bar is smartly traditional. Closed Monday.

Near Petersfield, Hampshire · *West Sussex* · Map 6 B4
Midhurst (073 081) 3724
*Free House* *Landlord* Mr C. S. Machin
John Smith Yorkshire Bitter; Badger Best Bitter; Huntsman Royal Oak, Dorchester; Ballards Best Bitter; Guinness; cider. *Real ale*

## Troutbeck *(Food, B & B)* — *Mortal Man*

Near Windermere · *Cumbria* · Map 3 B2
Ambleside (0966) 33193

*Free House*
*Landlord* C. J. Poulsom
**BEDROOMS 15 Grade 1 £A+**
Cumberland hot pot £1.50 Potted shrimps & salad £1.50 (No bar food eves)
Scottish & Newcastle Chieftain Mild, Newcastle Bitter; Guinness; Harp; Taunton cider.

This famous old inn enjoys a position of great beauty in a magnificent valley that sweeps down to Lake Windermere. Lunchtime in the cosy beamed bars brings simple, tasty snacks ranging from sandwiches and pâté to omelettes, cottage pie and a daily casserole. Ten of the comfortable, traditionally furnished bedrooms have private bathrooms. No under-fives overnight. Closed mid Nov–mid Feb. Garden.

## Tunbridge Wells *(Food)* — *Royal Wells Inn*

Mount Ephraim · *Kent* · Map 6 C3
Tunbridge Wells (0892) 23414

*Free House*
*Landlords* Robert & David Sloan

Steak & kidney pie £2 Toad in the hole £1.75 (Last order 10.30pm. No bar food Sun lunch)
Shepherd Neame Masterbrew; Courage Directors Bitter; Guinness; Hofmeister; Kronenbourg; Taunton cider. *Real ale*

Robert Sloan offers a tempting and imaginative menu in the large, elegant bar of this popular Regency inn. Dishes like vegetable terrine or blanquette of lamb provide tasty alternatives to the more familiar steak and kidney pie and toad in the hole. There's also a cold buffet at lunchtime, and a selection of gorgeous sweets like raspberry Pavlova.

**Family pub**

## Turville *(Food)* — *Bull & Butcher*

Near Henley-on-Thames, Oxfordshire
*Buckinghamshire* · Map 6 B3
Turville Heath (049 163) 283

*Brewery* Brakspear
*Landlords* Mr & Mrs Cowles

Cold seafood platter £3.50 Treacle tart 90p (Last order 10pm)
Brakspear's Bitter, Special, Old; Heineken. *Real ale*

Popular with car club enthusiasts (the landlord used to race saloons), this pleasant old village inn is a good stop for those in search of a simple, hearty snack. A soup usually heads the list of starters, followed perhaps by ploughman's, quiche or jacket potatoes (a winter favourite). Also daily specials (moussaka, steak & kidney pie), a summer cold buffet and nice sweets. Garden.

## Tutbury *(Food)* — *Ye Olde Dog & Partridge*

High Street · *Staffordshire* · Map 4 C4
Tutbury (0283) 813030

*Free House*
*Landlords* Mr & Mrs D. J. Martindale

Hot roast beef £4 Game pie £3.50 (Last order 10pm)
Worthington 'E'; Marston's Pedigree, Premium Bitter, Low 'C'; cider. *Real ale*

Succulent hot and cold joints, including boiled ham and tender sirloin, are the highlight of the bar food served in this fine old half-timbered coaching inn. There's also soup, sandwiches and popular daily specials such as game pie, Cumberland sausage and faggots with mushy peas. Patio and garden. *For accommodation see Egon Ronay's Lucas Hotel & Restaurant Guide 1985.*

**Family pub**

## Twickenham *(Food)* — *Prince Albert*

30 Hampton Road · *Middlesex* · Map 6 B3
01-894 3963

*Brewery* Fuller, Smith & Turner
*Landlords* Mr & Mrs B. Lunn
Pork with lemon cream sauce & vegetables £2 Chilli con carne £1.90 (Last order 9pm. No bar food Sun lunch)
Fuller's London Pride, ESB, Chiswick Bitter; Tennent's Extra; Guinness; Heineken. *Real ale*

Tasty lunchtime fare is the big draw in this friendly Victorian pub, where a bevy of ladies produces a wide range of hearty dishes from ham pâté, quiche and mushrooms bourguignon to appetising finnan haddock pancakes and liver and bacon. Nice fresh vegetables accompany, and there are delicious sweets like strawberry fool. Sandwiches only in the evening. Pretty garden with an aviary, rabbit and ducks.

## Twickenham *(Food)* — *White Swan*

Riverside · *Middlesex* · Map 6 B3
01-892 2166

*Brewery* Watney Combe Reid
*Landlord* Shirley Sutton

Hot pot £2.40 Pâté maison & salad £2 (No bar food Sun)
Watney's London Bitter; Manns IPA; Webster's Yorkshire Bitter; Guinness; Foster's; Carlsberg; cider. *Real ale*

Right beside the river, this cheerful pub is especially busy at lunchtime, when Shirley Sutton's excellent snacks are on offer. Delicious home-made soup makes a good start, and you can go on to dishes like steak and kidney pudding, chops in cider or a hearty beef and vegetable hot pot. Rolls only in the evening. Sunday lunch only by prior arrangement. Garden. **Family pub**

## Ufford *(Food)* — *Ye Olde White Hart Inn*

Near Stamford · *Lincolnshire* · Map 5 B1
Stamford (0780) 740250

*Brewery* Home
*Landlords* Marion & Nigel Adams

Bobotie £2.50 Pork & apricot tiffin £2.95 (Last order 8pm. No bar food Sat eve, all Sun & Mon eve)
Home Traditional Bitter; Skol. *Real ale*

Everything is appetising and carefully prepared at this friendly village pub. There's a colourful cold buffet in the cosy lounge bar, featuring home-cooked meats, pâtés and pies. If you want something hot, there are interesting dishes like spicy bobotie or pork and apricot tiffin. Soup, fresh local trout and ploughman's are other choices, with enjoyable sweets like cherry pie to finish. Patio and garden.

## Umberleigh *(B & B)* — *Rising Sun*

*Devon* · Map 8 C3
High Bickington (0769) 60447

*Owners* Wessex Hosts
*Landlord* Mr M. A. F. Tate

**BEDROOMS 8 Grade 1 £A**
Usher's Country Bitter, Triple Crown; Carlsberg.

Salmon and trout fishing on the river Taw brings a steady stream of anglers to stay at this pleasant country inn, whose little bars are full of fishy mementoes and chatter. Comfortable bedrooms, four with well-appointed private bathrooms, have pretty coordinated fabrics, modern units and tea-makers. Very good breakfasts. No children under six overnight. Accommodation closed mid Oct–1 March.

## Upper Basildon *(Food)* — *Beehive Inn*

Near Pangbourne · *Berkshire* · Map 6 B3
Upper Basildon (049 162) 269

*Free House*
*Landlord* Mr K. Peachey
Mexican baked potato £2.50 Seafood salad £2.75 (Last order 10pm. No bar food Sun eve)
Morland's Best Bitter, Ordinary; Hall's Harvest Bitter; Heineken; Stella Artois; cider. *Real ale*

Spuds, in some 20 different guises, are the speciality of this popular yellow-painted pub facing the village green. From an intriguing list of names like the Spanish Armada, Frenchman and Fisherman we selected the Indian – a huge baked potato filled with curried diced turkey and mango chutney, accompanied by a crisp green salad. Hot prawns in garlic butter make a tasty alternative. Garden. **Family pub**

## Upper Basildon *(Food)* — *Red Lion*

Near Pangbourne · *Berkshire* · Map 6 B3
Upper Basildon (049 162) 234

*Brewery* Courage
*Landlord* Mr Ken Woodward

Savoury omelette £1.60 Lasagne £1.85 (Last order 9.30pm. No bar food Sun)
Courage Best Bitter, Directors Bitter, John Courage; Guinness; Kronenbourg; Taunton cider. *Real ale*

The Woodwards do their own cooking at this welcoming red-brick village pub. In the neat, homely bar decorated with horse brasses and china plates, you can enjoy such tasty offerings as beef bourguignon served on a bed of rice mixed with mushrooms and baby onions or perhaps lasagne, gammon with Cumberland sauce or a fish dish. Freshly cut sandwiches and basket meals are also available. Garden.

## Upper Layham *(Food)* — *Marquis of Cornwallis*

Near Hadleigh · *Suffolk* · Map 5 D2
Hadleigh (0473) 822051

*Brewery* Ind Coope
*Landlords* John & Nicky Moss

Smoked salmon mousse £1.50 Prawn curry £3 (Last order 10pm)
Ind Coope Bitter, Double Diamond, Mild; Guinness; Skol; cider. *Real ale*

Crackling fires keep winter at bay in the oak-beamed bars of this friendly pub, where Nicky Moss offers a menu of capably prepared and attractively presented snacks. Her smoked salmon mousse is a finely flavoured, light-textured little masterpiece, and other choices range from soups and sandwiches to salads, steaks and pan-fried gammon. Nice sweets include old-fashioned sherry trifle and delicious raspberry parfait. Garden.

## Upper Oddington *(Food, B & B)* — *Horse & Groom Inn*

Near Stow-on-the-Wold · *Gloucestershire*
Map 5 A2
Cotswold (0451) 30584
*Free House*
*Landlords* Mr & Mrs G. Wilmot
**BEDROOMS 5 Grade 1 £B** (No dogs)
Cold buffet £3.25 Gloucestershire sausage £1.25 (No bar food eves)
Wadworth's Devizes Bitter, 6X; Worthington Best Bitter; Younger's Tartan; Heineken; Tuborg; cider. *Real ale*

Standing a couple of miles outside Stow-on-the-Wold, the Wilmots' immaculate 16th-century inn is a good base for a tour of the Cotswolds. Centrally heated bedrooms with beams and rustic doors have pretty fabrics, modern furniture and private showers (one bath). Lunchtime snacks served in the delightfully old-world bars include delicious soup, ploughman's, a summer cold table and winter hot specials. Garden. **Family pub**

## Uttoxeter *(B & B)* — *White Hart Hotel*

Carter Street · *Staffordshire* · Map 5 A1
Uttoxeter (088 93) 2437

*Brewery* Allied
*Landlord* Mrs H. V. Porteous

**BEDROOMS 24 Grades 1 & 2 £A**
Ind Coope Bitter, Burton Ale, Double Diamond; Guinness; Skol; Löwenbräu; cider. *Real ale*

This town-centre hostelry is noted for its friendly atmosphere and comfortable accommodation. The best bedrooms (in the annexe) have modern darkwood furnishings, thick carpets and TVs; some rooms in the main building have splendid panelling and antique furniture, whereas others are more up to date. Spacious private bathrooms have lovely large baths. There's a roomy lounge bar and a cosy TV lounge. **Family pub**

## Walkern *(Food)* — *White Lion*

High Street, Near Stevenage · *Hertfordshire*
Map 5 C2
Walkern (043 886) 251
*Brewery* Greene King
*Landlords* Mr & Mrs M. J. Windebank
Steak & kidney pie £2.50 Chilli con carne £2.50 (Last order 10pm. No bar food Sun & Mon eves)
Greene King IPA, Abbot Ale, Mild; Guinness; Harp; Kronenbourg; Taunton cider. *Real ale*

Mr & Mrs Windebank both take a share of the cooking in this pleasant, traditionally styled pub, whose characterful beamed bars feature an interesting collection of old clocks. His lamb curry and her delicious steak and kidney pie have many admirers, and pâté, pepper steaks, fish and chips and appetising salads are other popular choices. Sweets include a splendid sherry trifle. Garden.

## Wall *(B & B)* — *Hadrian Inn*

Near Hexham · *Northumberland* · Map 4 C1
Humshaugh (043 481) 232

*Brewery* Vaux
*Landlords* Mr & Mrs Mellors

**BEDROOMS 9 Grades 1 & 2 £C**
Vaux Samson, Lorimers Scotch, Sunderland Ale; Guinness; Tuborg; Taunton cider. *Real ale*

This homely roadside inn stands about four miles north of Hexham in a village largely built with stones taken from nearby Hadrian's Wall. Bedrooms, which command attractive views, are furnished in a mixture of traditional and more modern styles; some have TVs and five have their own bathrooms. (No children under 12 overnight.) The foyer-lounge features some fine old prints, and the bar is characterful. Garden. **Family pub**

## Waltham on the Wolds *(Food, B & B)* — *Royal Horseshoes*

Melton Road, Near Melton Mowbray
*Leicestershire* · Map 4 D4
Waltham (066 478) 289

*Brewery* John Smith
*Landlords* Mr & Mrs Wigglesworth
**BEDROOMS 4 Grade 1 £B** (No dogs)
Cock-a-leekie 60p Steak & kidney pie £2.40 (Last order 9pm)
John Smith's Bitter, Chestnut Mild; Hofmeister; John Smith's Lager. *Real ale*

A tempting cold table catches the eye in this friendly village pub, where anything from pâté and prawns to turkey and tender beef Wellington can be enjoyed with a selection of fresh, crisp salads. There is plenty of hot choice, too, including soup, scampi and a Sunday roast. Neat, modern bedrooms in a converted outbuilding have TVs, tea-makers and carpeted bathrooms. Patio. **Family pub**

## Waltham St Lawrence *(Food)* — *Bell*

*Berkshire* · Map 6 B3

*Free House*
*Landlord* Mr R. Bristow

Steak & kidney pie £1.95 Welsh rarebit £1.10 (Last order 10pm. No bar food Sun & Mon eves)
Adnams Mild; Bitter; Arkell's Bitter; Guinness; Carlsberg; cider. *Real ale*

This is truly a village pub, in that since 1608 it has been owned by a trust on behalf of the village. The atmospheric beamed bars offer a good variety of tasty snacks, from warming bowls of soup to steak sandwiches made with French bread, shepherd's pie and garlicky mushroom pancakes. There's a cold table in summer; jacket potatoes are the only choice Sunday lunchtime. Garden.
**Family pub**

## Waltham St Lawrence *(Food)* — *Plough Inn*

West End · *Berkshire* · Map 6 B3
Twyford (0734) 340015

*Brewery* Morland
*Landlord* Mrs Beryl Boulton-Taylor

Calf's liver & bacon £3.50 Treacle tart £1 (Last order 9.30pm. No bar food Mon)
Morland's Best Bitter, Bitter, Pale Ale; Heineken. *Real ale*

Red-clothed tables in the lounge bar of this delightful old timbered pub make an inviting setting for Mrs Boulton-Taylor's superb home cooking. Cold meats include tender rare roast beef and succulent ham off the bone, with grills and steaks at lunch-time and fowl and venison dishes at night. Sweets are a special treat: maybe a treacle tart topped with almonds, or a fruit pie bursting with blackberry and apple. Garden.

## Wansford *(Food)* — *Haycock Inn*

Near Peterborough · *Cambridgeshire*
Map 5 B1
Stamford (0780) 782223

*Owners* Poste Hotels
*Landlords* Mr Richard Neale
Braised silverside & salads £4.95 Cheese fondue (for 2) £7 (Last order 10.30pm)
Ruddle's County, Bitter; Bass; Younger's Tartan; Stone's Bitter; Kestrel; Stella Artois; Taunton cider. *Real ale*

A 17th-century coaching inn standing in pleasant grounds by the river Nene. A superb cold buffet is a winning feature in the River lounge, where hot snacks include home-made soups, baked mussels and chunky chicken and ham in a creamy cheese sauce. To finish, try treacle pudding or scrumptious lemon meringue pie. Garden. *For accommodation see Egon Ronay's Lucas Hotel & Restaurant Guide 1985.*
**Family pub**

## Wanstrow *(Food)* — *King William IV*

Near Shepton Mallet · *Somerset* · Map 8 D3
Upton Noble (074 985) 247

*Brewery* Usher
*Landlords* Mr & Mrs J. Geen

Chilli con carne with crusty bread £2 Chicken curry with chips £2 (Last order 9pm. No bar food Wed eve)
Usher's Country Bitter, Best Bitter; Ben Truman; Guinness; Carlsberg; cider. *Real ale*

Mrs Geen's tasty bar snacks are a popular draw at this pleasant pub on the Bruton–Frome road. The menu's not a large one, concentrating on familiar favourites like sandwiches, salads, chilli con carne and chicken curry (served with crisp, golden chips). To finish, perhaps fruit meringue or some good Stilton. The bar features an interesting collection of artefacts from the farmer's, farrier's and cheesemaker's trades. Patio.

## Warenford *(Food)* — *Warenford Lodge*

Near Belford · *Northumberland* · Map 2 D4
Belford (066 83) 453

*Free House*
*Landlords* Ray & Marian Matthewman

Cheese & asparagus savoury £1.95 Grilled trout £2.70 (Last order 9.30pm. No bar food Mon Nov–Easter)
Drybrough Heavy, Scotch; Carlsberg, Carlsberg Hof.

In a little village just off the A1, this warm, cosy pub is a splendid place to stop for a sustaining snack. The cooking is both imaginative and accomplished, and dishes range from delicious fresh tomato soup to Normandy-style guinea fowl, deep-fried lamb's kidneys and fillets of sole in a lovely light mornay sauce. Nice sweets, too. Closed Monday lunchtime November–Easter.

## Warfield *(Food)* — *Cricketers*

Cricket Lane · *Berkshire* · Map 6 B3
Winkfield Row (0344) 882910
*Free House*
*Landlords* Mr & Mrs R. Turner
Beef in old ale with jacket potato & salad £3.10 Minced lamb kebabs in pitta bread with salad £1.95 (Last order 10pm)
Brakspear's Ordinary Bitter; Wethered's Bitter; Pompey Royal; Flower's Original; Guinness; Stella Artois; Heineken; cider. *Real ale*

Once you've found this charming old pub (ask the way), the sign depicting a well-fed cricketer will show you what it's all about! Good, wholesome dishes – soups, pâtés, game pie, lamb vindaloo, roast beef, tempting sweets – are served in the cosily rustic bars. The barbecue house offering kebabs, spare ribs and the like is a major attraction on weekends May–Oct. Limited choice Sunday evening. **Family pub**

## Wark *(B & B)* — *Battlesteads Hotel*

Near Hexham · *Northumberland* · Map 4 C1
Bellingham (0660) 30209

*Free House*
*Landlords* Robert & Jane Dodd

**BEDROOMS 6 Grade 2 £C**
Drybrough Heavy, Scotch; Guinness; Carlsberg; cider.

Jane and Robert Dodd offer a warm welcome to visitors to their homely village pub near Hadrian's Wall. The spacious residents' lounge offers a lovely view of the pretty garden and countryside, and a striking carved serving counter dominates the beamed lounge bar. Well-maintained bedrooms have modern furniture and cheerful colour schemes, and the two old-fashioned bathrooms are spotless. **Family pub**

## Warminster *(Food, B & B)* — *Old Bell Hotel*

Market Place · *Wiltshire* · Map 8 D3
Warminster (0985) 216611

*Brewery* Wadworth
*Landlords* Mr & Mrs Howard Astbury

**BEDROOMS 16 Grades 1 & 2 £B**
Wiltshire special 90p Cherry pie 45p (Last order 9pm. No bar food eves in winter)
Bass; Wadworth's 6X, IPA, Northgate Bitter; Guinness; Harp. *Real ale*

Bar snacks are a popular feature of this fine old coaching inn with a distinguished colonnaded façade. The choice at lunchtime ranges from pâté and succulent roast beef salad to hot dishes like stuffed aubergines or sausage and mash. There's only cold food in the evening. Neat bedrooms have TVs and tea-makers, and ten have their own bath or shower rooms. Courtyard.

## Warren Street *(Food, B & B)* — *Harrow Inn*

Near Lenham · *Kent* · Map 6 C3
Maidstone (0622) 858727

*Free House*
*Landlord* Mark Watson
**BEDROOMS 5 Grade 1 £B** (No dogs)
Stilton soup with roll & butter 75p Spiced chicken with rice £2.95 (Last order 9.45pm)
Shepherd Neame Masterbrew, Bitter, Mild; Young's Special Bitter; Guinness; Hurlimann Sternbräu; Taunton cider. *Real ale*

You'll find a good choice of delicious bar food in the tastefully modernised surroundings of this village pub. In addition to sandwiches, pâté and salads, there are daily dishes such as superb home-made tomato soup, stuffed peppers and deliciously refreshing raspberry and redcurrant flan. Luxurious bedrooms have good furniture and pretty floral curtains; bathrooms are impeccable. There's a comfortable residents' lounge with TV. Garden.

## Warwick-on-Eden *(B & B)* — *Queen's Arms Inn & Motel*

Near Carlisle · *Cumbria* · Map 3 B1
Wetheral (0228) 60699

*Free House*
*Landlords* David, Lawrence, Jean & Barbara Keen

**BEDROOMS 8 Grade 1 £B**
Tetley's Bitter, Mild; Skol; Löwenbräu; Guinness; cider. *Real ale*

Handily placed close to Carlisle and the M6, this country inn is a nice blend of traditional and up-to-date features. The two bars have great appeal with their massive open fires and assorted bric-à-brac. Bedrooms are spacious and bright, with pretty floral curtains, TVs, tea-makers and radios, plus compact bath or shower rooms. The owners generate a very friendly atmosphere. Garden. **Family pub**

## Wasdale Head *(Food, B & B)* — *Wasdale Head Inn*

Near Gosforth · *Cumbria* · Map 3 B2
Wasdale (094 06) 229

*Free House*
*Landlord* Mr J. R. M. Carr
**BEDROOMS 8 Grade 1 £A**
Cumberland tattie pot £2.75 Beef ale casserole £2.75 (Last order 10pm)
Theakston's Best Bitter, Old Peculier; Jennings Bitter; Hartley's XB; Guinness; Carlsberg; Taunton cider. *Real ale*

Pleasant accommodation and tasty bar food available from 10.30am to 10pm make this inn popular with walkers and climbers. In the rustic bar you can enjoy simple, well-prepared offerings like pâté, quiche, Cumberland tattie pot with red cabbage and tender chicken and vegetable pie. Cosy bedrooms have duvets, tea-makers and tiled bath/shower rooms. No accommodation early Nov–28 Dec, when bars are open weekends only. **Family pub**

## Washbrook *(Food)* — *Brook Inn*

Back Lane, Near Ipswich · *Suffolk* · Map 5 D2
Copdock (047 386) 455

*Brewery* Tollemache & Cobbold
*Landlords* Mr & Mrs W. M. Freeth
Brook Special £2.50 Coffee & brandy gâteau 85p (No bar food eves, Sun or Bank Holidays)
Tolly Cobbold Original, Bitter, Best Bitter, Mild; Guinness; Hansa; Taunton cider. *Real ale*

Hungry businessmen make a beeline for this attractive village pub to enjoy some tasty lunchtime bar fare. Home-made soup is always a good bet (try the delicious tomato), and other enjoyable offerings might include chilli con carne, pork Stroganoff and salads with super home-cooked ham, or smoked fish. And there's always the Brook Special – soup, a roll and a mammoth plateful of ham, salami, superb Stilton and celery. Patio.

## Washington *(Food)* — *Frankland Arms*

Near Storrington · *West Sussex* · Map 6 B4
Ashington (0903) 892220

*Brewery* Whitbread
*Landlord* Mr Robert Carey

Lamb & apricot pie £2.45 Sandwiches from 70p (Last order 10.30pm)
Whitbread Country Bitter, Pompey Royal, Best Bitter; Guinness; Stella Artois; cider. *Real ale*

New hosts the Careys are maintaining the tradition of good home cooking at this attractive, whitewashed inn just off the A24. Tasty meat pies (lamb and apricot, steak and onion, chicken with sweetcorn) are great favourites, along with succulent home-boiled ham in sandwiches or salads. Freshly picked berries are used in delicious fruit puddings (usually available lunchtime only). Garden.

## Waterley Bottom *(B & B)* — *New Inn*

Near North Nibley, Dursley · *Gloucestershire*
Map 7 D2
Dursley (0453) 3659

*Free House*
*Landlord* Ruby Sainty
**BEDROOMS 2 Grade 2 £C** (No dogs)
Greene King Abbot Ale; Smiles Best Bitter; Cotleigh Tawny Bitter; Theakston's Old Peculier; New Inn WB; Hofmeister; cider. *Real ale*

Don't take the name literally, as this pleasant country inn is about as traditional as you can get: they play darts and dominoes in the public bar, and real ale comes from an old pewter beer engine. The two pretty bedrooms have modern units, duvets, colour TVs and tea-makers, and they share a good bathroom. Mrs Sainty gets guests off to a good start with a hearty breakfast. Nice garden.

## Wath-in-Nidderdale *(Food, B & B)* — *Sportsman's Arms*

Near Pately Bridge · *North Yorkshire* · Map 4 C2
Harrogate (0423) 711306

*Free House*
*Landlords* Mr & Mrs J. R. Carter
**BEDROOMS 6 Grade 2 £B**
Fresh Nidderdale trout & salad £2.45 Ploughman's platter £1.50 (No bar food eves)
Tetley's Bitter, Mild; Theakston's Bitter; Younger's Bitter, Export; Guinness; Carlsberg; cider.

A secluded setting is enjoyed by this mellow sandstone inn, which stands in attractive grounds just a stone's throw from the river Nidd. Six cosy bedrooms sharing two bathrooms offer simple overnight comforts, and there's a homely TV lounge. Bar luncheons include flavoursome home-made soup, wholemeal rolls generously topped with prawns and mayonnaise, local trout and sirloin steak. Nice sweets, too. Garden.
**Family pub**

## Watton-at-Stone *(Food)* — *George & Dragon*

*Hertfordshire* · Map 5 C2
Ware (0920) 830285

*Brewery* Greene King
*Landlord* Mr Kevin Dinnin

Omelette Arnold Bennett £2.50 Avocado with prawns & Danish caviar £3 (Last order 10pm. No bar food Sun)
Greene King IPA, Abbot Ale, Light Mild, Yeoman; Harp; Kronenbourg. *Real ale*

The bar snacks are a very popular feature at this friendly old roadside pub, where Kevin Dinnin looks after his customers with cheerful expertise. Favourites on the appealing menu include soups, sandwiches and salads, along with mushrooms in a gently curried cream sauce, seafood Thermidor and daily specials like home-made burgers. There's an excellent trifle among the puds. Garden.

## Weedon *(B & B)* — *Crossroads Hotel*

High Street · *Northamptonshire* · Map 5 B2
Weedon (0327) 40354

*Free House*
*Landlord* Mr T. Brown

**BEDROOMS 28 Grade 1 £A+** (No dogs)
Bass; Adnams Bitter; Litchborough Tudor; Younger's IPA; Guinness; Carlsberg Hof; cider. *Real ale*

This converted tollhouse close to the M1 (at the junction of the A5 and A45) is especially popular with motorway travellers. And no wonder, for the accommodation is superb. Traditionally furnished bedrooms in the main building and more modern annexe ones are all very comfortable and have colour TVs, radios, tea-makers and ample writing space. Bathrooms are plush. Attractive, welcoming bars too, one styled like a Victorian chemist's shop. **Family pub**

## Weldon *(B & B)* — *George Hotel*

Stamford Road, Near Corby
*Northamptonshire* · Map 5 B1
Corby (053 63) 67810

*Brewery* Melbourns
*Landlords* Mr & Mrs I. K. Watts

**BEDROOMS 4 Grade 2 £C** (No dogs)
Sam Smith's Old Brewery Bitter, Dark Mild, Taddy Bitter, Lager; Guinness; cider. *Real ale*

A charming stone pub, centuries old and once a coaching inn. The mellow beamed front bar is a quiet spot to relax with a drink, while pool, darts and video games generate a lively atmosphere in the public bar. Pleasant bedrooms (in the house next door) have decent freestanding furniture and good-quality fabrics. There's a spacious TV lounge. Children not accommodated overnight. **Family pub**

## Wellesbourne *(Food, B & B)* — *King's Head*

*Warwickshire* · Map 5 A2
Stratford-upon-Avon (0789) 840206

*Brewery* Bass
*Landlord* Mr Carl Watkins
**BEDROOMS 11 Grade 2 £B**
Baked fillet of cod Malaysian style £2.75
Lamb Shrewsbury £2.75 (Last order 9.30pm)
Bass; Mitchells & Butlers Brew XI; Worthington 'E'; Guinness; Carling Black Label; Hemeling. *Real ale*

You're bound to find something to tempt you on the menu of this large, creeper-clad pub. Taramasalata and Cornish mussel soup are among the interesting starters, and you could go on to Malaysian-style fillet of cod, pizza, steak or lamb curry. Blackcurrant ice-cream makes a delicious finish. Spacious, pleasant bedrooms have modern fittings, and bathrooms are well kept. **Family pub**

## Wells-next-the-Sea *(B & B)* — *Tinkers Hotel*

Polka Road · *Norfolk* · Map 5 C1
Fakenham (0328) 710288

*Brewery* Norwich
*Landlords* Mr & Mrs G. Hibbs

**BEDROOMS 9 Grade 2 £C**
Webster's Yorkshire Bitter; Norwich Castle Bitter, Mild; Ben Truman; Carlsberg; cider. *Real ale*

New tenants Mr and Mrs Hibbs provide basic, no-frills accommodation and hearty breakfasts at this former railway hotel, a tall building dating from the 17th century. Bedrooms are neat and simple, the roomiest being those on the top floor; all have washbasins and share a single bathroom. Bars, too, are unpretentious in style, and there's a bright, airy breakfast room. Garden.

## Wendron *(B & B)* — *New Inn*

Near Helston · *Cornwall* · Map 8 A4
Helston (032 65) 2683

*Brewery* Devenish
*Landlords* Bill & Spider Standcumbe

**BEDROOMS 2 Grade 2 £C** (No dogs)
Devenish Cornish Best Bitter, John Devenish Bitter, Falmouth; Guinness; Heineken Grünhalle; cider. *Real ale*

Friendly landlord Bill Standcumbe rises with the lark to polish the horse brasses, harnesses and bridles that adorn the stone-walled bars of this welcoming country pub. His wife Spider does an equally impressive job on the two spotless bedrooms, which are decorated in simple, homely style and have colour TVs and washbasins. There's a modern public bathroom. Children under ten not accommodated. Excellent breakfasts. Terrace.

## Wentworth *(Food)* — *George & Dragon*

Main Street, Near Rotherham
*South Yorkshire* · Map 4 C3
Barnsley (0226) 742440

*Free House*
*Landlord* Margaret Dickinson

Cold table £2.95 Home-made sweets 75p (Last order 9pm. No bar food Sun)
Taylor's Bitter, Landlord, Porter; Tetley's Bitter; Löwenbräu; cider. *Real ale*

Stuffed birds and hunting trophies lend a Victorian charm to this unpretentious greystone pub famous for Margaret Dickinson's superb lunchtime buffet laden with home-cooked meats, black pudding and the most imaginative salads. There are hot dishes in winter, and tempting sweets include a stunning chocolate crunch cake. Chunks of home-made bread with generous fillings are the only evening offerings. Patio.

## Weobley *(Food)* — *Red Lion Hotel*

Near Hereford · *Hereford & Worcester*
Map 7 D1
Weobley (0544) 318220
*Free House*
*Landlord* Mr Townley-Berry

Beef curry £3 Cold table buffet £3.50 (No bar food eves)
Flower's Best Bitter, Original; Ansells Bitter; Usher's Triple Crown; Carlsberg Hof; Red Stripe; cider. *Real ale*

Lunchtime bar snacks are served in the restaurant of this delightful 14th-century timbered inn. The centrepiece is a cold buffet offering a wide range of cooked meats and salads. There are also a couple of hot dishes – beef curry is a favourite – and a traditional roast on Sunday. Garden. *For accommodation see Egon Ronay's Lucas Hotel & Restaurant Guide 1985.*

**Family pub**

## West Adderbury *(Food)* — *White Hart*

Tanners Lane, Near Banbury · *Oxfordshire*
Map 5 A2
Banbury (0295) 810406

*Free House*
*Landlords* D. G. Benstead & Jane Purcell

Moussaka £2.50 Casserole of the day £3 (Last order 10pm)
Manns Bitter; Marston's Pedigree, Burton Bitter; Carlsberg. *Real ale*

Every visitor, whether regular or stranger, can be sure of a warm-hearted welcome at this attractive pub near the village centre. Excellent home-cooked fare is served in the well-furnished bar, from light, tasty salmon mousse to casseroled lamb cutlets and a tasty cold lemon soufflé. There's also an eye-catching cold buffet. Set three-course meal for Sunday lunch. Garden.

## West Bexington *(B & B)* — *Manor Hotel*

Bridport · *Dorset* · Map 8 D3
Burton Bradstock (0308) 897616

*Free House*
*Landlord* Mr Richard Childs

**BEDROOMS 11 Grade 1 £B** (No dogs)
Wadworth 6X; Manor Bitter; Eldridge Pope Royal Oak; Carlsberg; Taunton cider. *Real ale*

This ancient stone manor house enjoys a peaceful setting just a short stroll from the sea and the dramatic sweep of Chesil Bank. Fine oak panelling graces the flagstoned hall, and the original cellar is now a characterful bar. Light, airy bedrooms, all with colour TVs, are kept in spotless condition, and bathrooms are excellent. A comfortably traditional residents' lounge overlooks the garden. **Family pub**

## West Lavington *(Food)* — *Churchill*

High Street · *Wiltshire* · Map 6 A3
West Lavington (038 081) 2287

*Brewery* Bass
*Landlords* P. A. & S. Y. Smith & B. C. & M. R. Goram
Steak & kidney pie £2 Grilled gammon £2.50 (Last order 10pm)
Bass; Worthington Best Bitter; Toby Bitter; Guinness; Carling Black Label; Taunton cider. *Real ale*

This attractive red-brick pub draws an appreciative clientele with its enjoyable bar snacks. The list limits itself to familiar favourites, from sandwiches and home-made soup to grilled gammon, fried fish and a good tasty steak and kidney pie cooked in Guinness. Simple sweets include apple pie. Enjoy it all in the smartly furnished bar or outside in the beer garden. **Family pub**

## West Lavington *(B & B)* — *Wheatsheaf*

High Street · *Wiltshire* · Map 6 A3
West Lavington (0380 81) 3392

*Free House*
*Landlord* Mr T. Emery

**BEDROOMS 5 Grade 2 £C**
Wadworth's 6X; Ind Coope Bitter; Tetley's Bitter; Guinness; Löwenbräu; Skol. *Real ale*

A smart black and white pub at one end of the village, with two pleasant bars and a large beer garden. Well-carpeted bedrooms are bright and airy, nicely furnished with modern freestanding pieces; they all have central heating and TV and share an up-to-date bathroom and a shower cabinet. Additional rooms are planned, all with private facilities.

## West Witton *(B & B)* — *Wensleydale Heifer*

Near Leyburn · *North Yorkshire* · Map 4 C2
Wensleydale (0969) 22322

*Free House*
*Landlord* Nigel Holdsworth

**BEDROOMS 17 Grade 1 £B**
Younger's IPA; McEwan's Export, Lager; Guinness; Taunton cider. *Real ale*

Set in the splendid scenery of Wensleydale, this delightful 17th-century inn abounds in warmth and charm. A roaring log fire banishes winter from the comfortably furnished lounge, and the bar is cosy and convivial. Good-sized bedrooms (some in nearby buildings) have practical furnishings, TVs and tea-makers. One room boasts a four-poster, and nearly all have up-to-date private facilities. **Family pub**

## Westbury *(Food)* — *Reindeer Inn*

Near Brackley · *Buckinghamshire* · Map 5 B2
Brackley (0280) 704934

*Brewery* Manns
*Landlords* Mr & Mrs J. Clarke

Westbury country pie £1.60 Hot chocolate fudge cake 90p (Last order 10pm)
Usher's Founder's Ale; Webster's Yorkshire Bitter; Manns Traditional; Guinness; Holsten; Carlsberg; cider. *Real ale*

The large beer garden is a popular summer attraction at this cottagy, stone-built pub, while in cooler months the cosy bar beckons with its cheerful open fire. Freshly prepared snacks, available seven days a week, include flavoursome chicken liver pâté, pizzas and excellent cottage pie. Sandwiches and salads, too, along with good English cheeses and a wickedly rich hot chocolate fudge cake. **Family pub**

## Weston *(Food)* — *White Lion*

Near Crewe · *Cheshire* · Map 3 B4
Crewe (0270) 587011

*Free House*
*Landlords* Mr & Mrs G. Davies

Lionheart £1.85 Poached Dee salmon £3.85 (Last order 9.45pm)
Tetley's Traditional Bitter; Ind Coope Burton Ale, Bitter, Mild; Guinness; Skol; cider. *Real ale*

The food served in the pleasant snack bar is a major attraction at this rambling black and white inn proudly dated 1652. There's a lot of seafood on the menu, with tempting treats such as brown shrimps in garlic butter and Cornish crab. Soup, sandwiches, cold meat platters and an excellent cheeseboard provide further choice, along with a lunchtime roast or daily special like chicken provençale. Service is pleasantly attentive. **Family pub**

## Weston-on-the-Green *(Food)* — *Chequers Inn*

Near Bicester · *Oxfordshire* · Map 5 A2
Bletchington (0869) 50319

*Brewery* Halls
*Landlord* Patrick Bennett

Burgers from £1.30 Rump steak £3.95 (Last order 10.30pm)
Ind Coope Burton Ale, Mild; Halls Harvest Bitter; Double Diamond; Guinness; Löwenbräu; cider. *Real ale*

A very good local butcher supplies this pleasant old thatched inn that was once the village blacksmith's shop. Our rump steak was cooked to a turn – succulent, full of flavour and tender as butter – and the burgers are of the same high quality. Also available are soup, lunchtime sandwiches, ham salad and a dish of the day, sometimes beef curry. Garden. **Family pub**

## Westwood *(Food)* — *New Inn*

Near Bradford-on-Avon · *Wiltshire* · Map 8 D3
Bradford-on-Avon (022 16) 3123

*Brewery* Usher
*Landlord* Mr F. McFadden

Beef casserole £1.80 Sherry trifle 80p (Last order 10pm)
Usher's Country Bitter; Ben Truman; Carlsberg; Holsten; cider. *Real ale*

Local ladies take turns with the cooking at this pleasant village pub, producing anything from a light bite to a three-course meal that you can enjoy in the comfortable bar. Burgers, baked potatoes and lasagne are popular quick snacks, and other items on a varied menu range from rich, creamy fish soup and deep-fried clams to sirloin steak, roast duckling and turkey cordon bleu. Patio.

## Wetherby *(Food)* — *Alpine Inn*

*North Yorkshire* · Map 4 C3
Wetherby (0937) 62501

*Brewery* Samuel Smith
*Landlord* Mr Colin R. Hooton

Mushrooms in garlic butter £1.55 Fillet steak sandwich £2.25 (Last order 11pm)
Samuel Smith's Old Brewery Bitter, Dark Mild; Ayinger Bräu. *Real ale*

This modern, chalet-style pub beside the southbound carriageway of the A1 is just the place for hungry motorists and families. The choice of bar snacks is simple yet varied, and preparation is careful. If home-made soup or a ploughman's doesn't strike your fancy, you might opt for a sizzling fillet steak sandwich (the house speciality), fisherman's pie or a filled jacket potato. Light cream caramel makes a nice sweet. Patio. **Family pub**

## Weybridge *(Food)* — *Buffers*

Heath Road, Weybridge Station · *Surrey*
Map 6 B3
Weybridge (0932) 55332

*Free House*
*Landlord* James Heyward

Chilli & jacket potato £1.20 Steak & kidney pie £3.95 (No bar food eves or Sun lunch)
Whitbread Best Bitter, Best Scotch Bitter; Stella Artois; Heineken.

A cross between a wine bar and a hamburger restaurant in atmosphere, this popular place is a clever conversion of the former station booking office. Garlic mushrooms and grilled sardines are tasty ways of getting a meal under way, and to follow there are burgers, steaks, seafood and a good steak and kidney pie. Sweets are mainly ice cream-based. Live music most weekday nights. **Family pub**

## Weybridge *(B & B)* — *Kings Manor Hotel*

Oatlands Chase · *Surrey* · Map 6 B3
Walton-on-Thames (0932) 227790

*Brewery* Charrington
*Landlords* Mr & Mrs Braybrook

**BEDROOMS 16 Grade 2 £A** (No dogs)
Charrington IPA; Stones Bitter; Guinness; Carling Black Label; Tennent's; Taunton cider. *Real ale*

Situated in a smart residential road, this substantial white-painted pub with a large garden at the rear has a cheerful, friendly atmosphere. There's a comfortable, amply furnished bar, and accommodation ranges from simple, compact singles to good-sized twins (four with shower cubicles). All rooms have TVs, telephones and tea-makers, and there are three good modern bathrooms.

## Weymouth *(B & B)* — *Golden Lion*

19 St Edmund Street · *Dorset* · Map 8 D4
Weymouth (0305) 786778

*Brewery* Devenish
*Landlord* Mr B. I. Guarraci

**BEDROOMS 15 Grade 2 £C**
John Devenish Bitter, Wessex Best Bitter; John Grove's Weymouth Bitter; Guinness; Grünhalle; Heineken; Stella Atrois; cider. *Real ale*

Just a few steps from the harbour and cross-Channel ferries, this town-centre pub has been extensively modernised behind its handsome white and green facade. Bedrooms with neat, practical furnishings and pretty floral duvets offer good comfort for an overnight stop, and there are plenty of well-kept public bathrooms. There are two bars and a TV lounge. Accommodation closed end October–Easter.

## Whitefield *(Food)* — *Mason's Arms*

Bury New Road · *Greater Manchester*
Map 3 B3
061-766 2713

*Brewery* Whitbread
*Landlords* Phil & Carol Spires
Steak & kidney pie £1.60 Ploughman's lunch £1.30 (No bar food eves)
Whitbread Castle Eden Ale, Trophy, Traditional; Chester's Best Mild; Dutton's Light; Guinness; Heineken; cider. *Real ale*

Lunchtime bar snacks are brought to your table at this friendly red-brick pub. A hot steak sandwich is a popular choice, home-made steak and kidney pie is reliable and daily specials provide additional interest. If you fancy something cold, the display counter offers delicious-looking salad platters. Eye-catching puddings include things like cheesecake and lemon meringue pie.

## Whitewell *(Food, B & B)* — *Inn at Whitewell*

Near Clitheroe · *Lancashire* · Map 3 B3
Dunsop Bridge (020 08) 222
*Free House*
*Landlord* Mr Richard Bowman
**BEDROOMS 11 Grade 1 £B**
Chicken pie £2.85 Fresh Scottish salmon salad £3.85 (Last order 10pm. No bar food Sat eve)
Whitbread Trophy, Best Mild; Moorhouse's Bitter; Guinness; Heineken; Stella Artois. *Real ale*

This sturdy stone inn stands in the charming Forest of Bowland by the banks of the river Hodder. The large foyer-lounge is a welcoming place, and interesting prints and antiques are a feature throughout. Tasty bar snacks include superb home-made chicken soup and main courses like salads, seafood pancakes and savoury pies. Double-glazed bedrooms offer abundant space and comfort; roomy bathrooms are well fitted. **Family pub**

## Whitley *(Food)* — *Woolpack Inn*

Near Dewsbury · *West Yorkshire* · Map 4 C3
Mirfield (0924) 492718

*Free House*
*Landlord* Mr David Hall

Soup of the day 70p Uitsmyter £2.25 (Last order 10pm. No bar food Mon)
Tetley's Bitter, Mild; Bass; Stones Bitter; Guinness; Carling Black Label; cider. *Real ale*

This attractive stone pub on a hillside is a good spot to pause for a snack. The regular menu offers standard fare – soup, steak and kidney pie, hamburgers – and a blackboard lists daily specials such as lamb chops or goujons of halibut. A popular lunchtime treat is Dutch uitsmyter, a scrumptious open ham sandwich topped with three fried eggs. Terrace.

**Family pub**

## Whitney-on-Wye *(Food, B & B)* ★ — *Rhydspence Inn*

*Hereford & Worcester* · Map 7 C1
Clifford (049 73) 262
*Free House*
*Landlords* David & Flo Wallington
**BEDROOMS 3 Grade 1 £B** (No dogs)
Landlord's favourite diet portion £1.60 Curry of the day £4.25 (Last order 9.30pm)
Hook Norton Bitter; Bass; Robinson's Best Bitter; Mitchells & Butlers DPA; Bailey's Bitter; Guinness; Old Tom (winter only); cider (summer only). *Real ale*

A really marvellous pub, with an idyllic setting, delightful hosts, homely accommodation and superb food. The choice in the beamed bar ranges from stockpot soup and wonderful English cheeses to herby sausages, curries and seafood Thermidor, with delicious sweets to finish. Tastefully furnished bedrooms (no under-tens) are bright and comfortable; all have TVs. Bar closed Mondays and winter Tuesdays; pub closed 2 weeks in winter. Garden.

## Whittlesey *(B & B)* — *Falcon Hotel*

London Street · *Cambridgeshire* · Map 5 C1
Peterborough (0733) 203247

*Brewery* Tollemache & Cobbold
*Landlords* Mavis & Brian Ramsden

**BEDROOMS 8 Grade 2 £B**
Tolly's Best Bitter, Bitter, Original; Younger's Tartan; Hansa; Taunton cider. *Real ale*

A brick-built building tucked away behind the town square, this former coaching inn offers comfortable overnight accommodation in its spacious, well-kept bedrooms. All rooms have good carpets, colour TVs and tea-makers, and the elegant suite boasts a four-poster and its own lounge. There are two pleasant bars, one with a thatched serving area, the other with a fine carved wooden counter. Patio. **Family pub**

## Wickham *(Food, B & B)* — *Five Bells*

New Newbury · *Berkshire* · Map 6 A3
Boxford (048 838) 242

*Brewery* Watneys
*Landlord* Mrs D. A. Channing-Williams
**BEDROOMS 4 Grade 1 £C**
Steak & kidney pie £3 Ploughman's £1.50 (Last order 10pm)
Usher's Best Bitter, IPA; Watneys Special Bitter; Guinness; Carlsberg; cider. *Real ale*

The emphasis is on home cooking at Mrs Channing-Williams' 450-year old thatched pub. Winter specials like rabbit casserole supplement fish, fried chicken and steak and kidney pie, and there are crisp, fresh salads with locally baked ham. Home-made puddings include delicious treacle tart. All four bright bedrooms have washbasins and TVs, and the beds are comfortable. New features in the garden are a barbecue and swimming pool. **Family pub**

## Willian *(Food)* — *Three Horseshoes*

Letchworth · *Hertfordshire* · Map 5 B2
Letchworth (046 26) 5713

*Brewery* Greene King
*Landlord* Mr P. Jest

Quiche 80p Steak & kidney pie £1.75 (No bar food eves or Sun)
Greene King Abbot, IPA; Guinness; Harp; Kronenbourg; Taunton cider. *Real ale*

There's a loyal local following at this cheerful village pub, where simple lunchtime snacks are served in warm, friendly surroundings. The beamed bar has plenty of space for everyone to enjoy their choice from a short menu of rolls, sandwiches and ploughman's. Pâté and smoked salmon, too, plus tasty specials like Stilton and ham quiche or steak and kidney pie. Sandwiches and cheese only Saturday.

## Williton *(B & B)* — *Egremont Hotel*

Fore Street · *Somerset* · Map 8 C3
Williton (0984) 32500

*Brewery* Usher
*Landlord* Mr M. C. Smith

**BEDROOMS 12 Grade 2 £C**
Usher's Best Bitter, Triple Crown; Bass; Watneys Special; Guinness; Carlsberg Pilsner; cider. *Real ale*

The Smiths provide a warm welcome and simple, homely comforts in this solid 16th-century inn. Visitors can enjoy a drink in the basic public bar or the comfortable lounge bar; there's also a sturdily furnished TV lounge. Roomy bedrooms have a mixture of traditional and modern furniture; three have their own bathrooms. The two public bathrooms are modern and spotlessly clean. Enjoyable breakfasts. Garden.
**Family pub**

## Wilmcote *(B & B)* — *Swan House Hotel*

Near Stratford-upon-Avon · *Warwickshire*
Map 5 A2
Stratford-upon-Avon (0789) 67030

*Free House*
*Landlords* Mr & Mrs H. G. Poole

**BEDROOMS 11 Grade 2 £B** No dogs
Everards Old Original, Tiger; Tuborg Pils, Gold; cider. *Real ale*

Popular with both tourists and peace-seeking businessmen, this handsome black and white hotel stands near the house where Shakespeare's mother lived. Eight bedrooms are in the main building, three in the garden chalet; all have modern furniture, TVs and tea-makers. There's a cosy bar and a patio. The landlords are friendly and welcoming, and guests wake up to a splendid cooked breakfast. **Family pub**

## Wilson *(Food)* — *Bull's Head Inn*

Melbourne · *Derbyshire* · Map 4 C4
Melbourne (033 16) 2644

*Brewery* Allied
*Landlord* Mr Michael Johnson

Stilton ploughman's £1.20 Roast beef, Yorkshire pudding & 2 vegetables £3.50 (Last order 10pm. No bar food Sun & Mon eves)
Ind Coope Bitter, Mild; Guinness; Skol; Löwenbräu; cider. *Real ale*

The sight of cheerful window boxes decorating the smart exterior of this friendly pub suggests that somebody cares about the place. And that somebody is Michael Johnson, who also delights visitors with his delicious bar food. The impressive cold spread offers plenty of seafood choice and there are also jacket potatoes and sandwiches. The highlight is perhaps the juicy roast beef, packed into hunks of French bread and served with Yorkshire pudding.

## Wimborne St Giles *(Food, B & B)* — *Bull Inn*

Near Wimborne · *Dorset* · Map 6 A4
Cranborne (072 54) 284

*Brewery* Hall & Woodhouse
*Landlords* Tony & Sharon Sharp
**BEDROOMS 3 Grade 2 £C** (No dogs)
Rump steak £4.80 Home-made soup 85p (Last order 10pm)
Hall & Woodhouse Badger Best Bitter, Badger Export, Brock; Guinness; Carlsberg; Stella Artois; Taunton cider. *Real ale*

With its tranquil location in deepest rural Dorset, this well-kept inn is a pleasant spot for a snack or an overnight stop. The bar menu offers something to suit most tastes, from pâté and ploughman's to salads, grills, basket meals, vegetarian dishes, and fish fingers for the children. Three cheerful, spotless bedrooms provide simple comforts and nice views. Accommodation closed 2 weeks Christmas. Garden.

## Wincanton *(Food)* — *Hunter's Lodge*

Bourton · *Somerset* · Map 8 D3
Bourton (0747) 840660

*Free House*
*Landlord* Mr A. A. Dean

Jumbo local sausages £1.60 Beef & Guinness casserole £1.95 (Last order 10pm)
Hall & Woodhouse Badger Best Bitter; Guinness; Stella Artois; Carlsberg Hof; Brock; Taunton cider. *Real ale*

Just over the border from Wiltshire, this substantial old pub on the A303 offers a range of bar fare to satisfy even the hungriest hunter. Our turkey and vegetable soup was packed with goodness and flavour, a splendid prelude to a main-course salad, jumbo sausages or steak and Guinness casserole. Simple sweets include 12 ice creams. Breakfasts served Saturdays in the summer. There's a garden with children's play area. **Family pub**

## Wincham *(Food)* — *Black Greyhound Hotel*

Hall Lane, Near Northwich · *Cheshire*
Map 3 B3
Northwich (0606) 3053

*Brewery* Greenall Whitley
*Landlord* Mr David Buckley

Steak pie £2.15 Roast meat platter £2.95 (Last order 10pm)
Greenall Whitley Bitter, Festival; Guinness; Grünhalle; cider. *Real ale*

Mrs Buckley's hearty snacks bring the locals flocking to the homely bar of this large whitewashed pub. Generous portions of meat pies, sausages, chicken and scampi are served with superb crunchy chips that on their own justify a visit here! There are also generous ploughman's and filled baps, salads and a pleasing selection of English cheeses. **Family pub** (lunchtime)

## Winchcombe *(Food)* — *Corner Cupboard Inn*

Gloucester Street · *Gloucestershire* · Map 5 A2
Winchcombe (0242) 602303

*Brewery* Whitbread
*Landlords* Mr & Mrs M. Elliott

Cottage pie £2 Cheese stuffed pasta shells £2.20 (No bar food eves or Sun in winter)
Whitbread Best Bitter; Flowers IPA, Original, Pale Ale, Best Bitter; Guinness; Heineken; cider. *Real ale*

A friendly old sandstone inn, where Michael Elliott is the smiling host and his wife Jane the capable cook. Lunchtime snacks, which can be enjoyed in the beamed bar or out in the attractive walled garden, include toasted sandwiches, ploughman's and pâté. Salads are popular, too, with pasta, savoury pies and specials like moussaka to satisfy larger appetites. Garden.

## Winchelsea *(B & B)* — *Winchelsea Lodge Motel*

Sandrock, Hastings Road · *East Sussex*
Map 6 C4
Rye (0797) 226211

*Free House*
*Landlords* George Cunliffe & George Morgan

**BEDROOMS 20 Grade 1 £B**
Usher's Triple Crown; Websters Yorkshire Bitter; Carlsberg; Holsten; Fosters; cider. *Real ale*

A modern adaptation of a classic Sussex barn, this up-to-date complex west of Winchelsea on the A259 offers excellent accommodation. Motel-style bedrooms have neat contemporary fixtures and fittings, including built-in wardrobes, colour TVs and tea-makers, plus functional shower rooms. Exposed brickwork and a high raftered ceiling give the bar a pleasantly traditional atmosphere. Beer garden. **Family pub**

## Winfrith Newburgh *(B & B)* — *Red Lion*

Dorchester Road · *Dorset* · Map 8 D3
Warmwell (0305) 852814

*Brewery* Hall & Woodhouse
*Landlords* Mike & Libby Smeaton

**BEDROOMS 4 Grade 2 £C**
Hall & Woodhouse Hector's Bitter, Badger Best Bitter, Export, Tanglefoot; Guinness; Brock; Taunton cider. *Real ale*

All is cosy and cheerful in this popular, friendly pub on the A352, where caring hosts Mike and Libby Smeaton provide spotlessly clean accommodation. Bright bedrooms have pretty floral wallpapers, modern fitted units and tea-makers; the single public bathroom is immaculate. There's a rustic atmosphere about the pine-panelled bar, and the upstairs lounge is extremely comfortable. Accommodation closed 1 week Christmas. **Family pub**

## Wingham *(Food, B & B)* — *Red Lion Inn*

High Street · *Kent* · Map 6 D3
Canterbury (0227) 720217

*Brewery* Whitbread
*Landlords* Mr & Mrs Adam
**BEDROOMS 2 Grade 2 £C**
Stuffed mushrooms £1.25 Prawn risotto £2 (No bar food eves or Sun)
Whitbread Best Bitter, Best Mild, Trophy; Fremlins Bitter; Guinness; Heineken; Stella Artois. *Real ale*

Previously a canon's residence and sessions house, this ancient building assumed its current role of hostelry during the 17th century. Customers flock to the oak-beamed bar to enjoy the lunchtime snacks, all fresh, tasty and satisfying: ploughman's platters, stuffed mushrooms, honey-baked ham, super fish and chips. The traditionally furnished bedrooms share a spacious, well-kept bathroom. Excellent breakfasts. Garden. **Family pub**

## Winkfield *(Food)* — *Olde Hatchet*

Hatchet Lane, Near Windsor · *Berkshire*
Map 6 B3
Bracknell (0344) 882303

*Brewery* Charrington
*Landlord* Mr D. F. Davies

Flemish mussels £2.10 Trifle £1 (Last order 9pm. No bar food Sun eve)
Charrington's IPA; Bass; Guinness; Carling Black Label; Taunton cider. *Real ale*

Climbing plants and creepers hug the walls of this 16th-century roadside pub, which stands on the fringe of Windsor Great Park. A blackboard in the long beamed bar offers a good choice of well-prepared fare, from filled rolls and nourishing soups to hot smoked mackerel, mixed grill and outstanding lasagne verdi. Cold buffet only for Sunday lunch. **Family pub**

## Winkfield *(Food)* — *White Hart Inn*

Church Road, Near Windsor · *Berkshire*
Map 6 B3
Winkfield Row (0344) 882415

*Brewery* Courage
*Landlord* Ronald Edward Haywood
Steak & kidney pie £2.60 Seafood pancake £2.25 (Last order 9.30pm)
Courage Best Bitter, Directors Bitter, JC; Guinness; Kronenbourg; Hofmeister. *Real ale*

A welcoming open fire warms this 16th-century village pub, where locals and visitors gather to drink, chat and enjoy some tasty fare. Pride of place must go to the wholesome steak and kidney pie, but the menu also offers daily specials such as jugged hare and seafood pancakes, along with salads and grills. Start with a bowl of flavoursome soup and finish off with a seasonal fruit pie. Sandwiches only Sun eve. Garden.

## Winkleigh *(Food)* — *King's Arms*

*Devon* · Map 8 C3
Winkleigh (083 783) 384

*Free House*
*Landlords* Dennis Hawkes & Roy Falkner

Savoury cheese peach £1.25 Roast duck lunch £2.95 (Last order 10pm)
Usher's Best Bitter, Triple Crown; Carlsberg; Löwenbräu; cider. *Real ale*

It's well worth making a detour for the highly enjoyable snacks served in this delightful pub in a tiny village. One of the highlights is the daily roast lunch: our local duck was delicious and came with a spicy apple sauce. There's also excellent soup (perhaps thick vegetable) and a tempting cold buffet featuring savoury flans, terrines, rare roast beef and pies. Super sweets. Closed Monday, 2 weeks Feb & 3 weeks Nov.

## Winkton *(B & B)* — *Fisherman's Haunt*

Christchurch · *Dorset* · Map 6 A4
Christchurch (0202) 484071

*Free House*
*Landlords* Mr & Mrs J. Bochan

**BEDROOMS 17 Grades 1 & 2 £B**
Bass; John Smith's Bitter; Ringwood Best Bitter; Toby Bitter; Mc Ewan's Export; Guinness; Tennent's Extra; Taunton cider. *Real ale*

A mile from Christchurch on the B3347, this wistaria-covered inn overlooking the Avon offers a friendly welcome and homely accommodation. All bedrooms have TV, central heating and tea/coffee-makers. One room in the main house has a four-poster; nicest are the bedrooms in the adjacent cottages with their own little shower rooms. There's a pleasant residents' lounge on the first floor. Patio. **Family pub**

## Winscombe *(Food, B & B)* — *Woodborough*

Near Weston-super-Mare · *Avon* · Map 8 D3
Winscombe (093 484) 2167

*Brewery* Courage
*Landlords* Mary & Graham Ashdowne
**BEDROOMS 4 Grade 2 £C** (No dogs)
Chicken curry £1.50 Fresh salmon £2.50 (Last order 10pm. No bar food Sun eve)
Courage Best Bitter; Yorkshire Bitter; Guinness; Hofmeister; John Smith's Lager; Taunton cider. *Real ale*

Mary Ashdowne's tasty cooking is the attraction in this lively 1930s pub. She spends long hours preparing delicately spiced curries, which are served with excellent rice. She also offers sandwiches with a choice of fresh breads, seafood specialities, savoury flans and basket meals, and her apple pie is delicious. Sturdily furnished, old-fashioned bedrooms have TVs and tea-makers. Children not accommodated overnight.

## Winsford *(Food, B & B)* — *Royal Oak Inn*

Near Minehead · *Somerset* · Map 8 C3
Winsford (064 385) 232

*Free House*
*Landlords* Mr & Mrs C. Steven

**BEDROOMS 11 Grade 1 £A+**
Cold buffet £3.50 Seafood open sandwich £1.75 (Last order 9.30pm)
Flowers Original; Whitbread Best Bitter; Heineken; cider. *Real ale*

This enchanting thatched pub is a pleasant place for an overnight stay. Bedrooms, cottagy or modern, provide accommodation of a very high standard. In the attractive bar you can always enjoy sandwiches, ploughman's and a hot dish such as cottage pie or chunky steak and kidney pie. At lunchtime in summer the major attraction is the impressive buffet with splendid cold pies, home-cooked joints and delicious salads. Patio and garden.

## Winslow *(B & B)* — *Bell Hotel*

1 Sheep Street, Market Square
*Buckinghamshire* · Map 5 B2
Winslow (029 671) 2741

*Free House*
*Landlords* Mr & Mrs William Alston

**BEDROOMS 14 Grade 1 £B**
Adnams Bitter; Greene King Abbot Ale; Marston's Pedigree; Webster's Yorkshire Bitter; Foster's; Carlsberg; cider. *Real ale*

This fine old coaching inn, whose black and white facade dominates the market square, offers comfortable overnight accommodation and a choice of three characterful beamed bars. Bedrooms are of a high standard, with good-quality carpets, well-made reproduction furniture, tea-makers and colour TVs; most have their own smart up-to-date bath or shower room. Courtyard. **Family pub**

NOW'S
YOUR CHANCE
TO DRINK
CALIFORNIA
DRY.
PUSH UP HERE
ONE LITRE
Dry White Wine
PAUL MASSON
California Dry White Wine
1 Litre (e)
Paul Masson.
Now in Dry White.

**WE CORDIALLY INVITE**

# establishments not in this Guide

to write to us if they would like to be considered for inclusion next year – provided their standard of food *served in the bar* is exceptionally high, or their bedrooms clean and very pleasant, or both.

Write to **Egon Ronay's Guinness Pub Guide, Greencoat House, Francis Street, London SW1P 1DH**

We do not accept advertising, payment or free hospitality from any of the establishments we recommend.

# You'll find fussy Findus in everyone's good books.

SWISS CHEESE CRÊPES WITH HAM.

Our Swiss Cheese Crêpes with Ham are a perfect example of how Findus have become harder to please. Fussy, some might say.

Only fresh Emmental cheese from Switzerland, our chefs insist, will fit the bill. Lean, sweet-cured ham is an absolute must, too. As is a dash of Madeira wine and fresh cream for the filling.

Truth is, we have to be this fussy about our food. After all, aren't you?

Findus

The finest food-frozen

# Cater dish–a new thought for food from Simpsons.

Open up new market areas with Cater dish, the all in one way to present food. Just open, heat, and serve from the tray.

- Cater dish has applications in all areas of catering; especially for pubs, hotels and small restaurants. But it's also a great way to serve food at sports and social functions, or simply when entertaining friends.
- A ready meal needing no refrigeration
- Opens with a good can opener
- Reheats in a conventional oven
- Contains 1.5kg/3lb, enough to serve 6-8 people
- Simpsons, as the first users of Cater dish, include Lasagne, Hot Pot, Moussaka, Steak and Kidney Pie and Beef Casserole in their delicious range of dishes.

Simpson Ready Foods Ltd., Urmston, Manchester, M31 1WH, Tel: 061-865 2241.

**Cater dish**

another great idea from Metal Box Food Packaging Division.

## Winster *(Food, B & B)* — *Brown Horse Inn*

Near Bowness-on-Windermere · *Cumbria*
Map 3 B2
Windermere (096 62) 3443
*Free House*
*Landlords* Mr & Mrs G. Millar
**BEDROOMS 3 Grade 2 £C** (No dogs)
Steak & kidney pie £2.50 Lasagne £2.25 (Last order 9pm. No bar food Mon eve in winter)
Thwaites Bitter; Tetley's Bitter; McEwan's Scotch Bitter; Guinness; Stella Artois; Becks Bier; cider. *Real ale*

The hardworking Millars are your hosts at this exceptionally friendly pub in picturesque Lyth Valley. They offer a good choice of bar food, including thick vegetable soup, local Cumberland sausage, sandwiches, ploughman's platters and a really smashing meat and potato pie. The three centrally heated bedrooms, which share the landlord's bathroom, have smart furniture and TVs. No under-fours overnight. Closed Mon lunch in winter. **Family pub**

## Winterton-on-Sea *(Food, B & B)* — *Fisherman's Return*

The Lane · *Norfolk* · Map 5 D1
Winterton-on-Sea (049 376) 305

*Brewery* Norwich
*Landlords* John & Kate Findlay
**BEDROOMS 4 Grade 2 £C**
Mushrooms in garlic butter £1.25 Fisherman's omelette £2 (Last order 9.30pm)
Norwich S & P Bitter; Webster's Yorkshire Bitter; Bullard's Mild; Guinness; Carlsberg; Foster's; cider. *Real ale*

Two panelled bars and a family room provide plenty of space at this charming brick and flint pub just behind the dunes. Snacks range from pâtés and ploughman's to burgers, charcoal-grilled steaks and the filling fisherman's omelette with bacon, onions and mushrooms. Four neat, bright bedrooms share a spotless modern bathroom, and there's a little TV area. Tasty, generously served breakfasts. Garden.
**Family pub**

## Wisbech *(B & B)* — *Rose & Crown Hotel*

Market Square · *Cambridgeshire* · Map 5 C1
Wisbech (0945) 583187

*Brewery* Greene King
*Landlords* William & Sylvia Lloyd

**BEDROOMS 20 Grade 1 £B**
Greene King Abbot Ale, IPA; Guinness; Harp; Kronenbourg.

This impressive town-centre hostelry started life as a coaching inn and still provides a warm welcome and friendly hospitality. Bright, cheerful bedrooms are traditionally furnished to a high standard and equipped with TVs and tea-makers; most have spotlessly clean, up-to-date bathrooms. There's a cosy bar, a comfortable residents' lounge (with TV) and a delightful courtyard festooned with wistaria. **Family pub**

## Withington *(B & B)* — *Mill Inn*

Near Cheltenham · *Gloucestershire* · Map 5 A2
Withington (024 289) 204

*Free House*
*Landlords* Mr & Mrs D. T. Lawrence

**BEDROOMS 3 Grade 2 £B**
Younger's Tartan, IPA; Bass; Fussell's Best Bitter; Guinness; Foster's; Taunton cider. *Real ale*

You'll find bags of atmosphere at this delightful inn, which stands by the river Coln. Beams, sloping floors and rustic oak furniture characterise the charming, immaculately kept bedrooms, which share a similarly spotless bathroom. The bar and adjoining snugs are irresistible, too, with their inglenook fireplaces, comfortable old seats, interesting prints and bric-à-brac. There's an attractive riverside garden.
**Family pub**

## Withypool *(Food, B & B)* — *Royal Oak Inn*

Near Minehead · *Somerset* · Map 8 C3
Exford (064 383) 236

*Free House*
*Landlords* Mr & Mrs Bradley & Mr & Mrs Lucas
**BEDROOMS 8 Grade 1 £A**
Venison & bacon sausage & salad £2.75 Danish open prawn sandwich £1.80 (Last order 9.30pm)
Usher's Best Bitter, Country, Triple Crown; Guinness; Carlsberg; Taunton cider. *Real ale*

Lovers of the outdoor life appreciate both the surroundings and the hospitality at this lovely old Exmoor inn. Hearty fare is served in the public bar, from ploughman's and delicious home-cooked ham to daily hot specials and nice puds. Attractively decorated bedrooms provide excellent overnight accommodation (no under-tens); four have spotless private facilities, six are equipped with TVs. Terrace.

## Witney *(Food)* — *Butchers Arms*

104 Corn Street · *Oxfordshire* · Map 6 A3
Witney (0993) 5745

*Free House*
*Landlord* Mr Paul Loftus

Prawn salad £1.50 Jumbo sausage & chips £1.30 (No bar food eves or Sun)
Usher's Best Bitter; Morland's Bitter; Kronenbourg; Carlsberg; Foster's. *Real ale*

The atmosphere is bright and cheerful at this popular old pub, where well-chosen pop music entertains a predominantly youthful clientele. At lunchtime in the bar, with its attractive furnishings and exposed stone walls, visitors can tuck into a small selection of simple snacks: soup (served with good crusty bread), beefburgers, omelettes and tasty toasted sandwiches. Patio. **Family pub**

## Witney *(Food)* — *Red Lion*

1 Corn Street · *Oxfordshire* · Map 6 A3
Witney (0993) 3149

*Brewery* Morrell's
*Landlord* Mr R. Tams

Brunch muffin 85p Mushroom, mince & onion pie £2.25 (Last order 10pm)
Morrell's Bitter, Dark Mild, Friar; Harp; cider. *Real ale*

A homely town-centre pub, with an interesting menu of familiar favourites and some out-of-the-ordinary dishes. A wholemeal muffin filled with soft cheese, smoked ham and a poached egg makes an excellent snack, and other choices include roast beef (hot or cold), vegetable risotto in a sweet-sour sauce and a variety of savoury pies. Apple pie to finish. Courtyard.

## Woburn *(Food)* — *Black Horse Inn*

Bedford Street · *Bedfordshire* · Map 5 B2
Woburn (052 525) 210
*Free House*
*Landlord* Mr. T. Aldous
Pot of cottage cheese with jacket potato & salad £1.30 Hot seafood quiche & vegetables £1.50 (Last order 10pm)
Young's Special Bitter; Marston's Burton Bitter; Tetley's Bitter; John Marstons; Benskin's Pale; Guinness; Oranjeboom; Löwenbräu; cider. *Real ale*

This pleasant old inn offers a pretty walled garden for summer drinks, while the handsome bar hung with hunting scenes makes a welcoming retreat. Along with steaks at lunchtime you'll find well-prepared salads, ploughman's, pâté and Gloucester sausages, and at lunchtime look out for the hot dish of the day, which might be an appetising meat or fish pie served with vegetables. Sandwiches are also available.

## Woodbridge *(Food, B & B)* — *Bull Hotel*

Market Hill · *Suffolk* · Map 5 D2
Woodbridge (039 43) 2089
*Free House*
*Landlords* Mr & Mrs Allen
**BEDROOMS 26 Grade 2 £B**
Baked ham with parsley sauce & potatoes £2.30 Fisherman's pie with vegetables £2.30 (Last order 10pm)
Adnams Bitter; Tolly Cobbold Best Bitter; Bass; John Bull; Younger's Tartan; Whitbread Tankard; Taunton cider. *Real ale*

The welcoming Allens are the latest in a line of proprietors documented back to 1734 at this friendly town-centre pub. Popular bar snacks include lavishly filled omelettes, meaty Bullburgers, home-made cottage pie and a choice of grills, salads and sandwiches. Bedrooms, some in a courtyard annexe, vary from traditional to modern. Some have private bathrooms and TV, and there's a comfortable TV lounge.

**Family pub**

## Woodbury Salterton *(Food)* — *Digger's Rest*

Near Exeter · *Devon* · Map 8 C3
Woodbury (0395) 32375

*Free House*
*Landlord* Sally Jane Pratt
Cold gammon ham with chips £2.25 Roast chicken sandwich 85p (Last order 10pm)
Whitbread Best Bitter; Bass; Blackawton Bitter; Flowers Best Bitter; Younger's Tartan; Guinness; cider. *Real ale*

Pretty Sally Jane Pratt and her helpers keep things turning over in this charming thatched pub with its own skittle alley. The main attraction in the beamed bars is the nicely prepared food, which includes local pâté, home-made soup and sausages, the best bets undoubtedly being the cold meats cooked on the premises, which are served as salads or packed into hefty sandwiches. Hot dishes in winter. Garden.

**Family pub** (till 8pm)

## Woodditton *(Food)* — *Three Blackbirds*

Ditton Green · *Cambridgeshire* · Map 5 C2
Newmarket (0638) 730811

*Brewery* Tollemache & Cobbold
*Landlords* Ted & Joan Spooner

Beef provençale £2.25 Kidneys in red wine £1.95 (Last order 10.30pm)
Tolly Cobbold Original, Bitter, Old Strong; Guinness; Hansa; Taunton cider. *Real ale*

Racing folk and non-turfites alike enjoy the Spooner brand of hospitality at this white-painted thatched pub in a village near Newmarket. They also agree about the bar food – simple, satisfying fare ranging from flavoursome soup, pâté and prawns to gammon, pizzas and winning lunchtime hot specials like our splendidly robust beef and vegetable stew with dumplings. Cold buffet also in summer. Garden.

## Woodhall Spa *(Food)* — *Abbey Lodge Inn*

Kirkstead · *Lincolnshire* · Map 4 D4
Woodhall Spa (0526) 52538

*Brewery* John Smith
*Landlords* Tom & Eileen Sloan

Steak & kidney pie £1.90 Lasagne & salad £1.90 (Last order 10pm)
John Smith's Bitter, Lager; Guinness; Hofmeister; Taunton cider.

This whitewashed brick pub stands beside the B1192 south of town. In the farmhouse-style bar, genially presided over by Tom Sloan and his family, the food is of the wholesome, robust variety: full-bodied chicken and vegetable soup, flavoursome steak and kidney pie, lasagne, chilli con carne. Round things off in similar style with one of Eileen's good fruit pies. **Family pub**

## Woodstock *(Food)* — *Black Prince*

2 Manor Road · *Oxfordshire* · Map 5 A2
Woodstock (0993) 811530

*Free House*
*Landlords* Larry & Gabrielle O'Brien
Beef burrito £2.20 Mexican combination plate £4.20 (Last order 10pm. No bar food Mon eve)
Flowers Original; Ringwood Fortyniner; Adnams Southwold Bitter; Archers Village Bitter; Guinness; Stella Artois; Kronenbourg. *Real ale*

The garden of this old inn runs right down to the river Glyme, and interesting bar food is an additional attraction. The menu combines traditional British dishes like thick vegetable soup, ploughman's and steak and kidney pie with exotic Mexican specialities such as nachos, tacos, enchiladas and spicy beef burritos. **Family pub**

## Woodstock *(B & B)* — *Marlborough Arms*

Oxford Street · *Oxfordshire* · Map 5 A2
Woodstock (0993) 811227

*Free House*
*Landlords* McEwen family

**BEDROOMS 15 Grades 1 & 2 £A**
Charrington's IPA, Toby Bitter; Worthington 'E'; Carling Black Label. *Real ale*

Kings and dukes once took their rest in this historic 15th-century inn which still offers traditional comfort and hospitality. Neatly maintained bedrooms have mostly old-fashioned furniture plus modern touches like TVs and tea-makers; bathrooms have pretty patterned wallpaper. Guests can enjoy a drink round the fine old fireplace in the bar or relax in one of the pleasant lounges. Patio. **Family pub**

## Woodstock *(Food, B & B)* — *Punch Bowl Inn*

12 Oxford Street · *Oxfordshire* · Map 5 A2
Woodstock (0993) 811218

*Free House*
*Landlords* Mr & Mrs K. O'Malley
**BEDROOMS 14 Grade 2 £C** (No dogs)
Hot beef sandwich £1.25 Steak & mushroom pie £2 (Last order 9pm)
Wadworth's 6X; Flowers Bitter; Greenall Whitley Festival; Guinness; Stella Artois; Heineken; cider. *Real ale*

The home-made dish of the day is always a good bet in the attractive bar of the O'Malleys' friendly, town-centre inn: leek and ham in a cheese sauce, steak and kidney pie and roast lamb are typical tasty specials. You'll also find soup, sandwiches, salads and sweets. Bedrooms are neat and bright, with modern furnishings and TVs. Patio. **Family pub**

## Wooler *(B & B)* — *Tankerville Arms*

Cottage Road · *Northumberland* · Map 2 D4
Wooler (0668) 81581

*Free House*
*Landlords* Park & Morton families

**BEDROOMS 17 Grade 1 £B**
McEwan's 80/-; Drybrough's Heavy; Younger's Tartan; McEwan's Best Scotch; Cavalier; Harp; Taunton cider. *Real ale*

Standing alongside the A697 at the foot of the Cheviot Hills, this solidly built former coaching inn is run in friendly, welcoming style by the Park and Morton families. Guests can choose between the peaceful lounge bar and the cheerful public bar, and there's also a comfortable TV lounge. Spacious bedrooms have simple, warm colour schemes and mostly traditional furnishings. All have radios. Garden. **Family pub**

# Let TWA be your guide to the USA.

## TWA is the biggest airline across the Atlantic.

When you extend your visiting to America you want to go with the biggest and the best.

That's TWA.

TWA flies regular direct services from London to New York, Boston, Chicago, Philadelphia and Los Angeles.

And TWA flies more passengers across the Atlantic each year than any other airline.

As good guide-consulters you look for reputation and status. TWA has them both. Which is why you should make us your guide.

See your TWA Main Agent

You're going to like us TWA

## Woolhope *(Food, B & B)* — *Butchers Arms*

Near Hereford · *Hereford & Worcester*
Map 7 D2
Fownhope (043 277) 281
*Free House*
*Landlords* Mrs M. Bailey & Mr B. Griffiths
**BEDROOMS 3 Grade 2 £B** (No dogs)
Chilli con carne £1.95 Prawns in mayonnaise £2.85 (Last order 10pm)
Hook Norton Best Bitter, Old Hookey; Marston's Pedigree; Younger's Tartan, Mild; McEwan's Lager; cider. *Real ale*

A peaceful 14th-century inn offering a warm welcome, cosy accommodation and super bar food. Mary Bailey's tempting fare includes salads and basket meals, curries, casseroles and a delicious rabbit and bacon pie full of goodness and flavour. Soup and sandwiches are lunchtime extras. Beamed bedrooms with TVs and tea-makers have a simple, homely appeal, and breakfast is a hearty feast. Patio. **Family pub** (lunchtime)

## Woolverton *(Food)* — *Red Lion*

Near Frome · *Somerset* · Map 8 D3
Frome (0373) 830350

*Brewery* Wadworth
*Landlords* Barry & Penny Lander

Seafood platter £4.60 Traveller's lunch £1.80 (Last order 10pm)
Wadworth's 6X, IPA; Bass; Guinness; Harp; McEwan's Lager; Taunton cider. *Real ale*

King-size portions of excellent bar fare bring the crowds flocking to this hospitable stone-built pub alongside the A36. Barry Lander's repertoire is a splendidly varied one, ranging from deliciously fresh salad bowls (niçoise and Waldorf, for instance) and imaginatively filled jacket potatoes to lasagne, savoury pies, curries and a flavour-packed beef carbonnade made with real ale. Ice creams only for dessert. Garden. **Family pub**

## Worplesdon *(Food)* — *Jolly Farmer*

Burdenshott Road · *Surrey* · Map 6 B3
Guildford (0483) 234658
*Free House*
*Landlord* Mr Derek Rowley
Chicken & mushroom pancake £3.75 Home-made pâté £1.95 (Last order 10pm. No bar food Sun eve)
Fuller's HSB, ESB; Sam Smith's Old Brewery Bitter; Whitbread Pompey Royal; Guinness; Stella Artois; Heineken; cider. *Real ale*

This pleasant, cream-painted pub near the station is a popular place for bar snacks. Everything is home-prepared, from soup and very good pâté to steak and kidney pie, gammon and savoury pancakes. Salads, sandwiches and ploughman's make up the cold choice, and sweets include sherry trifle and gâteaux. Barbecues are a popular feature in the attractive garden in summer, when home-made ice cream makes a lovely finish.

## Wroughton *(Food)* — *White Hart*

High Street, Near Swindon · *Wiltshire*
Map 6 A3
Swindon (0793) 812436
*Brewery* Wadworth
*Landlords* Mr & Mrs A. Mitchener
Macaroni cheese £2.15 Cottage pie £2.30 (Last order 9.45pm. No bar food Mon & Tues eves or all Sun)
Wadworth's 6X, IPA, Old Timer; Guinness; Heineken; Löwenbräu; Taunton cider. *Real ale*

Sit at one of the tables in the lounge bar or eat in the skittle alley at this popular thatched pub. If you want a quick snack there are freshly cut sandwiches (our roast beef was pink and delicious), ploughman's and salads, while hearty appetites will be more than satisfied by a big steak with all the trimmings or a tasty home-made dish like cottage pie or chilli con carne. Fruit or mincemeat pies to finish.

## Wye *(Food, B & B)* — *Kings Head Hotel*

Church Street, Near Ashford · *Kent* · Map 6 D3
Wye (0233) 812418

*Brewery* Whitbread
*Landlords* Mr & Mrs A. Smith
**BEDROOMS 7 Grade 2 £C**
Beef roll with gravy £1 Seafood lasagne £2.75 (Last order 9pm)
Fremlins Bitter; AK Bitter; Whitbread Mild; Guinness; Stella Artois; Heineken; cider. *Real ale*

Visitors will find a good variety of tasty bar snacks to enjoy in this popular old coaching inn on the main street of the village. The range includes soup and pâté, sandwiches and salads, plus savoury pancakes, seafood lasagne and hearty casseroles. For overnight guests there are seven simple, comfortable bedrooms (one with private bath) and a cosy TV lounge. Nice walled garden. **Family pub**

## Wye *(Food, B & B)* — *New Flying Horse Inn*

Upper Bridge Street · *Kent* · Map 6 D3
Wye (0233) 812297

*Brewery* Shepherd Neame
*Landlord* Mr Barry Law
**BEDROOMS 10 Grades 1 & 2 £B**
Steak & kidney pie & vegetables £2.75 Smoked mackerel salad £2.75 (Last order 10pm)
Shepherd Neame Masterbrew, Abbey, Mild; Stock Ale; Guinness; Taunton cider. *Real ale*

Anita and Barry Law are carrying on a long tradition of hospitality at this fine old inn, once a posting house, on the A28. It's particularly popular for its excellent bar snacks, which range from sandwiches and salads to seafood and Sunday roasts. Best bedrooms are the annexe quartet, with neat tiled bathrooms. All rooms have TVs and tea-makers. Patio and garden. **Family pub**

## Wykeham *(B & B)* — *Downe Arms*

Near Scarborough · *North Yorkshire* · Map 4 D2
Scarborough (0723) 862471

*Free House*
*Manager* Mr Philip Mort

**BEDROOMS 7 Grade 1 £B**
Cameron's Best Bitter; Younger's Scotch Bitter; Guinness; Carling Black Label; McEwan's Lager; cider.

Philip Mort keeps everything in exemplary order at this fine stone inn, built as a farmhouse in 1725. An impressive entrance hall leads to the two attractive bars, and there's a children's summer room as well as a residents' TV lounge. Sparklingly clean bedrooms have pretty floral wallpaper and smart white furniture. The two tiled public bathrooms are spacious. Garden.
**Family pub**

## Wytham *(Food)* — *White Hart*

Near Oxford · *Oxfordshire* · Map 6 A3
Oxford (0865) 244372

*Brewery* Hall
*Landlord* Mr R. Godden
Stuffed peppers with salad £2.35 Flemish beef £3.55 (Last order 9.45pm. No bar food 1 week Christmas)
Hall's Harvest Bitter; Ind Coope Burton Ale; Guinness; Skol; Löwenbräu; cider. *Real ale*

A fine village pub, with a low-beamed, flagstone-floored bar and a delightful walled garden. A tempting cold buffet offers cooked meats, savoury pies and colourful salads. There's also a hot dish of the day (except summer lunch) such as tasty chicken and ham casserole. Evening fare is supplemented by steaks, a mixed grill and chicken Kiev. Delicious sweets too.

## Yarde Down *(Food)* — *Poltimore Arms*

Near South Moulton · *Devon* · Map 8 C3
Brayford (059 88) 381

*Free House*
*Landlords* Mr & Mrs R. M. E. Wright

Turkey pie £1.20 Treacle roly-poly 50p
(Last order 9.30pm)
Usher's Best Bitter, Triple Crown, Country Bitter; Guinness; Carlsberg; Taunton cider. *Real ale*

Fresh local produce is put to excellent use in this remote Exmoor pub, whose appearance has changed little in its 300-year history. Among the hunting mementoes in the cosy bar you can tuck into thick, flavour-packed vegetable soup, turkey pie or a mighty fry-up. Sandwiches, salads and grills provide further choice, and sweets include treacle roly-poly pudding. Garden. **Family pub**

## Yarmouth *(B & B)* — *Bugle Hotel*

The Square · *Isle of Wight* · Map 6 A4
Yarmouth (0983) 760272

*Brewery* Whitbread
*Landlords* Mr & Mrs McKillop

**BEDROOMS 10 Grade 1 £A**
Whitbread Strong Country Bitter, Best Bitter, Mild; Guinness; Heineken; Stella Artois; cider. *Real ale*

There's plenty of atmosphere inside this 300-year-old stone hostelry. The counter of the Galleon Bar is modelled like the stern of a sailing ship, while coaching lamps, horse brasses and wagon wheels evoke land travel in the other bar; there's also a cosy TV lounge. Comfortable bedrooms are well designed and neatly furnished in modern style; five have up-to-date bath or shower rooms. Garden.

## Yattendon *(Food, B & B)* ★ — *Royal Oak Hotel*

Near Newbury · *Berkshire* · Map 6 A3
Hermitage (0635) 201325

*Free House*
*Landlords* Kate & Richard Smith
**BEDROOMS 5 Grade 1 £A+**
Cream of spinach soup & roll £1.75 Plaice & chips £3.50 (Last order 10pm)
Bass; Charrington's IPA; Guinness; Carling Black Label; Taunton cider. *Real ale*

Kate & Richard Smith provide a cheerful welcome and really excellent bar snacks at this smart brick inn in the centre of the village. The menu might range from leek and potato soup and crispy duck salad to lamburger with green mustard sauce and calf's liver and bacon, with perhaps meringues or a home-made ice cream to finish. Smartly decorated bedrooms are most comfortable; all have their own bathrooms and TVs. Terrace. **Family pub**

# SCOTLAND

## Airdrie *(B & B)*

### *Staging Post*

8 Anderson Street · *Strathclyde* · Map 2 C3
Airdrie (023 64) 675251

*Brewery* Scottish & Newcastle
*Landlord* Mr M. Burns

**BEDROOMS 8 Grade 1 £A**
McEwan's Tartan, 80/-, Lager; Beck's Bier; Guinness; Taunton cider. *Real ale*

The name tells you that this long, low hostelry was once a staging post for horse-drawn coaches. Today's travellers still seek it out for its excellent accommodation: there are eight comfortable, well-kept bedrooms with built-in furniture, tea-makers, TVs and good modern bathrooms. The roomy main bar features some handsome horse brasses and harnesses, and there's a quiet cocktail bar. Garden. **Family pub**

## Anstruther *(Food)*

### *Craw's Nest Hotel*

Bankwell Road · *Fife* · Map 2 D3
Anstruther (0333) 310691

*Free House*
*Landlords* Mrs Clarke & family

Deep fried haddock £2.40 Steak pie £2.40 (Last order 10.30pm)
Younger's Tartan; McEwan's Export; Guinness; Carlsberg; Taunton cider.

Fresh local haddock and sole are popular choices among the simple snacks served at this modernised Scottish manse. Also available are sandwiches, omelettes and perhaps a curry or lamb dish. Smaller selection in the evening. There are two bars, one small and intimate, the other sunny and spacious. Garden. *For accommodation see Egon Ronay's Lucas Hotel & Restaurant Guide 1985.* **Family pub**

## Balerno *(Food)*

### *Marchbank Hotel*

Near Edinburgh · *Lothian* · Map 2 C3
031-449 3970

*Free House*
*Landlords* Mr & Mrs W. Waddell

Chicken pie & vegetables £1.75 Open sandwiches from 60p (Last order 9.45pm)
Lorimer's 80/-, 70/-; Younger's Tartan; Guinness; Carlsberg Deluxe; cider. *Real ale*

Eye-catching open sandwiches steal the show in this sturdy old house, with fillings of anything from prawns with mayonnaise to tasty salami with potato salad and raw onion. There are also plain sandwiches and salads, as well as hot dishes like appetising home-made soup and specials such as wine-flavoured beef stew, chicken fricassee or toad-in-the-hole. Sandwiches and basket meals in the evening. Garden. **Family pub**

## Busby *(Food, B & B)*

### *Busby Hotel*

Field Road, Clarkston, Glasgow · *Strathclyde*
Map 2 C3
041-644 2661

*Free House*
*Landlord* Mr J. Hebditch
**BEDROOMS 14 Grade 1 £A** (No dogs)
Lentil soup 35p Steak pie £2 (Last order 9pm)
Younger's No. 3 Ale, Tartan; McEwan's Export; Guinness; Harp; Taunton cider. *Real ale*

Excellent staff keep things running smoothly at this purpose-built modern hotel on the A726 a few miles from the centre of Glasgow. Simple, satisfying snacks served in the very busy bar include home-made soup, savoury pies, quiche and curries, plus filled rolls and salad platters. Attractively decorated bedrooms and bath/shower rooms are absolutely spotless and provide good facilities. **Family pub**

## Canonbie *(Food, B & B)* — *Riverside Inn*

*Dumfries & Galloway* · Map 2 D4
Canonbie (054 15) 295

*Free House*
*Landlords* Robert & Susan Phillips

**BEDROOMS 6 Grade 1 £A** (No dogs)
Ploughman's lunch £1.50 Angus sirloin steak £5.95 (Last order 9pm)
Theakston's Best Bitter; Bass; Guinness; Tennent's Lager. *Real ale*

It's a real treat to visit this beautifully maintained hostelry with its delightful, homely atmosphere. Charming bedrooms (including two in a converted cottage) are furnished in traditional style with careful attention to detail, and all have excellent bathrooms. Superb ploughman's and cheese platters top the comfy bar's bill of fare; other offerings include smooth pâté, curry, trout and steaks. Closed Sun lunch & 2 weeks Jan.

## Castle Douglas *(B & B)* — *King's Arms Hotel*

St Andrews Street · *Dumfries & Galloway*
Map 2 C4
Castle Douglas (0556) 2626

*Free House*
*Landlords* Mr & Mrs I. MacDonald

**BEDROOMS 15 Grade 1 £B**
Younger's Tartan, 60/-; Guinness (summer only); Holsten; Taunton cider.

An attractive sheltered patio stands at the rear of this former coaching house in the centre of a thriving market town. Tartan carpets and hunting trophies take the eye in the cosy bars, and there's a traditionally styled residents' lounge and modest TV room. Centrally heated bedrooms are quiet and comfortable, with practical fitted furniture and coordinated fabrics; six have their own bath/shower room. **Family pub**

## Catterline *(Food)* — *Creel Inn*

By Stonehaven · *Grampian* · Map 1 D2
Catterline (056 95) 254

*Free House*
*Landlords* Allan & Margaret Duncan

Catterline crab £3.95 Lentil broth 85p (No bar food eves or Sept–March)
McEwan's Export; Tennent's Lager.

Local seafood is a good bet for a lunchtime bar snack at this agreeable clifftop pub: tasty fresh Catterline crab can be enjoyed in soup or salads, or you might push the boat out with lobster or a mixed seafood platter. Cold ham or beef salads for carnivores, with simple sweets like meringues or apple pie. Terrace. Closed Monday.

## Comrie *(B & B)* — *Royal Hotel*

Melville Square · *Tayside* · Map 2 C3
Comrie (0764) 70200

*Free House*
*Landlords* Mr & Mrs I. Gordon

**BEDROOMS 16 Grade 2 £A**
Younger's Tartan; McEwan's Pale Ale; Skol; Harp; Taunton cider.

Welcoming travellers since 1765, this L-shaped hotel was dubbed royal after a visit by Queen Victoria. There are several golf courses nearby, so it's not surprising that the conversation swings towards bunkers and bogeys in the tartan-clad cocktail bar. Bedrooms, all with private facilities, have simple furniture (except one four-poster), tea-makers and TVs. There's a comfortable residents' lounge. Garden.
**Family pub** (lunchtime)

## Dulnain Bridge *(Food, B & B)* ★ *Muckrach Lodge Hotel*

Near Grantown-on-Spey · *Highland* · Map 1 C2
Dulnain Bridge (047 985) 257

*Free House*
*Landlords* Ogilvie & Fone families
**BEDROOMS 9 Grade 1 & 2 £B** (No dogs)
Sea trout sandwich £2.15 Home-cooked gammon sandwich £1.15 (No bar food eves)
Ind Coope Alloa's Archibald Arrol's 70/-, Diamond Heavy, Export; Skol. *Real ale*

The lunchtime bar snacks are simply superb at this friendly old shooting lodge set back from the A938. Sandwiches are packed to overflowing with goodies like gammon, garlic sausage and poached salmon, and there are soups, pâtés, winter hot dishes and some sublime sweets – chocolate pot to raspberry mousse. Booking advisable Sundays. Bedrooms are simply furnished in traditional style, and the bar and lounge have lovely views. **Family pub**

Prices given are as at the time of our research and are comparative indications rather than firm quotes.

## Dysart *(Food)* *Old Rectory Inn*

By Kirkcaldy · *Fife* · Map 2 C3
Kirkcaldy (0592) 51211

*Free House*
*Landlords* Roger & Marianne Worthy

Moussaka £2.10 Creamed kidneys in ginger £3.40 (Last order 9.30. No bar food Sat eve)
Ind Coope Diamond Export; Harp; Skol; cider.

The delightful walled garden is a popular summer alternative to the comfortable, characterful bars at this fine old house on the A955. Outside or in, there's a good variety of bar snacks to enjoy, from homely soups to cold meats and salads, moussaka and creamed kidneys in ginger. Nice simple sweets. Closed Sun and Mon eves and 1st 3 weeks January.

## Eddleston *(Food)* *Horse Shoe Inn*

*Borders* · Map 2 C3
Peebles (072 13) 225

*Free House*
*Landlord* Mr Alan McIntosh-Reid

Bookmaker's sandwich £3.45 Stilton soup 90p (Last order 10pm)
Broughton Greenmantle; McEwan's 80/-; Belhaven 60/-; Younger's Tartan; Guinness; Carlsberg; cider. *Real ale*

The village blacksmith's shop in Victorian times, this smart, white-painted inn is now sought out by lovers of good bar food. The menu is quite extensive: a different soup each day, fresh haddock, steak and Guinness casserole, rare roast beef with salad. The bookmaker's sandwich – rump steak in French bread – is a sure winner, and there are a few simple sweets. **Family pub**

## Edinburgh *(Food)* — *Beehive Inn*

18 Grassmarket · *Lothian* · Map 2 C3
031-225 7171

*Brewery* Scottish & Newcastle
*Landlord* Mr Alan Lawson Noble

Quiche & salad £1.80 Lentil soup 40p
Theakstons Best Bitter, Old Peculier; McEwans 70/-, 80/-, Lager; Youngers No. 3 Ale; Guinness; Taunton cider. *Real ale*

Businessmen and shoppers make a beeline for this comfortable pub to enjoy the tasty lunchtime snacks. The centre of attraction is the cold buffet, which offers a good selection of cooked meats, pies, quiches and interesting salads. There's also a soup of the day, along with hot specials (perhaps spaghetti bolognese or fresh haddock) and some nice home-made sweets. Filled rolls are the only evening choice. Closed Sun lunch.

## Edinburgh *(Food)* — *Cramond Inn*

Cramond Glebe Road, Cramond
*Lothian* · Map 2 C3
031-336 2035

*Free House*
*Landlord* Mr S. Proudfoot
Steak & kidney pie £2 Cold salmon salad £2 (No bar food eves)
Lorimer's 80/-; Tennent's Extra; Younger's Tartan; Guinness; Carlsberg; cider. *Real ale*

The Firth of Forth is just a short step from this pleasant white-painted inn, where tasty, well-prepared lunchtime snacks are just the thing after a bracing walk. Soup and pâté are popular starters, and main courses include attractive salads, quiche, herby sausage rolls and two unfailing favourites in the shape of cottage and steak and kidney pies. Terrace.

## Edinburgh *(B & B)* — *Rutland Hotel*

3 Rutland Street · *Lothian* · Map 2 C3
031-229 3402
*Owners* Welcome Inns
*Landlord* Mr G. Skinner

**BEDROOMS 18 Grade 1 £A**
Younger's Tartan; McEwan's 80/-, Export, Cavalier; Kestrel; Guinness; Taunton cider. *Real ale*

Pleasant accommodation is on offer at this modernised city-centre hotel on the corner of Princes Street. Spacious bedrooms have modern furnishings and are equipped with tea-makers and colour TV. Compact bathrooms with old-fashioned fittings are clean and adequate. Cheerful staff help to create a homely atmosphere. **Family pub**

## Elrick *(Food)* — *Broadstraik Inn*

Near Aberdeen · *Grampian* · Map 1 D2
Skene (033 05) 217

*Free House*
*Landlord* Mrs Anne Horn

Sizzle platter steak £4.60 Chilli con carne £2.55 (Last order 9.30pm)
Maclay's 80/-; Younger's Tartan; Guinness; Carlsberg Pilsner, Hof Export; Taunton cider. *Real ale*

Sizzling spectacularly on their cast-iron platters, tender, juicy steaks are a popular feature at this busy wayside pub. There's also fried fish, gammon and spicy things like chilliburgers or chilli con carne. A special children's menu including sausages and fish fingers is available until 7.30. This is a notably friendly and cheerful place. **Family pub** (till 7.30pm)

## Fochabers *(B & B)* — *Gordon Arms Hotel*

High Street · *Grampian* · Map 1 C2
Fochabers (0343) 820508

*Free House*
*Landlord* Mr C. Pern

**BEDROOMS 14 Grades 1 & 2 £B**
Alice Ale; McEwan's Export; Younger's Tartan, Light; Guinness; Harp; Taunton cider. *Real ale*

Rows of antlers adorn the outside of this smartly painted former coaching house, a popular local meeting place and a favourite of fishermen. Bedrooms – the majority in an extension – are very well equipped, with TVs, tea-makers, hair dryers and direct-dial telephones; nine have private facilities. The comfortable lounge bar stocks a wide selection of malt whiskies. Garden.
**Family pub** (lunchtime)

## Glasgow *(Food)* — *Archie's*

27 Waterloo Street · *Strathclyde* · Map 2 C3
041-221 3210

*Owners* Beard Hotels
*Landlord* Mr David Burns

Chicken provençale £1 Prawn salad £2.25 (Last order 10pm)
McEwan's 80/-; Guinness; Harp; Taunton cider. *Real ale*

Tasty snacks are available between 12.15pm and 10pm in this atmospheric modern bar, a series of rooms with mirrors, plants and bamboo furniture. A self-service counter displays cold meats, raised pies, seafood and a selection of good fresh salads, and a daily-changing hot choice could include lasagne, macaroni cheese, chicken provençale and chilli con carne. Closed Sunday.

## Glendevon *(Food, B & B)* — *Tormaukin Hotel*

Near Dollar · *Tayside* · Map 2 C3
Glendevon (025 982) 252

*Free House*
*Landlords* Jack & Annie Dracup

**BEDROOMS 6 Grade 1 £A**
Bacon burger £2.85 Chicken curry £2.65 (Last order 9.45pm)
Ind Coope Burton Ale, Double Diamond, Alloa's Export; Guinness; Skol; cider. *Real ale*

Tasty home-made snacks bring a loyal following to this smart roadside pub, whose traditional beamed bars are warm and welcoming: beefburgers and chicken curry are great favourites, with soup, colourful salads and succulent steaks also in constant demand. Attractive bedrooms, all with TVs and tea-makers, have smart pine furniture and neat little panelled bathrooms. Terrace.
**Family pub** (lunchtime)

## Glenfinnan *(B & B)* — *Stage House Inn*

*Highland* · Map 1 B2
Kinlocheil (039 783) 246

*Free House*
*Landlords* Helen & Andrew Brooks

**BEDROOMS 9 Grade 2 £B**
Younger's Tartan; Guinness; Tennent's Lager.

Fishing rights on nearby Loch Shiel lure anglers to this attractive wayside inn, which stands in breathtaking countryside on the road to Mallaig. Simple comforts are provided in the bedrooms, which all have private bath or shower rooms. There's a cheerful bar and two little sun lounges, the latter taking full advantage of the fabulous setting. Closed end October–mid March. Terrace.
**Family pub**

## Inverbeg *(B & B)* — *Inverbeg Inn*

Luss, Loch Lomond · *Strathclyde* · Map 2 B3
Luss (043 686) 678

*Free House*
*Landlord* Bill Porter

**BEDROOMS 14 Grade 1 £A**
McEwan's Tartan, Lager; Strathalbion Bitter; Guinness; Harp; Taunton cider.
*Real ale*

Cattle drovers have given way to tourists at this attractively modernised inn, which stands alongside the A82 on the west shore of Loch Lomond. A log fire burns in the pleasant lounge bar, which features fine paintings of Highland scenes; there's also a quiet residents' lounge. Bright bedrooms (half with well-kept private bathrooms) have tea-makers and radios. Most have TV's and command lovely loch views.
**Family pub**

## Invergarry *(B & B)* — *Inn on the Garry*

*Highland* · Map 1 B2
Invergarry (080 93) 206

*Free House*
*Landlords* Iain & Fiona Maclean

**BEDROOMS 10 Grade 2 £A**
Ind Coope Alloa's Archibald Arrol's 70/-, Heavy, Light; Burton's; Guinness; Skol; cider.
*Real ale*

Standing at the junction of the A82 and A87 (the 'Road to the Isles'), this sturdy Victorian inn is a popular base for anglers. Fishy yarns are spun in the rustic bar, and the comfortable lounges are good places to unwind. Best bedrooms are those on the first floor – simple, spacious and stoutly furnished. Accommodation closed October–March; bar closed at lunchtime mid November–March.
**Family pub**

## Invermoriston *(Food, B & B)* — *Glenmoriston Arms*

Glenmoriston, Near Inverness · *Highland*
Map 1 B2
Glenmoriston (0320) 51206
*Free House*
*Landlords* Mr & Mrs R. Shepherd
**BEDROOMS 8 Grade 2 £B**
Home-made soup 50p Fisherman's prawn salad with Marie Rose sauce £2 (Last order 8pm)
Younger's Tartan; McEwan's 80/-, Export; Guinness; Carlsberg Hof; Harp; Taunton cider.

A collection of guns and fishing rods underlines the sporting associations at this welcoming inn, which stands at the junction of the A82 and A887. Simple bar snacks include soup, sandwiches, pâté and a variety of meat, fish and cheese platters. Six of the modestly furnished bedrooms have TVs and shower or bathrooms. Accommodation closed November–April. Garden.
**Family pub**

## Killiecrankie *(Food)* — *Killiecrankie Hotel*

By Pitlochry · *Tayside* · Map 1 C2
Pitlochry (0796) 3220

*Free House*
*Landlords* Mr & Mrs Hattersley Smith & Emma

Venison steakette £1.95 Tayside trout £3.95 (Last order 10pm)
Younger's Tartan; Tennent's Extra

Bar food of good variety and quality attracts a large and loyal custom to this beautifully situated hotel. Lunchtime offers sandwiches, salads and tasty snacks like potted shrimps, pork sausages and an excellent smoked haddock flan. A shorter evening menu includes main courses like grilled trout and Angus steak. Closed mid Oct–end March. Garden. *For accommodation see Egon Ronay's Lucas Hotel & Restaurant Guide 1985.*
**Family pub**

## Killin *(Food, B & B)* — *Clachaig Hotel*

*Central* · Map 2 C3
Killin (056 72) 270

*Free House*
*Landlords* Colin & Jean Lewis

**BEDROOMS 8 Grade 2 £C**
Fresh herring £1.90 Haggis, tatties & neeps £2.40 (Last order 8.30pm)
Younger's Tartan; McEwan's 80/-; Harp; Taunton cider. *Real ale*

There's a real flavour of Scotland about the food served in this cheerful pub on the river Dochart. Tay salmon is a treat not to be missed, and other native specialities include fried herring, haggis, cloutie dumplings and oaty fruit crumbles. Also delicious bread and butter pudding. Spotless bedrooms offer simple comforts, and there's a cosy TV lounge. Accommodation closed late Nov–mid Jan. **Family pub**

## Killin *(Food, B & B)* — *Queen's Court Hotel*

*Central* · Map 2 C3
Killin (056 72) 349

*Landlords* Mr & Mrs S. Horn

**BEDROOMS 8 Grade 2 £C**
Scampi & chips £3 Home-made soup 65p
Tennent's 70/-, 80/-, Lager; Guinness. *Real ale*

The welcome couldn't be warmer at this solid, stone-built house standing on the outskirts of a pleasant Highland village. Neat bedrooms provide simple overnight comforts, and there's a traditionally furnished TV lounge. Snacks served in the convivial Coach House bar include hearty home-made soup, sandwiches, sausages and steaks, with a nice nutmeggy rice pudding to finish. **Family pub** (till 9pm)

## Kippen *(Food, B & B)* — *Cross Keys*

Main Street, Near Stirling · *Central* · Map 2 C3
Kippen (078 687) 293
*Free House*
*Landlords* Richard & Penny Miller
**BEDROOMS 3 Grade 2 £C**
Baked trout £3.50 Home-made special ice cream 80p (Last order 9pm. No bar food Mon eve)
Younger's No.3 Ale; McEwan's 80/-, Export, Pale; Guinness; Taunton cider. *Real ale*

A warm welcome, good food, comfortable accommodation, lovely views – this delightful old inn has them all. Filled rolls, sandwiches and pâté with oatcakes make tasty light snacks, while heartier fare includes casseroles, steak and kidney pie and succulent roast chicken, with home-made ice cream a popular sweet. (Less choice Mon lunch.) Three bright, tidy bedrooms (no smoking, please) share a spotless little bathroom. **Family pub**

## Lewiston *(B & B)* — *Lewiston Arms*

Near Drumnadrochit · *Highland* · Map 1 C2
Drumnadrochit (045 62) 225

*Free House*
*Landlords* Mr & Mrs N. Quinn

**BEDROOMS 8 Grade 2 £C**
Younger's Tartan, No. 3; McEwan's Export, Lager; Taunton cider. *Real ale*

A convivial 200-year-old pub in a tiny village close to Loch Ness. Thirsty guests can choose between the popular public bar and a modern lounge bar that opens on to the attractive garden. There's also a cosy lounge as well as a spacious TV room. Bedrooms (four in a cottage reached through the garden) offer simple comforts for an overnight stay. **Family pub**

## Linlithgow *(Food)* — *Champany Inn*

*Lothian* · Map 2 C3
Philipstoun (050 683) 4532

*Free House*
*Landlords* Anne & Clive Davidson

Pickled fish £1.65 Grilled lamb chops £2.75 (Last order 10pm. No bar food Sun eve)
Belhaven 80/-, 70/-; Skol; cider. *Real ale*

Choices on the bar menu at this welcoming roadside complex include juicy steaks, lamb and veal chops, burgers and deep-dish pizzas with a variety of toppings. At lunchtime you might have a bowl of nourishing soup or turn your attention to the laden cold table, which offers items like rich potted ham, tasty roast lamb, beef and duck, plus some very enjoyable salads.
**Family pub**

## Loch Eck *(Food)* — *Coylet Inn*

Dunoon · *Strathclyde* · Map 2 B3
Kilmun (036 984) 322

*Free House*
*Landlord* Mr R. Addis

Pâté & oatcakes £1.20 Open prawn sandwich £2.40 (Last order 10pm)
Younger's No. 3 Ale; McEwan 80/-; Heriot 80/-; Guinness; Tennant's Extra. *Real ale*

Excellent home-prepared bar snacks are served at this long, low pub 'twixt loch and forest. Scotch broth is a good warming starter, followed perhaps by home-cooked ham, chicken and chips or a tasty smoked haddock and egg pie. Traditional cloutie dumpling is a popular pud. Open fires keep the bar cosy in winter, while in summer the terrace comes into its own. **Family pub**

We neither seek nor accept hospitality, and we pay for all food, drinks and accommodation in full.

## Lybster *(Food, B & B)* — *Bayview Hotel*

*Highland* · Map 1 C1
Lybster (059 32) 346

*Free House*
*Landlords* Ranald & Norma Hutton

**BEDROOMS 3 Grade 1 £C**
Finnan haddock £1.50 Roast sirloin £2.50 (Last order 11pm)
McEwan's Export, Pale Ale; Younger's Tartan; Harp.

The Huttons' agreeable little haven of hospitality stands in a side street just a short stroll from the tiny harbour. Excellent fresh fish features among the enjoyable bar snacks, which also include tasty soup, salads, grills and lovely home-made sweets. The three neatly furnished bedrooms share a sparkling bathroom, and there's a cosy residents' lounge and two summery sun rooms. **Family pub**

## Melrose *(Food, B & B)* — *Burts Hotel*

Market Square · *Borders* · Map 2 D4
Melrose (089 682) 2285

*Free House*
*Landlords* Graham & Annie Henderson

**BEDROOMS 22 Grade 1 & 2 £B**
Prawns, bacon & mushrooms in garlic £1.50
Beef bourguignon £2.10 (Last order 9.30pm)
Belhaven 80/-, Export, Heavy, Light; Younger's Tartan; Taunton cider. *Real ale*

This distinctive black and white hotel in the town centre is a friendly, well-run place. The spacious bar, which features some deadly looking antique swords, offers a good selection of enjoyable snacks, from smoked mackerel pâté to basket meals, excellent ham salad and beef kidneys Turbigo. Attractively decorated bedrooms, some traditional, others more modern in style, have TVs and tea-makers. Garden.
**Family pub**

## Melrose *(B & B)* — *George & Abbotsford*

High Street · *Borders* · Map 2 D4
Melrose (089 682) 2308

*Free House*
*Landlord* Mr J. H. Brown

**BEDROOMS 36 Grade 1 & 2 £B**
Younger's Tartan; McEwan's Pale Ale; Greenmantle Ale; Guinness; Carlsberg Hof; Pilsner; cider. *Real ale*

Standing in the centre of town, this handsome hotel is a good base for exploring Sir Walter Scott country. Spacious, attractively coordinated bedrooms range from traditional to more modern; all have contemporary furniture, radios and tea-makers and most offer private facilities. There's a roomy, relaxing bar that opens on to an attractive rose garden. Upstairs, a modest lounge doubles as a TV room. **Family pub**

## Moffat *(Food, B & B)* — *Balmoral Hotel*

High Street · *Dumfries & Galloway* · Map 2 C4
Moffat (0683) 20288

*Free House*
*Landlords* Robin & Denise Stewart

**BEDROOMS 15 Grade 2 £B**
Breaded lamb chops £2.50 Madras curry £2 (Last order 10pm)
Younger's Tartan; McEwan's 80/-; Guinness; Carlsberg Hof; Harp; cider. *Real ale*

The bar snacks are homely and satisfying at this smartly painted town-centre hotel. Breaded lamb chops are a favourite choice, along with sandwiches, ploughman's, chicken curry and steak pie, and the cold luncheon buffet is popular in summer. Bedrooms with coordinated floral fabrics and wallpaper have whitewood furniture and tea-makers. There's a residents' lounge with TV. Patio. **Family pub**

## Moffat *(Food)* — *Black Bull*

Station Rd · *Dumfries & Galloway* · Map 2 C4
Moffat (0683) 20206

*Free House*
*Landlord* Mrs H. Poynton
Haggis £1.65 Shepherd's pie £1.85 (Last order 9pm. No bar food Sun eve & daily Jan–March)
Younger's No. 3 Ale, Tartan; McEwan's 80/-; Broughton Greenmantle; Guinness; Carlsberg Hof; cider. *Real ale*

There's a warm, friendly feel about this 16th-century inn, where simple, nourishing bar fare is the order of the day. Haggis and shepherd's pie are firm favourites, and other popular choices range from sandwiches and pâté to macaroni, cold meats and curries. Railway buffs should make tracks for the public bar, which is filled with relics from the Caledonian Railway.
**Family pub**

## Muir of Ord *(B & B)* — *Ord Arms Hotel*

Great North Road · *Highland* · Map 1 C2
Inverness (0463) 870286

*Free House*
*Landlords* John & Shirley Baillie

**BEDROOMS 15 Grade 1 £C**
Younger's Tartan; McEwan's Extra Pale Ale; Harp.

Just off the A9 on the northern outskirts of Muir of Ord, the Baillies' welcoming, sand-coloured inn provides excellent overnight accommodation. Bright, cheerful bedrooms, all with tea-makers and TVs, have plenty of cupboard space, good large mirrors and washbasins. Seven offer private facilities, and there are three public bathrooms. The two bars include one featuring pictures of some of the local regulars. Patio. **Family pub**

## New Abbey *(Food, B & B)* — *Criffel Inn*

Nr Dumfries · *Dumfries & Galloway* · Map 2 C4
New Abbey (038 785) 305
*Free House*
*Landlords* Mr & Mrs McCulloch

**BEDROOMS 5 Grade 2 £C**
Fresh salmon fishcakes £2.40 York ham salad, scones & cakes £3.60 (No bar food Sun lunch)
Younger's No.3 Ale; McEwan's 60/-, 70/-; Guinness; Tennent's Extra; Taunton cider. *Real ale*

A pleasant village pub, made more delightful by Janet McCulloch's homely snacks. Soup, salads, ploughman's and steak pies are popular lunchtime fare, along with York ham and fresh salmon, which also feature in the popular high teas served from 4.30 to 6. Sandwiches only in the evening. Bedrooms (two with shower cabinets) have simple modern furnishings; there's a residents' lounge with TV and a pleasant patio. **Family pub**

## Onich *(B & B)* — *Onich Hotel*

Near Fort William · *Highland* · Map 1 B2
Onich (085 53) 214

*Free House*
*Landlords* Messrs I. & R. Young

**BEDROOMS 25 Grade 2 £B**
Ind Coope Diamond Heavy; Alloa Light; Arrol's 70 Shilling; Burton Ale; Guinness; Skol; Taunton cider. *Real ale*

A magnificent setting on the banks of lovely Loch Linnhe is a major feature of this sizeable white-painted inn, a popular base for touring the Highlands. Compact bedrooms offer simple comforts, and, like other areas, are kept in very good order. The spacious main bar offers superb views, and there are two lounges (one with TV) and a games room. Good breakfasts. Garden.
**Family pub**

## Portree *(B & B)* — *Rosedale Hotel*

Isle of Skye · *Highland* · Map 1 B2
Portree (0478) 2531

*Free House*
*Landlord* Mr H. M. Andrew

**BEDROOMS 21 Grade 1 £B**
McEwan's Export; Younger's Tartan; Cavalier; Tennent's Extra; Taunton cider.

Right on the waterfront at Portree harbour, this agreeable white-painted hotel has been run by members of the Andrew family for more than 30 years. It's a good place for an overnight stop, with friendly service and comfortable, unpretentious accommodation. Bedrooms have simple fitted furniture and most offer private facilities. There are two lounges (one with TV) and a modern bar. **Family pub** (lunchtime)

## Spean Bridge *(B & B)* — *Letterfinlay Lodge Hote*

*Highland* · Map 1 B2
Invergloy (039 784) 222

*Free House*
*Landlords* Forsyth family

**BEDROOMS 15 Grades 1 & 2 £C**
Alloa's Export; Löwenbräu.

Seven miles north of Spean Bridge, this former shooting lodge has its own jetty on Loch Lochy. Huge picture windows in the bar provide breathtaking views of the mountains, and there is also a homely lounge. Most bedrooms are in sturdy traditional style and some have bathrooms with splendid antique fittings. The Forsyth family make guests feel thoroughly welcome. Closed end October to March. Garden. **Family pub**

## Spinningdale *(Food)* — *Old Mill Inn*

*Highland* · Map 1 C1
Whiteface (086 288) 242

*Free House*
*Landlord* Mr John Warner

Cream of salmon soup 60p Venison casserole £1.85 (Last order 8.45pm. No bar food Mon eve)
Younger's Tartan; McEwan's Pale Ale, Export; Tennent's Export; Taunton cider.

With its dramatic setting on the north side of Dornoch Firth, this old, whitewashed coaching inn is a splendid place to pause for a snack. In the mellow pine-clad bar there's a good choice of robust fare: salmon and venison appear in soups and pâtés as well as main courses, and other popular items include sandwiches and salads, burgers and flavoursome casseroles. **Family pub**

## Strathblane *(B & B)* — *Kirkhouse Inn*

Near Glasgow · *Central* · Map 2 C3
Blanefield (0360) 70621

*Free House*
*Landlord* Mr R. C. Aird

**BEDROOMS 19 Grade 1 £B**
McEwan's No. 3, Export, Tartan; Tennent's Lager; cider. *Real ale*

Follow the A81 north from Glasgow to find this handsome roadside inn, which has been much modernised over the years. The spacious foyer doubles as a comfortable lounge, and there are two roomy bars. Well-kept bedrooms are generally quite up to date in decor and furnishings, and ten have their own spick-and-span bathrooms. Patio. **Family pub**

## Strathmiglo *(Food)* — *Strathmiglo Inn*

High Street · *Fife* · Map 2 C3
Strathmiglo (033 76) 252

*Free House*
*Landlords* John & Barbara Winning

Fried fillet of sole £2.20 Steak & kidney pie £2.65 (Last order 9.30pm. No bar food Sun eve)
Tennent's 70/-, Export, Lager; Guinness.

The bar snacks are tasty and satisfying at this delightful little white-painted pub in the middle of the village. Start with the soup of the day – perhaps cream of cauliflower or deliciously thick bacon and lentil – and follow with grilled Arbroath smokies, gammon with steak or chilli con carne. Lighter bites include salads and sandwiches, and there's a small choice of sweets.

## Tarbert *(Food, B & B)* ★ *West Loch Hotel*

Loch Fyne · *Strathclyde* · Map 2 B3
Tarbert (088 02) 283

*Free House*
*Landlords* A. & J. Thom & D. & J. Thom
**BEDROOMS 6 Grade 1 £B**
Bobotie with rice £3.25 Grilled Loch Fyne herring with vegetables £2.50 (No bar food eves)
McEwan's Export; Younger's Pale; Guinness; Carlsberg; Taunton cider.

Warm and welcoming, this black and white roadside inn enjoys lovely views of the loch and surrounding countryside. The bar lunches are superb, with grilled herring, kidneys with rice and game pie typical delights on the daily-changing menu. Lovely sweets, too, like trifle, or caramel mousse. Bedrooms are neat and comfortable, and there's a pleasant little TV lounge. Closed November. **Family pub**

## Tayvallich *(Food)* *New Tayvallich Inn*

Near Lochgilphead · *Strathclyde* · Map 2 B3
Tayvallich (054 67) 282

*Free House*
*Landlords* Pat & John Grafton

Loch Scotnish mussels marinière £1.90
Soup 65p (Last order 7pm)
Ind Coope Alloa Export, Heavy; Guinness; Skol; Taunton cider.

This cheery little pub stands on the shores of Loch Sweet. The fare on offer in the cosy public bar includes soup of the day, steaks, burgers, salads and popular fish items such as plump mussels and Dublin Bay prawns. Home-made sweets like fruit crumble and a rich chocolate nut slice. **Family pub**

## Uig *(B & B)* *Ferry Inn*

Isle of Skye · *Highland* · Map 1 A2
Uig (047 042) 242

*Free House*
*Landlords* John & Betty Campbell

**BEDROOMS 6 Grade 2 £C**
McEwan's Export; Younger's Tartan; Guinness; Tennent's Export, Lager; Taunton cider.

A neatly kept, friendly little pub, which enjoys bird's-eye views of the ferry and fishing boats. Local fishermen are regular customers in the simple public bars; there's also a lounge bar and a small TV room. Spacious, plainly furnished bedrooms have tea-makers and central heating; one offers private facilities and there are two public bathrooms. Patio.
**Family pub**

## Ullapool *(B & B)* *Argyll Hotel*

Argyle Street · *Highland* · Map 1 B1
Ullapool (0854) 2422

*Free House*
*Landlords* Mr & Mrs I. Matheson

**BEDROOMS 8 Grade 2 £C**
McEwan's Export, 80/-, Heavy; Guinness; Carlsberg; Harp; Taunton cider. *Real ale*

Hospitality is a way of life at this white-painted inn near the quayside. The bars are convivial, and the place really buzzes on the nights when there's live entertainment. The TV room is a quieter spot. Overnight guests will find simply furnished, spotlessly kept bedrooms with fine views. They are equipped with tea-makers and electric blankets and there are three public bathrooms. Hearty breakfasts. **Family pub**

## Weem *(Food, B & B)* — *Ailean Chraggan Hotel*

By Aberfeldy · *Tayside* · Map 2 C3
Aberfeldy (0887) 20346

*Free House*
*Landlords* Gillespie family

**BEDROOMS 4 Grade 1 £B**
Chicken casserole £3.85 Cream meringue £1.10 (Last order 10pm, 8.30 in winter)
Younger's Tartan; Tennent's Extra.

A lot of care goes into the running of this friendly village pub, which has nice gardens and fine views. The bar snacks are simple and delicious, ranging from home-made soup and pasta to omelettes, Tay salmon and chicken casserole. Spick-and-span bedrooms, all with TVs and tea-makers, feature some fine traditional furniture; they share a single public bathroom.
**Family pub**

## Wester Howgate *(Food)* ★ — *Old Howgate Inn*

Near Penicuik · *Lothian* · Map 2 C3
Penicuik (0968) 74244

*Free House*
*Landlords* Mr & Mrs Di Rollo

Smørrebrød small £1.25 large £2.50 (Last order 10pm)
Belhaven 80/-; McEwan's 80/-; Younger's Tartan; Guinness; Carlsberg Pilsner, Export.
*Real ale*

Danish open sandwiches (smørrebrød) have for many years been the speciality at this delightful whitewashed pub alongside the A6094. The base is light or dark rye bread, and all the toppings are home-prepared. Forty mouthwatering varieties include chicken liver pâté, tomato rémoulade, ham with vegetable salad and superb sweet pickled herring with egg and curry mayonnaise. Garden. Closed Sun eve.
**Family pub**

# WALES

## Aberaeron *(Food)*

### *Harbourmaster Hotel*

Quay Parade · *Dyfed* · Map 7 B1
Aberaeron (0545) 570351

*Free House*
*Landlords* Mackay Family

Lasagne £1.85 Seafood piatter £3.25 (Last order 10pm)
Whitbread Best Bitter, Welsh Bitter; Flowers IPA; Guinness; Heineken; cider. *Real ale*

The harbour wall and the splendid little panelled bar are equally delightful settings for enjoying a drink and a snack at this handsome 19th-century pub. Seafood is something of a speciality, the choice ranging from garlic mussels to crab, lobster, salmon and a mixed platter. Other popular items include sandwiches, omelettes, tasty savoury pies and a cold buffet in summer. Closed Sunday. **Family pub**

## Abergavenny *(Food, B & B)*

### *Crowfield Inn*

Ross Road · *Gwent* · Map 7 C2
Abergavenny (0873) 5048

*Free House*
*Landlords* George & Sasha Crabb

**BEDROOMS 5 Grade 1 £A** (No dogs)
Crowfield smokies £1.50 Beef shobdon £4.65 (Last order 9.30pm. No bar food Sun)
Worthington Best Bitter; Bass; Carling Black Label. *Real ale*

A pleasant farmhouse inn, where Sasha Crabb's bar menu combines familiar favourites with delightful specialities such as zippy pepperpot beef or seafood in a mustardy cheese sauce. Spacious smartly furnished bedrooms (all in an annexe) have central heating and well-appointed bathrooms. There's a splendidly comfortable residents' lounge with a piano for guests to play. No children under 12 overnight; accommodation closed 1 week Christmas.

## Babell *(Food)*

### *Black Lion Inn*

Near Holywell · *Clwyd* · Map 3 B3
Caerwys (0352) 720239

*Free House*
*Landlords* Mr & Mrs H. G. Foster

Grilled sardines with salad & sautéed potatoes £2.60 Steak sandwich £2.95 (No bar food eves & all Sun)
Stones Bitter; Carling Black Label; Taunton cider.

Tucked away in the hills and lanes behind Holywell and the Dee Estuary, the Fosters' quaint little whitewashed inn serves very good lunchtime food in homely and hospitable surroundings. Soup, pâté and fresh sardines are popular starters, while main courses range from omelettes and steak sandwiches to flavoursome stews. Also salads and nice home-made sweets. Closed lunchtime Monday and Saturday.

## Beaumaris *(Food, B & B)*

### *Ye Olde Bull's Head*

Castle Street, Anglesey · *Gwynedd* · Map 3 A3
Beaumaris (0248) 810329

*Free House*
*Landlord* Mrs D. M. Barnett
**BEDROOMS 17 Grades 1 & 2 £B** (No dogs)
Florentine pie 90p Fresh local salmon salad £3 (No bar food eves)
Bass, Mild, 4X; Stones Bitter; Worthington 'E'; Younger's Scotch Bitter; Guinness; Carlsberg Hof. *Real ale*

This old posting house is steeped in history, and its beamed bar is a cosy setting for simple, satisfying lunchtime snacks. Sandwiches come with a variety of fillings – cheese and onion, roast duckling, even banana – and there are also salads and hot pies like sausage or fish. Less choice Sun. Individually furnished bedrooms offer good comforts, and there's a delightful residents' lounge. Rooms closed two weeks autumn. **Family pub**

## Betwys-yn-Rhos *(Food)* — *Ffarm Hotel*

*Clwyd* · Map 3 A3
Dolwen (049 260) 287

*Free House*
*Landlords* Lomax family

Ffarm liver pâté £1.25 Steak pipérade £4.40 (Last order 10pm)
Ind Coope Bitter, Dark Mild; Tetley Bitter; Wrexham Lager. *Real ale*

This crenellated Victorian Gothic building, owned by the Lomax family for many years, is an impressive setting in which to enjoy some excellent bar fare. Simple starters like soup, egg mayonnaise and smooth, flavoursome pâté precede splendid main courses such as trout amandine, chicken créole or kidneys in a sherry-based sauce. Other favourites include salads, steaks and basket meals. Closed Sunday in winter. Garden. **Family pub**

## Bodfari *(Food)* — *Dinorben Arms Inn*

Near Denbigh · *Clwyd* · Map 3 B4
Bodfari (074 575) 309

*Free House*
*Landlord* Mr G. T. Hopwood

Moussaka with vegetables & potatoes £3.50 Soused herrings £1.40 (Last order 10.15)
Border Bitter; Whitbread Mild; Younger's Tartan; Guinness; Heineken; Wrexham Lager; cider. *Real ale*

A splendid place for all the family, this 17th-century inn offers fine views from its attractive terraces and gardens. Soup and sandwiches are the fare in the bar, while in the dining room at lunchtime there's an impressive self-service selection of cold cuts and salads, plus some hot dishes. The evening choice, which is even wider, includes daily specials such as chicken Kiev. **Family pub**

## Brockweir *(B & B)* — *Brockweir Inn*

Chepstow · *Gwent* · Map 7 D2
Tintern (029 18) 548

*Free House*
*Landlords* Mavis & Granville Clegg

**BEDROOMS 4 Grade 2 £C**
Flower's Original; Hook Norton Best Bitter; Whitbread Best Bitter; Stella Artois; cider. *Real ale*

Mavis and Granville Clegg provide a warm welcome at this convivial little village inn by the river Wye. The cosy lounge bar is a splendid place for a drink and a chat, while pool is a popular pursuit in the public bar. Simply furnished bedrooms (two rooms under the eaves) are fine for an overnight stay, and guests wake up to a well-cooked breakfast. Garden. **Family pub**

## Cardigan *(B & B)* — *Black Lion Hotel*

High Street · *Dyfed* · Map 7 B2
Cardigan (0239) 612532

*Free House*
*Landlord* Mr T. L. Lowe

**BEDROOMS 11 Grade 1 £B**
Flower's IPA; Whitbread Welsh Bitter, Best Bitter; Stella Artois; Heineken; cider. *Real ale*

The greeting is warm and friendly at this popular town-centre hotel, whose red-brick Georgian façade hides 800 years of history. Comfortable accommodation is provided in the well-kept bedrooms, where modern pine units and tea-makers are standard. All have neat bath or shower rooms. Public areas include a TV lounge, snug little writing room and spacious bar. Closed Sunday. **Family pub**

## Cenarth *(Food)* — *White Hart*

Near Newcastle Emlyn · *Dyfed* · Map 7 B2
Newcastle Emlyn (0239) 710305

*Free House*
*Landlords* John & Anne Jones

Anglesey eggs £1.75 Teifi salmon £5.95 (Last order 10pm)
Whitbread Welsh Bitter, Mild; Buckley's Best Bitter; Guinness; Heineken. *Real ale*

John Jones in the bar and his wife Anne in the kitchen make a splendid team at this agreeable old inn near the river Teifi. The menu shows a strong Welsh influence, with dishes such as Anglesey eggs, Teifi salmon and the splendid catrin pie – a light pastry case enclosing minced lamb with raisins and brown sugar. More familiar fare includes sandwiches and basket-type meals. **Family pub**

## Chepstow *(Food, B & B)* — *Castle View Inn*

16 Bridge Street · *Gwent* · Map 7 D2
Chepstow (029 12) 70349

*Free House*
*Landlords* Mr & Mrs M. Gillett

**BEDROOMS 10 Grade 1 £A**
Aubergine & nut crumble £2.25 Rabbit pie & vegetables £3 (Last order 9.30pm)
John Smith's Bitter; Simond's Bitter; Kronenbourg.

The Gilletts' 300-year-old inn opposite the castle offers comfort, good food, friendly service and abundant period charm. Home-prepared bar snacks include omelettes, flavoursome pâtés, hearty pies and meaty casseroles, along with sandwiches, vegetarian dishes and nice sweets. Smartly modernised bedrooms have good-quality fitted furniture, TVs, tea-makers and well-equipped carpeted bathrooms. There's a lovely walled garden. **Family pub**

## Crickhowell *(Food, B & B)* — *Bear Hotel*

*Powys* · Map 7 C2
Crickhowell (0873) 810408

*Free House*
*Landlord* Mrs Joan Hindmarsh
**BEDROOMS 12 Grade 1 £B**
Fresh salmon & prawn béchamel with salad £4.95 Turkey américaine £4.50 (Last order 10pm)
Bass, Allbright; Whitbread Best Bitter; Stella Artois; Taunton cider. *Real ale*

A charming 15th-century hostelry, with a warm, welcoming bar, a cobbled courtyard and an attractive enclosed garden. The snack menu offers something for most tastes and appetites, from super smoked salmon pâté to savoury pies and pancakes, steaks and turkey américaine. Bedrooms (most with private facilities) are neatly appointed, and there's a comfortably furnished residents' lounge with television. **Family pub**

## Crickhowell *(Food)* — *Nantyffin Cider Mill Inn*

*Powys* · Map 7 C2
Crickhowell (0873) 810775

*Free House*
*Landlord* Mrs Barbara Ambrose

Smoked haddock kedgeree with salad £2.50 Cider syllabub £1.30 (Last order 10.30pm)
John Smith's Bitter; Marston's Pedigree; Worthington Best Bitter; Guinness; Carlsberg Export; cider. *Real ale*

Pork and cider pie and superb cider syllabub are two of Barbara Ambrose's specialities at this attractive pink-washed pub that was once a cider mill. Her smoked haddock kedgeree is another great favourite, along with flavoursome soups, cold meats and salads, quiches and treacle tart. The inn stands west of Crickhowell at the junction of the A40 and A479. Garden. **Family pub**

## Dollgellau *(B & B)* — *Gwernan Lake Hotel*

*Gwynedd* · Map 7 C1
Dolgellau (0341) 422488

*Free House*
*Landlords* Mr & Mrs P. Hall

**BEDROOMS 10 Grade 2 £B** (No dogs)
Bass; Carling Black Label. *Real ale*

Trout-filled Lake Gwernan provides a peaceful setting for this whitewashed inn outside Dolgellau. There's a friendly little bar and a panelled lounge adorned with a fine collection of plates and pottery. Bright, cheerful bedrooms, which share two public bathrooms, are simply furnished. No children under three overnight. Accommodation is closed between October and Easter. Garden.

## Felindre Farchog *(B & B)* — *Old Salutation Inn*

Near Cardigan · *Dyfed* · Map 7 B2
Newport (0239) 820564

*Free House*
*Landlords* Peter & Joan Voyce

**BEDROOMS 8 Grade 1 £C**
John Smith's Bitter; Sam Powell Traditional; Courage Best Bitter; Ind Coope Double Diamond; Hofmeister; cider.

Overnight accommodation is in a modern annexe at this charming old whitewashed inn, whose garden slopes down to the banks of the river Nevern. All the bedrooms have TVs, tea-makers and sparkling bathrooms and offer plenty of space and comfort. The two beamed bars are pleasant spots for a drink and a chat and there's a relaxing residents' lounge. **Family pub**

## Hay-on-Wye *(Food, B & B)* — *Old Black Lion*

26 Lion Street · *Powys* · Map 7 C2
Hay-on-Wye (0497) 820841

*Free House*
*Landlords* Mr & Mrs C. Vaughan
**BEDROOMS 10 Grade 1 £A**
Ploughman's £1.10 Steak & kidney pudding £3.95 (Last order 10pm)
Flowers Best Bitter; Worthington Best Bitter; Guinness; Carlsberg Export; cider. *Real ale*

Low ceilings and creaking floors add to the antique charm of this delightful hostelry in a pleasant market town. Excellent bar fare includes a tempting cold buffet and other delights ranging from pasties and toasted sandwiches to steak and kidney pudding and home-pickled salmon. Delicious ice cream to finish. Characterful bedrooms, most with neat bath/shower rooms, have handsome furnishings, TVs and tea-makers. **Family pub**

## Henllan *(B & B)* — *Henllan Falls Inn*

Near Newcastle Emlyn · *Dyfed* · Map 7 B2
Velindre (0559) 370437

*Free House*
*Landlords* Mr & Mrs T. J. Revell

**BEDROOMS 4 Grade 2 £C** (No dogs)
Buckley's Bitter, Mild; John Smiths; Guinness; Celtic; Hofmeister; Kronenbourg; cider.

Close to the river Teifi, the Revells' agreeable little pub is a peaceful spot to spend the night. Simply furnished bedrooms (one suitable for families) have tea-makers and washbasins, and share an up-to-date bathroom. Pool and darts are played in the rustic public bar, and there's a quiet lounge bar and pleasant TV room. Accommodation closed Christmas week. Pub closed Sunday. **Family pub**

## Holywell *(B & B)* — *Stamford Gate Hotel*

Halkyn Road · *Clwyd* · Map 3 B3
Holywell (0352) 712942

*Free House*
*Landlords* A. J. & K. L. Newell

**BEDROOMS 12 Grade 1 £A** (No dogs)
Wilson's Great Northern Bitter; Watney's Special Mild; Guinness; Carlsberg; cider. *Real ale*

This go-ahead little hotel above the Dee estuary offers spotlessly clean overnight accommodation that appeals equally to business visitors and holiday-makers. Bedroom decor is smartly cheerful, and TVs, radio-alarms and well-supplied bathrooms are standard throughout. Public rooms include a comfortable reception lounge and two bars, one with a nautical theme. Breakfast is served in bedrooms.

**Family pub**

## Llanarmon Dyffryn Ceiriog *(B & B)* — *West Arms Hotel*

Near Llangollen · *Clwyd* · Map 3 B4
Llanarmon Dyffryn Ceiriog (069 176) 665

*Free House*
*Landlords* Mr & Mrs A. J. Edge

**BEDROOMS 16 Grade 2 £A**
Younger's Scotch Bitter, Mild; Harp; McEwan's Export; Carlsberg Hof.

Situated in a little village at the head of a lovely valley, this 400-year-old inn has gardens running down to the river Ceiriog. Trout fishing is available to guests, who can swap anglers' tales in the charming bars or catch a TV programme in the lounge. Bedrooms, some with splendid views, are pleasantly furnished in cottagy style. Six have private facilities. **Family pub**

## Llanarthney *(Food, B & B)* — *Golden Grove Arms*

Near Carmarthen · *Dyfed* · Map 7 B2
Dryslwyn (055 84) 551

*Free House*
*Landlords* Mr & Mrs R. J. Jones

**BEDROOMS 7 Grade 2 £C**
Barbecued spare ribs £2 King prawns in garlic butter £3 (Last order 10pm)
Buckley's Bitter; Whitbread Welsh Bitter, Tankard; Heineken; cider. *Real ale*

Evening snacks are a popular attraction at this welcoming stone-built farmhouse, which stands just off the B4300 about eight miles from Carmarthen. The choice is nicely varied, from soup and sandwiches to local trout, spare ribs and speciality steaks. Comfortable bedrooms of various sizes have tea-makers and neat pine furnishings. Closed lunch and Sun to non-residents, also 14 January–1 March. **Family pub**

## Llandissilio *(Food)* — *Bush Inn*

Near Clynderwen · *Dyfed* · Map 7 B2
Clynderwen (099 12) 626

*Free House*
*Landlords* K. J. & J. E. Honeker

Lasagne & salad £2.90 Cheese & onion pie £2.20 (Last order 10.30pm)
Worthington Best Bitter; Harp; Double Diamond; Guinness; Kronenbourg; Whitbread Tankard. *Real ale*

This modest little roadside inn is a good place to drop in and enjoy some very tasty snacks. Cold meats and salads make a tempting lunchtime and evening display in the low-ceilinged bar, with locally reared turkey one of the most popular choices. There are also plenty of hot dishes, from soup and lasagne to curries, casseroles and delicious pies, both savoury and sweet.

## Llandogo *(B & B)* — *Sloop Inn*

Near Monmouth · *Gwent* · Map 7 D2
Dean (0594) 530291

*Free House*
*Landlords* George Morgan & Grace Evans

**BEDROOMS 4 Grade 1 £B**
Smiles Best Bitter; Wadworth's 6X; Worthington Best Bitter; Guinness; Harp; Stella Artois; cider. *Real ale*

George Morgan is a most hospitable and caring host at this carefully modernised little inn in the heart of the Wye valley. There are fine views from the panelled lounge bar, while the pool table and fruit machines are popular features of the front bar. Accommodation is excellent: spotless bedrooms (one with a four-poster) are very attractively decorated and have colourful modern bathrooms. Delicious breakfasts. Garden.

## Llandovery *(B & B)* — *King's Head Inn*

Market Square · *Dyfed* · Map 7 C2
Llandovery (0550) 20393

*Free House*
*Landlords* Mr & Mrs Madeira-Cole

**BEDROOMS 4 Grades 1 & 2 £B**
Worthington Dark Mild, Best Bitter; Allbright; Hancock's Traditional Ale; Guinness; Carling Black Label. *Real ale*

This pleasant little inn, parts of which date back to the reign of Charles I, stands right on the market square. The delightfully rustic public bar is a popular place with the locals, and there's a relaxing lounge bar as well as spacious first-floor residents' lounge. Bedrooms have a fresh, modern appeal, with neat fitted furniture and sparkling tiled bathrooms. **Family pub**

## Llanfihangel Crucorney *(Food, B & B)* ★ — *Skirrid Inn*

Near Abergavenny · *Gwent* · Map 7 C2
Crucorney (087 382) 258

*Free House*
*Landlords* Mr & Mrs D. Foster
**BEDROOMS 1 Grade 2 £B**
Shrimp scramble £3.10 Casserole of wild rabbit £3.95 (Last order 9.30pm)
Robinson's Bitter; Wadworth's 6X; Felinfoel Bitter; Allbright; Guinness; Carlsberg; Taunton cider. *Real ale*

The oldest pub in Wales, with a fascinating history going back to the 12th century, is renowned for the excellence of its food. In the atmospheric flagstoned bars you can tuck into Mr Foster's marvellous meat pies or savour the delights of his splendid soups, quiches and casseroles. Lovely old-fashioned puds like figgy duff to finish. There's one large, comfortable bedroom. **Family pub**

## Llanfrynach *(Food)* — *White Swan*

Near Brecon · *Powys* · Map 7 C2
Llanfrynach (087 486) 276

*Free House*
*Landlords* Mr & Mrs David Bell
Range of curries from £2.75 Welsh-style trout & bacon £4.95 (Last order 10.30pm. No bar food Mon except Bank Holidays)
Brain's Bitter; Whitbread Traditional, Best, Welsh Bitter; Guinness; Heineken; cider. *Real ale*

You'll find this attractive, centuries-old pub opposite the church boasting the largest graveyard in Wales. The roomy, open-plan beamed bar is full of character, and here you can sample Mrs Bell's legendary pies, baked to order, or tasty French onion soup. Her careful cooking ranges from vegetable goulash to baked crab, roasts and grills to curries and casseroles. Closed Mon lunch & last 3 weeks January. **Family pub**

## Llangollen *(Food, B & B)* — *Britannia Inn*

Horseshoe Pass · *Clwyd* · Map 3 B4
Llangollen (0978) 860144

*Free House*
*Landlords* Cyril & Maureen Ashton

**BEDROOMS 7 Grade 1 £B**
Chicken & mushroom pie £2.50 Fresh fruit pie 80p (Last order 10pm)
Border Bitter, Mild; Stones Bitter; Tetley's Bitter; Guinness; Wrexham lager; cider.

Nestling at the foot of Horseshoe Pass, this delightful old inn numbers prize-winning gardens and fine mountain views among its attractions. The rustic, spotlessly kept bars are the setting for good simple snacks like toasted sandwiches, salads, savoury pies and chicken curry. Comfortable, homely bedrooms with TVs and tea-makers share three modern bath/shower rooms. Closed Monday evenings in Jan and Feb.

## Llangorse *(B & B)* — *Red Lion*

Near Brecon · *Powys* · Map 7 C2
Llangorse (087 484) 238

*Free House*
*Landlords* Mr & Mrs C. Cocker

**BEDROOMS 10 Grade 1 £B**
Robinson's Best Bitter; Felinfoel Double Dragon; Whitbread Best Bitter, Welsh Bitter; Guinness; cider. *Real ale*

Occupying a picturesque position complete with babbling stream, this charming rose-clad inn in the village centre is a cosy overnight stop for visitors to the Brecon Beacons National Park. The stone-walled bars are popular with the locals, and the public bar features darts and pool. Neat, bright bedrooms have cheerful floral wall-paper, simple white furniture and private bathrooms or shower cubicles. Garden.
**Family pub**

## Llangurig *(B & B)* — *Blue Bell Inn*

Near Llanidloes · *Powys* · Map 7 C1
Llangurig (055 15) 254

*Free House*
*Landlords* Bill & Diana Mills

**BEDROOMS 10 Grade 2 £C** (No dogs)
Whitbread Bitter, Welsh Bitter, Best Mild; Banks's Traditional Bitter; Stella Artois; Heineken. *Real ale*

Converted 16th-century farm cottages make up this pink-washed roadside inn, where landlords Bill and Diana Mills extend a warm and friendly welcome. The rustic bars are cosy and convivial, and there's a traditionally furnished residents' lounge with colour TV. Well-kept bedrooms (front ones double-glazed) offer simple comforts, and overnight guests can look forward to a hearty cooked breakfast.

## Llannefydd *(Food, B & B)* — *Hawk & Buckle Inn*

Near Denbigh · *Clwyd* · Map 3 A4
Llannefydd (074 579) 249

*Free House*
*Landlords* K. C. & M. Johnson

**BEDROOMS 10 Grade 1 £B**
Steak & kidney pie £2.25 Chicken provençale with rice £2.65 (Last order 10pm)
Wilson's Bitter, Special Mild; Carlsberg; Foster's; cider.

Winding roads lead up to this remote stone inn, which enjoys spectacular views from its vantage point above the Vale of Clwyd. Comfortable accommodation (no children under eight) is provided in well-kept bedrooms that range from traditional to smartly modern; all rooms have excellent private facilities. Splendid bar snacks include home-made soups and pâtés, steaks and fresh salmon. Closed weekday lunchtime Nov–Easter.

## Llanrug *(Food)* — *Glyntwrog*

*Gwynedd* · Map 3 A4
Caernarfon (0286) 2191

*Brewery* Lloyd & Trouncer
*Landlords* David & Gill Rochell

Local trout £2 Lamb kebabs £1.75 (Last order 9pm. No bar food Sun lunch)
Ansells Bitter, Mild; Ind Coope Bitter, Double Diamond; Guinness; Skol; cider. *Real ale*

There's a lively local atmosphere in this delightful whitewashed pub, whose two traditionally furnished bars are the convivial setting for some excellent lunchtime and evening snacks. Fresh fish, kebabs and hamburgers are always in demand, along with grills and cold cuts, casseroles and roast chicken. A simple selection of sweets includes ice cream and a delicious apple pie. Garden.

## Llantrissent *(B & B)* — *Royal Oak Inn*

Near Usk · *Gwent* · Map 7 D2
Usk (029 13) 2632

*Free House*
*Landlords* Mr & Mrs G. Rossiter

**BEDROOMS 20 Grade 1 £B** (No dogs)
Flower's Original; Felinfoel Double Dragon; Whitbread Best Bitter, Welsh Bitter; Heineken; cider. *Real ale*

Graham and Maureen Rossiter put out the welcome mat for both old friends and new arrivals at this charming old village inn. Stone walls and oak beams give period character to the cosy main bar, while smartly furnished bedrooms (divided between the original building, a converted cottage and motel-style block) offer a more modern appeal. All have colour TVs and well-equipped shower rooms. Garden.

## Llantilio Crossenny — *Hostry Inn*

'1459', proclaims the sign outside this attractive whitewashed inn a few yards from the B4233. But it's certainly no museum piece, with locals gathering nightly for a drink, a chat and a game of darts. The place has considerable rustic charm, highlighted by the country prints and paraphernalia that adorn the public bar. Patio.

Near Abergavenny · *Gwent* · Map 7 D2
Llantilio (060 085) 278
*Free House* *Landlord* Douglas McAdam
Usher's Best Bitter, Triple Crown; Ben Truman; Carlsberg. *Real ale*

## Llowes *(Food)* ★ — *Radnor Arms*

Near Hay-on-Wye · *Powys* · Map 7 C2
Glasbury (049 74) 460

*Free House*
*Landlords* Brian & Tina Gorringe

Hot avocado £2.75 Fresh salmon & asparagus quiche £3.50 (Last order 10pm)
Felinfoel Double Dragon; Marston's Bitter; Guinness; Carlsberg Hof; cider. *Real ale*

Prime local produce, from fruit and vegetables to lamb and Wye salmon, is put to superb use in the marvellous bar fare served in this delightful stone pub. Our dark, rich mushroom soup was a masterpiece, the lamb hot pot simply delicious. Other tempting dishes include quiches, hot stuffed avocado, seafood omelette and traditional faggots. The sweets are hard to resist, too. Less choice Sunday evenings. Garden.

## Llyswen *(Food, B & B)* — *Griffin Inn*

Near Brecon · *Powys* · Map 7 C2
Llyswen (087 485) 241
*Free House*
*Landlords* Richard & Di Stockton
**BEDROOMS 6 Grade 1 £C**
Fresh Wye Salmon salad £2.75 Fruit crumble 75p (Last order 9pm)
Whitbread Welsh Bitter, Best Bitter; Flower's Best Bitter; Brain's Draught Bitter; Guinness; Stella Artois; Heineken; cider. *Real ale*

Much changed since its coaching inn days, this convivial inn is a good base for touring Wales. Comfortable bedrooms, all with private facilities, have practical modern furnishings and tea-makers, and there's a little upstairs lounge. Tasty snacks served in the characterful bars include sandwiches, salads and hot specials like chicken curry or beef in red wine. Less choice Sunday.

## Menai Bridge *(B & B)* — *Gazelle Hotel*

Glyn Garth · *Gwynedd* · Map 3 A4
Menai Bridge (0248) 713364

*Brewery* Robinson
*Landlords* Kenneth & Barbara Moulton

**BEDROOMS 13 Grade 2 £B**
Robinson's Bitter, Mild, Cock Robin, Old Tom; Guinness; Einhorn; cider. *Real ale*

Popular with fishermen and yachtsmen, the Moultons' friendly quayside pub was once the ferry house for the crossing to Bangor Pier. There are fine views from many of the bedrooms, which have neat modern furnishings, TVs and tea-makers. The spacious bar is a cheerful place for a drink and a chat, and upstairs there's a comfortable residents' lounge. Garden.
**Family pub**

## Mold *(B & B)* — *Arches Inn*

Alltami Road, New Brighton · *Clwyd* · Map 3 B4
Mold (0352) 58646

*Free House*
*Landlords* Mr & Mrs A. S. Meeton

**BEDROOMS 14 Grade 1 £B** (No dogs)
Ansell's Bitter, Mild; Tetley's Bitter; Guinness; Löwenbräu; Wrexham Lager; cider. *Real ale*

Set back from the Mold–Flint road, this attractive red-brick hotel offers modern accommodation of a high standard. Well-equipped bedrooms (no children overnight) are furnished in a modern style that is both smart and practical, and all rooms have spotless bathrooms with coloured suites and shower units. The big lounge bar is comfortable and elegant, with acres of gold plush under its panelled ceiling. Garden.
**Family pub**

## Monmouth *(B & B)* — *Queen's Head Hotel*

St James' Street · *Gwent* · Map 7 D2
Monmouth (0600) 2767

*Free House*
*Landlords* Margaret & Alan Statham

**BEDROOMS 5 Grade 1 £B**
Piston Bitter, 1035 Bitter; Flower's Best Bitter; Whitbread Welsh Bitter; Guinness; cider. *Real ale*

Jovial landlords and cheerful staff create a happy, relaxed atmosphere in this 350-year-old black and white coaching inn. Home-brewed beer brings a large local clientele to the comfortable lounge bar (note the ornate plasterwork ceiling), and the pool table is a popular feature in the tiny public bar. Accommodation comprises two beamed singles sharing a shower room and three larger rooms with modern private facilities.
**Family pub**

## Morfa Nefyn *(Food)* — *Bryncynan Inn*

Near Pwllheli · *Gwynedd* · Map 3 A4
Nefyn (0758) 720879

*Brewery* Lloyd & Trouncer
*Landlord* Mr A. Wilson

Leek & bacon soup 80p Cockle pie £2.75 (Last order 9.30pm)
Ansells Mild, Bitter; Guinness; Double Diamond; Wrexham Lager; Skol; Löwenbräu; cider. *Real ale*

The bar snacks are fresh, tasty and satisfying at this neat little stone inn, which stands at a crossroads on the outskirts of the town. The menu extends to some 40 items, from soup and spaghetti to salads and seafood, pâtés and pies, curries and grills. Nice sweets, too, including a tongue-tingling lemon meringue pie. Closed Sunday.

## Nottage *(B & B)* — *Rose & Crown*

Near Porthcawl · *Mid Glamorgan* · Map 7 C2
Porthcawl (065 671) 4850

*Brewery* Usher
*Landlords* Mr & Mrs D. Parry

**BEDROOMS 7 Grade 1 £B**
Usher's Best Bitter, Triple Crown; Carlsberg; Ben Truman; Guinness; Foster's; cider. *Real ale*

This cheery white-painted pub is a really comfortable place to stay the night: seven attractively furnished bedrooms, all with TV and bathroom, are sparklingly clean, with useful writing and cupboard space. There's a TV lounge for residents and a good hearty breakfast on rising. The three little stone-walled bars with copper-topped tables are hung with hunting cartoons, and the Parrys make excellent hosts.

**Family pub**

## Penallt *(Food)* — *Bush Inn*

Near Monmouth · *Gwent* · Map 7 D2
Monmouth (0600) 2503

*Free House*
*Landlords* Mr & Mrs J. A. Wilson

8oz sirloin steak, chips & peas £4.75 Chicken curry £2 (Last order 10.15pm)
Hancocks Bitter; Bass; Hook Norton Bitter; Worthington Dark; Carlsberg; Carling Black Label; cider. *Real ale*

High above the beautiful Wye valley, this sturdy, slate-roofed inn serves carefully prepared bar snacks from a menu that changes with the seasons. Smooth, creamy chicken liver pâté makes a nice start to a meal, followed perhaps by plaice or a steak, home-cooked ham or chunky chicken curry. Save some room for one of Mrs Wilson's lovely puds. Enjoy it all outside in summer.

## Penmaenpool *(B & B)* — *George III Hotel*

Near Dolgellau · *Gwynedd* · Map 3 A4
Dolgellau (0341) 422525

*Free House*
*Landlord* Gail Hall

**BEDROOMS 13 Grade 1 £B**
Border Bitter; John Marston's Bitter; Younger's Tartan; Guinness; Carlsberg Hof Export, Pilsner; cider.

This attractive old inn overlooking a quaint wooden tollbridge enjoys superb views over the Mawddach estuary to the darkly looming hills beyond. Two characterful bars provide a choice for the thirsty, and there's a delightfully cosy lounge. Best bedrooms are those in the annexe, with cheerful coordinated fabrics and good modern bathrooms. Main-house rooms are more traditionally appointed. Patio.

**Family pub**

## Penybont *(B & B)*

### *Severn Arms*

Near Llandrindod Wells · *Powys* · Map 7 C1
Penybont (059 787) 224

*Free House*
*Landlords* Mr & Mrs W. G. Lloyd

**BEDROOMS 10 Grades 1 & 2 £C**
Bass, Allbright; Worthington Best Bitter, Dark Mild; Whitbread Welsh Bitter; Guinness; Carling Black Label; cider. *Real ale*

The Lloyds extend a friendly welcome to their pleasant whitewashed inn, which dates back to about 1840. The two bars retain a good deal of period character, and there's also a games room and a large residents' lounge with TV. The style is traditional, too, in the spacious bedrooms, which all have tea-makers and good modern bathrooms. Garden.
**Family pub** (lunchtime)

## Raglan *(Food, B & B)*

### *Beaufort Arms Hotel*

High Street · *Gwent* · Map 7 D2
Raglan (0291) 690412

*Free House*
*Landlords* Jeanes family
**BEDROOMS 12 Grade 1 £B**
Pâté-filled mushrooms £2.40 Beef mexicaine £2.95 (Last order 10pm)
Ansell's Traditional Bitter; John Bull Bitter; Double Diamond; Guinness; Löwenbräu; cider. *Real ale*

Run in fine style by the Jeanes family, this town-centre hostelry plays a dual role of friendly local and comfortable hotel. The well-furnished lounge bar is a refined and relaxed setting for enjoying tasty snacks that range from soup and stuffed mushrooms to seafood, coq au vin and a nice spicy beef mexicaine. Warm bedrooms (most with private facilities) have TVs, radios and tea-makers. Patio. **Family pub**

## Three Cocks *(B & B)*

### *Three Cocks Hotel*

Near Brecon · *Powys* · Map 7 C2
Glasbury (049 74) 215

*Free House*
*Landlords* Barry & Jill Cole

**BEDROOMS 7 Grade 1 £A**
Worthington Best Bitter

South-west of Hay-on-Wye on the A438, this family-run stone inn offers homely comforts in peaceful surroundings. Heavy beams and carved oak furniture give an old-world charm to the pretty bedrooms, which share three well-kept bathrooms. There's a comfortable lounge and, across the road, the cheerful Old Barn pub. Overnight guests can look forward to a well-cooked breakfast. Closed Jan–mid Feb.

## Trecastle *(Food)*

### *Castle Hotel*

Near Brecon · *Powys* · Map 7 C2
Senny Bridge (087 482) 354

*Free House*
*Landlords* Dick & Joan Ward

Curried eggs £1.60 Lasagne & salad £2.95 (Last order 9.45pm)
Usher's Best Bitter, Founders Ale; Ben Truman; Webster's Yorkshire Bitter; Guinness; Carlsberg; cider. *Real ale*

In the centre of a village on the A40, this sturdy, grey-painted hostelry attracts a sizable following with some good, wholesome snacks served in the traditionally styled bar. Mushrooms in a crisp breadcrumb coating make a tasty starter, and the main-course choice could include salads, lasagne or a richly flavoured lamb curry served with carefully cooked saffron rice. Simple sweets. Garden. **Family pub**

## Whitebrook *(Food, B & B)* — *Crown at Whitebrook*

Near Monmouth · *Gwent* · Map 7 D2
Monmouth (0600) 860254

*Free House*
*Landlords* John & David Jackson

**BEDROOMS 8 Grade 1 £A+**
Pâté de truite £2.75 Coeur d'artichaut £3.25 (Last order 10pm)
Whitbread Bitter; Heineken; cider.
*Real ale*

The Jackson brothers set high standards at this remote 300-year old hostelry, where starters from the restaurant menu make up the very interesting snacks offered in the cocktail lounge: truffled duck terrine, perhaps, or tartlets filled with Gruyère and cream cheese. Finish with a sorbet or ice cream. Excellent bedrooms in cottagy style have spotlessly clean shower rooms. Glorious breakfasts. Closed 2–20 January.
**Family pub**

## Wolf's Castle *(Food)* — *Wolfe Inn*

Near Haverfordwest · *Dyfed* · Map 7 B2
Treffgarne (043 787) 662
*Free House*
*Landlords* Mr & Mrs Fritz Neumann
Smoked trout pâté £1.85 Sirloin steak chasseur £5.85 (Last order 10pm. No bar food Sun & Mon eves & all Mon in winter)
Felinfoel Double Dragon; George's Best Bitter; Worthington Best Bitter; Guinness; Carling Black Label; Carlsberg Hof; cider.
*Real ale*

Locals like to gather in the tiny public bar of this well-kept stone inn on the A40. Meanwhile, in the lounge and the charming conservatory-style dining area, a good choice of bar snacks is available, ranging from soup, prawns and home-made pâté to a huge and succulent sirloin steak with onion and mushroom sauce. Desserts like cheesecake, lemon mousse and gâteaux are a particular attraction. Closed Mon evening in winter.
**Family pub**

# CHANNEL ISLANDS

## Pleinmont *(B & B)* — *Imperial Hotel*

Torteval · *Guernsey* · Map 8 C4
Guernsey (0481) 64044

*Brewery* Randall
*Landlords* Mr & Mrs J. W. Hobbs

**BEDROOMS 12 Grade 1 £C**
Randall's Bitter; Worthington 'E'; Guinness; Breda; Holsten; cider.

A popular base for family holidays, this friendly, white-painted inn overlooks lovely Rocquaine Bay with its clifftop walks and sandy beaches. The views are particularly fine from the picture-windowed lounge bars, and the convivial public bar is a popular local meeting place. Bedrooms are bright and cheerful, with bold geometric-patterned wallpaper, TVs and tea-makers. Ten have private facilities. Excellent housekeeping. **Family pub**

## St Aubin's Harbour *(Food, B & B)* — *Old Court House Inn*

*Jersey* · Map 8 D4
Jersey (0534) 41156

*Free House*
*Landlords* Jonty & Vicky Sharp

**BEDROOMS 9 Grade 2 £A**
Lasagne £1.50 Moules marinière £2.30
(No bar food eves or Sun)
Mary Ann Special; John Smith's Bitter; Harp; Taunton cider.

There's character aplenty about this rambling harbourside inn, one of whose bars is decked out in the style of an old galleon. Lunchtime snacks announced on a blackboard menu range from hearty, flavoursome minestrone to well-presented salads, spare ribs and outstanding moules marinière. Ship-shape bedrooms are homely, with antique furniture and colour TVs. There's a cosy residents' lounge. Patio. **Family pub**

# ISLE OF MAN

## Andreas *(Food)*

### *Grosvenor*

*Isle of Man* · Map 3 A2
Kirk Andreas (0624 88) 576

*Brewery* Heron & Brearly
*Landlords* Mr & Mrs B. Hamer

Steak & kidney pie £1.75 Fresh crab salad £2 (Last order 10.45pm. No bar food Sun eve)
Okells Bitter, Mild; Guinness; Harp; Tennent's Lager; Taunton cider. *Real ale*

Lunchtime bar snacks bring the crowds to this well-kept modern pub not far from the sea. Toasted baps with grilled steak or gammon are very popular, as are black pudding, fishy things such as cockles and crab salad, and a good meaty steak and kidney pie served with super chips. To finish, a selection of familiar sweets from the trolley. Sandwiches only evenings and Sunday lunch. Terrace.

## Peel *(Food)*

### *Creek Inn*

The Quayside · *Isle of Man* · Map 3 A2
Peel (062 484) 2216

*Brewery* Okells
*Landlords* Robert & Jean McAleer

Open prawn sandwich £1.50 Lasagne & salad £1.45 (Last order 10.45pm)
Okells Bitter, Mild; Guinness; Harp; Carlsberg; Taunton cider. *Real ale*

Down on the harbour amidst the bustle of the boats, this welcoming pub is a friendly and convivial place to meet for a drink and a snack at any time of day. Sandwiches, salads and pizzas are favourite choices, and an ever-changing blackboard menu announces specials like lasagne, scallops mornay and the popular Creek pie – a delicious concoction of sausage meat, onions, apples and potatoes. Terrace.

**Family pub**

# JUST A BITE

## Egon Ronay's Lucas Guide

**for Gourmets on a Family Budget**

**— 1985 —**

for the best British light meals and snacks in some 1,000 cafés, tearooms, wine bars, wholefood and vegetarian restaurants, fish and chip shops, pizzerias and hamburger places, coffee shops and many other modest eating places serving high-quality food:

including **EATING ON & OFF MOTORWAYS**

With many new recommendations replacing the old ones after reappraisal.

£3.95 from bookshops everywhere or £4.50 to include postage and packing (limited to addresses in the United Kingdom) from:

Egon Ronay Organisation Ltd,
Greencoat House, Francis Street
LONDON SW1P 1DH

*See colour pages following page 96 for news of another 1985 Egon Ronay publication.*

# AN OFFER FOR ANSWERS – A DISCOUNT ON A GUIDE NEXT YEAR

If you kindly complete the questionnaire below (your answers will be treated in confidence), we will offer you one of our next year's Guides before publication at a very substantial discount, as our readers' reactions are of invaluable help in planning for the future. *After you have made use of the Guide for a few weeks*, please tear out this page and post it to:

**Egon Ronay's Pub Guide**
**Greencoat House, Francis Street**
**London SW1P 1DH**

*This offer is valid until 31 December 1985 and is limited to addresses within the United Kingdom.*

1 Are you (*please tick*) ✓

male ☐ female ☐

under 21 ☐ 21–30 ☐ 31–45 ☐ 46–65 ☐ over 65 ☐

2 Your occupation .....

3 Do you refer to this Guide (*please tick*)

(a) four times a week? (b) three times a week? (c) twice a week? (d) once a week? (e) once a fortnight? (f) once a month?

How many people, apart from yourself, refer to this Guide (including those in your home and place of work)?

..... males ..... females

4 Do you own our Pub Guide? 1983 ☐ 1984 ☐

5 Do you have our Egon Ronay's Lucas Guide to Hotels and Restaurants?

1983 ☐ 1984 ☐ 1985 ☐

6 Do you have our Just a Bite Guide?

1983 ☐ 1984 ☐ 1985 ☐

*continued*

7 Do you own the house you live in? | Yes | No |

8 Do you and members of your family residing with you possess
one car? ☐ two cars? ☐ three cars? ☐

9 What year is your car? .....

10 What is your daily newspaper? .....

11 Which of the following credit cards do you use?

| | | | |
|---|---|---|---|
| Access | ☐ | Diners | ☐ |
| American Express | ☐ | Visa | ☐ |

12 In a pub, do you usually drink

| | |
|---|---|
| beer or cider? | ☐ |
| wine? | ☐ |
| spirits, sherry or other short drinks? | ☐ |

13 Are you generally happy with the quality of wines served in pubs?
| Yes | No |

14 Are you in favour of accompanied children being served food in pubs?

| | |
|---|---|
| Yes, at any time | ☐ |
| Lunchtimes only | ☐ |
| No, not at all | ☐ |

Please *print* your name and address here if you would like us to send you the order form according to our offer on the preceding page.

Name .....

Address .....

.....

.....

# Readers' comments

Please use this sheet to recommend bar snacks or inn accommodation of very high quality – *not* full restaurant or hotel facilities. Your complaints about any of the Guide's entries are also welcome.

Please post to:
PUB GUIDE 1985
Egon Ronay Organisation
Greencoat House, Francis Street, London SW1P 1DH

NB We regret that owing to the enormous volume of readers communications received each year, we will be unable to acknowledge these forms but they will certainly be seriously considered.

| Name and address of establishment (*Please state whether food or accommodation*) | Your recommendation or complaint |
|---|---|
| | |
| | |
| | |
| | |
| | |
| | |
| | |

PUB

Name of sender (in block letters) _____

Address of sender (in block letters) _____

# Readers' comments

Please use this sheet to recommend bar snacks or inn accommodation of very high quality – *not* full restaurant or hotel facilities. Your complaints about any of the Guide's entries are also welcome.

Please post to:
PUB GUIDE 1985
Egon Ronay Organisation
Greencoat House, Francis Street, London SW1P 1DH

NB We regret that owing to the enormous volume of readers communications received each year, we will be unable to acknowledge these forms but they will certainly be seriously considered.

| Name and address of establishment (*Please state whether food or accommodation*) | Your recommendation or complaint |
|---|---|
| | |
| | |
| | |
| | |
| | |
| | |
| | |

PUB

Name of sender (in block letters) _____

Address of sender (in block letters) _____

# Readers' comments

Please use this sheet to recommend bar snacks or inn accommodation of very high quality – *not* full restaurant or hotel facilities. Your complaints about any of the Guide's entries are also welcome.

Please post to:
PUB GUIDE 1985
Egon Ronay Organisation
Greencoat House, Francis Street, London SW1P 1DH

NB We regret that owing to the enormous volume of readers communications received each year, we will be unable to acknowledge these forms but they will certainly be seriously considered.

| Name and address of establishment (*Please state whether food or accommodation*) | Your recommendation or complaint |
|---|---|
| | |
| | |
| | |
| | |
| | |
| | |
| | |

PUB

Name of sender (in block letters) _____

Address of sender (in block letters) _____

# Readers' comments

Please use this sheet to recommend bar snacks or inn accommodation of very high quality – *not* full restaurant or hotel facilities. Your complaints about any of the Guide's entries are also welcome.

Please post to:
PUB GUIDE 1985
Egon Ronay Organisation
Greencoat House, Francis Street, London SW1P 1DH

NB We regret that owing to the enormous volume of readers communications received each year, we will be unable to acknowledge these forms but they will certainly be seriously considered.

| Name and address of establishment (*Please state whether food or accommodation*) | Your recommendation or complaint |
|---|---|
| | |
| | |
| | |
| | |
| | |
| | |
| | |

PUB

Name of sender (in block letters) _____

Address of sender (in block letters) _____

# Readers' comments

Please use this sheet to recommend bar snacks or inn accommodation of very high quality – *not* full restaurant or hotel facilities. Your complaints about any of the Guide's entries are also welcome.

Please post to:
PUB GUIDE 1985
Egon Ronay Organisation
Greencoat House, Francis Street, London SW1P 1DH

NB We regret that owing to the enormous volume of readers communications received each year, we will be unable to acknowledge these forms but they will certainly be seriously considered.

| Name and address of establishment (*Please state whether food or accommodation*) | Your recommendation or complaint |
|---|---|
| | |
| | |
| | |
| | |
| | |
| | |
| | |

PUB

Name of sender (in block letters) _____

Address of sender (in block letters) _____

# Readers' comments

Please use this sheet to recommend bar snacks or inn accommodation of very high quality – *not* full restaurant or hotel facilities. Your complaints about any of the Guide's entries are also welcome.

Please post to:
PUB GUIDE 1985
Egon Ronay Organisation
Greencoat House, Francis Street, London SW1P 1DH

NB We regret that owing to the enormous volume of readers communications received each year, we will be unable to acknowledge these forms but they will certainly be seriously considered.

| Name and address of establishment (*Please state whether food or accommodation*) | Your recommendation or complaint |
|---|---|
| | |
| | |
| | |
| | |
| | |
| | |
| | |

PUB

Name of sender (in block letters) _____

Address of sender (in block letters) _____

# ADVERTISERS' INDEX

Bejam see colour section between 192–193

Carlsberg inside front cover, inside back cover, 320

Crosse & Blackwell see colour section between 192–193

Distillers Company (Home Trade) 160, map section

English Country Cheese Council 162–165

Findus see colour section between 272–273

Food & Wine from France see colour sections between 96–97 and 192–193

Guinness outside back cover, 48–53

Metal Box see colour section between 272–273

Paul Masson California Carafe see colour section between 272–273

Philip Morris see colour section between 96–97

Schweppes 23–32

Scottish & Newcastle 119

Trans World Airlines 63, 149, 277

Uncle Ben's (Dornay Foods) see map section

Whitbread 59

# English beers, Flemish settlers.

## And probably the best lager in the world.

### A Short Guide To What Goes Into Your Drink

**Ale** – Originally a liquor made from an infusion of malt by fermentation, as opposed to beer, which was made by the same process but flavoured with hops.
**Beer** – "Beer" and "Ale" were the words to describe all malt liquors until the 16th Century, when Flemish settlers re-introduced hops for flavouring. The hopped variety was then called "Beer" and the unhopped liquors were called "Ale."
**Bitter** – The driest and one of the most heavily hopped beers served on draught.
**Burton** – A strong ale, dark in colour, made with a proportion of highly dried or roasted malts. It is not necessarily brewed in Burton and a variety of strong or old ales were given the term.
**Carlsberg** – A Danish lager brewery, founded in 1847, based in Copenhagen and specialising solely in the production of lagers. The company has a major brewery at Northampton, England, where these lagers are produced by Danish brewers. Carlsberg is unique because it is owned by a philanthropic foundation which gives all its profits to art, scientific and medical research.
**India Pale Ale** – The name given to a fine pale ale first made for export to the troops in India. The term became popular with a number of brewers for their bottled pale ales.
**Lager** – Light coloured beer brewed principally on the Continent. Fewer hops are used than in English beer, and fermentation is carried out at a much lower temperature. Bottom fermentation is caused by special yeasts which descend to the bottom of the fermenting vessels, and character is achieved by the length of the fermentation and storage.
**Mulled Ale** – A hot drink for cold weather. Beer flavoured with sugar and spices and sometimes the yolk of an egg.
**Pale Ale** – Also known as light ale. Made of the highest quality malts, it is dry and highly hopped.
**Pilsner** – The German name for the Czechoslovakian town of Plzen which gave its name to Pilsner. Carlsberg first exported a pilsner type lager from Copenhagen to Scotland in 1868.
**Special Brew** – A strong, high quality lager produced by Carlsberg. First introduced to commemorate a visit by Winston Churchill to Copenhagen in 1950.
**Stout** – Heavy dark beer prepared with well roasted barley or malt, and sometimes caramel.

**Carlsberg Brewery Ltd. Tel 0604 21621.**